The Cross-Platform Prep Course

Welcome to the Cross-Platform Prep Course Edition! McGraw-Hill Education's multi-platform course gives you a variety of tools to raise your scores and get in to the school of your choice. Whether you're studying at home, the library, or on-the-go, you can find practice content in the format you need—print, online, or mobile.

Print Book

This print book gives you the tools you need to ace the test. In its pages you'll find smart test-taking strategies, in-depth reviews of key topics, and ample practice questions and tests. See the Welcome section of your book for a step-by-step guide to its features.

Online Platform

The Cross-Platform Prep Course's online platform gives you additional study and practice content that you can access *anytime, anywhere*. You can create a personalized study plan based on your test date that sets daily goals to keep you on track. Integrated lessons provide important review of key topics. Practice questions, exams, and flashcards give you the practice you need to build test-taking confidence. The game center is filled with challenging games that allow you to practice your new skills in a fun and engaging way. You can interact with other test-takers in the discussion section and gain valuable peer support.

Getting Started

To get started, open your account on the online platform:

Go to www.xplatform.mhprofessional.com

↓

Enter your access code, which you can find on the inside back cover of your book

↓

Provide your name and e-mail address to open your account and create a password

↓

Click "Start Studying" to enter the platform

It's as simple as that. You're ready to start studying online.

Your Personalized Study Plan

First, select your test date on the calendar, and you're on your way to creating your personalized study plan. Your study plan will help you stay organized and on track and will guide you through the course in the most efficient way. It is tailored to *your* schedule and features daily tasks that are broken down into manageable goals. You can adjust your end date at any time and your daily tasks will be reorganized into an updated plan.

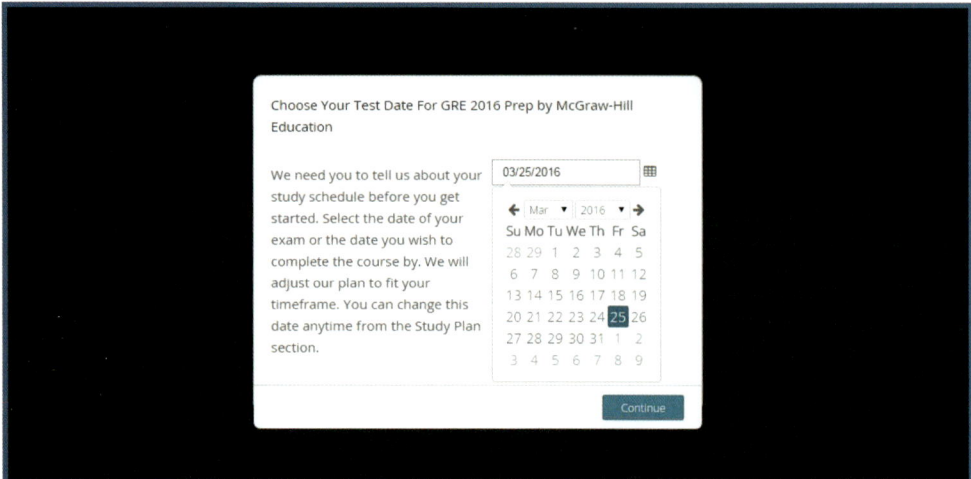

You can track your progress in real time on the Study Plan Dashboard. The Today's Knowledge Goal progress bar gives you up-to-the minute feedback on your daily goal. Fulfilling this is the most efficient way to work through the entire course. You can get an instant view of where you stand in the entire course with the Study Plan Progress bar.

If you need to exit the program before completing a task, you can return to the Study Plan Dashboard at any time. Just click the Study Task icon and you can automatically pick up where you left off.

Practice Tests

One of the first tasks in your personalized study plan is to take the Diagnostic Test. At the end of the test, a detailed evaluation of your strengths and weaknesses shows the areas where you need to focus most. You can review your practice test results either by the question category to see broad trends or question-by-question for a more in-depth look.

The full-length tests are designed to simulate the real thing. Try to simulate actual testing conditions and be sure you set aside enough time to complete the full-length test. You'll learn to pace yourself so that you can get the best possible score on test day.

Lessons

The lessons in the online platform are divided into manageable pieces that let you build knowledge and confidence in a progressive way. They cover the full range of topics that appear on your test.

After you complete a lesson, mark your confidence level. (You must indicate a confidence level in order to count your progress and move on to the next task.) You can also filter the lessons by confidence levels to see the areas you have mastered and those that you might need to revisit.

> *Use the bookmark feature to easily refer back to a concept or leave a note to remember your thoughts or questions about a particular topic.*

Practice Questions

All of the practice questions are based on real-life exams and simulate the test-taking experience. The Review Answer gives you immediate feedback on your answer. Each question includes a rationale that explains why the correct answer is right and the others are wrong. To explore any topic further, you can find detailed explanations by clicking the "Help me learn about this topic" link.

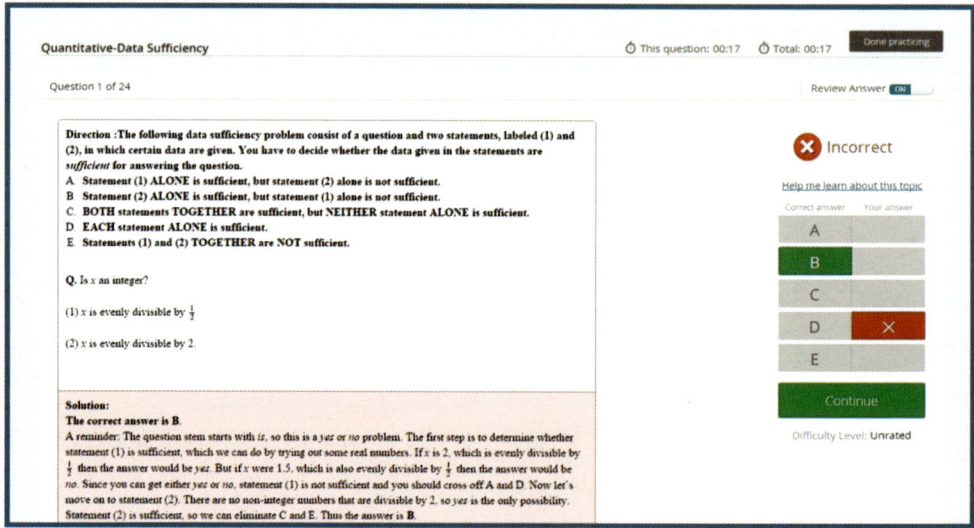

You can go to the Practice Dashboard to find an overview of your performance in the different categories and sub-categories.

Dashboard

Visit the dashboard to see personalized information on your progress and performance. The Percentile Rank icon shows your position relative to all the other students enrolled in the course. You can also find information on your average scores in practice questions and exams.

A detailed overview of your strengths and weaknesses shows your proficiency in a category based on your answers and difficulty of the questions. By viewing your strengths and weaknesses, you can focus your study on your weaker spots.

Flashcards

Hundreds of flashcards are perfect for learning key terms quickly, and the interactive format gives you immediate feedback. You can filter the cards by category and confidence level for a more organized approach. Or, you can shuffle them up for a challenge.

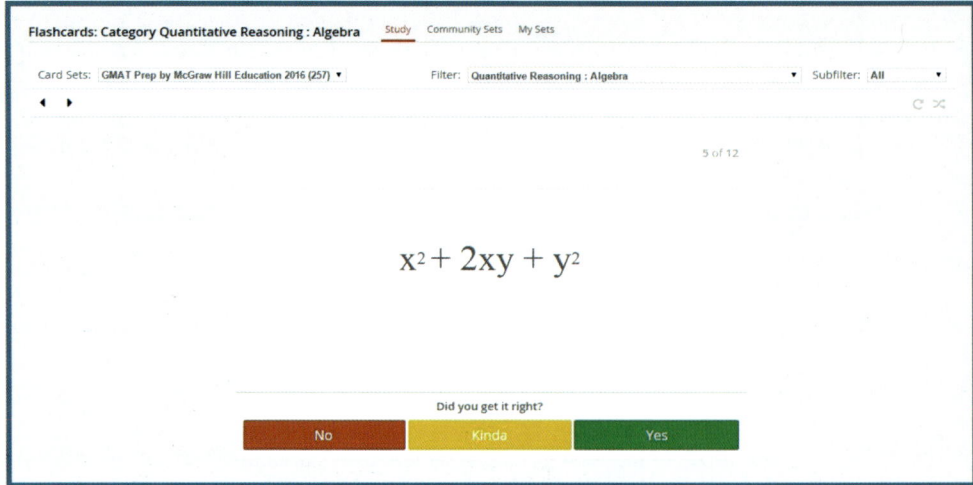

Another way to customize the flashcards is to create your own sets. You can keep these private or share or them with the public. Subscribe to Community Sets to access sets from other students preparing for the same exam.

Game Center

Play a game in the Game Center to test your knowledge of key concepts in a challenging but fun environment. Up the difficulty level and complete the games quickly to build the highest score. Be sure to check the leaderboard to see who's on top.

Social Community

Interact with other students who are preparing for your test. Start a discussion, reply to a post, or even upload files to share. You can search the archives for common topics or start your own private discussion with friends.

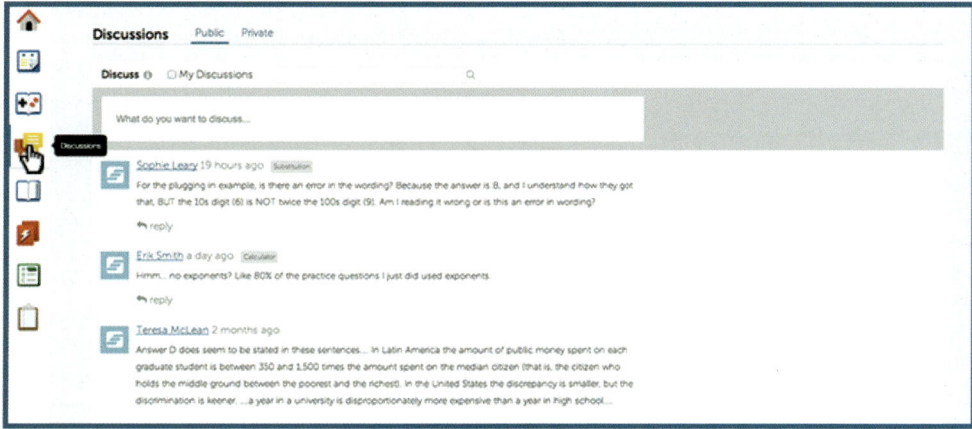

Mobile App

The companion mobile app lets you toggle between the online platform and your mobile device without missing a beat. Whether you access the course online or on your smartphone or tablet, you'll pick up exactly where you left off.

Go to the iTunes or Google Play stores and search "BenchPrep Companion" to download the companion iOS or Android app. Enter your e-mail address and the same password you created for the online platform to open your account.

Now, let's get started!

5 STEPS TO A 5™
AP Macroeconomics
2018

ELITE STUDENT EDITION

5 STEPS TO A 5™

AP Macroeconomics
2018

Eric R. Dodge, PhD

New York   Chicago   San Francisco   Athens   London   Madrid   Mexico City
Milan   New Delhi   Singapore   Sydney   Toronto

Copyright © 2017 by McGraw-Hill Education. All rights reserved. Printed in the United States of America. Except as permitted under the United States Copyright Act of 1976, no part of this publication may be reproduced or distributed in any form or by any means, or stored in a database or retrieval system, without the prior written permission of the publisher.

1 2 3 4 5 6 7 8 9   LHS   22 21 20 19 18 17 (Cross-Platform Prep Course only)
1 2 3 4 5 6 7 8 9   LHS   22 21 20 19 18 17 (Elite Student Edition)

ISBN   978-1-259-86386-8 (Cross-Platform Prep Course only)
MHID   1-259-86386-7

e-ISBN 978-1-259-86387-5 (e-book Cross-Platform Prep Course only)
e-MHID   1-259-86387-5

ISBN   978-1-259-86390-5 (Elite Student Edition)
MHID   1-259-86390-5

e-ISBN 978-1-259-86388-2 (e-book Elite Student Edition)
e-MHID   1-259-86388-3

Trademarks: McGraw-Hill Education, the McGraw-Hill Education logo, *5 Steps to a 5*, and related trade dress are trademarks or registered trademarks of the McGraw-Hill Education and/or its affiliates in the United States and other countries and may not be used without written permission. All other trademarks are the property of their respective owners. McGraw-Hill Education is not associated with any product or vendor mentioned in this book.

AP, Advanced Placement Program, and *College Board* are registered trademarks of the College Board, which was not involved in the production of, and does not endorse, this product.

The series editor was Grace Freedson, and the project editor was Del Franz. Series design by Jane Tenenbaum.

McGraw-Hill Education products are available at special quantity discounts to use as premiums and sales or for use in corporate training programs. To contact a representative, please visit the Contact Us pages at www.mhprofessional.com.

CONTENTS

Preface vii
Acknowledgments ix
About the Author xi
Introduction: The Five-Step Program xiii

STEP 1 **Set Up Your Study Program**
1 What You Need to Know About the AP Macroeconomics Exam 3
2 How to Plan Your Time 12

STEP 2 **Determine Your Test Readiness**
3 Take the Diagnostic Exam 19
   Diagnostic Exam: AP Macroeconomics 23

STEP 3 **Develop Strategies for Success**
4 How to Approach Each Question Type 33
   Section I: Multiple-Choice Questions 33
   Section II: Free-Response Questions 36

STEP 4 **Review the Knowledge You Need to Score High**
5 Fundamentals of Economic Analysis 41
   5.1 Scarce Resources 42
   5.2 Production Possibilities 45
   5.3 Functions of Economic Systems 51
6 Demand, Supply, Market Equilibrium, and Welfare Analysis 55
   6.1 Demand 55
   6.2 Supply 61
   6.3 Market Equilibrium 64
   6.4 Welfare Analysis 69
7 Macroeconomic Measures of Performance 74
   7.1 The Circular Flow Model 75
   7.2 Accounting for Output and Income 76
   7.3 Inflation and the Consumer Price Index 82
   7.4 Unemployment 86
8 Consumption, Saving, Investment, and the Multiplier 92
   8.1 Consumption and Saving 93
   8.2 Investment 96
   8.3 The Multiplier Effect 99
9 Aggregate Demand and Aggregate Supply 106
   9.1 Aggregate Demand (AD) 106
   9.2 Aggregate Supply (AS) 109
   9.3 Macroeconomic Equilibrium 112
   9.4 The Trade-Off Between Inflation and Unemployment 119

10 Fiscal Policy, Economic Growth, and Productivity 126
    10.1 Expansionary and Contractionary Fiscal Policy 126
    10.2 Difficulties of Fiscal Policy 130
    10.3 Economic Growth and Productivity 134

11 Money, Banking, and Monetary Policy 141
    11.1 Money and Financial Assets 141
    11.2 Fractional Reserve Banking and Money Creation 148
    11.3 Monetary Policy 151

12 International Trade 160
    12.1 Comparative Advantage and Gains from Trade 160
    12.2 Balance of Payments 164
    12.3 Foreign Exchange Rates 166
    12.4 Trade Barriers 169

STEP 5

Build Your Test-Taking Confidence
    AP Macroeconomics Practice Exam 1 177
    AP Macroeconomics Practice Exam 2 197

ELITE STUDENT EDITION

5 Minute to a 5
    90 AP Macroeconomics
        Activities and Questions in 5 Minutes a Day 215
    90 AP Microeconomics
        Activities and Questions in 5 Minutes a Day 351

Appendixes
    Further Reading 493
    Websites 495
    Glossary 497
    Important Formulas and Conditions 503

PREFACE

So, you've decided to bite the bullet and invest in a book designed to help you earn a 5 on your AP Macroeconomics exam. Congratulations! You have taken the first of many small steps toward this goal. An important question remains: Why this book?

Priority number one, both for your AP course and for this book, is to prepare you to do well enough on the AP Macroeconomics exam to earn college credit. I firmly believe that this book has a comparative advantage over your other options. First, I have written this text with a certain conversational approach, rather than a flurry of formulas and diagrams that you must remember. Sure, some memorization is required for any standardized test, but a memorizer of formulas is in deep trouble when asked to analyze the relative success of several possible economic policies or to draw fine distinctions between competing economic theories. Using this book to supplement and reinforce your understanding of the theories and relationships in economics allows you to apply your analytical skills to the exam, and this gives you a significant advantage over the formula-memorizing exam taker. If you spend less time memorizing formulas and take the extra time to understand the basics, you will get along just fine with this book, and you will do extremely well on the AP Macroeconomics exam.

Second, as a college professor who has taught economics to thousands of students, I have a strong understanding of where the learning happens and where the mistakes are made.

Third, as a reader and writer of AP exams, I can tell you where points are lost and where a 5 is made on the free-response questions. Most important, I am a realist. You want to know what it takes to earn a 5 and not necessarily the finer points of the Federal Reserve System, the Sherman Antitrust Act, or the NAFTA.

Take the time to read the first four chapters of this book, which are designed to help you understand the challenge that lies ahead and to provide you with tips for success on the exam.

Take the diagnostic exam to see where you stand before beginning your review. The bulk of this book is a comprehensive review of macroeconomics with practice questions at the end of each chapter. These questions are designed to quickly test your understanding of the material presented in each chapter, not necessarily to mirror the AP exam. For exam questions that are more typical of what you will experience in May, I have provided you with two practice exams in macroeconomics, complete with essay questions, sample responses, and scoring guidelines.

Since the first edition of the book, several updates have been made to adapt to changes in the AP Macroeconomics exams. Earlier editions expanded coverage of the balance of payments and provided an explanation for how changes to the current account affect changes to the capital account. In the last edition, I added an alternative approach to how government deficits affect the market for loanable funds. This "demand side" treatment of the loanable funds market has since become the preferred way of modeling the crowding-out effect, and because it has the advantage of being much more intuitive, I have emphasized it rather than the original "supply-side" approach in this edition. I have also included more graphical coverage of the model of aggregate demand and aggregate supply, with an emphasis on the theoretical treatment of the adjustment from short-run to long-run equilibrium.

I do not see any reason to continue talking about the book when we could just dive in. I hope that you enjoy this book and that you find it a useful resource. Good luck!

ACKNOWLEDGMENTS

This book is dedicated to my wife, Dr. Melanie Fox, and our three sons, Eli, Max, and Theo. My utility for you is increasing at an increasing rate. Thank you.

ABOUT THE AUTHOR

Eric R. Dodge was born in Portland, Oregon, and attended high school in Tigard, Oregon. He received a bachelor's degree in Business Administration from the University of Puget Sound in Tacoma, Washington, before attending the University of Oregon for his master's and doctoral degrees in Economics. While at the University of Oregon, he received two graduate student awards for teaching and became a die-hard fan of the Ducks. Since 1995, he has been teaching economics at Hanover College in Hanover, Indiana, the oldest private college in the state. The author teaches principles of microeconomics and macroeconomics, intermediate microeconomic theory, labor economics, environmental economics, industrial organization, statistics, econometrics, and the economics of dams.

Since 2000, Eric Dodge has served as a faculty consultant for the AP economics program, and has been a reader and writer of free-response questions, table leader, and question leader at the annual AP Economics Reading. With coauthor Melanie Fox, he has also written three recently published books: *Economics Demystified*, *500 Microeconomics Questions: Ace Your College Exams*, and *500 Macroeconomics Questions: Ace Your College Exams*. He lives in historic Madison, Indiana, with his wife, Melanie; sons Eli, Max, and Theo; and a dog and a cat.

INTRODUCTION: THE FIVE-STEP PROGRAM

The Basics

Not too long ago, you agreed to enroll in AP Macroeconomics. Maybe you saw a flyer and the allure of economic knowledge was just too much to resist, or maybe a respected teacher encouraged you to challenge yourself and you took the bait. Either way, you find yourself here, flipping through a book that promises to help you culminate this life-changing experience with the highest of honors, a 5 in AP Macroeconomics. Can it be done without this book? Sure, there are many excellent teachers of AP Macroeconomics out there who teach, coax, and cajole their students into a 5 every year. But for the majority of students in your shoes, the marginal benefits of buying this book far outweigh the marginal costs.

Introducing the Five-Step Preparation Program

This book is organized as a five-step program to prepare you for success on the exams. These steps are designed to provide you with the skills and strategies vital to the exam and the practice that can lead you to that perfect 5. Each of the five steps provides you with the opportunity to get closer and closer to that prize trophy 5.

Following are the five steps:

Step 1: Set Up Your Study Program

In this step you'll read a brief overview of the AP Macroeconomics exam, including an outline of topics and the approximate percentage of the exam that will test knowledge of each topic. You will also follow a process to help determine which of the following preparation programs is right for you:

- Full school year: September through May.
- One semester: January through May.
- Six weeks: Basic training for the exam.

Step 2: Determine Your Test Readiness

In this step you'll take a diagnostic exam in macroeconomics. This pretest should give you an idea of how prepared you are to take the real exam before beginning to study for it.

- Go through the diagnostic exam step-by-step and question-by-question to build your confidence level.
- Review the correct answers and explanations so that you see what you do and do not yet fully understand.

Step 3: Develop Strategies for Success

In this step you'll learn strategies to help you do your best on the exam. These strategies cover both the multiple-choice and free-response sections of the exam. Some of these tips are based upon my understanding of how the questions are designed, and others have been gleaned from my years of experience reading (grading) the AP exams.

- Learn to read multiple-choice questions.
- Learn how to answer multiple-choice questions, including whether or not to guess.
- Learn how to plan and write the free-response questions.

Step 4: Review the Knowledge You Need to Score High

In this step you'll review the material you need to know for the test. This review section takes up the bulk of this book. It contains a comprehensive review of macroeconomics.

There is a lot of material here, enough to summarize a yearlong experience in AP Macroeconomics and highlight the, well, highlights. Some AP courses will have covered more material than yours; some will have covered less. The bottom line is that if you thoroughly review this material, you will have studied all that is tested on the exam, and you will significantly increase your chances of scoring well. This edition gives new emphasis to some areas of macroeconomics to bring your review more in line with recent exams. For example, there is more coverage of how the economy can adjust from the short run to the long run in the macroeconomics review.

Step 5: Build Your Test-Taking Confidence

In this step you'll complete your preparation by testing yourself on practice exams. This section contains two complete exams in macroeconomics, solutions, and, sometimes more importantly, advice on how to avoid the common mistakes. Be aware that these practice exams are *not* reproduced questions from actual AP Macroeconomics exams, but they mirror both the material tested by AP and the way in which it is tested.

Lastly, at the back of this book you'll find additional resources to aid your preparation. These include the following:

- A brief bibliography
- A list of websites related to AP Macroeconomics
- A glossary of terms related to the AP Macroeconomics exam
- A summary of formulas related to the AP Macroeconomics exam

Introduction to the Graphics Used in this Book

To emphasize particular skills and strategies, several icons appear in the margins, alerting you to pay particular attention to the accompanying text:

This icon indicates a very important concept or fact that you should not pass over.

This icon calls your attention to a strategy that you might want to try.

This icon alerts you to a tip that you might find useful.

Boldfaced words indicate terms that are included in the glossary. Throughout the book you will also find marginal notes, boxes, and starred areas. Pay close attention to these areas because they can provide tips, hints, strategies, and further explanations to help you reach your full potential.

5 STEPS TO A 5™
AP Macroeconomics
2018

Set Up Your Study Program

CHAPTER 1 What You Need to Know About the AP Macroeconomics Exam
CHAPTER 2 How to Plan Your Time

What You Need to Know About the AP Macroeconomics Exam

IN THIS CHAPTER
Summary: Learn what topics are tested, how the test is scored, and basic test-taking information.

Key Ideas
✪ Most colleges will award credit for a score of 4 or 5.
✪ Multiple-choice questions account for two-thirds of your final score.
✪ Free-response questions account for one-third of your final score.
✪ Your composite score on the two test sections is converted to a score on the 1-to-5 scale.

Background Information

The AP Economics exams that you are taking were first offered by the College Board in 1989. Since then, the number of students taking the tests has grown rapidly. In 1989, 3,198 students took the Macroeconomics exam, and by 2014 that number had increased to 117,209.

Frequently Asked Questions About the AP Economics Exams

Why Take the AP Economics Exams?

Although there might be some altruistic motivators, let's face it: most of you take the AP Economics exams because you are seeking college credit. The majority of colleges and universities will accept a 4 or 5 as acceptable credit for their Principles of Microeconomics or Macroeconomics courses. Many private colleges will give you credit if you take both exams and receive a combined score of a 9 or 10. A small number of schools will even accept a 3 on an exam. This means you are one or two courses closer to graduation before you even begin working on the "freshman 15." Even if you do not score high enough to earn college credit, the fact that you elected to enroll in AP courses tells admission committees that you are a high achiever and serious about your education. In recent years, close to two-thirds of students have scored a 3 or higher on the AP Macroeconomics exam.

What Is the Format of the Exams?

Table 1.1 The Format of the AP Macroeconomics and Microeconomics Exams

AP MACROECONOMICS		
Section	Number of Questions	Time Limit
I. Multiple-Choice Questions	60	1 hour and 10 minutes
II. Free-Response Questions	3	Planning time: 10 minutes Writing time: 50 minutes

AP MICROECONOMICS		
Section	Number of Questions	Time Limit
I. Multiple-Choice Questions	60	1 hour and 10 minutes
II. Free-Response Questions	3	Planning time: 10 minutes Writing time: 50 minutes

Who Writes the AP Economics Exams?

Development of each AP exam is a multiyear effort that involves many education and testing professionals and students. At the heart of the effort is the AP Macroeconomics Development Committee, a group of college and high school economics teachers who are typically asked to serve for three years. The committee and other college professors create a large pool of multiple-choice questions. With the help of the testing experts at Educational Testing Service (ETS), these questions are then pretested with college students enrolled in Principles of Microeconomics and Macroeconomics for accuracy, appropriateness, clarity, and assurance that there is only one possible answer. The results of this pretesting allow each question to be categorized by degree of difficulty. Several more months of development and refinement later, Section I of the exam is ready to be administered.

The free-response essay questions that make up Section II go through a similar process of creation, modification, pretesting, and final refinement so that the questions cover the necessary areas of material and are at an appropriate level of difficulty and clarity. The committee also makes a great effort to construct a free-response exam that allows for clear and equitable grading by the AP readers.

At the conclusion of each AP reading and scoring of exams, the exam itself and the results are thoroughly evaluated by the committee and by ETS. In this way, the College Board can use the results to make suggestions for course development in high schools and to plan future exams.

What Topics Appear on the Exams?

The College Board, after consulting with teachers of economics, develops a curriculum that covers material that college professors expect to cover in their first-year classes. Based upon this outline of topics, the multiple-choice exams are written such that those topics are covered in proportion to their importance to the expected economics understanding of the student. If you find this confusing, think of it this way: Suppose that faculty consultants agree that foreign currency markets are important to the Macroeconomics curriculum, maybe to the tune of 10 percent. So if 10 percent of the curriculum in your AP Macroeconomics course is devoted to foreign currency markets, you can expect roughly 10 percent of the multiple-choice exam to address this topic. Following are the general outlines for both the Microeconomics and Macroeconomics curriculum and exams. Remember, this is just a guide and each year the percentages differ slightly.

Microeconomics

Content Area	Approximate percentage for exam (multiple-choice)

I. Basic Economic Concepts
   A. Scarcity, choice, and opportunity cost
   B. Production possibilities curve
   C. Comparative advantage, absolute advantage, specialization, and trade
   D. Economic systems
   E. Property rights and role of incentives
   F. Marginal analysis
	8–14%

II. The Nature and Functions of Product Markets
   A. Supply and demand (15–20%)
      1. Market equilibrium
      2. Determinants of supply and demand
      3. Price and quantity controls
      4. Elasticity
         a. Price, income, and cross-price elasticities of demand
         b. Price elasticity of supply
      5. Consumer surplus, producer surplus, and allocative efficiency
      6. Tax incidence and deadweight loss
   B. Theory of consumer choice (5–10%)
      1. Total utility and marginal utility
      2. Utility maximization: equalizing marginal utility per dollar
      3. Individual and market demand curves
      4. Income and substitution effects
	55–70%

C. Production and costs (10–15%)
   1. Production functions: short and long run
   2. Marginal product and diminishing returns
   3. Short-run costs
   4. Long-run costs and economies of scale
   5. Cost minimizing input combination and productive efficiency
D. Firm behavior and market structures (25–35%)
   1. Profit
      a. Accounting versus economic profits
      b. Normal profit
      c. Profit maximization: MR = MC rule
   2. Perfect competition
      a. Profit maximization
      b. Short-run supply and shutdown decision
      c. Behavior of firms and markets in the short run and long run
      d. Efficiency and perfect competition
   3. Monopoly
      a. Sources of market power
      b. Profit maximization
      c. Inefficiency of monopoly
      d. Price discrimination
      e. Natural monopoly
   4. Oligopoly
      a. Interdependence, collusion, and cartels
      b. Game theory and strategic behavior
      c. Dominant strategy
      d. Nash equilibrium
   5. Monopolistic competition
      a. Product differentiation and role of advertising
      b. Profit maximization
      c. Short-run and long-run equilibrium
      d. Excess capacity and inefficiency

III. Factor Markets   10–18%
   A. Derived factor demand
   B. Marginal revenue product
   C. Hiring decisions in the markets for labor and capital
   D. Market distribution of income

IV. Market Failure and the Role of Government   12–18%
   A. Externalities
      1. Marginal social benefit and marginal social cost
      2. Positive externalities
      3. Negative externalities
      4. Remedies
   B. Public goods
      1. Public versus private goods
      2. Provision of public goods

    C. Public policy to promote competition
        1. Antitrust policy
        2. Regulation
    D. Income distribution
        1. Equity
        2. Sources and measures of income inequality

Macroeconomics

Content Area	Approximate percentage for exam (multiple-choice)

I. Basic Economic Concepts
  A. Scarcity, choice, and opportunity costs
  B. Production possibilities curve
  C. Comparative advantage, specialization, and exchange
  D. Demand, supply, and market equilibrium
  E. Macroeconomic issues: business cycle, unemployment, inflation, growth
	8–12%

II. Measurement of Economic Performance
  A. National income accounts
    1. Circular flow
    2. Gross domestic product
    3. Components of gross domestic product
    4. Real versus nominal gross domestic product
  B. Inflation measurement and adjustment
    1. Price indices
    2. Nominal and real values
    3. Costs of inflation
  C. Unemployment
    1. Definition and measurement
    2. Types of unemployment
    3. Natural rate of unemployment
	12–16%

III. National Income and Price Determination
  A. Aggregate demand
    1. Determinants of aggregate demand
    2. Multiplier and crowding-out effects
  B. Aggregate supply
    1. Short-run and long-run analyses
    2. Sticky versus flexible wages and prices
    3. Determinants of aggregate supply
  C. Macroeconomic equilibrium
    1. Real output and price level
    2. Short and long run
    3. Actual versus full-employment output
    4. Business cycle and economic fluctuations
	10–15%

IV. Financial Sector
  A. Money, banking, and financial markets
    1. Definition of financial assets: money, stocks, bonds
	15–20%

    2. Time value of money (present and future value)
    3. Measures of money supply
    4. Banks and the creation of money
    5. Money demand
    6. Money market and the equilibrium nominal interest rate
  B. Loanable funds market
    1. Supply of and demand for loanable funds
    2. Equilibrium real interest rate
    3. Crowding out
  C. Central bank and control of the money supply
    1. Tools of central bank policy
    2. Quantity theory of money
    3. Real versus nominal interest rates

V. Stabilization Policies   20–30%
  A. Fiscal and monetary policies
    1. Demand-side effects
    2. Supply-side effects
    3. Policy mix
    4. Government deficits and debt
  B. The Phillips curve
    1. Short-run and long-run Phillips curves
    2. Demand-pull versus cost-push inflation
    3. Role of expectations

VI. Economic Growth.   (5–10%)
  A. Definition of economic growth
  B. Determinants of economic growth
    1. Investment in human capital
    2. Investment in physical capital
    3. Research and development, and technological progress
  C. Growth policy

VII. Open Economy: International Trade and Finance   10–15%
  A. Balance of payments accounts
    1. Balance of trade
    2. Current account
    3. Financial account (formerly known as capital account)
  B. Foreign exchange market
    1. Demand for and supply of foreign exchange
    2. Exchange rate determination
    3. Currency appreciation and depreciation
  C. Imports, exports, and financial capital flows
  D. Relationships between international and domestic financial and goods markets

Who Grades My AP Economics Exam?

From confidential sources, I can tell you that nearly 100,000 free-response essay booklets are dropped from a three-story building, and those that fall into a small cardboard box are given a 5, those that fall into a slightly larger box are given a 4, and so on until those that fall into a dumpster receive a 1. It's really quite scientific!

Okay, that's not really how it's done. Instead, every June a group of economics teachers gather for a week to assign grades to your hard work. Each of these "Faculty Consultants," or "Readers," spends a day or so getting trained on one question and one question only. Because each reader becomes an expert on that question, and because each exam book is anonymous, this process provides a very consistent and unbiased scoring of that question. During a typical day of grading, a random sample of each reader's scores is selected and cross-checked by other experienced "Table Leaders" to ensure that the consistency is maintained throughout the day and the week. Each reader's scores on a given question are also statistically analyzed to make sure that they are not giving scores that are significantly higher or lower than the mean scores given by other readers of that question. All measures are taken to maintain consistency and fairness for your benefit.

Will My Exam Remain Anonymous?

Absolutely. Even if your high school teacher happens to randomly read your booklet, there is virtually no way he or she will know it is you. To the reader, each student is a number, and to the computer, each student is a bar code.

What About That Permission Box on the Back?

The College Board uses some exams to help train high school teachers so that they can help the next generation of economics students to avoid common mistakes. If you check this box, you simply give permission to use your exam in this way. Even if you give permission, your anonymity is maintained.

How Is My Multiple-Choice Exam Scored?

The multiple-choice section of each Economics exam is 60 questions and is worth two-thirds of your final score. Your answer sheet is run through the computer, which adds up your correct responses. The total scores on the multiple-choice sections are based on the number of questions answered correctly. The "guessing penalty" has been eliminated, and points are no longer deducted for incorrect answers. As always, no points are awarded for unanswered questions. The formula looks something like this:

$$\text{Section I Raw Score} = N_{right}$$

How Is My Free-Response Exam Scored?

Your performance on the free-response section is worth one-third of your final score. The exams in both microeconomics and macroeconomics consist of three questions. Because the first question is longer than the other two, and therefore scored on a higher scale, it is given a different weight in the raw score. For example, question 1 might be graded on a scale of 10 points, while question 2 is graded on a scale of 7 points and question 3 on a scale of 5 points. Every year, ETS, the Test Development Committee, and the Chief Faculty Consultant tinker with the weighting formulas. However, if you use the following sample formula as a rough guide, you'll be able to gauge your approximate score on the practice questions.

$$\text{Section II Raw Score} = (1.50 \times \text{Score 1}) + (1.0714 \times \text{Score 2}) + (1.50 \times \text{Score 3})$$

So How Is My Final Grade Determined and What Does It Mean?

With a total composite score of 90 points, and 60 being determined on Section I, the remaining 30 must be divided among the three essay questions in Section II. The total composite score is then a weighted sum of the multiple-choice and the free-response sections. In the end, when all of the numbers have been crunched, the Chief Faculty Consultant converts the range of composite scores to the 5-point scale of the AP grades.

Table 1.2 gives you a very rough example of a conversion, and as you complete the practice exam, you may use this table to give yourself a hypothetical grade, keeping in mind that every year the conversion changes slightly to adjust for the difficulty of the questions from year to year. You should receive your grade in early July.

Table 1.2

MACROECONOMICS		
Score Range	AP Grade	Composite Interpretation
71–90	5	Extremely well qualified for college credit
53–70	4	Well qualified
43–52	3	Qualified
31–42	2	Possibly qualified
0–30	1	No recommendation

Example:

In Section I, you receive 50 correct and 10 incorrect responses on the macroeconomics practice exam. In Section II, your scores are 7/10, 6/7, and 5/5.

$$\text{Weighted Section I} = 50$$

$$\text{Weighted Section II} = (1.50 \times 7) + (1.0714 \times 6) + (1.50 \times 5)$$
$$= 10.50 + 6.4284 + 7.5 = 24.4284$$

Composite Score = 50 + 24.4284 = 74.4284, which would be assigned a 5.

How Do I Register and How Much Does It Cost?

If you are enrolled in AP Macroeconomics in your high school, your teacher is going to provide all of these details, but a quick summary wouldn't hurt. After all, you do not have to enroll in the AP course to register for and complete the AP exam. When in doubt, the best source of information is the College Board's Website: www.collegeboard.com.

In 2015, the fee for taking an AP exam was $91 for each exam. Students who demonstrate financial need may receive a partial refund to help offset the cost of testing. The fee and the amount refunded to students demonstrating financial need vary from year to year, so check the College Board Website for the latest information. There are also several *optional* fees that *can* be paid if you want your scores rushed to you or if you wish to receive multiple grade reports.

The coordinator of the AP program at your school will inform you where and when you will take the exam. If you live in a small community, your exam might not be administered at your school, so be sure to get this information.

What If My School Only Offered AP Macroeconomics and Not AP Microeconomics, or Vice Versa?

Because of budget and personnel constraints, some high schools cannot offer both Microeconomics and Macroeconomics. The majority of these schools choose the macro side of the AP program, but some choose the micro side. This puts students at a significant disadvantage when they sit down for the Microeconomics exam without having taken the course. Likewise, Macroeconomics test takers have a rough time when they have not taken the Macroeconomics course. If you are in this situation, and you put in the necessary effort, I assure you that buying this book will give you more than a fighting chance on either exam even if your school did not offer that course.

What Should I Bring to the Exam?

On exam day, I suggest bringing the following items:

- Several pencils and an eraser that doesn't leave smudges.
- Black- or blue-colored pens for the free-response section. Some students like to use two colors to make their graphs stand out for the reader.
- A watch so that you can monitor your time. You never know whether the exam room will have a clock on the wall. Make sure you turn off the beep that goes off on the hour.
- Your school code.
- Your photo identification and social security number.
- Tissues.
- Your quiet confidence that you are prepared!

What Should I *Not* Bring to the Exam?

It's probably a good idea to leave the following items at home:

- A calculator. It is not allowed for the Microeconomics or Macroeconomics exam. However, this does not mean that math will not be required. Questions involving simple computations have recently appeared on the exams, and later in the book I point out a few places where knowing a little math can earn you some points.
- A cell phone, smart watch, camera, tablet, laptop computer, or walkie-talkie.
- Books, a dictionary, study notes, flash cards, highlighting pens, correction fluid, a ruler, or any other office supplies.
- Portable music of any kind.
- Clothing with any economics on it.
- Panic or fear. It's natural to be nervous, but you can comfort yourself that you have used this book well and that there is no room for fear on your exam.

CHAPTER 2

How to Plan Your Time

IN THIS CHAPTER
Summary: The right preparation plan depends on your study habits and the amount of time you have before the test.

Key Idea
✪ Choose the study plan that's right for you.

Three Approaches to Preparing for AP Exams

What kind of preparation program for the AP exam should you use? Should you carefully follow every step, or are there perhaps some steps you can bypass? That depends not only on how much time you have, but also on what kind of student you are. No one knows your study habits, likes, and dislikes better than you do. So you are the only one who can decide which approach to use. This chapter presents three possible study plans, labeled A, B, and C. Look at the brief profiles that follow. These will help you determine which plan is right for you.

You're a **full-school-year prep student** if:

1. You are the kind of person who likes to plan for everything very far in advance.
2. You buy your best friend a gift two months before his or her birthday because you know exactly what to choose, where you will buy it, and how much you will pay for it.
3. You like detailed planning and everything in its place.
4. You feel that you must be thoroughly prepared.
5. You hate surprises.

If you fit this profile, consider **Plan A**.

You're a **one-semester prep student** if:

1. You buy your best friend a gift one week before his or her birthday because it sort of snuck up on you, yet you have a clear idea of exactly what you will be purchasing.
2. You are willing to plan ahead to feel comfortable in stressful situations, but are okay with skipping some details.
3. You feel more comfortable when you know what to expect, but a surprise or two is cool.
4. You're always on time for appointments.

If you fit this profile, consider **Plan B**.

You're a **6-week prep student** if:

1. You buy your best friend a gift for his or her birthday, but you need to include a belated card because you missed it by a couple of days.
2. You work best under pressure and tight deadlines.
3. You feel very confident with the skills and background you've learned in your AP Economics classes.
4. You decided late in the year to take the exam.
5. You like surprises.
6. You feel okay if you arrive 10 to 15 minutes late for an appointment.

If you fit this profile, consider **Plan C**.

Table 2.1 Three Different Study Schedules

MONTH	PLAN A: FULL SCHOOL YEAR	PLAN B: ONE SEMESTER	PLAN C: 6 WEEKS
September to October	Introduction; Chapters 1 to 4	—	—
November	Chapters 5 to 6	—	—
December	Chapters 7 to 8	—	—
January	Chapter 9	Chapters 1 to 4	—
February	Chapter 10	Chapters 5 to 7	—
March	Chapter 11	Chapters 8 to 10	—
April	Chapter 12; Practice Exam 1	Chapters 11 to 12; Practice Exam 1	Skim Chapters 1 to 9; all rapid reviews; take Practice Exam 1
May	Review everything; take Practice Exam 2	Review everything; take Practice Exam 2	Skim Chapters 10 to 12; take Practice Exam 2

Calendar for Each Plan

Plan A: You Have a Full School Year to Prepare

Use this plan to organize your study during the coming school year.

SEPTEMBER–OCTOBER (Check off the activities as you complete them.)

_____ Determine the student mode (A, B, or C) that applies to you.
_____ Carefully read Chapters 1 to 4 of this book.
_____ Take the diagnostic exam.
_____ Pay close attention to your walk-through of the diagnostic exam.
_____ Get on the Web and take a look at the AP website(s).
_____ Skim the review chapters in Step 4 of this book. (Reviewing the topics covered in this section will be part of your yearlong preparation.)
_____ Buy a few color highlighters.
_____ Flip through the entire book. Break the book in. Write in it. Toss it around a little bit . . . highlight it.
_____ Get a clear picture of your own school's AP Economics curriculum.
_____ Begin to use this book as a resource to supplement the classroom learning.

NOVEMBER (the first 10 weeks have elapsed)

_____ Read and study Chapter 5, "Fundamentals of Economic Analysis."
_____ Read and study Chapter 6, "Demand, Supply, Market Equilibrium, and Welfare Analysis."

DECEMBER

_____ Read and study Chapter 7, "Macroeconomic Measures of Performance."
_____ Read and study Chapter 8, "Consumption, Saving, Investment, and the Multiplier."
_____ Review and study Chapters 5 to 8.

JANUARY

_____ Read and study Chapter 9, "Aggregate Demand and Aggregate Supply."
_____ Review Chapters 5 to 9.

FEBRUARY

_____ Read and study Chapter 10, "Fiscal Policy, Economic Growth, and Productivity."
_____ Review and study Chapters 5 to 10.

MARCH

_____ Read and study Chapter 11, "Money, Banking, and Monetary Policy."
_____ Review and study Chapters 5 to 11.

APRIL

_____ Read and study Chapter 12, "International Trade."
_____ Review Chapters 5 to 12.
_____ Take Practice Exam 1 in the last week of April.
_____ Evaluate your Macro strengths and weaknesses.
_____ Study appropriate chapters to correct your Macro weaknesses.

MAY (first two weeks) (THIS IS IT!)

_____ Review Chapters 5 to 12—all the material!
_____ Take Practice Exam 2.
_____ Score yourself.
_____ Get a good night's sleep before the exam. Fall asleep knowing that you are well prepared.

GOOD LUCK ON THE TEST!

Plan B: You Have One Semester to Prepare

If you have already completed one semester of economic studies, the following plan will help you use those skills you've been practicing to prepare for the May exam.

JANUARY–FEBRUARY
_____ Carefully read Chapters 1 to 4 of this book.
_____ Take the diagnostic exam.
_____ Pay close attention to your walk-through of the diagnostic exam.
_____ Read and study Chapter 5, "Fundamentals of Economic Analysis."
_____ Read and study Chapter 6, "Demand, Supply, Market Equilibrium, and Welfare Analysis."
_____ Read and study Chapter 7, "Macroeconomic Measures of Performance."

MARCH (10 weeks to go)
_____ Read and study Chapter 8, "Consumption, Saving, Investment, and the Multiplier."
_____ Read and study Chapter 9, "Aggregate Demand and Aggregate Supply."
_____ Read and study Chapter 10, "Fiscal Policy."
_____ Review Chapters 5 to 10.

APRIL
_____ Read and study Chapter 11, "Money, Banking, and Monetary Policy."
_____ Read and study Chapter 12, "International Trade."
_____ Take Practice Exam 1 in the last week of April.
_____ Evaluate your Macro strengths and weaknesses.
_____ Study appropriate chapters to correct your Macro weaknesses.
_____ Review Chapters 5 to 12.

MAY (first two weeks) (THIS IS IT!)
_____ Review Chapters 5 to 12—all the material!
_____ Take Practice Exam 2.
_____ Score yourself.
_____ Get a good night's sleep before the exam. Fall asleep knowing that you are well prepared.

GOOD LUCK ON THE TEST!

Plan C: You Have Six Weeks to Prepare

Use this plan if you have been studying economics for six months or more and intend to use this book primarily as a specific guide to the AP Macroeconomics exam. If you have only six weeks to prepare, now is not the time to try to learn everything. Focus instead on the essential points you need to know for the test.

APRIL 1–15
_____ Skim Chapters 1 to 4 of this book.
_____ Skim Chapters 5 to 9.
_____ Carefully go over the Rapid Review sections of Chapters 5 to 9.
_____ Skim and highlight the Glossary at the end of the book.

APRIL 15–MAY 1
_____ Skim Chapters 10 to 12.
_____ Carefully go over the Rapid Review sections of Chapters 10 to 12.
_____ Complete the Macroeconomics Practice Exam 1.
_____ Score yourself and analyze your errors.
_____ Continue to skim and highlight the Glossary at the end of the book.

MAY (first two weeks) (THIS IS IT!)
_____ Carefully go over the Rapid Review sections of Chapters 5 to 12.
_____ Take Practice Exam 2.
_____ Score yourself and analyze your errors.
_____ Get a good night's sleep before the exam. Fall asleep knowing that you are well prepared.

GOOD LUCK ON THE TEST!

Determine Your Test Readiness

CHAPTER 3 Take the Diagnostic Exam

Take the Diagnostic Exam

IN THIS CHAPTER

Summary: This chapter includes a diagnostic exam for macroeconomics. It is only half the length of the real thing and is restricted to multiple-choice questions. It is intended to give you an idea of where you stand with your preparation. The questions have been written to approximate the coverage of material that you will see on the AP exam and are similar to the review questions that you see at the end of each chapter in this book. Once you are done with the exam, check your work against the given answers, which also indicate where you can find the corresponding material in this book. Also provided is a way to convert your score to a rough AP score.

Key Ideas
- Practice the kind of multiple-choice questions you will be asked on the real exam.
- Answer questions that approximate the coverage of topics on the real exam.
- Check your work against the given answers.
- Determine your areas of strength and weakness.
- Earmark the pages that you must give special attention.

Diagnostic Exam: AP Macroeconomics

SECTION I
Time—35 Minutes
30 Questions

For the following multiple-choice questions, select the best answer choice and record your choice on the answer sheet provided.

1. Which of the following is an example of capital as an economic resource?

    (A) A cement mixer
    (B) A barrel of crude oil
    (C) A registered nurse
    (D) A share of corporate stock
    (E) A bachelor's degree

Question 2 is based on the production possibilities of two nations that can produce both crepes and paper.

NATION X		NATION Y	
Crepes	Paper	Crepes	Paper
0	3	0	5
9	0	5	0

2. Which of the following statements is true of these production possibilities?

    (A) Nation X has comparative advantage in paper production and should trade paper to Nation Y in exchange for crepes.
    (B) Nation X has comparative advantage in crepe production and should trade crepes to Nation Y in exchange for paper.
    (C) Nation X has absolute advantage in paper production, and Nation Y has absolute advantage in crepe production. No trade is possible.
    (D) Nation Y has absolute advantage in paper production, and Nation X has absolute advantage in crepe production. No trade is possible.
    (E) Nation Y has comparative advantage in crepe production and should trade paper to Nation X in exchange for crepes.

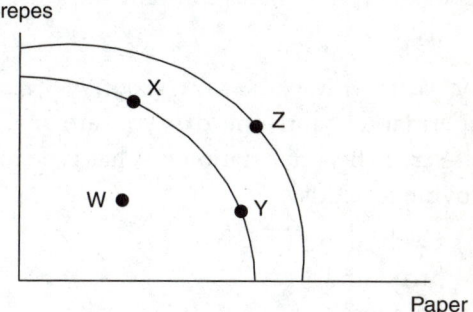

Figure D.1

3. Using Figure D.1, which of the following movements would be described as economic growth?

    (A) W to X
    (B) X to Y
    (C) W to Y
    (D) Z to W
    (E) X to Z

4. Suppose DVD players are a normal good and are exchanged in a competitive market. All else equal, an increase in household income will

    (A) increase the equilibrium quantity and increase the price.
    (B) decrease the equilibrium quantity and increase the price.
    (C) increase the equilibrium price, but the change in quantity is ambiguous.
    (D) decrease the equilibrium quantity and decrease the price.
    (E) increase the equilibrium quantity but the change in price is ambiguous.

5. An American firm moves a manufacturing plant from the United States to Brazil. How will this affect gross domestic product (GDP) in the United States and in Brazil?

   (A) U.S. GDP falls and Brazil's GDP falls.
   (B) U.S. GDP rises and Brazil's GDP falls.
   (C) U.S. GDP falls and Brazil's GDP remains constant.
   (D) U.S. GDP falls and Brazil's GDP rises.
   (E) U.S. GDP remains constant and Brazil's GDP rises.

6. For years you work as a grocery checker at a supermarket, and one day you are replaced by self-serve checkout stations. What type of unemployment is this?

   (A) Cyclical
   (B) Structural
   (C) Seasonal
   (D) Frictional
   (E) Discouraged

7. If the consumer price index (CPI) increases by 2 percent and your nominal income increases by 8 percent, your real income has approximately

   (A) increased by 4 percent.
   (B) decreased by 4 percent.
   (C) increased by 6 percent.
   (D) decreased by 6 percent.
   (E) increased by 10 percent.

8. To deflate nominal gross domestic product (GDP), you must

   (A) divide nominal GDP by the GDP deflator.
   (B) multiply real GDP by the GDP deflator.
   (C) divide real GDP by the GDP deflator.
   (D) multiply nominal GDP by the GDP deflator.
   (E) divide nominal GDP by real GDP.

9. A stronger stock market is likely to cause which of the following changes in the consumption function and aggregate demand?

	CONSUMPTION	AGGREGATE DEMAND
(E)	Decrease	Decrease

10. An increase in corporate optimism will have which of the following effects in the market for loanable funds?

    (A) An increase in supply, lowering the interest rate.
    (B) A decrease in demand, increasing the interest rate.
    (C) An increase in both supply and demand, and an ambiguous change in interest rates.
    (D) A decrease in supply, decreasing the interest rate.
    (E) An increase in demand, increasing the interest rate.

11. If the economy is operating below full employment, which of the following will have the greatest positive impact on real gross domestic product?

    (A) The government decreases spending with no change in taxes.
    (B) The government increases spending with no change in taxes.
    (C) The government decreases spending and matches it with a decrease in taxes.
    (D) The government holds spending constant while decreasing taxes.
    (E) The government increases spending and matches it with an increase in taxes.

12. Suppose the economy is operating beyond full employment. Which of the following is true at this point?

    (A) The short-run aggregate supply curve is horizontal.
    (B) Further increases in aggregate demand will result in a lower price level.
    (C) A decrease in aggregate demand will result in a lower price level if prices are sticky.
    (D) Further increases in aggregate demand will not lower the unemployment rate but will create inflation.
    (E) The unemployment rate is higher than the natural rate of unemployment.

13. When government uses expansionary fiscal policy, the spending multiplier is often smaller than predicted because of

    (A) lower taxes.
    (B) increasing net exports.
    (C) falling unemployment.
    (D) lower interest rates.
    (E) rising price levels.

14. The best example of a negative supply shock to the economy would be

    (A) a decrease in government spending.
    (B) a decrease in the real interest rate.
    (C) an increase in the money supply.
    (D) unexpectedly higher resource prices.
    (E) technological improvements.

15. The Phillips curve represents the relationship between

    (A) inflation and the money supply.
    (B) unemployment and the money supply.
    (C) the money supply and the real interest rate.
    (D) inflation and unemployment.
    (E) investment and the real interest rate.

16. If the economy is experiencing a recession, how will a plan to decrease taxes for consumers and increase spending on government purchases affect real gross domestic product (GDP) and the price level?

    (A) real GDP rises and the price level falls.
    (B) real GDP falls and the price level rises.
    (C) real GDP rises and the price level rises.
    (D) real GDP falls and the price level falls.
    (E) real GDP stays the same and the price level rises.

17. Of the following choices, the one most likely to be preferred by supply-side economists would be

    (A) increased government spending.
    (B) higher tariffs on imported goods.
    (C) lower taxes on household income.
    (D) higher welfare payments.
    (E) a tax credit on capital investment.

18. Automatic stabilizers in the economy serve an important role in

    (A) increasing the length of the business cycle.
    (B) balancing the budget.
    (C) increasing a budget surplus in a recession.
    (D) decreasing net tax revenue during economic growth.
    (E) lessening the impact of a recession.

19. The "crowding-out" effect is the result of

    (A) decreasing interest rates from contractionary fiscal policy.
    (B) increasing interest rates from expansionary fiscal policy.
    (C) increasing interest rates from expansionary monetary policy.
    (D) increasing unemployment rates from expansionary monetary policy.
    (E) a depreciating dollar versus other currencies.

20. In a recession, expansionary monetary policy is designed to

    (A) decrease aggregate demand so that real prices will decrease, which is good for the economy.
    (B) increase aggregate demand, which will increase real output and increase employment.
    (C) increase unemployment, but low prices negate this effect.
    (D) keep interest rates high, which attracts foreign investment.
    (E) boost the value of the dollar in foreign currency markets.

21. A contractionary monetary policy will cause the nominal interest rate, aggregate demand, output, and the price level to change in which of the following ways?

	NOMINAL INTEREST RATE	AGGREGATE DEMAND	OUTPUT	PRICE LEVEL
(A)	Decrease	Increase	Increase	Increase
(B)	Decrease	Decrease	Decrease	Increase
(C)	Increase	Decrease	Decrease	Increase
(D)	Increase	Decrease	Decrease	Decrease
(E)	Increase	Increase	Increase	Increase

22. Which of the following is a tool used by the Fed to increase the money supply?

    (A) A lower discount rate.
    (B) Selling Treasury securities to commercial banks.
    (C) A higher reserve ratio.
    (D) A lower personal income tax rate.
    (E) A lower investment income tax rate.

23. Which of the following monetary policies would lessen the effectiveness of expansionary fiscal policy?

    (A) Decreasing the value of the domestic currency.
    (B) Lowering the income tax rate.
    (C) Selling Treasury securities to commercial banks.
    (D) Lowering the discount rate.
    (E) Lowering the reserve ratio.

24. Which of the following is an accurate statement of the money supply in the United States?

    (A) The money supply is backed by gold reserves.
    (B) The least liquid measure of money is $M2$.
    (C) $M1$ is larger than $M3$.
    (D) Paper money can be exchanged at commercial banks for an equal amount of gold.
    (E) The most liquid measure of money is $M1$.

25. Excess reserves in the banking system will increase if

    (A) the reserve ratio is increased.
    (B) the checking deposits increase.
    (C) the discount rate is increased.
    (D) the Fed sells Treasury securities to commercial banks.
    (E) income tax rates increase.

26. If a bank has $1,000 in checking deposits and the bank is required to reserve $250, what is the reserve ratio? How much does the bank have in excess reserves? What is the size of the money multiplier?

    (A) 25%, $750, $M = ¼$
    (B) 75%, $250, $M = 4$
    (C) 25%, $750, $M = 4$
    (D) 75%, $750, $M = ¼$
    (E) 25%, $250, $M = 4$

27. Suppose the reserve ratio is 10 percent and the Fed buys $1 million in Treasury securities from commercial banks. If money demand is perfectly elastic, which of the following is likely to occur?

    (A) Money supply increases by $10 million, lowering the interest rate and increasing AD.
    (B) Money supply remains constant, the interest rate does not fall, and AD does not increase.
    (C) Money supply increases by $10 million, the interest rate does not fall, and AD does not increase.
    (D) Money supply decreases by $10 million, raising the interest rate and decreasing AD.
    (E) Money supply decreases by $10 million, the interest rate does not rise, and AD does not decrease.

28. If the world price of copper exceeds the domestic (U.S.) price of copper, we would expect

    (A) the United States to be a net exporter of copper.
    (B) the United States to impose a tariff on imported copper to protect domestic producers.
    (C) the demand for U.S. copper to fall.
    (D) a growing trade deficit in the United States in goods and services.
    (E) the dollar to depreciate relative to the currencies of other copper-producing nations.

29. Suppose the Japanese economy is suffering a prolonged recession. Lower Japanese household incomes will affect U.S. exports to Japan, demand for the dollar, and the value of the dollar relative to the yen in which of the following ways?

	EXPORTS TO JAPAN	DEMAND FOR $	VALUE OF $
(A)	Decrease	Decrease	Decrease
(B)	Decrease	Decrease	Increase
(C)	Decrease	Increase	Decrease
(D)	Increase	Decrease	Decrease
(E)	Increase	Decrease	Increase

30. Which of the following is a likely effect of a higher tariff imposed by the United States on imported automobiles?

    (A) Net exports will fall and the dollar will appreciate in value.
    (B) Net exports will fall and the dollar will depreciate in value.
    (C) The price of automobiles in the United States will fall.
    (D) Net exports will rise and the dollar will depreciate in value.
    (E) Net exports will rise and the dollar will appreciate in value.

Macroeconomics Answers and Explanations, Section I

This test was designed to test you on topics that you will see on the AP Macroeconomics exam in the approximate proportions that you will see them. Chronologically they appear in the approximate order of their review in Step 4 of this book, but this is not the case on the AP exam. Topics on your practice exams will be shuffled.

Questions from Chapter 5

1. **A**—Economic capital includes machinery, like a cement mixer, used to produce goods and services. A barrel of oil is a natural resource, and a nurse is a unit of labor. A share of corporate stock is a financial instrument used to raise money so that a firm can purchase more economic resources.

2. **B**—A quick calculation of opportunity costs shows that the opportunity cost of one more paper is three crepes in Nation X and one crepe in Nation Y. The opportunity cost of one more crepe is one-third paper in Nation X and one crepe in Nation Y. Nations benefit by specializing in the goods for which they have a comparative advantage. Thus, Nation Y can specialize in paper production, and Nation X can specialize in crepe production. Nation X trades some crepes to Nation Y in exchange for paper.

3. **E**—Economic growth occurs when the production possibility frontier shifts outward. A movement from W to X or to Y is an improved allocation of unemployed resources, but the potential production has not grown for this nation.

Questions from Chapter 6

4. **A**—If DVDs are normal goods, an increase in household income increases demand for DVDs, which increases quantity and price. Even though this is a macroeconomics exam, be prepared for simple supply and demand questions to test your understanding of markets.

Questions from Chapter 7

5. **D**—The GDP of a nation includes the value of production done within the borders of that nation, regardless of the nationality of the owners. If a U.S. factory moves to Brazil, U.S. GDP falls and it rises in Brazil.

6. **B**—Structural unemployment is the result of changing demand for skills, not the business cycle. Automation decreases the demand for human grocery checkers, and this trend is unlikely to reverse itself.

7. **C**—The percentage change in real income is approximately equal to the percentage change in nominal income minus the percentage change in the price level.

8. **A**—Nominal values must be adjusted to take into account rising prices. To deflate nominal values to real values, divide the nominal value by the price index (in hundredths).

Questions from Chapter 8

9. **D**—A strong stock market increases consumer wealth and optimism, shifting the consumption function upward. Since aggregate demand includes consumption, aggregate demand increases.

10. **E**—In the market for loanable funds, investment (I) represents demand and saving represents supply. More I increases the demand for loanable funds and increases the interest rate.

11. **B**—The spending multiplier is larger than the tax multiplier, which is larger than the balanced budget multiplier (equals 1). If you want the largest increase in real GDP, you should increase government spending and leave taxes unchanged. The largest impact would be seen if we increased spending and decreased taxes, but this is not one of your options.

Questions from Chapter 9

12. **D**—If the economy is beyond full employment, the short-run AS curve is nearly vertical. At this point, increasing aggregate demand cannot increase output and will only increase prices.

13. **E**—The full multiplier is only felt if short-run aggregate supply is horizontal. Any increase in the price level decreases the impact of the spending multiplier.

14. **D**—Higher resource prices shift the short-run aggregate supply (SRAS) curve to the left. All other choices either do not impact the SRAS curve or they would act as positive shocks to the SRAS curve.

15. **D**—The Phillips curve shows the short-run inverse relationship between the inflation rate and the unemployment rate. In the long run, this curve is vertical at the natural rate of unemployment.

Questions from Chapter 10

16. **C**—In the aggregate demand (AD) and aggregate supply (AS) model, lower taxes and more government spending increases AD. This rightward shift increases real GDP and begins to increase the price level.

17. **E**—Supply-side economists advocate increased aggregate supply through incentives for investment and productivity. These would likely come in the form of lower taxes on interest income from savings or tax credits for investment.

18. **E**—As a recession deepens, a progressive tax system and transfer programs like welfare assistance kick in and shorten the downturn in the business cycle. These automatic stabilizers produce recessionary deficits and inflationary surpluses.

19. **B**—Expansionary fiscal policy, intended to boost aggregate demand, that requires borrowing increases interest rates and lessens private investment spending. The decrease in investment spending weakens the impact of expansionary fiscal policy.

Questions from Chapter 11

20. **D**—Increasing the money supply lowers interest rates and increases investment spending (I), aggregate demand (AD), real GDP, and employment.

21. **D**—A contractionary money supply increases nominal interest rates, decreases aggregate demand and real GDP, and decreases the price level.

22. **A**—A lower discount rate increases excess reserves by making it less costly for commercial banks to borrow from the Fed. This is one of the Fed's tools of monetary policy. Remember that the Fed does not impact taxes, as taxes are fiscal policy made by the executive and legislative branches.

23. **C**—Selling securities would draw down excess reserves in the banks, decrease the money supply, and increase the interest rate. This would work counter to expansionary fiscal policy.

24. **E**—Nearest to cash, $M1$ is the most liquid of monetary measures. The U.S. dollar is not backed by gold. Our fiat money has value because the Fed ensures stable prices.

25. **B**—When more deposits are made, the bank increases required reserves by the fraction of the reserve ratio, and increased excess reserves are lent to borrowers to create more money.

26. **C**—The reserve ratio is required reserves divided by deposits, so rr = 0.25. With $250 in required reserves, excess reserves are $750. The money multiplier is equal to $1/rr = 4$.

27. C—The money multiplier is 10 because the reserve ratio is 0.10. If money demand is horizontal, a $1 million increase in excess reserves shifts the money supply curve rightward by $10 million but will not lower the nominal interest rate. If the interest rate does not fall, aggregate demand does not rise.

Questions from Chapter 12

28. A—Nations are net exporters of a good when the world price is greater than the domestic price. A higher world price creates a surplus in the domestic market and the surplus is exported. This situation improves the U.S. balance of trade and would not foster any U.S. protective trade policy. In currency markets, the dollar likely appreciates, as foreign consumers need dollars to buy U.S. copper.

29. A—When relative incomes are falling in Japan, fewer U.S. goods are demanded, so U.S. exports fall. The decrease in the demand for U.S. dollars causes the dollar to depreciate.

30. E—A tariff causes imports to fall, so net exports rise for the U.S. With fewer consumers demanding foreign-built cars, the demand for foreign currency falls, decreasing the value of foreign currency, appreciating the value of the U.S. dollar.

Scoring and Interpretation

Now that you have completed the diagnostic exam and checked your answers, it is time to assess your knowledge and preparation. If you saw some questions that caused you to roll your eyes and mutter "What the . . . ?" then you can focus your study on those areas. If you breezed through some questions, great!

Calculate your raw score with the formula that follows. If you left any questions blank, there is no penalty. Take this raw score on the diagnostic exam and compare it to the table that follows to estimate where you might score at this point.

Section I Raw Score = N_{right}

MACROECONOMICS	
Raw Diagnostic Score	AP Grade
22–30	5
18–21	4
15–17	3
9–14	2
0–8	1

Remember, on the real exam, Section I will account for two-thirds of your composite score, with one-third coming from the free-response Section II. Given this important difference between your diagnostic exam and the real thing, the table above is a *very* preliminary way to convert your diagnostic raw score to an AP grade. No matter how you scored on the diagnostic exam, it is time to begin to review for your AP Macroeconomics Exam.

Develop Strategies for Success

CHAPTER 4 How to Approach Each Question Type

How to Approach Each Question Type

IN THIS CHAPTER
Summary: Use these question-answering strategies to raise your AP score.

Key Ideas

Multiple-Choice Questions
✪ Read the question carefully.
✪ Try to answer the question yourself before reading the answer choices.
✪ Guess if you can eliminate one or more answer choices.
✪ Remember that drawing a picture can help.
✪ Don't spend too much time on any one question.

Free-Response Questions
✪ Write clearly and legibly.
✪ Be consistent from one part of your answer to another.
✪ Draw a graph if one is required.
✪ If the question can be answered with one word or number, don't write more.
✪ Pay attention to the prompts.

Section I: Multiple-Choice Questions

Because you are a seasoned student accustomed to the educational testing machine, you have surely participated in more standardized tests than you care to count. You probably know some students who always seem to ace the multiple-choice questions and some students who would rather set themselves on fire than sit for another round of "bubble trouble." I hope that, with a little background and a few tips, you might improve your scores in this important component of the AP Macroeconomics exam.

First, the background. Every multiple-choice question has three important parts:

1. The **stem** is the basis for the actual question. Sometimes this comes in the form of a fill-in-the-blank statement, rather than a question.

   Example
   Average fixed cost is computed by dividing total fixed cost by

   Example
   If the economy is operating below full employment, which of the following fiscal policies is most likely to decrease the unemployment rate?

2. The **correct answer option.** Obviously, this is the one selection that best completes the statement, or responds to the question in the stem. Because you have purchased this book, you will select this option many, many times.

3. **Distractor options.** Just as it sounds, these are the incorrect answers intended to distract the person who decided not to purchase this book. You can locate this person in the exam room by searching for the individual who is repeatedly smacking his or her forehead on the desktop.

Students who do well on multiple-choice exams are so well prepared that they can easily find the correct answer, but other students do well because they are savvy enough to identify and avoid the distractors. Much research has been done on how to best study for, and complete, multiple-choice questions. You can find some of this research by using your favorite Internet search engine, but here are a few tips that many economics students find useful.

1. *Let's be careful out there.* You must carefully read the question. This sounds pretty obvious, but you would be surprised how tricky those test developers can be. For example, rushing past and failing to see the use of a negative can throw a student.

   Example
   Which of the following is *not* true of firms in perfect competition?
   A. Firms produce a homogenous good.
   B. Firms engage in price discrimination.
   C. Firms earn a normal profit in the long run.
   D. Firms have no ability to influence the market price.
   E. Firms produce the output where price is equal to marginal cost.

   A student who is going too fast and ignores the negative *not* might select option (A) because it is true of perfectly competitive firms, and it was the first option that the student saw.

2. *See the answer, be the answer.* Many people find success when they carefully read the question and, before looking at the alternatives, visualize the correct answer. This allows the person to narrow the search for the correct option and identify the distractors. Of course, this visualization tip is most useful for students who have used this book to thoroughly review the economic content.

Example

The profit-maximizing monopolist sets output where

> Before you even look at the options, you should know that the answer is MR = MC. Find that option, and then quickly confirm to yourself that the others are indeed wrong.

3. *Never say never.* Words like "never" and "always" are called absolute qualifiers. If these words are used in one of the choices, it is rarely the correct choice.

Example

Which of the following is true about production in the short run?

A. MP is always greater than AP.
B. MP is never increasing.

> If you can think of any situation where the statements in (A) and (B) are untrue, then you have discovered distractors and can eliminate these as valid choices.

4. *Easy is as easy does.* It's exam day and you're all geared up to set this very difficult test on its ear. The first question looks like a no-brainer. Of course! The answer is 7, choice (C). But rather than smiling at the satisfaction that you knew the answer, you doubt yourself. Could it be that easy? Sometimes they are just that easy.

5. *Sometimes a blind squirrel finds an acorn.* Should you guess? If you have no clue which choice is correct, guessing is a no-lose strategy. Even with a wild guess, you have a 20 percent chance of getting it right. If you leave it blank, you have no chance. I am sure that you can do the math.

6. *Draw it, nail it.* Many questions can be easily answered if you do a quick sketch in the margins of your test book. Hey, you paid for that test book; you might as well use it.

Example

In an economy with a vertical aggregate supply curve, a decrease in consumer confidence will cause output and the price level to change in which of the following ways?

	OUTPUT	PRICE LEVEL
(A)	No change	Increase
(B)	Decrease	Decrease
(C)	Increase	No change
(D)	No change	No change
(E)	No change	Decrease

> These types of questions are particularly difficult because the answer requires two ingredients. It also requires a very thorough understanding of the AD/AS model, and here is where your graph comes in. The first thing you should do is quickly draw the situation given to you in the question: a vertical AS curve. Show a downward-sloping AD curve shifting to the left and you can see that option (E) is correct. The graph speaks for itself.

7. *Come back, come back!* There are 60 questions, and none of these is worth more than the other. If you are struggling with a particular question, circle it in your **exam book**

and move on. Another question deeper into the exam might jog a memory of a theory you studied or something you learned from a practice exam in this book. You can then go back and quickly slay the beast. But if you spend a ridiculous amount of time on one question, you will feel your confidence and your time slipping away. Which leads me to my last tip.

8. *Timing is everything, kid.* You have about 70 seconds of time for each of the 60 questions. Keep an eye on your watch as you pass the halfway point. If you are running out of time and you have a few questions left, skim them for the easy (and quick) ones so that the rest of your scarce time can be devoted to those that need a little extra reading or thought.

Other things to keep in mind:

- Take the extra half of a second required to clearly fill in the bubbles.
- Don't smudge anything with sloppy erasures. If your eraser is smudgy, ask the proctor for another.
- Absolutely, positively check that you are bubbling the same line on the answer sheet as the question you are answering. I suggest that every time you turn the page you double-check that you are still lined up correctly.

Section II: Free-Response Questions

Your score on the FRQs amounts to one-third of your grade, and as a longtime reader of essays, I assure you there is no other way to score highly than to know your stuff. While you can guess on a multiple-choice question and have a one-in-five chance of getting the correct answer, there is no room for guessing in this section. There are, however, some tips that you can use to enhance your FRQ scores.

1. *Easy to Read = Easy to Grade.* Organize your responses around the separate parts of the question and clearly label each part of your response. In other words, do not hide your answer; make it easy to find and easy to read. It helps you, and it helps the reader to see where you're going. *Trust me, helping the reader can never hurt.* Which leads me to a related tip: Write in English, not Sanskrit. Even the most levelheaded and unbiased reader has trouble keeping his or her patience while struggling to read sloppy handwriting. I have seen three readers waste almost 10 minutes using the Rosetta stone to decipher a paragraph of text that was obviously written by a time-traveling student from the Byzantine Empire.

2. *Consistently wrong can be good.* The free-response questions are written in several parts, each building upon the first. If you are looking at an eight-part question, it can be scary. However, these questions are graded so that you can salvage several points even if you do not correctly answer the first part. The key thing for you to know is that you must be consistent, even if it is consistently wrong. For example, you might be asked to draw an AD/AS graph showing how expansionary monetary policy can eliminate a recessionary gap. Following sections might ask you to show the change in the aggregate price level and real GDP—each being determined by the AD/AS graph you drew earlier. So let's say you draw your graph, but you show *contractionary* monetary policy. Obviously you are not going to receive that graphing point. But if you proceed by showing correct changes to the aggregate price level and real GDP for your *incorrect* graph, you would be surprised how forgiving the grading rubric can be.

3. *Have the last laugh with a well-drawn graph.* There are some points that require an explanation (i.e., "Describe how . . ."). Not all free-response questions require a graph, but a garbled paragraph of explanation can be saved with a perfect graph that tells the reader you know the answer to the question. This does not work in reverse.

4. *If I say draw, you better draw, Tex.* There are what readers call "graphing points," and these cannot be earned with a well-written paragraph. For example, if you are asked to draw the monopoly scenario described above, certain points will be awarded for the graph, and only the graph. A delightfully written and entirely accurate paragraph of text will not earn the graphing points. You also need to clearly label graphs. You might think that downward-sloping line is obviously a demand curve, but some of those graphing points will not be awarded if lines and points are not clearly, and accurately, identified.

5. *Give the answer, not a dissertation.* There are some parts of a question where you are asked to simply "identify" something. For example, "Identify the price if this firm were a monopolist" or "Identify the area that corresponds to deadweight loss." This type of question requires a quick piece of analysis that can literally be answered in one word or number. That point will be given if you provide that one word or number whether it is the only word you write or the fortieth that you write. For example, you might be given a table that shows how a firm's output changes as it hires more workers. One part of the question asks you to identify the optimal number of workers that the firm should hire. Suppose the correct answer is 4. The point is given if you say "4," "four," and maybe even "iv." If you write a 500-word Magna Carta concluding with the word "four," you will get the point, but will have wasted precious time. This brings me to . . .

6. *Welcome to the magical kingdom.* If you surround the right answer to a question with a paragraph of economic wrongness, you will usually get the point, so long as you say the magic word. The only exception is a direct contradiction of the right answer. For example, suppose that when asked to *identify* the optimal number of workers, you spend a paragraph describing how the workers are unionized and therefore are subject to a price ceiling and that the exchange rate between those workers and the production possibility frontier means the answer is four. You will get the point! You said they should hire four, and "four" was the magic word. However, if you say that the answer is four, but that it is also five and on Mondays it is seven, you have contradicted yourself and the point will not be given.

7. *Marginally speaking.* This point is made in the first two chapters of review in this book, but it bears repeating here as a valuable test-taking strategy. In economics, anything that is optimal, or efficient, or rational, or cost minimizing, or profit maximizing can be answered by telling the reader that the marginal benefits must equal the marginal costs. Depending upon the situation, you might have to clarify that "marginal benefit" to the firm is "marginal revenue," or to the employer "marginal revenue product." If the question asks you *why* the answer is four, there is always a very short phrase that readers look for so that they may award the point. This answer often includes the appropriate marginal comparison.

8. *Identify, Illustrate, Define, Indicate, and Explain.* Each part of a free-response question includes a prompt that tells you what the reader will be looking for so that the points can be awarded. If the question asks you to "identify" something, you may need only one word or a short phrase to receive all of the points. Writing a paragraph here will only waste your time. As mentioned, any reference to "illustrate" will require you to

draw, or redraw, a graph to receive points. If the question asks you to "define" a concept, you need to devote more time to providing your best definition of that concept. If you are prompted to "indicate" something, you must simply state what is expected to happen. For example, suppose you are told that the central bank has sold bonds in an open market operation and you are asked to indicate what will happen to interest rates. All you need to do to earn the point is to indicate that interest rates will increase. You may also get the point if you clearly indicate, preferably with an arrow, in a graph of the money market that interest rates are rising. The most time-intensive prompt is usually one that involves "explain." Suppose you are told that the Canadian dollar is appreciating relative to the U.S. dollar. Then you are asked to explain how this will impact domestic output and the price level in the United States. To give yourself the best chance at receiving all of the points, your response must provide two parts. First, give a clear statement of what exactly will happen; second, explain why it is going to happen.

Here are some other things to keep in mind:

- The free-response section begins with a 10-minute reading period. Use this time well to jot down some quick notes to yourself so that when you actually begin to respond, you will have a nice start.
- The first parts of the free-response questions are the easiest parts. Spend just enough time to get these points before moving on to the more difficult sections.
- The questions are written in logical order. If you find yourself explaining Part C before responding to Part B, back up and work through the logical progression of topics.
- Abbreviations are your friends. You can save time by using commonly accepted abbreviations for economic variables and graphical curves, and you will get more adept at their use as your mastery improves. For example, in macroeconomics you can save some time by using "OMO" rather than "open market operation," and in microeconomics you can use "MRP" rather than "marginal revenue product."
- *Show your work.* In recent years, the exam has included more mathematical components that allow you to demonstrate that you know a particular economic concept by computing something. Virtually all of these problems include the prompt "show your work," and you will *not* earn points if you have not set up the mathematical problem correctly and shown your work clearly. For example, suppose that price is $5 and 10 units are sold at this price; you are asked to compute total revenue and show your work. You know that total revenue (P × Q) is obviously $50, but if you simply state that total revenue is $50, you will not earn the point, because you did not show your work. The simple fix for this is to write: TR = P × Q = $5 × 10 = $50. Point earned!

Review the Knowledge You Need to Score High

CHAPTER 5 Fundamentals of Economic Analysis
CHAPTER 6 Demand, Supply, Market Equilibrium, and Welfare Analysis
CHAPTER 7 Macroeconomic Measures of Performance
CHAPTER 8 Consumption, Saving, Investment, and the Multiplier
CHAPTER 9 Aggregate Demand and Aggregate Supply
CHAPTER 10 Fiscal Policy, Economic Growth, and Productivity
CHAPTER 11 Money, Banking, and Monetary Policy
CHAPTER 12 International Trade

CHAPTER 5

Fundamentals of Economic Analysis

IN THIS CHAPTER
Summary: If there are two concepts that you should have down pat, they are: (1) scarce resources require decision makers to make decisions that involve costs and benefits, and (2) these decisions are best made when the additional benefits of the action are exactly offset by the additional costs of the action. This chapter presents material that, at least on the surface, appears to be "Econ-lite." Some readers might make the mistake of simply glossing over it on the way to meatier topics. I urge you to take the time to reinforce these early concepts, for they should, like a bad commercial jingle, stick in your subconscious throughout your preparation for the AP exam.

Key Ideas
✪ Scarcity
✪ Opportunity Cost
✪ Marginal Analysis
✪ Production Possibilities
✪ Functions of Economic Systems

5.1 Scarce Resources

Main Topics: *Economic Resources, Scarcity, Trade-Offs, Opportunity Cost, Marginal Analysis*

Economic Resources

Economics is the study of how people, firms, and societies use their scarce productive resources to best satisfy their unlimited material wants. Resources, or Factors of Production, are commonly separated into four groups:

- *Labor.* Human effort and talent, physical and mental. This can be augmented by education and training (human capital).
- *Land or natural resources.* Any resource created by nature. This may be arable land, mineral deposits, oil and gas reserves, or water.
- *Physical capital.* Manmade equipment like machinery, but also buildings, roads, vehicles, and computers.
- *Entrepreneurial ability.* The effort and know-how to put the other resources together in a productive venture.

Scarcity

All of the above resources are scarce, or in limited supply. Since productive resources are scarce, it makes sense that the production of goods and services must be scarce.

Example:

Sometimes it is easier to see this if you look at the production of something familiar, like the production of a term paper.

- *Labor.* Your hours of research, writing, and rewriting. As we all know, these hours are scarce, or limited to the number of waking hours in the day.
- *Land/natural resources.* Paper (trees) and electricity (rivers, coal, natural gas, wind, solar). Not only are these in scarce supply, but your ability to acquire these resources is limited by your income, which is a result of using some of your scarce labor hours to work for a wage.
- *Capital.* Your computer, printer, desk, pens and pencils, the library and sources within.
- *Entrepreneurial ability.* The skill that it takes to compile the research into a coherent, thoughtful, and articulate piece of academic work.

Trade-Offs

The fact that we are faced with scarce resources implies that individuals, firms, and governments are constantly faced with trade-offs.

Individuals

Consumers choose between housing arrangements (Do I rent an apartment or buy a home?), transportation options, grocery store items, and many other daily purchases. Workers and students must choose from a wide range of employment and education opportunities. (Do I pick up an extra shift? Do I pursue my MBA or Ph.D.?)

Firms

For the firm, decisions are often centered upon which good or service can be provided, how much should be produced, and how to go about producing those goods and services.

A local restaurant considers whether or not to stay open later on Saturday night. A steel company must decide whether to open a plant in Indiana or in Indonesia.

Governments

Every society, in one form or another, places many tough decisions in the hands of government, both local and national. Not surprisingly, local government is faced with issues that are likely to have an immediate impact on the lives of local citizens. (Should we use tax revenues to pave potholes in the streets or buy a new city bus?) At the national level, not all citizens might/would feel the impact immediately, but the stakes are likely much higher. (Should we open protected wilderness areas to oil and gas exploration? Should we impose a tariff on imported rice?)

Regardless of the decision maker—individual, firm, or government—the reality of scarce resources creates a trade-off between the opportunity that is taken and the opportunity that was not taken and thus forgone. The value of what was given up is called the **opportunity cost**.

Opportunity Cost

At the most basic level, the opportunity cost of doing something is what you sacrifice to do it. In other words, if you use a scarce resource to pursue activity X, the opportunity cost of activity X is activity Y, the next best use of that resource.

> **Example:**
> You have one scarce hour to spend between studying for an exam or working at a coffee shop for $8 per hour. If you study, the opportunity cost of studying is $8.

> **Example:**
> You have one scarce hour to spend between studying for an exam or working at a coffee shop for $8 per hour or mowing your uncle's lawn for $10 per hour. If you choose to study, what is the opportunity cost of studying?
>
> *Be careful!* A common mistake is to add up the value of *all* of your other options ($18), but this misses an important point. In this scenario, and in many others, you have one hour to allocate to one activity, thus giving up the others. By choosing to study, you really only gave up one thing: mowing the lawn *or* serving cappuccinos, not both.
>
> The opportunity cost of using your resource to do activity X is the value the resource would have in its *next best alternative use*. Therefore, the opportunity cost of studying is $10, the better of your two alternatives.
>
> *At this point, you might be wondering, "Does everything have a dollar figure attached to it? Can't we just enjoy something without slapping a price tag on it?"*

"Pay close attention here; this is a very common mistake."
—Hillary, AP Student

This is an excellent question, and the concept can often be a difficult point to make. If you have one scarce hour and you could either work at the coffee shop for $8 or take a restful nap, the opportunity cost of working is the nap, which certainly has value. How can we place a dollar value on the nap? Maybe you are giving serious thought to taking the nap, but your employer at the coffee shop really needs you to work. Maybe your employer offers you $10 to forgo the nap and come to work. After some consideration, you still choose the nap. Surely there is a price (the wage) that would be high enough to entice you to come to work at the coffee shop. If your employer offered you just enough to compensate you for the nap you gave up, you have found the value that you placed on the nap.

Marginal Analysis

Most decisions are made based upon a change in the status quo. You have one cup of coffee (the status quo) and are deciding whether to have another. You have studied five hours for an economics exam (the status quo) and need to decide if it is in your best interest to study another hour.

These decisions are said to be made at the margin. The next cup of coffee brings with it *additional* (or marginal) benefits to the consumer but comes at *additional* (marginal) costs. The rational consumer weighs the additional benefits against the additional costs.

Marginal analysis. This is a concept that is seen throughout economics, and throughout this book, but let's briefly look at it from a consumer's point of view.

Marginal cost (MC). The additional cost incurred from the consumption of the next unit of a good or service.

Marginal benefit (MB). The additional benefit received from the consumption of the next unit of a good or service. Another way of measuring marginal benefit is to ask yourself, "How much would I pay for the next unit of this good?"

Example:

The soda machine down the hall charges me $1.00 for every can of pop.

The decision to buy another soda is another example of marginal analysis. If I expect to receive at least $1 in additional benefit, or if I am willing to pay $1 or more to have it, buying another soda is a rational decision. This decision is shown in Figure 5.1.

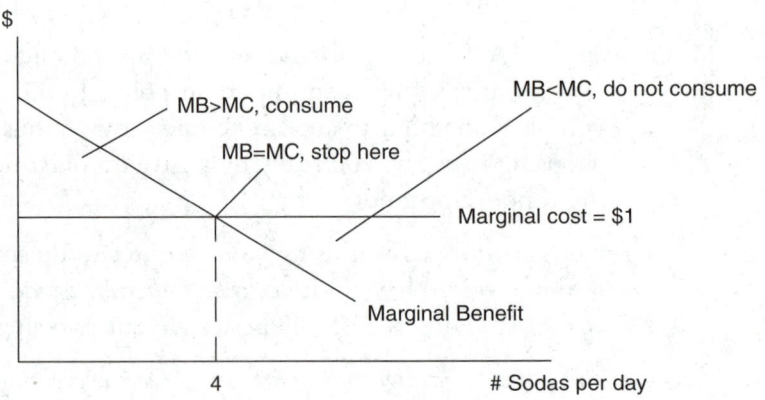

Figure 5.1

So how many sodas will I consume in a typical day? For each of the first three sodas, my MB > $1, the marginal cost of the next soda. The fourth soda provides me with exactly $1 in marginal benefit, so I find it exactly worth my while to buy it. The fifth soda is not bought because the MC > MB. Notice that my MB declines as I consume more sodas. This is a fairly predictable relationship, since I am likely to enjoy my first soda of the day more than my fifth.

> **Rule:**
>
> Do something if the marginal benefits ≥ marginal costs of doing it.
>
> Stop doing something when the marginal benefits = marginal costs of doing it.
>
> Never do something when the marginal benefits < marginal costs of doing it.

You will find this to be true in consumption, production, hiring, and many other economic decisions.

5.2 Production Possibilities

Main Topics: *Production Possibilities Curve, Resource Substitutability, Law of Increasing Costs, Comparative Advantage and Specialization, Efficiency, Growth*

Production Possibilities Curve

To examine production and opportunity cost, economists find it useful to create a simplified model of an individual, or a nation, that can choose to allocate its scarce resources between the production of two goods or services. For now we assume that those resources are being fully employed and used efficiently.

Example:

The owner of a small bakery can allocate a fixed amount of labor (the chef and her helpers), capital (mixers, pans, and ovens), natural resources (raw materials), and her entrepreneurial talent toward the production of pastries and pizza crusts.

The **production possibilities** table (Table 5.1) lists the different combinations of pastries and crusts that can be produced with a fixed quantity of scarce resources.

Table 5.1

PASTRIES	PIZZA CRUST
0	10
1	8
2	6
3	4
4	2
5	0

If the chef wishes to produce one more pastry, she must give up two pizza crusts. If she wishes one more crust, she must give up one-half of a pastry.

In other words:

The opportunity cost of a pastry is two crusts.
The opportunity cost of a pizza crust is one-half of a pastry.

We can graphically depict Table 5.1 in a **production possibility curve.** Each point on the curve represents some maximum output combination of the two products. Some refer to this curve as a **production possibility frontier** because it reflects the outer limit of production. Any point outside the frontier (e.g., 4, 8) is currently unattainable, and any point inside the frontier (e.g., 1, 2) fails to use all of the bakery's available resources in an efficient way. We talk more about efficiency at the end of this section.

So here you might wonder, "Why is there a limit to the production of these goods? In other words, why doesn't the frontier just expand to allow an unlimited amount of either?"

Over the course of time, the frontier is believed to expand. But at any given point in time, we must confront the scarcity problem again. The resources used to produce these goods are scarce, and thus the production frontier is going to act as a binding constraint. The concept of economic growth is introduced in this chapter and also discussed in Chapter 10, but for the time being, the frontier looks like Figure 5.2.

Figure 5.2

The opportunity cost of each good is also apparent in the production possibility curve itself. We ignore the fact that the curve slopes downward and simply focus on its magnitude, or absolute value.

- The slope of the curve, 2 in our case, measures the opportunity cost of the good on the *x*-axis.
- The inverse of the slope, ½ in our case, measures the opportunity cost of the good on the *y*-axis.

Notice that with a straight line, the opportunity cost of producing more of each good is always a constant. Is this realistic?

Resource Substitutability

Suppose our bakery chef is currently producing 10 pizza crusts and zero pastries. But today she decides that she should produce one pastry and eight crusts. In Figure 5.2, this decision appears fairly straightforward.

What we often forget is that resources must be reallocated from pizza crust production to pastry production. Labor, capital, and natural resources must be removed from crust production and moved into pastry production.

Perhaps some of the capital (i.e., pans) in the bakery are better suited to pizza crust production than pastry production. Certainly raw materials like chocolate and frosting are not very useful for pizza crust production, but extremely valuable to the pastry production.

The same could be said for individual laborers. Maybe the entrepreneur herself was trained as a French pastry chef and can make pizza crusts, but not as well as she can make éclairs. The fact that these resources are better suited to the production of one good, and less easily adaptable to the production of the other good, gives us the concept of . . .

Law of Increasing Costs

Law of increasing costs tells us that the more of a good that is produced, the greater its opportunity cost. This reality gives us a production possibility curve that is concave to the origin, or *bowed outward*, as shown in Figure 5.3.

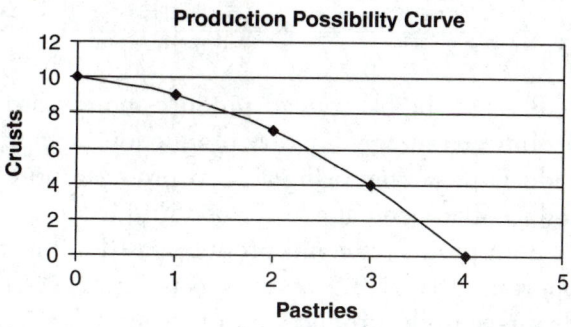

Figure 5.3

Now as the bakery produces more pastries, the opportunity cost (slope) begins to rise. Of course, the same is happening if the chef chooses to produce more crusts.

- Because resources are not perfectly adaptable to alternative uses, our production possibility curve is unlikely to be linear and will probably become steeper as production moves downward along the curve.

Comparative Advantage and Specialization

I went to the dentist's office the other day. For 30 minutes the dental hygienist took an x-ray and then cleaned and flossed my teeth. When she was done, the dentist popped in, peeked at her handiwork, studied my x-ray, and sent me on my way with a new toothbrush. Why did my dentist let the hygienist do all the cleaning and flossing when he is perfectly capable of doing the task? Because the dentist's scarce time resource is better used performing tasks like oral surgery. The opportunity cost of the dentist flossing my teeth is the revenue earned from a procedure that only he is qualified to perform. Forgoing the revenue from the oral surgery is avoided by assigning the cleaning tasks to the hygienist, whose specialty is oral hygiene, but not oral surgery.

The law of increasing costs tells us that it becomes more costly to produce a good as you produce more of it. This reality prompts us to find other, less expensive ways to get our hands on additional units. The concepts of **specialization** and **comparative advantage** describe the way that individuals, nations, and societies can acquire more goods at lower cost.

Example:

Suppose our bakery, which can produce both pizza crusts and pastries, shares the local market with a pizza parlor. The pizza parlor can also produce pastries, but it might rather produce pizza crusts. Each firm would like to produce more goods at lower cost. Table 5.2 shows the production possibilities of these two firms and the opportunity costs of producing more of each good.

Table 5.2

BAKERY		PIZZA PARLOR	
Pastries	Crusts	Pastries	Crusts
10	0	5	0
0	5	0	10
OPPORTUNITY COSTS		**OPPORTUNITY COSTS**	
1 pastry costs	1 crust costs	1 pastry costs	1 crust costs
½ crust	2 pastries	2 crusts	½ pastry

Because the bakery can produce more pastries than the pizza parlor, the bakery has **absolute advantage** in pastry production. The pizza parlor has absolute advantage in crust production. Simply being able to produce more of a good does not mean that the firm produces that good at a lower opportunity cost.

Both producers could produce pastries, but the bakery can produce pastries at lower opportunity cost (0.5 crusts versus 2 crusts). The bakery is said to have **comparative advantage** in the production of pastries. Likewise, the table illustrates that the pizza parlor has the comparative advantage in pizza crusts (0.5 pastries versus 2 pastries). These producers can, and indeed should, **specialize** by producing only pastries at the bakery and only crusts at the pizza parlor. Because these firms are specializing and producing at lower cost, not only do they benefit by earning more profit, but consumers across town benefit from purchasing goods at lower prices.

In microeconomics, the principle of comparative advantage explains why the pediatrician delivers the babies while the electrician wires the house, and not the other way around. In macroeconomics, this principle is the basis for showing how nations can gain from free trade. We explore trade among nations in the last chapter. To see the microeconomics gains from specialization, we do a game called "before and after."

Before. Each firm devotes half of its resources to pastry production and half to crust production.

Total citywide pastry production = 5 + 2.5 = 7.5
Total citywide crust production = 2.5 + 5 = 7.5

After. Each firm specializes in the production of the good for which it has comparative advantage.

Total citywide pastry production = 10 + 0 = 10
Total citywide crust production = 0 + 10 = 10

Figure 5.4 shows both production possibility frontiers and how a combination of 10 crusts and 10 pastries (specialization) was previously unattainable and is superior to when each firm produced at the midpoint (50/50) of their individual frontiers.

> "Know the different ways of showing comparative advantage. This is a potential free-response question."
> —AP Teacher

- If firms and individuals produce goods based upon their comparative advantage, society gains more production at lower cost.

KEY IDEA

Efficiency

If not all available resources are being used to their fullest, the economy is operating at some point inside the production possibility frontier. This is clearly inefficient. But even if the economy is operating at some point on the frontier, who is to say that it is the point that is

Figure 5.4

most desired by the citizens? If it does not happen to be the point that society most wants, we are also facing an inefficient situation.

In this production possibility model, there are two types of efficiency:

Productive efficiency. The economy is producing the maximum output for a given level of technology and resources. All points on the production frontier are productively efficient.

Allocative efficiency. The economy is producing the optimal mix of goods and services. By optimal, we mean that it is the combination of goods and services that provides the most net benefit to society. If society is allocatively efficient, it is operating at the best point on the frontier.

How do we determine which point is the best point? Remember how I determined the optimal number of sodas to consume every day? Suppose we could measure, societywide, the marginal benefit received from the consumption of pizza crusts. Like my MB for sodas, the societal MB for crusts is falling as more crusts are consumed. We already know that the marginal cost of producing pizza crusts increases. The marginal cost of producing and marginal benefit of consuming more pizza crusts are illustrated in Figure 5.5.

Figure 5.5

The allocatively efficient amount of pizza crusts is Q^*, the quantity where the MB of the next crust is exactly equal to the MC of producing it. If we produce anything beyond this point, we have created a situation where the MC of producing it exceeds our marginal enjoyment of it. Clearly we should devote those resources to other goods that we desire to a greater degree, and that are produced at a lower marginal cost.

Growth

At a given point in time, the bakery (or a nation's economy) cannot operate beyond the production frontier. However, as time passes, it is likely that firms and nations experience economic growth. This results in a production frontier that moves outward, expanding the set of production and consumption. More discussion of growth follows in the macroeconomic section of the review.

Economic growth, the ability to produce a larger total output over time, can occur if one or all of the following occur:

- An increase in the quantity of resources. For example, the bakery acquires another oven.
- An increase in the quality of existing resources. For example, the chef acquires the best assistants in the city.
- Technological advancements in production. For example, electric mixers versus hand mixers.

Figure 5.6 illustrates economic growth for the bakery.

Figure 5.6

Notice that the above frontier has not increased proportionally. The maximum number of crusts that could possibly be produced has increased by 50 percent, while the maximum number of pastries has increased by 100 percent.

Economic growth almost always occurs in this way. For example, technological advancements in wireless technology have certainly increased the nation's capacity to produce cell phones and tablet computers but has not likely measurably increased our capacity to produce tomatoes.

5.3 Functions of Economic Systems

Main Topic: *Market Systems*

Market Systems

In the twenty-first century, most industrially advanced nations have gravitated toward a **market economy—capitalism.**

Keys to a Market System

- *Private Property*. Individuals, not government, own most economic resources. This private ownership encourages innovation, investment, growth, and trade.

   Example:

   If the state owned the bakery ovens, mixers, and even the building itself, how much of an incentive would our entrepreneur have to maintain the equipment, the inventory, or even the quality of the product? Knowing that the state could take these resources with very little notice, our chef might just do the bare minimum, and if this situation happened all over town, the local economy would languish.

- *Freedom*. Individuals are free to acquire resources to produce goods and services, and free to choose which of their resources to sell to others so that they may buy their own goods and services.

   Example:

   The bakery can freely use its resources to produce rolls, pastries, croissants, and anything else it believes leads to profitability. Of course, this freedom is limited by legal constraints. The bakery cannot sell illegal drugs from the back door, and the chef is not free to offer open-heart surgery with her bagels.

- *Self-Interest and Incentives*. Individuals are motivated by self-interest in their use of resources. Entrepreneurs seek to maximize profit, while consumers seek to maximize happiness. With these incentives, goods are sold and bought.

   Example:

   Our bakery owner, motivated by profit, seeks to offer products that appeal to her customers. Customers, seeking to maximize their happiness, consume these bakery products only if they satisfy their personal tastes and wants.

- *Competition*. Buyers and sellers, acting independently, and motivated by self-interest, freely move in and out of individual markets. Again, the issue of incentives is powerful. A new firm, eager to compete in a market, only enters that market if profits are available.

   Example:

   Competition implies that prices are determined in the marketplace and not controlled by individual sellers, buyers, or the government. Our bakery owner employs labor at the going market wage, which is determined in the competitive local labor market. She offers baked products at the going price, which is determined in the competitive local market for those goods.

> "This concept, although an easy one, is a definite MC question. Don't miss it."
> —Adam, AP Student

- *Prices.* Prices send signals to buyers and sellers, and resource allocation decisions are made based upon this information. Prices also serve to ration goods to those consumers who are most willing and able to pay those prices. Prices coordinate the decentralized economic activity of millions of individuals and firms in a way that no one central economic figure can hope to achieve. Prices, not just for goods and services but also for labor and other resources, are the delivery mechanism for the above incentives—profit for the firm and happiness for the consumer.

Example:
As the price of labor, relative to capital, changes, the bakery chef might be motivated to readjust her employment of assistants. Changes in the relative price of her products might prompt consumers to readjust their purchasing decisions.

Review Questions

1. Economics is best described as

   (A) the study of how scarce material wants are allocated between unlimited resources.
   (B) the study of how scarce labor can be replaced by unlimited capital.
   (C) the study of how decision makers choose the best way to satisfy their unlimited material wants with a scarce supply of resources.
   (D) the study of how unlimited material wants can best be satisfied by allocating limitless amounts of productive resources.
   (E) the study of how capitalism is superior to any other economic system.

2. A student decides that, having already spent three hours studying for an exam, she should spend one more hour studying for the same exam. Which of the following is most likely true?

   (A) The marginal benefit of the fourth hour is certainly less than the marginal cost of the fourth hour.
   (B) The marginal benefit of the fourth hour is at least as great as the marginal cost of the fourth hour.
   (C) Without knowing the student's opportunity cost of studying, we have no way of knowing whether or not her marginal benefits outweigh her marginal costs.
   (D) The marginal cost of the third hour was likely greater than the marginal cost of the fourth hour.
   (E) The marginal benefit of the third hour was less than the marginal cost of the third hour.

The island nation of Beckham uses economic resources to produce tea and crumpets. Use the following production possibilities frontier for questions 3 to 4.

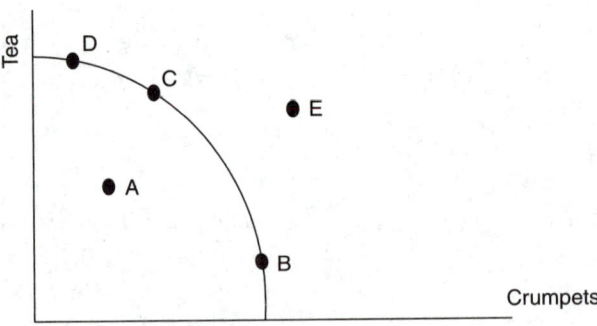

3. Economic growth is best represented by a movement from
   (A) A to B
   (B) B to C
   (C) C to D
   (D) D to E
   (E) E to A

4. The shape of this PPF tells us that

   (A) economic resources are perfectly substitutable from production of tea to production of crumpets.
   (B) citizens prefer that an equal amount of tea and crumpets be produced.
   (C) the opportunity cost of producing crumpets rises as more crumpets are produced.
   (D) the opportunity cost of producing crumpets is constant along the curve.
   (E) the opportunity cost of producing tea falls as you produce more tea.

5. Ray and Dorothy can both cook and can both pull weeds in the garden on a Saturday afternoon. For every hour of cooking, Ray can pull 50 weeds and Dorothy can pull 100 weeds. Based on this information,

   (A) Ray pulls weeds, since he has absolute advantage in cooking.
   (B) Dorothy pulls weeds, since she has absolute advantage in cooking.
   (C) Dorothy cooks, since she has comparative advantage in cooking.
   (D) Ray cooks, since he has comparative advantage in cooking.
   (E) Dorothy pulls weeds, since she has comparative advantage in cooking.

› Answers and Explanations

1. **C**—It is important to remember that society has a limitless desire for material wants, but satisfaction of these wants is limited by scarce economic resources. Economics studies how to solve this problem in the best possible way.

2. **B**—If we observe her studying for the fourth hour, then it must be the case that the MB ≥ MC of studying for that next hour. If we observe her putting her books away and doing something else, the opposite must be true.

3. **D**—Economic growth is an outward expansion of the entire PPF. A movement from the interior to the frontier (A to B) is not growth, it just tells us that some unemployed resources (A) are now being used to their full potential (B).

4. **C**—When the PPF is concave to the origin (or bowed outward) it is an indicator of the law of increasing costs. This is a result of economic resources not being perfectly substitutable between tea and crumpets. A baking sheet used to bake crumpets might be quite useless in producing tea leaves.

5. **D**—For Ray, the opportunity cost of cooking is 50 weeds, while Dorothy's opportunity cost of cooking is 100 unpulled weeds. Ray does not pull weeds because he has comparative advantage in cooking. Dorothy does not cook because she has comparative advantage in weed pulling.

› Rapid Review

Economics: The study of how people, firms, and societies use their scarce productive resources to best satisfy their unlimited material wants.

Resources: Called factors of production, these are commonly grouped into the four categories of labor, physical capital, land or natural resources, and entrepreneurial ability.

Scarcity: The imbalance between limited productive resources and unlimited human wants. Because economic resources are scarce, the goods and services a society can produce are also scarce.

Trade-offs: Scarce resources imply that individuals, firms, and governments are constantly faced with difficult choices that involve benefits and costs.

Opportunity cost: The value of the sacrifice made to pursue a course of action.

Marginal: The next unit or increment of an action.

Marginal benefit (MB): The additional benefit received from the consumption of the next unit of a good or service.

Marginal cost (MC): The additional cost incurred from the consumption of the next unit of a good or service.

Marginal analysis: Making decisions based upon weighing the marginal benefits and costs of that action. The rational decision maker chooses an action if the MB ≥ MC.

Production possibilities: Different quantities of goods that an economy can produce with a given amount of scarce resources. Graphically, the trade-off between the production of two goods is portrayed as a production possibility curve or frontier (PPC or PPF).

Production possibility curve or frontier (PPC or PPF): A graphical illustration that shows the maximum quantity of one good that can be produced, given the quantity of the other good being produced.

Law of increasing costs: The more of a good that is produced, the greater the opportunity cost of producing the next unit of that good.

Absolute advantage: This exists if a producer can produce more of a good than all other producers.

Comparative advantage: A producer has comparative advantage if he can produce a good at lower opportunity cost than all other producers.

Specialization: When firms focus their resources on production of goods for which they have comparative advantage, they are said to be specializing.

Productive efficiency: Production of maximum output for a given level of technology and resources. All points on the PPF are productively efficient.

Allocative efficiency: Production of the combination of goods and services that provides the most net benefit to society. The optimal quantity of a good is achieved when the MB = MC of the next unit. This only occurs at one point on the PPF.

Economic growth: This occurs when an economy's production possibilities increase. It can be a result of more resources, better resources, or improvements in technology.

Market economy (capitalism): An economic system based upon the fundamentals of private property, freedom, self-interest, and prices.

Demand, Supply, Market Equilibrium, and Welfare Analysis

IN THIS CHAPTER

Summary: A thorough understanding of the way in which the market system determines price and quantity pays dividends both in microeconomics and macroeconomics. In the absence of government intervention and/or externalities, the competitive market also provides the most efficient outcome for society.

Key Ideas
✪ Demand
✪ Supply
✪ Equilibrium
✪ Consumer and Producer Surplus

6.1 Demand

Main Topics: *Law of Demand, Income and Substitution Effects, The Demand Curves, Quantity Demanded versus Demand Determinants of Demand*

For many years now, you have understood the concept of demand. On the surface, the concept is rather simple: people tend to purchase fewer items when the price is high than they do when the price is low. This is such an intuitively appealing concept that your typical consumer cares little about the rationale and still manages to live a happy life. As someone knee-deep in reviewing to take the AP Macroeconomics exam, you need to go "behind the scenes" of demand. Intuition will take you only so far: you need to know the underlying theory of what is perhaps the most widely understood, and sometimes misunderstood, economic concept.

You might be asking yourself, "Self, I'm studying for a macroeconomics exam. Why do I need to learn about demand, supply, equilibrium, and efficiency in microeconomics markets?" Well, the quick answer is that this does appear on the AP Macroeconomics outline of topics so it is fair game on the multiple-choice section of the exam. But, as you will see in the review later, demand and supply and equilibrium appear in macroeconomic models too. It is important to build a good foundation of how this simple model works so that you can apply it later and score big points on the free-response questions that are sure to appear on the AP Macroeconomics exam.

Law of Demand

Let's get this part out of the way. The **law of demand** is commonly described as: *Holding all else equal, when the price of a good rises, consumers decrease their quantity demanded for that good*. In other words, there is an inverse, or negative, relationship between the price and the quantity demanded of a good.

"Holding all else equal"? Economic models—demand is just one of many such models—are simplified versions of real behavior. In addition to the price, there are many factors that influence how many units of a good consumers purchase. In order to predict how consumers respond to changes in one variable (price), we must assume that all other relevant factors are held constant. Say we observed that last month the price of orange juice fell, consumer incomes rose, the price of apple juice increased, and consumers bought more orange juice. Was this increased orange juice consumption because the price fell, because incomes rose, or perhaps because apple juice became more expensive? Maybe it increased for all of these reasons. Maybe for none of these reasons. It is impossible to isolate and measure the effect of one variable (i.e., orange juice prices) on the consumption of orange juice if we do not control (hold constant) these other external factors. At the heart of the law of demand is a consumer's willingness and ability to pay the going price. If the consumer becomes more willing, or more able, to consume a good, then either the price has fallen or one of these external factors has changed. We spend more time on these demand "determinants" a little later in this chapter.

Income and Substitution Effects

One of the important factors behind the scenes of the law of demand is the economic mantra "*only relative prices matter.*" I'm sure you have heard the stories from your parents or grandparents about how the price of a cup of coffee back in the good old days was just a nickel. Today you might get the same coffee for $1.75. These prices are simply **money** (or **absolute**, or **nominal**) **prices**, and when it comes to a demand decision, a money price alone is near useless. However, if you think about the money price in terms of (1) what other goods $1.75 could buy, or (2) how much of your income is absorbed by $1.75, then you're talking **relative** (or **real**) **prices**. These are what matter. The number of units of any other good Y that must be sacrificed to acquire the first good X, measures the relative price of good X.

> **Example:**
> Let's keep things simple and say that you divide your $10 daily income between apple fritters at today's prices of $1 each and chocolate chip bagels at $2 each. These are the money prices of your labor and of these two yummy snacks.

Table 6.1

	MONEY PRICE		RELATIVE PRICE		SHARE OF INCOME	
	Today	Tomorrow	Today	Tomorrow	Today	Tomorrow
Fritter	$1	$2	1/2 bagel	1 bagel	1/10	1/5
Bagel	$2	$2	2 fritters	1 fritter	1/5	1/5

Today at the price of $1, the relative cost of a fritter is one-half of a bagel (see Table 6.1). Relative to your income, it amounts to one-tenth of your budget.

Tomorrow, when the price doubles to $2 per fritter, two things happen to help explain, and lay the foundation for, the law of demand:

1. The relative price of a fritter has risen to one bagel, and the relative price of a bagel has fallen from two fritters to one fritter. Since fritters are now *relatively more expensive*, we would expect you to consume more bagels and fewer fritters. This is known as the **substitution effect**.

2. Relative to your income, the price of a fritter has increased from one-tenth to one-fifth of your budget. In other words, if you were to buy only fritters, today you can purchase 10 but tomorrow the same income would only buy you 5. This lost purchasing power is known as the **income effect**.

- ***Substitution effect.*** The change in quantity demanded resulting from a change in the price of one good relative to the price of other goods.
- ***Income effect.*** The change in quantity demanded resulting from a change in the consumer's purchasing power (or real income).

When the price of fritters increased, both of these effects caused our consumer (you) to decrease the quantity demanded, thus predicting a response consistent with the law of demand.

So at this point you might ask, "How would a consumer react if the prices of fritters and bagels, and daily income had all doubled?"

Since the price of fritters, relative to the price of bagels, and relative to daily income, has not changed, the consumer is unlikely to alter behavior. This is why we say that only relative prices matter.

The Demand Curve

The residents of a small Midwestern town love to quench their summer thirsts with lemonade. Table 6.2 summarizes the townsfolk's daily consumption of cups of lemonade at several prices, holding constant all other factors that might influence the overall demand for lemonade. This table is sometimes referred to as a **demand schedule**.

Table 6.2

PRICE PER CUP ($)	QUANTITY DEMANDED (CUPS PER DAY)
.25	120
.50	100
.75	80
1.00	60
1.25	40

The values in Table 6.2 reflect the law of demand: *Holding all else equal, when the price of a cup of lemonade rises, consumers decrease their quantity demanded for lemonade*. It is often quite useful to convert a demand schedule like the one above into a graphical representation, the **demand curve** (Figure 6.1).

Figure 6.1

Quantity Demanded versus Demand

The law of demand predicts a downward (or negative) sloping demand curve (Figure 6.1). If the price moves from $1 to $1.25, and all other factors are held constant, we observe a decrease in the *quantity demanded* from 60 to 40 cups. It is important to place special emphasis on "quantity demanded." If the price of the good changes and all other factors remain constant, the demand curve is held constant and we simply observe the consumer moving along the fixed demand curve. If one of the external factors change, the entire demand curve shifts to the left or right.

Determinants of Demand

So, what are all of these factors that we insist on holding constant? These **determinants of demand** influence both the willingness and ability of the consumer to purchase units of the good or service. In addition to the price of the product itself, there are a number of variables that account for the total demand for a good like lemonade:

- Consumer income.
- The price of a substitute good such as iced tea.
- The price of a complementary good such as a Popsicle.
- Consumer tastes and preferences for lemonade.
- Consumer expectations about future prices of lemonade.
- Number of buyers in the market for lemonade.

- *Consumer Income*

Demand represents the consumer's willingness and ability to pay for a good. Income is a major factor in that "ability" to pay component. For most goods, when income increases, demand for the good increases. Thus, for these **normal goods**, increased income results in a graphical rightward shift in the entire demand curve. There are other

inferior goods, fewer in number, where higher levels of income produce a decrease in the demand curve.

Example:
When looking to furnish a first college apartment, many students increase their demand for used furniture at yard sales. Upon graduation and employment in their first real job, new graduates increase their demand for new furniture and decrease their demand for used furniture. For them, new furniture is a normal good, while used furniture is an inferior good.

- An *increase in demand* is viewed as a *rightward shift* in the demand curve. There are two ways to think about this shift.
    a. At all prices, the consumer is willing and able to buy more units of the good. In Figure 6.2 you can see that at the constant price of $1, the quantity demanded has risen from two to three.
    b. At all quantities, the consumer is willing and able to pay higher prices for the good.

- Of course, the opposite is true of a *decrease in demand*, or *leftward shift* of the demand curve. In Figure 6.2 you can see that at the constant price of $1, the quantity demanded has fallen from two to one.

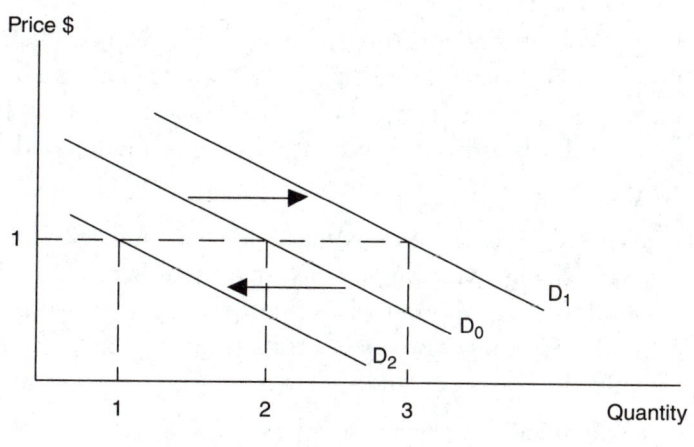

Figure 6.2

- *Price of Substitute Goods*

Two goods are substitutes if the consumer can use either one to satisfy the same essential function, therefore experiencing the same degree of happiness (utility). If the two goods are substitutes, and the price of one good X falls, the consumer demand for the substitute good Y decreases.

Example:
Ivy Vine College (IVC) and Mammoth State University (MSU) are considered substitute institutions of higher learning in the same geographical region. Ivy Vine College, shamelessly (wink, wink) seeking to increase its reputation as an "elite" institution, increases tuition, while Mammoth State's tuition remains the same. We expect to see, holding all else constant, a decrease in quantity demanded for IVC degrees, and an increase in the overall demand for MSU degrees. (See Figures 6.3 and 6.4.)

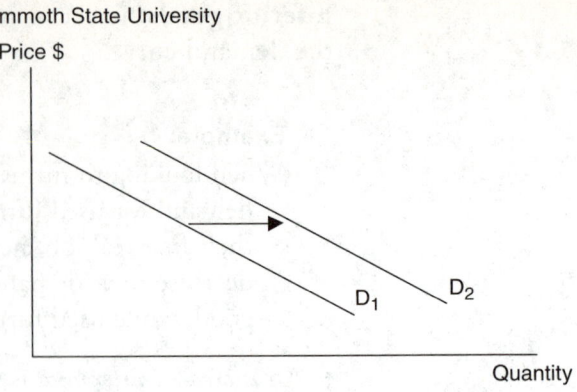

Figure 6.3   Figure 6.4

- *Price of Complementary Goods*

Two goods are complements if the consumer receives more utility from consuming them together than she would receive consuming each separately. I enjoy consuming tortilla chips by themselves, but my utility increases if I combine those chips with a complementary good like salsa or nacho cheese dip. If any two goods are complements, and the price of one good X falls, the consumer demand for the complement good Y increases.

Example:

College students love to order late-night pizza delivered to their dorm rooms. The local pizza joint decreased the price of breadsticks, a complement to the pizzas. We expect to see, holding all else constant, an increase in quantity demanded for breadsticks, and an increase in the demand for pizzas.

> "Finally, something in a textbook that I can fathom!"
> —Adam, AP Student

- *Tastes and Preferences*

We have different internal tastes and preferences. Collectively, consumer tastes and preferences change with the seasons (more gloves in December, fewer lawn chairs); with fashion trends (increased popularity of tattoos, return of bell-bottoms); or with advertising (low-carb foods). A stronger preference for a good is an increase in the willingness to pay for the good, which increases demand.

- *Future Expectations*

The future expectation of a price change or an income change can cause demand to shift today. Demand can also respond to an expectation of the future availability of a good.

Example:

On a Wednesday, you have reason to believe that the price of gasoline is going to rise $0.05 per gallon by the weekend. What do you do? Many consumers, armed with this expectation, increase their demand for gasoline today. We might predict the opposite behavior, a decrease in demand today, if consumers expect the price of gasoline to fall a few days from now.

Demand can also be influenced by future expectations of an income change.

Example:

One month prior to your college graduation day, you land your first full-time job. You have signed an employment contract that guarantees a specific salary, but you will not receive your first paycheck until the end of your first month on the job. This future expectation of a sizable increase in income often prompts consumers to increase their demand for normal goods now. Maybe you would start shopping for a car, a larger apartment, or several business suits.

Example:

For years, auto producers have been promising more alternative-fuel cars, but so far these cars are relatively difficult to find on dealership lots. Suppose the major auto producers promise widespread availability of affordable electric and hydrogen fuel cell cars in the next 12 months. This expectation of increased availability in the future will likely decrease the demand for these cars today.

- *Number of Buyers*

An increase in the number of buyers, holding other factors constant, increases the demand for a good. This is often the result of demographic changes or increased availability in more markets.

Example:

When the Soviet Union fractured and the Russian government began allowing more foreign investment, corporations such as Coca-Cola, Apple, and McDonald's found millions of new buyers for their products. Globally, the demand for colas, iPods, and burgers increased.

6.2 Supply

Main Topics: *Law of Supply, Increasing Marginal Costs, The Supply Curve, Quantity Supplied versus Supply, Determinants of Supply*

If there are three words that you need to have in your arsenal for the AP exams, they are "Demand and Supply," or "Supply and Demand" if you are the rebellious type. The previous section covered the demand half of this duo, and so it stands to reason that we should spend a little time studying the other side. Unlike demand, few of us have ever had up close and personal experience as suppliers. Because you likely lack such personal experience with supply, it is helpful to put yourself in the shoes of someone who wishes to profit from the production and sale of a product. If something happens that would increase your chances of earning more profit, you increase your supply of the product. If something happens that will hurt your profit opportunities, you decrease your supply of the product.

Law of Supply

Drumroll, please. The **law of supply** is commonly described as: "*Holding all else equal, when the price of a good rises, suppliers increase their quantity supplied for that good.*" In other words, there is a direct, or positive, relationship between the price and the quantity supplied of a good.

Again, we insist on qualifying our law with the phrase, "Holding all else equal." Similar to the *demand model*, the *supply model* is a simplified version of real behavior. In addition to the price, there are several factors that influence how many units of a good producers supply. In order to predict how producers respond to fluctuations in one variable (price), we must assume that all other relevant factors are held constant. Before we talk about these external supply determinants, let's examine what is happening behind the scenes of the law of supply.

Increasing Marginal Costs

The more you do something (e.g., a physical activity), the more difficult it becomes to do the next unit of that activity. Anyone who has run laps around a track, lifted weights, or raked leaves in the yard understands this. If you were asked to rake leaves, as more hours of raking are supplied, it becomes physically more and more difficult to rake the next hour. We also include the opportunity cost of the time involved in the raking, and you surely know that time is precious to a student. If you have a paper to write or an exam to cram for, raking leaves for an hour comes at a dear cost. In terms of forgone opportunities, the marginal cost of raking leaves rises as you postpone that paper or study session.

When we discussed production possibilities in Chapter 5, we addressed a key economic concept: as more of a good is produced, the greater is its marginal cost.

- As suppliers increase the quantity supplied of a good, they face rising marginal costs.
- As a result, they only increase the quantity supplied of that good if the price received is high enough to at least cover the higher marginal cost.

The Supply Curve

A small town has a thriving summer sidewalk lemonade stand industry. Table 6.3 summarizes the daily quantity of cups of lemonade offered for sale at several prices, holding constant all other factors that might influence the overall supply of lemonade. This table is sometimes referred to as a **supply schedule**.

Table 6.3

PRICE PER CUP ($)	QUANTITY SUPPLIED (CUPS PER DAY)
.25	40
.50	60
.75	80
1.00	100
1.25	120

"Make sure on the AP test to include all labels, especially arrows." —Adam, AP Student

The values in this table reflect the law of supply: "*Holding all else equal, when the price of a cup of lemonade rises, suppliers increase their quantity supplied for lemonade.*" Remember those profit opportunities? If kids can sell more cups of lemonade at a higher price, they will do so. It is often quite useful to convert a supply schedule like the one in Table 6.3 into a graphical representation: the **supply curve** (Figure 6.5).

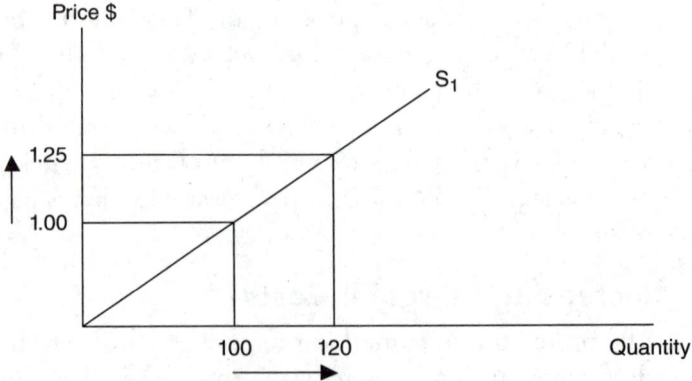

Figure 6.5

Quantity Supplied versus Supply

> "This is an important distinction to make."
> —AP Teacher

The law of supply predicts an upward- (or positive-) sloping supply curve (Figure 6.5). When the price moves from $1 to $1.25, and all other factors are held constant, we observe an increase in the *quantity supplied* from 100 cups to 120 cups. Just as with demand, it is important to place special emphasis on "quantity supplied." When the price of the good changes, and all other factors are held constant, the supply curve is held constant; we simply observe the producer moving along the fixed supply curve. If one of the external factors changes, the entire supply curve shifts to the left or right.

Determinants of Supply

Lemonade producers are willing and able to supply more lemonade if something happens that promises to increase their profit opportunities. In addition to the price of the product itself, there are a number of variables, or **determinants of supply**, that account for the total supply of a good like lemonade:

- The cost of an input (e.g., sugar) to the production of lemonade
- Technology and productivity used to produce lemonade
- Taxes or subsidies on lemonade
- Producer expectations about future prices
- The price of other goods that could be produced
- The number of lemonade stands in the industry

- *Cost of Inputs*

If the cost of sugar, a key ingredient in lemonade, unexpectedly falls, it has now become less costly to produce lemonade, and so we should expect producers all over town, seeing the profit opportunity, to increase the supply of lemonade at all prices. This results in a graphical rightward shift in the entire supply curve.

- An *increase in supply* is viewed as a *rightward shift* in the supply curve. There are two ways to think about this shift:
  1. At all prices, the producer is willing and able to supply more units of the good. In Figure 6.6 you can see that at the constant price of $1, the quantity supplied has risen from two to three.
  2. At all quantities, the marginal cost of production is lower, so producers are willing and able to accept lower prices for the good.
- Of course, the opposite is true of a decrease *in supply*, or *leftward shift* of the supply curve. In Figure 6.6 you can see that at the constant price of $1, the quantity supplied has fallen from two to one.

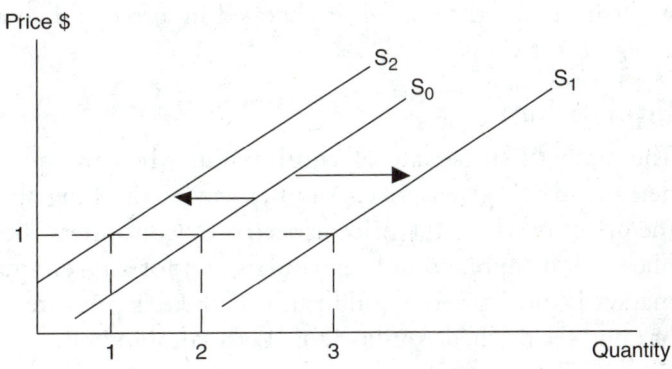

Figure 6.6

> "Remember, the tax goes to the government and is NOT included in the profit."
> —Hillary, AP Student

- *Technology or Productivity*

A technological improvement usually decreases the marginal cost of producing a good, thus allowing the producer to supply more units, and is reflected by a rightward shift in the supply curve. If kids all over town began using electric lemon squeezers rather than their sticky bare hands, the supply of lemonade would increase.

- *Taxes and Subsidies*

A per unit tax is treated by the firm as an additional cost of production and would therefore decrease the supply curve, or shift it leftward. Mayor McScrooge might impose a 25-cent tax on every cup of lemonade, decreasing the entire supply curve. A subsidy is essentially the anti-tax, or a per unit gift from the government because it lowers the per unit cost of production.

- *Price Expectations*

A producer's willingness to supply today might be affected by an expectation of tomorrow's price. If it were the 2nd of July and lemonade producers expected a heat wave and a 4th of July parade in two days, they might hold back some of their supply today and hope to sell it at an inflated price on the holiday. Thus, today's quantity supplied at all prices would decrease.

- *Price of Other Outputs*

Firms can use the same resources to produce different goods. If the price of a milkshake were rising and profit opportunities were improving for milkshake producers, the supply of lemonade in a small town would decrease and the quantity of milkshakes supplied would increase.

- *Number of Suppliers*

When more suppliers enter a market, we expect the supply curve to shift to the right. If several of our lemonade entrepreneurs are forced by their parents to attend summer camp, we would expect the entire supply curve to move leftward. Fewer cups of lemonade would be supplied at each and every price.

6.3 Market Equilibrium

Main Topics: *Equilibrium, Shortage, Surplus, Changes in Demand, Changes in Supply, Simultaneous Changes in Demand or Supply*

Demanders and suppliers are both motivated by prices, but from opposite camps. The consumer is a big fan of low prices; the supplier applauds high prices. If a good were available, consumers would be willing to buy more of it, but only if the price is right. Suppliers would love to accommodate more consumption by increasing production, but only if justly compensated. Is there a price and a compatible quantity where both groups are content? Amazingly enough, the answer is a resounding "maybe." Discouraged? Don't be. For now we assume that the good is exchanged in a free and competitive market, and if this is the case, the answer is "yes."

Equilibrium

The market is in a state of **equilibrium** when the quantity supplied equals the quantity demanded at a given price. Another way of thinking about equilibrium is that it occurs at the quantity where the price expected by consumers is equal to the price required by suppliers. So if suppliers and demanders are, for a given quantity, content with the price, the market is in a state of equilibrium. If there is pressure on the price to change, the market has not yet reached equilibrium. Let's combine our lemonade tables from the earlier sections in Table 6.4.

Table 6.4

PRICE PER CUP ($)	QUANTITY DEMANDED (CUPS PER DAY)	QUANTITY SUPPLIED (CUPS PER DAY)	$Q_d - Q_s$	SITUATION	PRICE SHOULD
.25	120	40	80	Shortage	Rise
.50	100	60	40	Shortage	Rise
.75	80	80	0	Equilibrium	Stable
1.00	60	100	−40	Surplus	Fall
1.25	40	120	−80	Surplus	Fall

At a price of 75 cents, the daily quantity demanded and quantity supplied are both equal to 80 cups of lemonade. The equilibrium (or market clearing) price is therefore 75 cents per cup. In Figure 6.7 the equilibrium price and quantity are located where the demand curve intersects the supply curve. Holding all other demand and supply variables constant, there exists no other price where $Q_d = Q_s$.

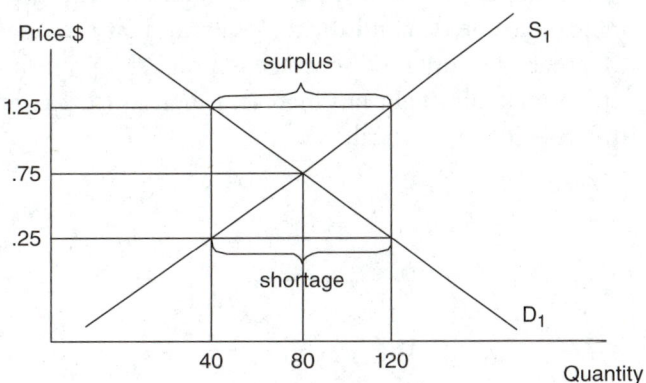

Figure 6.7

Shortage

> "In a free market, shortages and surpluses always return to equilibrium in the long run."
> —Adam, AP Student

A **shortage** exists at a market price when the quantity demanded exceeds the quantity supplied. This is why a shortage is also known as **excess demand**. At prices of 25 cents and 50 cents per cup, you can see the shortage in Figure 6.7. Remember that consumers love low prices so the quantity demanded is going to be high. However, suppliers are not thrilled to see low prices and therefore decrease their quantity supplied. At prices below 75 cents per cup, lemonade buyers and sellers are in a state of **disequilibrium**. The disparity between what the buyers want at 50 cents per cup and what the suppliers want at that price should remedy itself. Thirsty demanders offer lemonade stand owners prices slightly higher than 50 cents, and, receiving higher prices, suppliers accommodate them by squeezing lemons. With competition, the shortage is eliminated at a price of 75 cents per cup.

Surplus

A **surplus** exists at a market price when the quantity supplied exceeds the quantity demanded. This is why a surplus is also known as **excess supply**. At prices of $1 and $1.25 per cup, you can see the surplus in Figure. 6.7. Consumers are reluctant to purchase as much lemonade as suppliers are willing to supply, and, once again, the market is in disequilibrium. To entice more consumers to buy lemonade, lemonade stand owners offer slightly discounted cups of lemonade and buyers respond by increasing their quantity demanded. Again, with competition, the surplus would be eliminated at a price of 75 cents per cup.

- Shortages and surpluses are relatively short-lived in a free market as prices rise or fall until the quantity demanded again equals the quantity supplied.

"Explain your logic every time you shift a curve, no matter what!"
—Jake, AP Student

Changes in Demand

While our discussion of market equilibrium implies a certain kind of stability in both the price and quantity of a good, changing market forces disrupt equilibrium, either by shifting demand, shifting supply, or shifting both demand and supply.

Increase in Demand

About once a winter a freak blizzard hits southern states like Georgia and the Carolinas. You can bet that the national media show video of panicked southerners scrambling for bags of rock salt and bottled water. Inevitably a bemused reporter tells us that the price of rock salt has skyrocketed to $17 per bag. What is happening here? In Figure 6.8, the market for rock salt is initially in equilibrium at a price of $2.79 per bag. With a forecast of a blizzard, consumers expect a lack of future availability for this good. This expectation results in a feverish increase in the demand for rock salt, and, at the original price of $2.79, there is a shortage. The market's cure for a shortage is a higher equilibrium price. (Note: The equilibrium quantity of rock salt might not increase much, since blizzards are short-lived and the supply curve might be nearly vertical.)

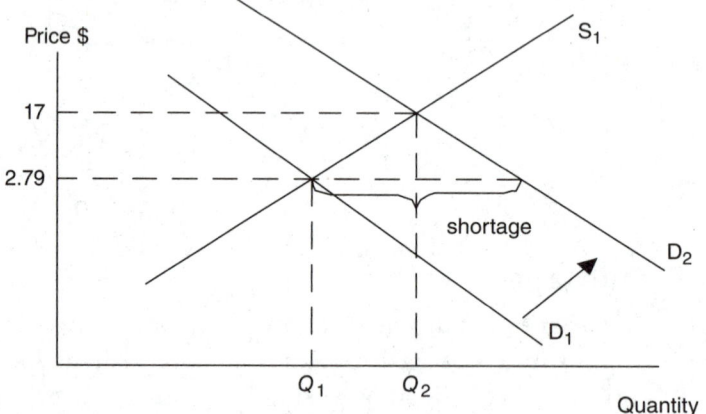

Figure 6.8

Decrease in Demand

The most recent recession was damaging to the automobile industry. When average household incomes fell in the United States, the demand for cars, a normal good, decreased. Manufacturers began offering deeply discounted sticker prices, zero-interest financing, and other incentives to reluctant consumers so that they might purchase a new car. In Figure 6.9 you can see that the original price of a new car was $18,000. Once the demand for new cars fell, there was a surplus of cars on dealer lots at the original price. The market cure for a surplus is a lower equilibrium price; therefore, fewer new cars were bought and sold.

Figure 6.9

- When demand increases, equilibrium price and quantity both increase.
- When demand decreases, equilibrium price and quantity both decrease.

Changes in Supply

Increase in Supply

Advancements in computer technology and production methods have been felt in many markets. Figure 6.10 illustrates how, because of better technology, the supply of laptop computers has increased. At the original equilibrium price of $4,000, there is now a surplus of laptops. To eliminate the surplus, the market price must fall to P_2 and the equilibrium quantity must rise to Q_2.

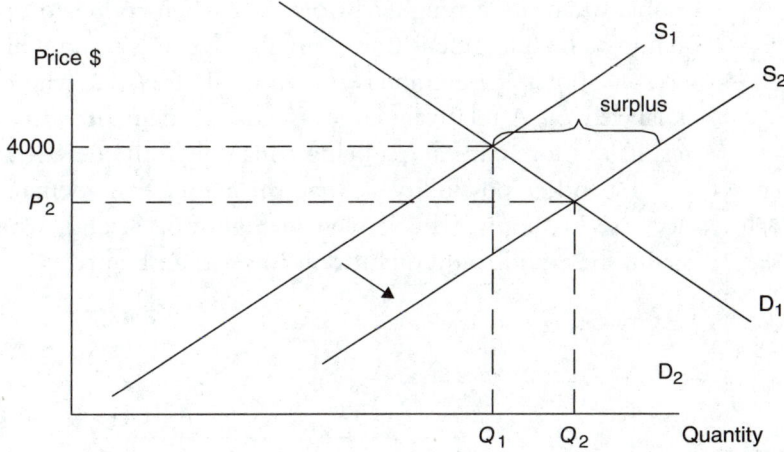

Figure 6.10

Decrease in Supply

Geopolitical conflict in the Middle East usually slows the production of crude oil. This decrease in the global supply of oil can be seen in Figure 6.11. At the original equilibrium price of $60 per barrel, there is now a shortage of crude oil on the global market. The market eliminates this shortage through higher prices, and, at least temporarily, the equilibrium quantity of crude oil falls.

Figure 6.11

- When supply increases, equilibrium price decreases and quantity increases.
- When supply decreases, equilibrium price increases and quantity decreases.

Simultaneous Changes in Demand and Supply

When both demand and supply change at the same time, predicting changes in price and quantity becomes a little more complicated. An example should illustrate how you need to be careful.

An extremely cold winter results in a higher demand for energy such as natural gas. At the same time, environmental safeguards and restrictions on drilling in protected wilderness areas have limited the supply of natural gas. An increase in demand, by itself, creates an increase in both price and quantity. However, a decrease in supply, by itself, creates an increase in price and a decrease in quantity. When these forces are combined, we see a double-whammy on higher prices. But when trying to predict the change in equilibrium quantity, the outcome is uncertain and depends upon which of the two effects is larger.

One possible outcome is shown in Figure 6.12, where the initial equilibrium outcome is labeled E_1. A relatively large increase in demand with a fairly small decrease in supply results in more natural gas being consumed. The new equilibrium outcome is labeled E_2.

The other possibility is that the increase in demand is relatively smaller than the decrease in supply. This is seen in Figure 6.13, and, while the price is going to increase again, the equilibrium quantity is lower than before.

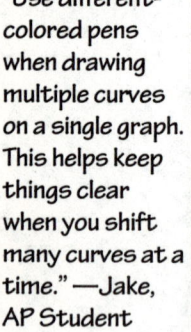

"Use different-colored pens when drawing multiple curves on a single graph. This helps keep things clear when you shift many curves at a time." —Jake, AP Student

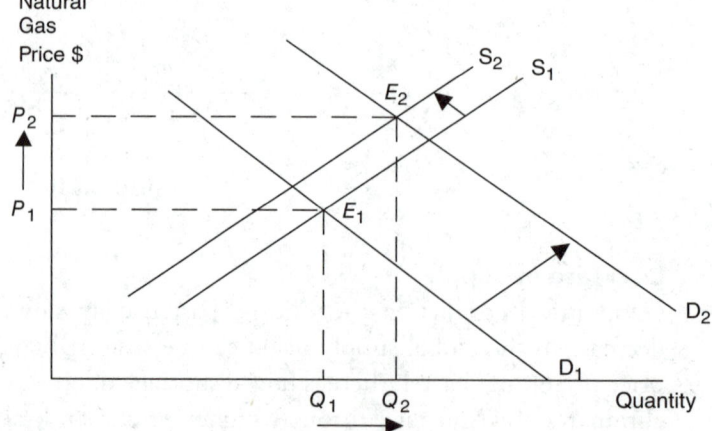

Figure 6.12

Demand, Supply, Market Equilibrium, and Welfare Analysis   69

> "If you don't know the answer, it is probably where the sticks cross." —Chuck, AP Student

Figure 6.13

- When both demand and supply are changing, one of the equilibrium outcomes (price or quantity) is predictable and one is ambiguous.
- Before combining the two shifting curves, predict changes in price and quantity for each shift, by itself.
- The variable that is rising in one case and falling in the other case is your ambiguous prediction.

6.4 Welfare Analysis

Main Topics: *Total Welfare, Consumer Surplus, Producer Surplus*

Total Welfare

The competitive market, free of government and externalities, produces an equilibrium outcome that provides the maximum amount of total welfare for society. Society consists of all consumers and all producers, and, in the marketplace, each party seeks the other so that they can make an acceptable transaction at the going market price. Each party expects to gain in these transactions. **Total welfare** is the sum of two measures of these gains: consumer surplus and producer surplus.

Consumer Surplus

You know that great feeling you get when you pay a price that is lower than you expected, or is lower than you were willing to pay? That's **consumer surplus**, the difference between your willingness to pay and the price you actually pay. The market demand curve, at each quantity, measures society's willingness to pay (the price). You can see consumer surplus in Figure 6.14. At a price of $5, three units of the good are purchased. The first two units receive some amount of consumer surplus because the willingness to pay exceeds $5. The consumer of the third unit pays a price exactly equal to his willingness to pay so he earns no consumer surplus. Total consumer surplus is the total amount earned by these three consumer transactions.

Producer Surplus

Producers are ecstatic when they receive a price for their product that is above the marginal cost of producing it. This is **producer surplus**, the difference between the price received and the marginal cost of producing the good. The market supply curve, at each quantity, measures society's marginal cost. You can see producer surplus in Figure 6.15. At a price of $5, three units of the good are produced. The first two units earn producer surplus because

$5 is above the marginal cost. The third unit earns no additional producer surplus, since the marginal cost is exactly equal to the price received. Total producer surplus is the total amount earned by these three producer transactions.

Figure 6.14

- The area under the demand curve and above the market price is equal to total consumer surplus.

Figure 6.15

- The area above the supply curve and below the market price is equal to total producer surplus.

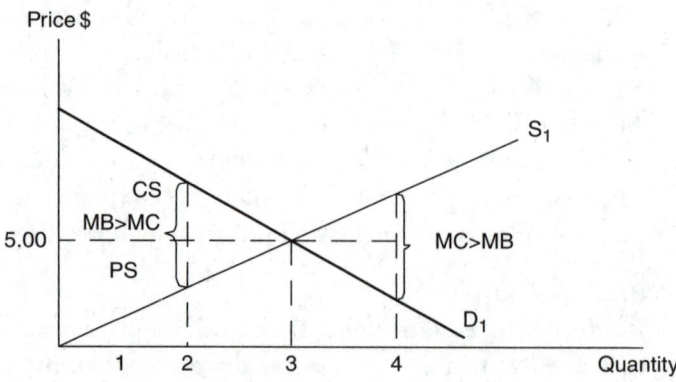

Figure 6.16

So, is market equilibrium conducive to increasing total welfare for society? Combining Figures 6.14 and 6.15 completes the market pictured in Figure 6.16. We see that the combined consumer and producer surplus, or total welfare, is greatest at the equilibrium price of $5 and quantity of three units.

At a lesser quantity (e.g., two units), the combined area is smaller than at a quantity of three. At greater quantities (i.e., $q = 4$) the price of $5 exceeds MB, so consumer surplus is being lost. If this weren't bad enough, the MC exceeds the price at $q = 4$, so producer surplus is being lost. Thus, if total welfare is falling at quantities less than three and at quantities greater than three, total welfare must be maximized at the market equilibrium quantity of three and price of $5.

» Review Questions

1. When the price of pears increases, we expect the following:

    (A) Quantity demanded of pears rises.
    (B) Quantity supplied of pears falls.
    (C) Quantity demanded of pears falls.
    (D) Demand for pears falls.
    (E) Supply of pears rises.

2. If average household income rises and we observe that the demand for pork chops increases, pork chops must be

    (A) an inferior good.
    (B) a normal good.
    (C) a surplus good.
    (D) a public good.
    (E) a shortage good.

3. Suppose that aluminum is a key production input in the production of bicycles. If the price of aluminum falls, and all other variables are held constant, we expect

    (A) the demand for aluminum to rise.
    (B) the supply of bicycles to rise.
    (C) the supply of bicycles to fall.
    (D) the demand for bicycles to rise.
    (E) the demand for bicycles to fall.

4. The market for denim jeans is in equilibrium, and the price of polyester pants, a substitute good, rises. In the jean market

    (A) supply falls, increasing the price and decreasing the quantity.
    (B) supply falls, increasing the price and increasing the quantity.
    (C) demand falls, increasing the price and decreasing the quantity.
    (D) demand rises, increasing the price and increasing the quantity.
    (E) supply and demand both fall, causing an ambiguous change in price but a definite decrease in quantity.

5. The apple market is in equilibrium. Suppose we observe that apple growers are using more pesticides to increase apple production. At the same time, we hear that the price of pears, a substitute for apples, is rising. Which of the following is a reasonable prediction for the new price and quantity of apples?

    (A) Price rises, but quantity is ambiguous.
    (B) Price falls, but quantity is ambiguous.
    (C) Price is ambiguous, but quantity rises.
    (D) Price is ambiguous, but quantity falls.
    (E) Both price and quantity are ambiguous.

6. The competitive market provides the best outcome for society because

    (A) consumer surplus is minimized, while producer surplus is maximized.
    (B) the total welfare is maximized.
    (C) producer surplus is minimized, while consumer surplus is maximized.
    (D) the difference between consumer and producer surplus is maximized.
    (E) the total cost to society is maximized.

Answers and Explanations

1. **C**—If the price of pears rises, either quantity demanded falls or quantity supplied rises. Entire demand or supply curves for pears can shift, but only if an external factor, not the price of pears, changes.

2. **B**—When income increases and demand increases, the good is a normal good. Had the demand for pork chops decreased, they would be an inferior good.

3. **B**—This is a determinant of supply. If the raw material becomes less costly to acquire, the marginal cost of producing bicycles falls. Producers increase the supply of bicycles. Recognizing this as a supply determinant allows you to quickly eliminate any reference to a demand shift.

4. **D**—When a substitute good becomes more expensive, the demand for jeans rises, increasing price and quantity.

5. **C**—Increased use of pesticides increases the supply of apples. If the price of a substitute increases, the demand for apples increases. Combining these two factors predicts an increase in the quantity of apples, but an ambiguous change in price. *To help you see this, draw these situations in the margin of the exam.*

6. **B**—When competitive markets reach equilibrium, no other quantity can increase total welfare (consumer + producer surplus).

Rapid Review

Law of demand: Holding all else equal, when the price of a good rises, consumers decrease their quantity demanded for that good.

All else equal: To predict how a change in one variable affects a second, we hold all other variables constant. This is also referred to as the *ceteris paribus* assumption.

Absolute (or money) prices: The price of a good measured in units of currency.

Relative prices: The number of units of any other good Y that must be sacrificed to acquire the first good X. Only relative prices matter.

Substitution effect: The change in quantity demanded resulting from a change in the price of one good relative to the price of other goods.

Income effect: The change in quantity demanded that results from a change in the consumer's purchasing power (or real income).

Demand schedule: A table showing quantity demanded for a good at various prices.

Demand curve: A graphical depiction of the demand schedule. The demand curve is downward sloping, reflecting the law of demand.

Determinants of demand: The external factors that shift demand to the left or right.

Normal goods: A good for which higher income increases demand.

Inferior goods: A good for which higher income decreases demand.

Substitute goods: Two goods are consumer substitutes if they provide essentially the same utility to the consumer. A Honda Accord and a Toyota Camry might be substitutes for many consumers.

Complementary goods: Two goods are consumer complements if they provide more utility when consumed together than when consumed separately. Cars and gasoline are complementary goods.

Law of supply: Holding all else equal, when the price of a good rises, suppliers increase their quantity supplied for that good.

Supply schedule: A table showing quantity supplied for a good at various prices.

Supply curve: A graphical depiction of the supply schedule. The supply curve is upward sloping, reflecting the law of supply.

Determinants of supply: One of the external factors that influences supply. When these variables change, the entire supply curve shifts to the left or right.

Market equilibrium: Exists at the only price where the quantity supplied equals the quantity demanded. Or, it is the only quantity where the price consumers are willing to pay is exactly the price producers are willing to accept.

Shortage: Also known as *excess demand*, a shortage exists at a market price when the quantity demanded exceeds the quantity supplied. The price rises to eliminate a shortage.

Disequilibrium: Any price where quantity demanded is not equal to quantity supplied.

Surplus: Also known as *excess supply*, a surplus exists at a market price when the quantity supplied exceeds the quantity demanded. The price falls to eliminate a surplus.

Total welfare: The sum of consumer surplus and producer surplus. The free market equilibrium provides maximum combined gain to society.

Consumer surplus: The difference between your willingness to pay and the price you actually pay. It is the area below the demand curve and above the price.

Producer surplus: The difference between the price received and the marginal cost of producing the good. It is the area above the supply curve and under the price.

Macroeconomic Measures of Performance

Technically, this is the first chapter in the review of macroeconomics, but both AP Microeconomics and Macroeconomics courses begin with coverage of "Basic Economic Concepts," a section that includes the following topics:

- *Scarcity, choice, and opportunity costs*
- *Production possibilities curve*
- *Comparative advantage, specialization, and exchange*
- *Demand, supply, and market equilibrium*

IN THIS CHAPTER

Summary: Should we raise or lower interest rates? Should we cut or increase taxes? The media is always buzzing about some macroeconomic policy intended to make our lives better. What does it mean to do better? How is "better" measured in something as large and complex as the macroeconomy? In general, macroeconomic policies share the goal of stabilizing and improving the economy, and they also share reliance upon statistical measures of economic performance. Though "statistics" might sound like a dirty word to you and your classmates, as AP Macroeconomics test takers, you need to understand how some important measures are, well, measured. Knowing how they are measured provides you with a much better way of responding to exam questions that ask you to use theoretical models to fix a macroeconomic problem. You cannot speak intelligently about growing the economy until you know how economic growth is measured. Likewise, if you want to perform better on the AP Macroeconomics exam, you might want to know exactly how those statistics (your grade) are compiled and study accordingly.

This chapter introduces measurement of economic production and paves the way for models of the macroeconomy and policies intended to improve this economic performance.

Key Ideas:
- The Circular Flow Model
- Gross Domestic Product
- Real versus Nominal
- Inflation and the Consumer Price Index
- Unemployment

7.1 The Circular Flow Model

Main Topic: *Circular Flow Model of a Closed Economy*

The Circular Flow Model

"What comes around goes around." If you remember nothing else about the circular flow model, remember this old phrase. The **circular flow of goods and services** (or **circular flow of economic activity**) is a model of an economy showing the interactions among households, firms, and government as they exchange goods and services and resources in markets. In other words, it is a game of "follow the dollars."

Figure 7.1 illustrates a model of a **closed economy**, where the foreign markets are not assumed (yet) to exist. Domestic households offer their resources to firms in the resource market so that those firms can produce goods and services. The households are paid competitive prices for those resources. They use that income to consume the very goods that were produced through the employment of their productive resources. Revenues from the sale of goods and services are then used to provide income to those households. In this simplified model, every dollar of income in the household ends up as revenue for the firm.

"What About the Government?"

Though not pictured in Figure 7.1, the government plays an important role in the circular flow model. The government is an employer of inputs and a producer of goods and services. The government collects taxes both from households and firms and uses the funds to pay for the inputs that they employ.

"How Much Economic Activity Is Being Generated?"

We can add up all of the dollars earned as income by resource owners, or we can add up all of the spending done on goods and services, or we can add up the value of all of those goods and services.

"Where Does It Begin, Where Does It End?"

It doesn't matter; it's the counting of the dollars that is the important first step in measuring economic performance.

Figure 7.1

Macroeconomic Goals

Figure 7.1 implies that a steady flow of goods and dollars circulating throughout the economy is necessary or commerce ceases. The big issue is how we keep this flow strong, and how we know when it is weak. Measuring success is the focus of the sections that follow. Most modern societies maintain the fairly broad goal of keeping spending and production in the macroeconomy strong without drastically increasing prices.

7.2 Accounting for Output and Income

Main Topics: *Valuing Production, Gross Domestic Product (GDP), National Income Concepts, Real and Nominal GDP, The GDP Deflator, Business Cycles*

Valuing Production

The key here is to measure the value of the goods that are produced, not just the amount of goods that are produced. Remember the circular flow? If we need to follow the dollars to measure economic activity, we need to know prices of these goods.

Value of Production, Not Just Production

When you track the monthly production of a small coffee shop, you could sum up all of the cappuccinos, café lattes, and scones that were purchased. Table 7.1 represents the output in two recent months. At first glance, the two months produced the same amount (100) of goods, but clearly the mix of goods at the coffee shop is different.

Table 7.1 Production

JANUARY			FEBRUARY		
# of Cappuccinos	# of Café Lattes	# of Scones	# of Cappuccinos	# of Café Lattes	# of Scones
25	25	50	30	30	40

Valuing Production

To paint a more accurate picture of production, we need to incorporate the value of these items as shown in Table 7.2.

Table 7.2

JANUARY	QUANTITY	PRICES	VALUE OF PRODUCTION
Cappuccinos	25	$3.00	$75
Café Lattes	25	$2.50	$62.50
Scones	50	$1.50	$75
Totals	100		$212.50
FEBRUARY			
Cappuccinos	30	$3.00	$90
Café Lattes	30	$2.50	$75
Scones	40	$1.50	$60
Totals	100		$225

While the total production at the coffee shop remained the same from month to month, the value of that production has increased in February. There are now more dollars circulating.

- Don't just add up the quantities; multiply by prices and add up the values.

Gross Domestic Product (GDP)

Aggregation, Not Aggravation

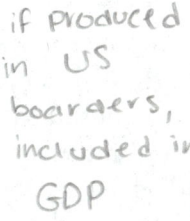
if produced in US boarders, included in GDP

To move from valuing production of one firm to the entire town, to the state, or to the U.S. economy, we need to **aggregate**. Simply stated, we need to value all production of all firms and then add them up to get the value of production for the entire domestic economy. It is this aggregated measure of the total value of domestic production that allows us to calculate our first important macroeconomic statistic, **GDP**. GDP is the market value of the final goods and services produced within a nation in a year. If the good or service is produced within the borders of the United States, it counts toward U.S. GDP. It does not matter if the firm is headquartered in Indonesia; so long as it is producing in Indiana, it appears in the U.S. GDP.

What's In, What's Out

Final goods are those that are ready for consumption. A bottle of ketchup at the Piggly Wiggly is counted. **Intermediate goods** are those that require further processing before they are counted as a final good. When the tomatoes used to make ketchup are purchased from a grower, they are not counted toward the GDP. At least not until those tomatoes, and their value, find themselves in a bottle of ketchup and sold at the supermarket. A raw material like a tomato might be bought and sold several times before it appears as a final product. If we were to count the dollars at every stage of this process, we would be **double counting,** and this is to be avoided. Suppose the tomatoes go through three stages: harvest, processing, and retail sale as a bottle of ketchup. Along the way a pound of tomatoes is sold, bought, and altered. The pound of tomatoes was sold from the grower to the processor for 50 cents. The bottle of ketchup was sold to a grocery store for $1.50, and eventually the ketchup was sold to a consumer for $3. If we added all of these transactions, we come up with $5, which overstates the value of the good in its final use. GDP only adds the final transaction as the value of the final good produced and consumed.

Second-hand sales are not counted. This falls under the "do not double count" rule. If you buy a new Xbox at Best Buy in 2012, it would count in the GDP for 2012. If you resell it on eBay in 2015, it is not counted again. Final goods and services are only counted once, in the year in which they were produced.

Nonmarket transactions are not counted toward GDP. For example, if I have a clogged drain in my kitchen, I have two choices: fix it myself or call the plumber and pay to have it fixed. Doing it myself does not contribute to GDP, but paying a plumber to do it does. The same job is done, but only the latter ends up in the books. In a similar way, regular housework done at home by an unpaid member of the household is not counted, though it is very much a productive effort. This reality is sometimes cited as a criticism of GDP accounting: some valuable services are counted and others are not.

Underground economy transactions are not counted. For obvious reasons, the illegal sale of goods or services or paying someone cash "under the table" for work are not counted. Informal bartering between individuals is also not counted. You might help a friend study for economics, while she helps you study for biology, but this kind of bartering would not appear on any official ledger of production, even though it might be quite productive.

As a practical matter, official tabulation of GDP is never 100 percent accurate because the value of final goods and services is based upon a survey of representative firms, not a complete census of all firms throughout the nation. Despite this methodology, economists work very hard to get a fairly accurate picture of the value of a nation's production.

Aggregate Spending

Since GDP is measured by adding up the value of the final goods and services produced in a given year, we just need to figure out from where this spending is coming. Spending on output is done by four sectors of the macroeconomy.

Consumer Spending (*C*). The largest component of GDP is the spending done by consumers. Consumers purchase services, like tax preparation or a college degree. Consumers also consume nondurable goods, like food, which are those goods that are consumed in under a year. Durable goods, like a Jet Ski, are goods expected to last a year or more.

Investment Spending (*I*). Investment is defined as current spending in order to increase output or productivity later. There are three general types of investment that are included in GDP:

- *New capital machinery purchased by firms.* Examples are a fleet of delivery trucks produced for UPS, or a new air-conditioning system at a Holiday Inn.
- *New construction for firms or consumers.* A new store built for Gap Inc. is investment spending. New residential housing (apartments or homes) is considered investment spending, since it is expected to provide housing services for years.
- *Market value of the change in unsold inventories.* If GM produces a new Cadillac in 2015, but it remains unsold on December 31, 2015, it would not be counted as consumer spending in 2015. It would appear in *I* as unsold inventory. Later, when it is eventually sold, it is added to *C* and deducted from *I*.

Government Spending (*G*). The government, at all levels, purchases final goods and services and invests in infrastructure. These include police cars, the services provided by social workers, computers for the Pentagon, or Humvees for the Marines. Infrastructure investments include highways, an airport, and a new county jail.

Note: Government transfer payments to citizens who qualify for government benefits (e.g., retired veterans) amount to sizable government expenditures but do not count toward GDP because these are not dollars spent on the production of goods and services.

Net Exports ($X - M$). We should add any domestically produced goods purchased by foreign consumers (exports = X) but subtract any spending by our citizens on purchases of goods made within other nations (imports = M). This way we include dollars flowing into our economy and acknowledge that some dollars flow out and land in other economies.

Most macroeconomic policies, directly or indirectly, influence GDP. Knowing the components of GDP is very useful when you are tested on policies.

$$\text{Aggregate spending (GDP)} = C + I + G + (X - M)$$

National Income Concepts

The basic circular flow model tells us that if we add up all of the spending, it equals all of the income, and either measure provides us with GDP. This simplicity is a bit deceiving, because in practice there are several necessary accounting entries that complicate matters. We keep it simple enough for the AP exam and leave the accounting to those who wear the pocket protectors.

Aggregate Income

Calculating GDP from the income half of the circular flow (aka "the income approach") must begin with incomes that are paid to the suppliers of resources. These are the households, and they supply labor, land, capital, and entrepreneurial talents. See Table 7.3. Payments to these resources are usually referred to as wages, rents, interest, and profits. With some accounting adjustments, the sum of all income sources is approximately equal to the sum of all spending sources, or GDP.

Table 7.3

RESOURCE SUPPLIED	INCOME RECEIVED
Labor	Wages
Land	Rent
Capital	Interest
Entrepreneurial Talent	Profits

K.I.S.S.: Keep It Simple, Silly

National income accounting makes my head spin, and studying it usually sends students off to their guidance counselors to investigate majoring in Scandinavian poetry. If we focus on the simplicities of the circular flow model, we can use the relationships between income and spending with some powerful results.

$$\text{GDP} = C + I + G + (X - M) = \text{Aggregate spending}$$
$$= \text{Aggregate income } (Y)$$

- The most recent AP Macroeconomics curriculum focuses on GDP, or total spending, as the nation's measure of economic output. Your study should therefore focus on the components of GDP.

Real and Nominal GDP

Remember that calculation of GDP requires that we take production of goods and services and apply the value of those items. But we know that prices change, so when we compare GDP from one year to the next, we have to account for changing prices. Reporting that GDP has risen without acknowledging that this is simply because prices have risen doesn't tell a very accurate story. We need a way to compare GDP over time by accounting for different prices over time.

Example:

In 2014, our small coffee shop sold 1,000 café lattes at a price of $2 each. The total value of this production was $2,000. In 2015, firms and residents in town experienced a higher cost of living, and our coffee shop increased the price of a latte to $3 and still sold 1,000. The total value of the production has shown an increase of $1,000, but production didn't increase at all.

Nominal GDP. The value of current production at the current prices. Valuing 2015 production with 2015 prices creates nominal GDP in 2015. This is also known as current-dollar GDP or "money" GDP.

Real GDP. The value of current production, but using prices from a fixed point in time. Valuing 2015 production at 2014 prices creates real GDP in 2015 and allows us to compare it to 2014. This is also known as constant-dollar or real GDP.

Keepin' It Real: An Espresso Example

Suppose GDP is made up of just one product, cups of latte. Table 7.4 shows how many lattes have been made in a four-year period, the prices, and a price index. We need a **price index** in order to calculate real GDP. This index is a measure of the price of a good in a given year, when compared to the price of that good in a **reference** (or **base**) **year.** Using 2012 as the base year, I'll create a latte index and use it to adjust nominal GDP to real GDP for this one good. First the latte price index, or LPI:

LPI in year t = 100 × (Price of a latte in year t)/(Price of a latte in base year)

Table 7.4

YEAR	# OF LATTES	PRICE PER CUP	NOMINAL GDP	PRICE INDEX	REAL GDP
2012	1,000	$2	$2,000	= 100 × $2/$2 = 100	= $2,000
2013	1,200	$3	$3,600	150	$2,400
2014	1,800	$4	$7,200	200	$3,600
2015	1,600	$5	$8,000	250	$3,200

Notice that a price index always equals 100 in the base year. Even if you didn't know the actual price of a latte in 2012, by looking at the LPI, you can see that the price doubled by 2014, since the LPI is 200 compared to the base value of 100.

Deflating Nominal GDP

To deflate a nominal value, or adjust for inflation, you do a simple division:

Real GDP = 100 × (Nominal GDP)/(Price index) or you can think of it as

Real GDP = (Nominal GDP)/(Price index; in hundreds)

Making this adjustment provides the final column of the above table. While nominal GDP appears to be rapidly rising from 2012 to 2015, you can see that, in real terms, the value of latte production has risen more modestly from 2012 to 2014 but actually fell in 2015.

Using Percentages

Another way to look at the relationship among a price index, real GDP, and nominal GDP is to look at them in terms of percentage change.

%Δ real GDP = %Δ nominal GDP − %Δ price index

Example:

If nominal GDP increased by 5 percent and the price index increased by 1 percent, we could say that real GDP increased by 4 percent.

The GDP Deflator

GDP is constructed by aggregating the consumption and production of thousands of goods and services. The prices of these many goods that compose GDP are used to construct a price index informally called the **GDP price deflator.** Nominal GDP is deflated, with this price index, to create real GDP. Economists watch real GDP to look for signs of economic growth and recession. We see these changes in real GDP by looking at the business cycle.

Business Cycles

The **business cycle** is the periodic rise and fall in economic activity, and can be measured by changes in real GDP. Figure 7.2 is a simplification of a complete business cycle. In general, there are four phases of the cycle.

- **Expansion.** A period where real GDP is growing.
- **Peak.** The top of the cycle where an expansion has run its course and is about to turn down.

Figure 7.2

- **Contraction.** A period where real GDP is falling. There is no specific criteria for defining one, but a **recession** is unofficially described as two consecutive quarters of falling real GDP. If the contraction is prolonged or deep enough, it is called a **depression.**
- **Trough.** The bottom of the cycle where a contraction has stopped and is about to turn up.

- *Though it is an imperfect measure, GDP is used as a measure of economic prosperity and growth.*
- *You must focus on real GDP, not nominal.*
- *Nominal GDP is deflated to real GDP by dividing by the price index known as the GDP deflator.*

This chapter has stressed that we need to know how economic activity is measured so that we can understand how and why policies can be used to strengthen the economy. Real GDP is one of these important economic indicators and is probably the most all-encompassing of macroeconomic measures of performance, but it is not the only one. The economic indicators of inflation and unemployment are also targets of economic policy and are widely covered by the media. Before getting to macroeconomic models and policy, the next two sections spend some time learning more about what these statistics do, and do not, tell us.

7.3 Inflation and the Consumer Price Index

Main Topics: *Consumer Price Index, Inflation, Is Inflation Bad?, Measurement Issues*

My "Latte Price Index" illustrates that a price index can be constructed to measure changes in the price of anything. Another price index, the GDP price deflator, measures the increase in the price level of items that compose GDP. But not all goods that fall into GDP are goods that the everyday household shops for. If United Airlines buys a 767 from Boeing, it falls in GDP, but the price of a new 767 doesn't exactly fall within what we might call consumer spending. We need a statistic that focuses on consumer prices.

The Consumer Price Index (CPI)

To measure the average price level of items that consumers actually buy, use the **consumer price index (CPI)**. The Bureau of Labor Statistics (BLS) selects a base year, and a **market basket** is compiled of approximately 400 consumer goods and services bought in that year. A monthly survey is conducted in 50 urban areas around the country, and based on the results of this survey, the average prices of the items in the base year market basket is factored into the CPI. Confused yet? Let's do a simple example of a price index for a typical consumer (see Table 7.5).

Table 7.5

		2015 (BASE PERIOD)		2016 (CURRENT PERIOD)	
Items in the Basket	Quantity Purchased	Price	2015 Spending using 2015 Prices and Quantities	Price	2016 Spending using 2016 Prices and 2015 Quantities
Chocolate Bars	12	$1.50	$18	$1.75	$21
Concert Tickets	4	$45	$180	$60	$240
Large Pizzas	18	$16	$288	$15	$270
Total Spending			= $486		= $531

Price index current year = 100 × (Spending current year)/(Spending base year)

2016 price index = 100 × (531)/(486) = 109.26

Inflation

In the above example, the price index increased from 100 in the base year to 109.26 in 2016. In other words, the average price level increased by 9.26 percent.

On a much larger scale, the official CPI is constructed and used to measure the increase in the average price level of consumer goods. The annual rate of **inflation** on goods consumed by the typical consumer is the percentage change in the CPI from one year to the next.

> "Know these things for multiple-choice especially."
> —Lucas, AP Student

So What Is the Difference Between the CPI and the GDP Deflator?

This concept can be confusing. The difference between these two price indices lies in the content of the market basket of goods. The CPI is based upon a market basket of goods bought by consumers, even those goods that are produced abroad. The GDP deflator includes all items that make up domestic production. Because GDP includes more than just consumer goods, the index is a broader measure of inflation, while the CPI is a measure of inflation of only consumer goods. Since consumer spending is so important to the economy, making up about 70 percent of U.S. GDP each year, the CPI is a very important indicator of what is happening in the broader economy.

- *Consumer inflation rate = 100 × (CPI new – CPI old)/CPI old*
- *If you wished to calculate the rate of price inflation for all goods produced in a nation, you would use the GDP deflator and not the CPI.*

Nominal and Real Income

As a consumer, I am also a worker and an income earner. Rising consumer prices hurt my ability to purchase the items that make me happy. In other words, rising prices can cause a decrease in my purchasing power. Ideally, I would like to see my income rise at a faster rate than the price of consumer goods. One way to see if this is happening is to deflate nominal income by the CPI to calculate my real income. Real income is calculated in the same way that real GDP is calculated.

- **Real income this year = (Nominal income this year)/CPI (in hundredths)**

Example:

In 2014 Kelsey's nominal income was $40,000, and it increases to $41,000 in 2015. Curious about her purchasing power, she looks up the CPI in 2014 and finds that at the end of that year it was 234.8; at the end of 2015 it was 236.5. This is compared to the base year value of 100 in 1984.

Real income 2015 = $40,000/2.348 = $17,036

Real income 2016 = $41,000/2.365 = $17,336

What we have done here is converted Kelsey's nominal incomes in 2014 and 2015, which were each a function of prices on those two years, into constant 1984 dollars. In other words, we have adjusted (or deflated) incomes measured in two different years so they are measured with the prices that existed in one year. After accounting for inflation, Kelsey's real income increased by $300. Her nominal income increased at a rate slightly faster than the rate of inflation, and so her purchasing power has slightly increased.

Example:

What if Kelsey's wages were frozen, and she did not receive that raise in 2015?

Real income 2015 = $40,000/2.365 = $16,913,

or a $123 decrease in purchasing power

Is Inflation Bad?

The previous example illustrates that inflation erodes the purchasing power of consumers if nominal wages do not keep up with prices. In general, inflation impacts different groups in different ways. It can actually help some individuals! The main thing to keep in mind with inflation is that it is the unexpected or sudden inflation that creates winners and losers. If the inflation is predictable and expected, most groups can plan for it and adjust behavior and prices accordingly.

"Make sure you understand the difference between expected and unexpected inflation."
—AP Teacher

Expected Inflation

If my employer and I agree that the general price level is going to increase by 3 percent next year, then my salary can be adjusted by at least 3 percent so that my purchasing power does not fall. This **cost of living adjustment** doesn't hurt my employer so long as the prices of the firm's output and any other inputs also increase by 3 percent. Many unions and government employees have cost of living raises written into employment contracts to recognize predictable inflation over time.

Banks and other lenders acknowledge inflation by factoring expected inflation into interest rates. If they do not, savers and lenders can be hurt by rising prices. For this reason, the bank adds an inflation factor on the **real rate** of interest to create a **nominal rate** of interest that savers receive and borrowers pay.

Nominal interest rate = Real interest rate + Expected inflation

Savings Example 1:

When I see the bank offering an interest rate of 1 percent for a savings account and I put $100 in the bank, I expect to have $101 worth of purchasing power a year from now. But if prices increase by 2 percent, my original deposit is only worth $98. So even when I receive my $1 of interest, I have lost purchasing power.

If you have a savings account, the real rate is the rate the bank pays you to borrow your money for a year. You must be compensated for this because you do not have $100 to spend at the mall if you put it into the bank. Look at my savings example again with an inflation expectation of 2 percent and a real interest rate of 1 percent.

Savings Example 2:

- January 1: The purchasing power of my $100 is $100, and the bank offers me a 3 percent nominal interest rate on a savings account.
- Throughout the year, inflation is indeed 2 percent.
- December 31: My bank balance says $103, but $2 of purchasing power on my original deposit has been lost to inflation, leaving me with $1 as payment from the bank for having my money for one year.

Borrowing Example:

If you are looking for a loan of $100, the real interest is the rate the bank will charge you for borrowing the bank's money for a year. After all, if the bank lends the money to you, it will not have those funds for some other profitable opportunity. Again, let's assume that the expected inflation is 2 percent but the real rate of interest is 3 percent.

- January 1: The purchasing power of the bank's $100 is $100, and the bank lends it to me with a 5 percent nominal interest rate.
- Throughout the year, inflation is indeed 2 percent.
- December 31: I pay the bank back $105, but $2 of the bank's purchasing power on the original $100 has been lost to inflation, leaving it with $3 as payment from me for having its money for one year.

- So long as the actual inflation is identical to the expected inflation, workers, employers, savers, lenders, and borrowers are not harmed by the inflation.

Unexpected Inflation

When price levels are unpredictable or increase by a much larger or much smaller amount than predicted, some sectors of the economy gain and others lose. Though not a comprehensive list, some of the groups that win and lose from unexpected inflation include the following:

- *Employees and employers.* If the real income of workers is falling because of rapid inflation, it is possible that firms are benefiting at the expense of the workers. In a simple case, you work at a grocery store and the price of groceries unexpectedly rises by 10 percent a year, but your nominal wages rise by 8 percent. Your employer is clearly benefiting by selling goods at higher and higher prices but paying you wages that are rising more slowly.
- *Fixed income recipients.* A retiree receiving a fixed pension can expect to see it slowly eroded by rising prices. Likewise, a landlord who is locked into a long-term lease receives payments that slowly decline in purchasing power. If the minimum wage is not adjusted for inflation, then minimum-wage workers see a decline in their purchasing power.
- *Savers and borrowers.* If I put my money in the bank and leave it for a year when inflation is higher than expected, and then withdraw it, the purchasing power is greatly diminished. On the other hand, if I borrow from the bank at the beginning of that year and pay it back after higher-than-expected inflation, I am giving back dollars that are not worth as much as they used to be. This benefits me and hurts the bank.

- Rapid unexpected inflation usually hurts employees if real wages are falling, as well as fixed-income recipients, savers, and lenders.
- Rapid unexpected inflation usually helps firms if real wages are falling, as well as borrowers. It might also increase the value of some assets like real estate or other properties.

Difficulties with the CPI

Like all statistical measures, we should be careful not to read too much into them and acknowledge that they all have some problematic issues.

- *Consumers substitute.* The market basket uses consumption patterns from the base year, which could be several years ago. As the price of goods begins to rise, we know that consumers seek substitutes. This substitution might make the base year market basket a poor representation of the current consumption pattern.
- *Goods evolve.* Imagine if the CPI market basket were using 1912 as a base year. The basket would include the price of buggy whips and stove pipe hats in the inflation rate. The emergence of new products (smartphones) and extinction of others (manual typewriters) is understood by firms and consumers, but the market basket must reflect this or it risks becoming irrelevant.

- *Quality differences.* Some price increases are the result of improvements in quality. As automakers improve safety features, luxury options, and mechanical sophistication, we should expect the price to rise. Prices that increase because the product is fundamentally better are not an indication of overall inflation. Because the Bureau of Labor Statistics (BLS) has a difficult time telling the difference between quality improvements and actual inflation, the CPI can be overstated for this reason.

If the market basket is not altered to account for the above effects, the CPI is not very accurate. The BLS reviews the market basket from time to time and updates it if necessary. Comparisons over long periods of time are not very useful, but from month to month and year to year, the CPI is a fairly useful measure of how the average price level of consumer items is changing.

7.4 Unemployment

Main Topics: *Measuring the Unemployment Rate, Types of Unemployment*

Whenever an economy has idle, or unemployed, resources, it is operating inside the production possibility frontier. Though unemployment can describe any idle resource, it is almost always applied to labor.

Measuring the Unemployment Rate

Is an infant unemployed? What about an 85-year-old retiree? A parent staying home with young children? Before we can calculate an unemployment rate, we must first define who is a candidate for employment. Once again, a monthly survey is conducted by the BLS, and through a series of questions, it classifies all persons in a surveyed household above the age of 16 into one of three groups: "Employed" for pay at least one hour per week, "Unemployed" but looking for work, or "Out of the Labor Force." If a person is out of the labor force, he has chosen to not seek employment. Our retiree and stay-at-home parent of young children would fall into this category. Many students, at least those who choose not to work, also fall into this latter category.

The non-institutionalized civilian **labor force** (LF) is the sum of all individuals 16 years and older, not in the military or in prison, who are either currently employed (E) or unemployed (U). To be counted as one of the unemployed, you must be actively searching for work.

$$LF = E + U$$

The **unemployment rate** is the ratio of unemployed to the total labor force:

$$UR = (U/LF) \times 100$$

Example:

Table 7.6 summarizes the 2015 and 2016 labor market in Smallville.

Table 7.6

	POPULATION	OUT OF THE LABOR FORCE	EMPLOYED	UNEMPLOYED	LABOR FORCE = E + U	UNEMPLOYMENT RATE = (U/LF) × 100
2015	1,800	800	900	100	1,000	= 10%
2016	1,800	820	900	80	980	= 8.2%

In 2015, 100 citizens are unemployed but are seeking work and the reported unemployment rate is 10 percent. After a year of searching, 20 of these unemployed citizens become tired of looking for work and move back home to live in the basement of their parents' home. These **discouraged workers** are not counted in the ranks of the unemployed, and this results in an unemployment rate that falls to 8.2 percent. On the surface, the economy looks to be improving, but these 20 individuals have *not* found employment. The statistic hides their presence.

To give you an idea of the statistical impact that discouraged workers have on the official unemployment rate, we can look at labor force data from January 2016. The BLS estimated a U.S. labor force of 158,335,000, people and of those, 7,791,000 were counted as unemployed. The January 2016 official unemployment rate was 4.9 percent. However, there were an estimated 623,000 people who were not in the labor force because they were discouraged over their job prospects. If you add these people to the ranks of the unemployed and also to the labor force, the adjusted unemployment rate increases to 5.3 percent.

- The presence of discouraged workers understates the true unemployment rate.

Types of Unemployment

"Be sure to give examples of each type."
—AP Teacher

People are unemployed for different reasons. Some of these reasons are predictable and relatively harmless, and others can even be beneficial to the individual and the economy. Others reasons for lost jobs are quite damaging, however, and policies need to target these types of job loss.

Frictional Unemployment. This type of unemployment occurs when someone new enters the labor market or switches jobs. Frictional unemployment can happen voluntarily if a person is seeking a better match for his or her skills, or has just finished schooling, and is usually short-lived. Employers who fire employees for poor work habits or subpar performance also contribute to the level of frictional unemployment. The provision of unemployment insurance for six months allows for a cushion to these events and assists the person in finding a job compatible with his or her skills. Because frictional unemployment is typically a short-term phenomenon, it is considered the least troublesome for the economy as a whole.

Seasonal Unemployment. This type of unemployment emerges as the periodic and predictable job loss that follows the calendar. Agricultural jobs are gained and lost as crops are grown and harvested. Teens are employed during the summers and over the holidays, but most are not employed during the school year. Summer resorts close in the winter, and winter ski lodges close in the spring. Workers and employers alike anticipate these changes in employment and plan accordingly, thus the damage is minimal. The BLS accounts for the seasonality of some employment, so such factors are not going to affect the published unemployment rate.

Structural Unemployment. This type of unemployment is caused by fundamental, underlying changes in the economy that can create job loss for skills that are no longer in demand. A worker who manually tightened bolts on the assembly line can be structurally replaced by robotics. In cases of technological unemployment like this, the job skills of the worker need to change to suit the new workplace. In some cases of structural employment, jobs are lost because the product is no longer in demand, probably because a better product has replaced it. This market evolution is inevitable, so the more flexible the skills of the workers, the less painful this kind of structural change. Government-provided job training and subsidized public universities help the structurally unemployed help themselves.

Cyclical Unemployment. Jobs are gained and lost as the business cycle improves and worsens. The unemployment rate rises when the economy is contracting, and the unemployment rate falls as the economy is expanding. This form of unemployment is usually felt throughout the economy rather than on certain subgroups, and therefore policies are going to focus on stimulating job growth throughout the economy. Structural unemployment might be forever, but cyclical unemployment only lasts as long as it takes to get through the recession.

Full Employment

Economists acknowledge that frictional and structural unemployment are always present. In fact, in a rapidly evolving economy, these are often beneficial in the long run. Because of these forms of unemployment, the unemployment rate can never be zero. Economists define **full employment** as the situation when there is no cyclical unemployment in the economy. The unemployment rate associated with full employment is called the **natural rate of unemployment**, and in the United States, this rate has traditionally been 5 to 6 percent.

❯ Review Questions

1. Which of the following transactions would be counted in GDP?

    (A) The cash you receive from babysitting your neighbor's kids
    (B) The sale of illegal drugs
    (C) The sale of cucumbers to a pickle manufacturer
    (D) The sale of a pound of tomatoes at a supermarket
    (E) The eBay resale of a sweater you received from your great aunt at Christmas

2. GDP is $10 million, consumer spending is $6 million, government spending is $3 million, exports are $2 million, and imports are $3 million. How much is spent for investments?

    (A) $0 million
    (B) $1 million
    (C) $2 million
    (D) $3 million
    (E) $4 million

3. If Real GDP = $200 billion and the price index = 200, Nominal GDP is

    (A) $4 billion
    (B) $400 billion
    (C) $200 billion
    (D) $2 billion
    (E) Impossible to determine since the base year is not given

For Questions 4 to 5 use the following information for a small town:

Total population: 2,000
Total employed adults: 950
Total unemployed adults: 50

4. What is the size of the labor force?

    (A) 2,000
    (B) 950
    (C) 900
    (D) 1,000
    (E) 1,950

5. What is the official unemployment rate?

    (A) 5 percent
    (B) 2.5 percent
    (C) 5.5 percent
    (D) 7 percent
    (E) Unknown, as we do not know the number of discouraged workers

6. You are working at a supermarket bagging groceries, but you are unhappy about your wage, so you quit and begin looking for a new job at a competing grocery store. What type of unemployment is this?

    (A) Cyclical
    (B) Structural
    (C) Seasonal
    (D) Frictional
    (E) Discouraged

Answers and Explanations

1. **D**—The supermarket tomatoes are the only final good sale and are counted. Babysitting is a nonmarket, cash "under the table" service. The sale of illegal drugs is a part of an underground economy. The sale of the cucumbers is an intermediate good. The resale of the sweater, even though it was never worn, is a second-hand sale. When your great aunt originally purchased it at the mall, it was counted in GDP.

2. **C**—GDP = $C + I + G + (X - M)$. This would mean that $10 = 6 + I + 3 + (2 - 3)$; therefore, $I = \$2$ million.

3. **B**—Nominal GDP/price index (in hundredths) = Real GDP. Use this relationship to solve for Nominal GDP. $\$200 = $ (Nominal GDP)/2. Nominal GDP = $400 billion.

4. **D**—Labor force is the employed + the unemployed. LF = 950 + 50 = 1,000. The remaining citizens are out of the labor force.

5. **A**—The unemployment rate is the ratio of unemployed to the total labor force. UR = U/LF = 50/1,000 = 5%.

6. **D**—Frictional unemployment occurs when a person is in between jobs. This person has not been laid off due to a structural change in the demand for skills, or because of a cyclical economic downturn, or because of a new season. A low wage might be discouraging; a discouraged worker is a worker who has been unemployed for so long that he or she has ceased the search for work.

Rapid Review

Circular flow of economic activity: A model that shows how households and firms circulate resources, goods, and incomes through the economy. This basic model is expanded to include the government and the foreign sector.

Closed economy: A model that assumes there is no foreign sector (imports and exports).

Aggregation: The process of summing the microeconomic activity of households and firms into a more macroeconomic measure of economic activity.

Gross domestic product (GDP): The market value of the final goods and services produced within a nation in a given period of time.

Final goods: Goods that are ready for their final use by consumers and firms, for example, a new Harley-Davidson motorcycle.

Intermediate goods: Goods that require further modification before they are ready for final use, e.g., steel used to produce the new Harley.

Double counting: The mistake of including the value of intermediate stages of production in GDP on top of the value of the final good.

Second-hand sales: Final goods and services that are resold. Even if they are resold many times, final goods and services are only counted once, in the year in which they were produced.

Nonmarket transactions: Household work or do-it-yourself jobs are missed by GDP accounting. The same is true of government transfer payments and purely financial transactions like the purchase of a share of IBM stock.

Underground economy: These include unreported illegal activity, bartering, or informal exchange of cash.

Aggregate spending (GDP): The sum of all spending from four sectors of the economy. GDP = $C + I + G + (X - M)$.

Aggregate income (AI): The sum of all income—Wages + Rents + Interest + Profit—earned by suppliers of resources in the economy. With some accounting adjustments, aggregate spending equals aggregate income.

Nominal GDP: The value of current production at the current prices. Valuing 2015 production with 2015 prices creates nominal GDP in 2015.

Real GDP: The value of current production, but using prices from a fixed point in time. Valuing 2015 production at 2014 prices creates real GDP in 2015 and allows us to compare it back to 2014.

Base year: The year that serves as a reference point for constructing a price index and comparing real values over time.

Price index: A measure of the average level of prices in a market basket for a given year, when compared to the prices in a reference (or base) year. You can interpret the price index as the current price level as a percentage of the level in the base year.

Market basket: A collection of goods and services used to represent what is consumed in the economy.

GDP price deflator: The price index that measures the average price level of the goods and services that make up GDP.

Real rate of interest: The percentage increase in purchasing power that a borrower pays a lender.

Expected (anticipated) inflation: The inflation expected in a future time period. This expected inflation is added to the real interest rate to compensate for lost purchasing power.

Nominal rate of interest: The percentage increase in money that the borrower pays the lender and is equal to the real rate plus the expected inflation.

Business cycle: The periodic rise and fall (in four phases) of economic activity.

Expansion: A period where real GDP is growing.

Peak: The top of a business cycle where an expansion has ended.

Contraction: A period where real GDP is falling.

Recession: Unofficially defined as two consecutive quarters of falling real GDP.

Trough: The bottom of the cycle where a contraction has stopped.

Depression: A prolonged, deep contraction in the business cycle.

Consumer price index (CPI): The price index that measures the average price level of the items in the base year market basket. This is the main measure of consumer inflation.

Inflation: The percentage change in the CPI from one period to the next.

Nominal income: Today's income measured in today's dollars. These are dollars unadjusted by inflation.

Real income: Today's income measured in base year dollars. These inflation-adjusted dollars can be compared from year to year to determine whether purchasing power has increased or decreased.

Employed: A person is employed if she has worked for pay at least one hour per week.

Unemployed: A person is unemployed if he is not currently working but is actively seeking work.

Labor force: The sum of all individuals 16 years and older who are either currently employed (E) or unemployed (U). $LF = E + U$.

Out of the labor force: A person is classified as out of the labor force if he has chosen to not seek employment.

Unemployment rate: The percentage of the labor force that falls into the unemployed category. Sometimes called the *jobless rate*. $UR = 100 \times U/LF$.

Discouraged workers: Citizens who have been without work for so long that they become tired of looking for work and drop out of the labor force. Because these citizens are not counted in the ranks of the unemployed, the reported unemployment rate is understated.

Frictional unemployment: A type of unemployment that occurs when someone new enters the labor market or switches jobs. This is a relatively harmless form of unemployment and not expected to last long.

Seasonal unemployment: A type of unemployment that is periodic, is predictable, and follows the calendar. Workers and employers alike anticipate these changes in employment and plan accordingly, thus the damage is minimal.

Structural unemployment: A type of unemployment that is the result of fundamental, underlying changes in the economy such that some job skills are no longer in demand.

Cyclical unemployment: A type of unemployment that rises and falls with the business cycle. This form of unemployment is felt economy-wide, which makes it the focus of macroeconomic policy.

Full employment: Exists when the economy is experiencing no cyclical unemployment.

Natural rate of unemployment: The unemployment rate associated with full employment, somewhere between 4 to 6 percent in the United States.

Consumption, Saving, Investment, and the Multiplier

IN THIS CHAPTER
Summary: Having described GDP as the macroeconomic measure of a nation's output, we begin to build a model that helps to explain how and why GDP fluctuates. As the largest component of GDP, we spend some time on consumption. Investment is also a component of GDP, but because investment plays an important role in monetary policy, we investigate it as well. The market for loanable funds combines savings and investment and is a prelude to the interaction of interest rates and the role of financial institutions. This chapter begins to show how changes in spending affect output and employment through the multiplier process. Discussion of the spending multiplier previews how policy affects the macroeconomy and leads to the aggregate demand and supply model in the next chapter.

Key Ideas
✪ Consumption and Saving Functions
✪ Investment
✪ Market for Loanable Funds
✪ The Spending Multiplier, Tax Multiplier, and Balanced-Budget Multiplier

8.1 Consumption and Saving

Main Topics: *Consumption and Saving Functions, Marginal Propensity to Consume and Save, Changes in Consumption and Saving*

The circular flow model illustrates the importance of consumption in the production of goods and the employment of resources. A better understanding of consumption allows us to build a model of the macroeconomy and see the role of policy in affecting macroeconomic indicators like GDP, employment, and inflation.

Consumption and Saving Functions

Though not the only factor, the most important element affecting consumption (and savings) is disposable income. **Disposable income (DI)** is what consumers have left over to spend or save once they have paid out their net taxes.

$$DI = \text{Gross income} - \text{Net taxes}$$

where Net taxes = (Taxes paid − Transfers received).

With no government transfers or taxation, $DI = C + S$. Though not all consumers save part of their income, typical consumers spend the majority of their disposable income and save whatever is left over. To see the relationship between disposable income and consumption, we create a **consumption function**.

Consumption and Saving Schedules

The consumption and saving schedules are the direct relationships between disposable income and consumption and savings. As DI increases for a typical household, C and S both increase. Table 8.1 provides an example.

Table 8.1

DISPOSABLE INCOME (DI)	CONSUMPTION (C)	SAVINGS (S)
0	40	−40
100	120	−20
200	200	0
300	280	20
400	360	40
500	440	60

Consumption

Even with zero disposable income, households still consume as they liquidate wealth (sell assets), spend some savings, or borrow (dissavings). For every additional $100 of disposable income, consumers increase their spending by $80 and increase saving by $20. We can convert the above consumption schedule to a linear equation or **consumption function**:

$$C = 40 + .80(DI)$$

The constant $40 is referred to as **autonomous consumption** because it does not change as DI changes. The slope of the consumption function is .80. This function is plotted in Figure 8.1.

Figure 8.1

At every level of DI, the consumption function tells us how much is consumed. Both Table 8.1 and Figure 8.1 tell us that at incomes below $200, the consumer is consuming more than his income. As a result, saving is negative, and this is referred to as **dissaving**. But at incomes above $200, the consumer is spending less than his income, and so saving is positive.

Saving

The saving schedule above can also be converted into a linear equation, or **saving function**:

$$S = -40 + .20(DI)$$

The constant $-40 is referred to as **autonomous saving** because it does not change as DI changes. With zero disposable income, the household would need to borrow $40 to consume $40 worth of goods. The slope of the saving function is .20. This function is plotted in Figure 8.2.

Figure 8.2

Marginal Propensity to Consume and Save

An important lesson from the study of microeconomics is the marginal concept. You can think of it in two equivalent ways. Marginal always means an incremental change caused by an external force, or it is always the slope of a "total" function. The same is true here.

The **marginal propensity to consume (MPC)** is the change in consumption caused by a change in disposable income. Another way to think about it is the slope of the consumption function.

$$\text{MPC} = \Delta C/\Delta DI = \text{Slope of consumption function}$$

Using Table 8.1, we see that for every additional $100 of DI, C increases by $80, so the MPC = .80.

The **marginal propensity to save (MPS)** is the change in saving caused by a change in disposable income. Another way to think about it is the slope of the saving function:

$$\text{MPS} = \Delta S/\Delta DI = \text{Slope of saving function}$$

Using Table 8.1, we can see that for every additional $100 of DI, S increases by $20, so the MPS = .20.

There is a nice relationship between the MPC and the MPS. For every additional dollar not consumed, it is saved. So if the consumer gains $100 in disposable income, he increases his consumption by $80 and increases saving by $20. In other words, MPC + MPS = 1. If you know one, you can find the other.

- MPC = $\Delta C/\Delta DI$ = Constant slope of consumption function
- MPS = $\Delta S/\Delta DI$ = Constant slope of saving function
- MPC + MPS = 1

Changes in Consumption and Saving

A change in disposable income causes a movement along the consumption and savings functions. Economists typically recognize four external determinants of household consumption and saving that shift the functions upward or downward.

Determinants of Consumption and Saving

- *Wealth.* When the value of accumulated wealth increases, consumption functions shift upward, and the saving function shifts downward, because households can sell stock or other assets to consume more goods at their current level of disposable income.
- *Expectations.* Uncertainty or a low expectation about future income usually prompts a household to decrease consumption and increase saving. An expectation of a higher future price level spurs higher consumption right now and less saving.
- *Household debt.* Households can increase consumption with borrowing, or debt. However, as households accumulate more and more debt, they need to use more and more disposable income to pay off the debt, and thus decrease consumption.
- *Taxes and transfers.* A change in taxes impacts both consumption and saving in the same direction. If the government increases taxes, households see both consumption and saving decrease because more of their gross income is sent to the government. On the other hand, an increase in government transfer payments increases both consumption and saving functions. In the case of taxes and transfers, consumption and saving functions shift in the same way.

An upward shift in consumption tells us that at all levels of disposable income, consumption is greater (C_{High}). If consumption is greater at all levels of disposable income, saving must be lower (S_{Low}), and vice versa. The only exception is the case of taxes and transfers described above. Figures 8.3 and 8.4 illustrate these simultaneous shifts in the opposite directions.

Figure 8.3

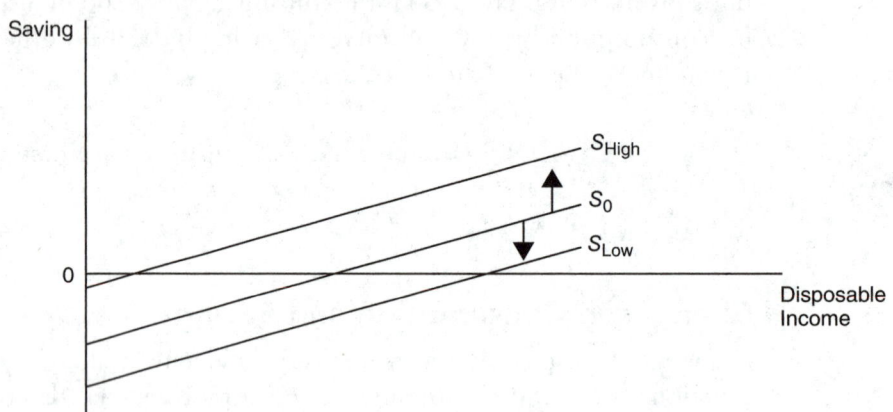

Figure 8.4

- With the exception of taxes and transfers, when the consumption function shifts upward, the saving function shifts downward.
- With the exception of taxes and transfers, when the consumption function shifts downward, the saving function shifts upward.
- When taxes increase (or transfers decrease), both consumption and saving functions shift downward.
- When taxes decrease (or transfers increase), both consumption and saving functions shift upward.

8.2 Investment

Main Topics: *Decision to Invest, Investment Demand, Investment and GDP, Market for Loanable Funds*

Investment is the other source of private domestic spending. We spend a little time examining why firms increase or decrease investment, build the investment demand curve, and then introduce the market for loanable funds.

Decision to Invest

The decision of a firm to spend money on new machinery or construction is simply a decision based upon marginal benefits and marginal costs. The marginal benefit of an investment is the expected real rate of return (r) the firm anticipates receiving on the expenditure. The marginal cost of the investment is the real rate of interest (i), or the cost of borrowing. Let's look at this concept with examples.

Expected Real Rate of Return
A local pizza firm invests $10,000 in a new delivery car. The owner expects this to help to deliver more pizzas, increasing revenues and profits. The car lasts exactly one year and the increased real profits are anticipated to be $2,000. This expected real rate of return is $2,000/$10,000 = .20 or 20 percent. Of course an actual car lasts more than one year, but this decision to invest is shown for one year to keep it simple, while still making the point.

Real Rate of Interest
The owner goes to the bank and asks for a one-year loan to purchase the new delivery car. The bank offers a nominal rate of interest of 15 percent; this includes 5 percent for expected inflation and 10 percent as the real rate of borrowing the money for a year. At the end of the year, he spends $1,000 as real interest on the $10,000 loan.

The Decision
Since the new delivery car provides $2,000 in additional real profits ($r = 20\%$), and the loan costs $1,000 in real interest ($i = 10\%$), this investment should be made. Another way to make this decision is with a comparison of interest rates.

- If $r\% \geq i\%$, make the investment.
- If $r\% < i\%$, do not make the investment.

Investment Demand
Like any demand curve, the quantity demanded increases as the price falls. The same is true for investment demand. The rational firm invests in all projects up to the point where the real rate of interest equals the expected real rate of return ($i = r$). Very few investment projects are available at extremely high rates of return and so those opportunities are taken first. As the real rate of return (r) falls, those very profitable opportunities are gone, but many less profitable investments remain. So as the expected real rate falls, the cumulative amount of investment dollars rises. Likewise, as the real cost of borrowing (i) falls, more and more projects become worthwhile, so dollars of investment rises. Either way, as interest rates fall, the total amount of investment rises. Figure 8.5 illustrates the **investment demand curve**, which shows the inverse relationship between the interest rate and the cumulative dollars invested. At an interest rate of 5 percent, $20 billion dollars might be invested.

Investment and GDP
In the simple model of private investment outlined in Figure 8.5, there is no mention of GDP or disposable income. With no government or foreign sector, GDP = DI. To keep the model simple, we assume that investment spending (I) is determined from the investment demand curve and is constant at all levels of GDP.

> Example:
> In Figure 8.5 if the interest rate was 5%, firms would invest $20 billion this year, regardless of the level of disposable income or GDP. This **autonomous investment** is illustrated in Figure 8.6 as a horizontal line with GDP on the x axis.
> If something happened to interest rates, or to investment demand, autonomous

Figure 8.5

Figure 8.6

investment could increase or decrease, but at that new level, would once again be constant at any value of GDP.

Market for Loanable Funds

It is useful to see the relationship between saving and investment by looking at the **market for loanable funds.** When savers place their money in banks or buy bonds, those funds are available to be borrowed by firms for private investment.

Demand for Loanable Funds

The inverse relationship between investment and the real interest rate is fairly straightforward. As the real interest rate falls, borrowing becomes less costly, and large investment projects become more attractive to firms. This investment demand curve can also be thought of as a **demand for loanable funds,** and this demand is the result of the borrowing by private firms and the government.

Supply of Loanable Funds

The **supply of loanable funds** comes from saving on the part of households, both domestic and foreign. If disposable income is greater than consumption, this **private saving** exists, and is positively related to the real interest rate.

The market for loanable funds is shown in Figure 8.7, and the equilibrium interest rate is found at the intersection of the supply and demand curves. In upcoming chapters, we investigate the role of this market in the banking system, fiscal and monetary policy, and economic growth.

> "Make the connections between concepts learned in a previous chapter to what you are learning now, because everything is cumulative." —Caroline, AP Student

Figure 8.7

- The supply of loanable funds comes from saving, and lending.
- The demand for loanable funds comes from investment, and borrowing.
- Equilibrium is at the real interest rate where dollars saved equals dollars invested.

8.3 The Multiplier Effect

Main Topics: *Multiplier Effect and Spending Multiplier, Public and Foreign Sectors, Tax Multiplier, Balanced-Budget Multiplier*

The most simple circular flow consists solely of consumers and firms; in other words, GDP = $C + I$. But the public sector (G) and foreign sector ($X - M$) are also important sources of domestic spending and income. Inclusion of these two sectors provides very little in the way of complications; they introduce the concept of the spending multiplier, the tax multiplier, and the balanced budget multiplier. This also paves the way for fiscal policy aimed at macroeconomic stability.

Multiplier Effect and Spending Multiplier

When you buy an ear of corn at the farmers' market, those dollars serve as income to several people. The farmers use those dollars to pay employees, to run their farm equipment, and to buy their own food. Farm employees use those wages to buy bacon, pay the rent, and many other goods and services. The circular flow explains how the injection of a few dollars of spending creates many more dollars of spending. Follow the dollars for a few rounds to see how it works. With the marginal propensity to consume of .80, if households receive a $1 of new income they spend $.80 and save $.20.

Round 1: Firms *increase* **investment spending by $10**, which acts as an injection of new money into the economy.
Round 2: The **$10** acts as income to resource suppliers (households) and with an MPC = .80, **households spend $8** and save $2.
Round 3: The **$8** of new consumption spending (*C*) is income for other households, and they also spend 80 percent, or **$6.40** and save $1.60.
Round 4: The **$6.40** of new *C* is income for other households, and they spend 80 percent, or **$5.12**, and save $1.28.

This process repeats. Each time the dollars circulate through the economy, 80 percent is spent and 20 percent is saved. After only four rounds, there has been $10 + 8 + 6.40 + 5.12 = **$29.52 of new GDP**. The process continues until households are trying to consume 80 percent of virtually nothing and the increase in new GDP comes to an eventual stop.

This is called the **multiplier effect**. A change in any component of autonomous spending creates a larger change in GDP. The discussion of the "rounds" of spending above implies that the marginal propensities to consume and save play a critical role in determining the magnitude of the multiplier. There are two equivalent ways to calculate the multiplier if you know the MPC or MPS. The magnitude of the **spending multiplier** is found by taking a ratio:

$$\text{Multiplier} = 1/(1 - \text{MPC}) = 1/(1 - .80) = 5$$
Since MPC + MPS = 1,
$$\text{Multiplier} = 1/\text{MPS} = 1/.20 = 5.$$

The spending multiplier can be found by using one of the following equations:

- Multiplier = 1/MPS
- Multiplier = 1/(1−MPC)
- Multiplier = (Δ GDP)/(Δ Spending)

Some common spending multipliers are as follows:

- MPC = .90, Multiplier = 1/.10 = 10
- MPC = .80, Multiplier = 1/.20 = 5
- MPC = .75, Multiplier = 1/.25 = 4
- MPC = .50, Multiplier = 1/.5 = 2

Public and Foreign Sectors

The inclusion of government spending (*G*) and net exports (*X* − *M*) act in the very same way as the change in investment illustrated in the preceding example.

Government Spending (G)

With the MPC =.80, we have found the spending multiplier equal to 5. If autonomous government spending is incorporated into the circular flow model, the multiplier effect is again felt throughout the economy. If *G* = $20, we could expect those $20 to multiply to $100 in new GDP.

Net Exports (X−M)

The final sector of the macroeconomy is the foreign sector. The addition or subtraction (if imports exceed exports) of autonomous net exports is an increase (or decrease) of dollars in the circular flow. Using a spending multiplier of 5, if $(X - M) = \$10$, GDP would increase by $50.

Tax Multiplier

The preceding discussion of the public sector shows that when the government injects money into the economy (G), it multiplies by a factor of the spending multiplier. But the government can also have an impact on aggregate expenditures and real GDP by changing taxes and/or transfers.

The Multiplier Effect

Recipients of a decrease in taxes treat it as an increase in disposable income. The typical household increases consumption by a factor of the MPC and increases saving by a factor of the MPS. It is important to keep in mind that less than 100 percent of this increase in disposable income circulates through the economy because most households save a proportion of it.

> **Example:**
> The MPC is equal to .90, and the government transfers back tax revenue to consumers by sending each taxpayer a $200 check. With an MPC = .90, $180 is consumed and $20 is saved. The multiplier process kicks in, but not on the entire $200, only on the consumed portion of $180. The multiplier being $1/.10 = 10$, GDP increases by $1,800.
> In other words, a $200 change in tax policy (a tax rebate in this case) caused an $1,800 change in real GDP. This tax multiplier of 9 measures the magnitude of the multiplier process when there is a change in taxes.

The Difference in Multipliers

"Remember that taxes will have a smaller multiplier than government spending!"
--Richard, AP Student

With an MPC = .90, the spending multiplier is 10, but the tax multiplier is smaller, Tm = 9. Why? The spending multiplier begins to work as soon as there is a change in autonomous spending (C, I, G, net exports), but the tax multiplier must first go through a person's consumption function as disposable income. In that first "round" of spending, some of those injected dollars are leakages in the form of savings. In the example above, 10 percent of those injected dollars fail to be recirculated, and therefore the final multiplier effect is smaller. The relationship between the spending multiplier and the tax multiplier (Tm) is as follows:

$$\text{Tm} = \text{MPC} \times (\text{Spending multiplier}) = .90 \times (1/.10) = 9 \text{ in our example}$$

Be prepared to respond to a free-response question that asks you to explain why the tax multiplier is smaller than the spending multiplier.

> **Example:**
> The MPC = .80 and the government decides to impose a $50 increase in taxes. What happens to GDP?
>
> $$\text{Tm} = .80 \times \text{Multiplier} = .80 \times (1/.20) = 4$$
>
> Because the tax multiplier is equal to 4, we determine that GDP falls by $200. How do we know? Because taxes were *increased*, disposable income falls, consumption falls, causing GDP to fall, in this case by a factor of 4.

The tax multiplier is found by:

- Tm = (Δ GDP)/(Δ taxes)
- Tm = MPC × M = MPC/MPS

Balanced-Budget Multiplier

The government both collects and spends tax revenue. In a simplified model, if the dollars spent equal the dollars collected, the budget is balanced. We have already discussed how the spending multiplier and tax multiplier are different. A quick example of a balanced budget policy illustrates what is called the **balanced-budget multiplier.**

Example:
The government wants to spend $100 on a federal program and pay for it by collecting $100 in additional taxes. The MPC = .90 in this example.

Spending Effect
The spending multiplier = 10 implies that the $100 of new spending (G) creates a $1,000 *increase* in real GDP.

Taxation Effect
The tax multiplier Tm = 9 implies that a $100 increase in taxes *decreases* real GDP by $900.

Balanced Budget Effect

$$\text{Change in real GDP} = +\$1{,}000 - \$900 = +\$100$$

So a $100 increase in spending, financed by a $100 increase in taxes, created only $100 in new GDP. *The balanced-budget multiplier is always equal to 1, regardless of the MPC.*

- Balanced-budget multiplier = 1

> Review Questions

1. When disposable income increases by $X,

   (A) consumption increases by more than $X.
   (B) saving increases by less than $X.
   (C) saving increases by exactly $X.
   (D) saving remains constant.
   (E) saving decreases by more than $X.

2. Which of the following is true about the consumption function?

   (A) The slope is equal to the MPC.
   (B) The slope is equal to the MPS.
   (C) The slope is equal to MPC + MPS.
   (D) It shifts upward when consumers are more pessimistic about the future.
   (E) It shifts downward when consumer wealth increases in value.

3. Which of the following events most likely increases real GDP?

   (A) An increase in the real rate of interest
   (B) An increase in taxes
   (C) A decrease in net exports
   (D) An increase in government spending
   (E) A lower value of consumer wealth

4. Which of the following choices is most likely to create the greatest decrease in real GDP?

   (A) The government decreases spending, matched with a decrease in taxes.
   (B) The government increases spending with no increase in taxes.
   (C) The government decreases spending with no change in taxes.
   (D) The government holds spending constant while increasing taxes.
   (E) The government increases spending, matched with an increase in taxes.

5. The tax multiplier increases in magnitude when

   (A) the MPS increases.
   (B) the spending multiplier falls.
   (C) the MPC increases.
   (D) government spending increases.
   (E) taxes increase.

6. Which of the following is the source of the supply of loanable funds?

   (A) The stock market
   (B) Investors
   (C) Net exports
   (D) Banks and mutual funds
   (E) Savers

› Answers and Explanations

1. **B**—A $1 increase in DI increases consumption by a factor of the MPC and increases saving by a factor of the MPS. Because both MPC and MPS represent the fraction of new income that is consumed and saved, consumption and saving increase by less than the increase in DI.

2. **A**—The slope of the consumption function is the MPC. The slope of the saving function is the MPS.

3. **D**—An increase in GDP is the result of an increase in C, I, G, or (X – M). All other choices represent less spending in some economic sector.

4. **C**—Look for choices that decrease GDP by the largest magnitude. Choices B and E actually improve the economy (and GDP), so they are eliminated. A decrease in spending lowers GDP by a magnitude equal to the spending multiplier, which is larger than the tax multiplier, which in turn is larger than the balanced budget multiplier. This question is a prelude to fiscal policy.

5. **C**—Knowing the relationship between the tax and spending multipliers allows you to make the right choice. Tm = MPC × Multiplier = MPC/MPS.

6. **E**—Banks help facilitate lending to investors, but the real supply of those loanable funds are the savers who choose to place some of their disposable income dollars in those banks as saving.

› Rapid Review

Disposable income (DI): The income a consumer has left over to spend or save once he or she has paid out net taxes. DI = $Y - T$.

Consumption and saving schedules: Tables that show the direct relationships between disposable income and consumption and saving. As DI increases for a typical household, C and S both increase.

Consumption function: A linear relationship showing how increases in disposable income cause increases in consumption.

Autonomous consumption: The amount of consumption that occurs no matter the level of disposable income. In a linear consumption function, this shows up as a constant and graphically it appears as the *y* intercept.

Saving function: A linear relationship showing how increases in disposable income cause increases in saving.

Dissaving: Another way of saying that saving is less than zero. This can occur at low levels of disposable income when the consumer must liquidate assets or borrow to maintain consumption.

Autonomous saving: The amount of saving that occurs no matter the level of disposable income. In a linear saving function, this shows up as a constant and graphically it appears as the *y* intercept.

Marginal Propensity to Consume (MPC): The change in consumption caused by a change in disposable income, or the slope of the consumption function: MPC = $\Delta C/\Delta$DI.

Marginal propensity to save (MPS): The change in saving caused by a change in disposable income, or the slope of the saving function: MPS = $\Delta S/\Delta$DI.

Determinants of consumption and saving: Factors that shift the consumption and saving functions in the opposite direction are wealth, expectations, and household debt. The factors that change consumption and saving functions in the same direction are taxes and transfers.

Expected real rate of return (r): The rate of real profit the firm anticipates receiving on investment expenditures. This is the marginal benefit of an investment project.

Real rate of interest (i): The cost of borrowing to fund an investment. This can be thought of as the marginal cost of an investment project.

Decision to invest: A firm invests in projects as long as $r \geq i$.

Investment demand: The inverse relationship between the real interest rate and the cumulative dollars invested. Like any demand curve, this is drawn with a negative slope.

Autonomous investment: The level of investment determined by investment demand. It is autonomous because it is assumed to be constant at all levels of GDP.

Market for loanable funds: The market for dollars that are available to be borrowed for investment projects. Equilibrium in this market is determined at the real interest rate where the dollars saved (supply) is equal to the dollars borrowed (demand).

Demand for loanable funds: The negative relationship between the real interest rate and the dollars invested and borrowed by firms and by the government.

Private saving: Saving conducted by households and equal to the difference between disposable income and consumption.

Supply of loanable funds: The positive relationship between the dollars saved and the real interest rate.

Multiplier effect: Describes how a change in any component of aggregate expenditures creates a larger change in GDP.

Spending multiplier: The magnitude of the spending multiplier effect is calculated as = (ΔGDP)/(Δ spending) = 1/MPS = 1/(1 − MPC).

Tax multiplier: The magnitude of the effect that a change in taxes has on real GDP. Tm = (ΔGDP)/(Δ taxes) = MPC × Multiplier = MPC/MPS.

Balanced-budget multiplier: When a change in government spending is offset by a change in lump-sum taxes, real GDP changes by the amount of the change in *G*; the balanced-budget multiplier is thus equal to 1.

Aggregate Demand and Aggregate Supply

"This is the bulk of the Macro exam—very important!"
—AP Teacher

IN THIS CHAPTER

Summary: Chapter 7 addressed three widely used measures of macroeconomic performance: real GDP, inflation, and unemployment. Economists have built upon the models of supply and demand for microeconomic markets to model an aggregate picture of the macroeconomy. The models of Aggregate Demand (AD) and Aggregate Supply (AS) have been extremely useful to predict how real GDP, employment, and the average price level are affected by external factors and government policy. Before discussing macroeconomic policy, we first need to describe the AD/AS model.

Key Ideas
- Aggregate Demand (AD)
- Aggregate Supply (AS)
- Short-Run and Long-Run AS
- Macroeconomic Equilibrium
- The Inflation and Unemployment Trade-Off

9.1 Aggregate Demand (AD)

Main Topics: *What Is Aggregate Demand?, Components of AD, The Shape of AD, Changes in AD*

When we discussed microeconomic markets, we described the shape of any microeconomic demand curve with the Law of Demand, income, and substitution effects. Both effects work to change quantity demanded in the opposite direction of any price change.

What tends to be the case for the demand of a microeconomic good is also the case for AD, but for different theoretical reasons.

What Is Aggregate Demand?

A microeconomic demand curve for peaches illustrates the relationship between the quantity of peaches demanded and the price of peaches. When economists aggregate all microeconomic markets to build AD, we include peaches and all other items that are domestically produced. **Aggregate demand** is the relationship between all spending on domestic output and the average price level of that output.

Components of AD

Demand in the macroeconomy comes from four general sources, and we have already seen these components when we described how total production is measured in the economy. In the previous chapter we defined real GDP as $= C + I + G + (X - M)$.

So AD measures, for any price level, the sum of consumption spending by households, investment spending by firms, government purchases of goods and services, and the net exports bought by foreign consumers.

The Shape of AD

When the price of peaches rises, consumers find another microeconomic good (with a lower relative price) to substitute for peaches, and this helps explain why the demand for peaches is downward sloping. But if the overall price level is rising, the price of peaches, pears, and apples might all be rising. Remember that this average price level is not the same as the price of one good relative to another. Where are the substitutes when the "good" we are discussing is a unit of real GDP? Macroeconomists describe three general groups of substitutes for national output:

- Goods and services produced in other nations (foreign sector substitution effect)
- Goods and services in the future (interest rate effect)
- Money and financial assets (wealth effect)

Foreign Sector Substitution Effect. When the average price of United States output (as measured by the CPI or some other price index) increases, consumers naturally begin to look for similar items produced elsewhere. A Japanese computer, a German car, and a Mexican textile all begin to look more attractive when inflation heats up in the United States. The resulting increase in imports pushes real GDP down at a higher price level.

Interest Rate Effect. Remember that consumers have two general choices with their disposable income: they can consume it or they can save it for future consumption. If the average price level rises, consumers might need to borrow more money for big-ticket items like autos or college tuition. When more and more households seek loans, the real interest rate begins to rise, and this increases the cost of borrowing. Firms postpone their investment in plant and equipment, and households postpone their consumption of more expensive items for a future when their spending might go further and borrowing might be more affordable. This wait-and-see mentality reduces current consumption of domestic production as the price level rises and real GDP falls.

Wealth Effect. Wealth is the value of accumulated assets like stocks, bonds, savings, and especially cash on hand. As the average price level rises, the purchasing power of wealth and savings begins to fall. Higher prices therefore tend to reduce the quantity of domestic output purchased.

The combination of the foreign sector substitution, interest rate, and wealth effects predict a downward-sloping AD curve. For all three reasons, as the overall price level rises, consumption of domestic output (real GDP) falls along the AD curve. This is seen as a movement from points *a* to *b* in Figure 9.1.

Figure 9.1

- Aggregate demand is not the vertical or horizontal summation of the demand curves for all microeconomic goods and services.
- AD is a model of how domestic purchasing changes when the aggregate price level changes.

Changes in AD

Since AD is the sum of the four components of domestic spending [$C, I, G, (X - M)$], if any of these components increases, holding the price level constant, AD increases, which increases real GDP. This is seen as a shift to the right of AD. If any of these components decreases, holding the price level constant, AD decreases, which decreases real GDP. This is seen as a shift to the left of AD. Figure 9.2 illustrates these shifts in AD.

Figure 9.2

This is a preview for policy to manipulate the macroeconomy. If you want to stimulate real GDP and lower unemployment, you need to boost any or all of the components of AD. If you feel AD must slow down, you need to rein in the components of AD. Policies are tackled in more depth in the next chapter, but for now we'll take a quick look at some variables that can increase $C, I, G,$ or $(X - M)$.

Consumer Spending (C). If you put more money in the pockets of households, expect them to consume a great deal of it and save the rest. Consumers also increase their consumption if they are more optimistic about the future.

Investment Spending (I). Firms increase investment if they believe the investment will be profitable. This expected return on the investment is increased if investors are optimistic about the future profitability, or if the necessary borrowing can be done at a low rate of interest.

Government Spending (G). The government injects money into the economy by spending more on goods and services, by reducing taxes, or by increasing transfer payments.

1. *Government spending* on goods and services acts as a direct increase in AD.
2. *Taxes and transfers*. Lowering taxes and increasing transfer payments increase AD through C by increasing DI.

Net Exports (X – M). When we sell more goods to foreign consumers and buy fewer goods from foreign producers, this component of AD increases.

1. *Foreign incomes.* Exports (X) increase with a strong Canadian, Mexican, or Brazilian economy. When foreign consumers have more disposable income, this increases the AD in the United States because those consumers spend some of that income on U.S.-made goods.
2. *Consumer tastes.* Consumer tastes and preferences, both foreign and domestic, are constantly changing. If American blue jeans become more popular in France, American AD increases. If French wines become more preferred by American consumers, AD in France increases.
3. *Exchange rates.* Imports (M) decrease when the exchange rate between the U.S. dollar and foreign currency falls. The model of foreign currency exchange is covered in a later chapter, but the idea is that foreign goods become relatively more expensive and so domestic consumers buy fewer foreign-produced items.

9.2 Aggregate Supply (AS)

Main Topics: *What Is Aggregate Supply?, Short-Run and Long-Run Shape of AS, Changes in AS*

Again, there are parallels between our coverage of supply in micro markets and aggregate supply. The law of supply describes the positive relationship between the micro price of a product and the quantity of that product that firms supply, and is explained in part by increasing marginal cost as output rises. What tends to be the case for the supply of a micro good is also the case for AS, but for different theoretical reasons.

What Is Aggregate Supply?

A microeconomic supply curve for salt illustrates the relationship between the price of salt and the quantity of salt supplied. When economists aggregate all microeconomic markets to build AS, we include salt and all other items that are domestically supplied. **Aggregate supply** is the relationship between the average price level of all domestic output and the level of domestic output produced.

Short-Run and Long-Run Shape of AS

The model of AS and the resulting shape of the AS curve depend upon whether the economy has fully adjusted to market forces and price changes.

Macroeconomic Short Run

In the **macroeconomic short run** period of time, the prices of goods and services are changing in their respective markets, but input prices have not yet adjusted to those product market changes. This lag between the increase in the output price and the increase in input prices gives us a shape of the short-run AS curve that is described in three stages. Figure 9.3 illustrates the stages of short-run AS.

Figure 9.3

If the economy is in a recession with low production (GDP_u), there are many unemployed resources. Increasing output from this low level puts little pressure on input costs and subsequent minimal increase in the overall price level. The first stage of AS is drawn as almost horizontal. The Keynesian school of economics believes that when aggregate spending is extremely weak, the economy can be modeled in this way.

As real GDP increases in the second stage of AS and approaches full employment (GDP_f), available resources become more difficult to find, and so input costs begin to rise. If the price level for output rises at a faster rate than the rising costs, producers have a profit incentive to increase output. Most of the time the economy is operating in this upward-sloping range of AS, and so you see short-run AS commonly drawn with a positive slope.

If the economy grows and approaches the nation's productive capacity (GDP_c), firms cannot find unemployed inputs. Input costs and the price level rise much more sharply, and so in this third stage of AS, the curve is almost vertical.

Macroeconomic Long Run

The period of time known as the **macroeconomic long run** is long enough for input prices to have fully adjusted to market forces. Now all product and input markets are in equilibrium, and the economy is at full employment. In this long-run equilibrium, the AS curve is vertical at GDP_f. The Classical school of economics asserts that the economy always gravitates toward full employment; so a cornerstone of classical macroeconomics is a vertical AS curve. Figure 9.4 illustrates the long-run AS curve.

- When drawing the AD/AS graph for a free-response question, it is *not* acceptable to label the vertical axis "P" or "$" and the horizontal axis "Q." You want to be *very* careful to use terms like "Aggregate price level" or "PL" on the vertical axis and "Real output" or "Real GDP" on the horizontal axis to earn these graphing points.

Figure 9.4

Changes in AS

In the short run, AS may fluctuate without changing the level of full employment. There are some factors, however, that can cause a fundamental shift in the long-run AS curve because they can change the level of output at full employment.

Short-Run Shifts

The most common factor that affects short-run AS is an economy-wide change in input (or factor) prices. Taxes, government policy, and short-term political or natural events can change the short-term ability of a nation to supply goods and services.

- *Input prices.* If input prices fall, the short-run AS curve increases (shifting to the right) without changing the level of full employment.
- *Tax policy.* Some taxes are aimed at producers rather than consumers. If these "supply-side taxes" are lowered, short-run AS shifts to the right.
- *Deregulation.* In some cases, the regulation of industries can restrict their ability to produce (for good reasons in many cases). If these regulations are lessened, the short-run AS likely increases.
- *Political or environmental phenomena.* For a nation as large as the United States, wars and natural disasters can decrease the short-run AS without permanently decreasing the level of full employment. For a smaller nation or a large nation hit by an epic disaster, this could be a permanent decrease in the ability to produce.

Long-Run Shifts

There are a few main factors that affect both long-run and short-run AS and fundamentally affect the level of full employment in a nation's macroeconomy:

- *Availability of resources.* A larger labor force, larger stock of capital, or more widely available natural resources can increase the level of full employment.
- *Technology and productivity.* Better technology raises the productivity of both capital and labor. A more highly trained or educated populace increases the productivity of the labor force. These factors increase long-run AS over time.
- *Policy incentives.* Different national policies like unemployment insurance provide incentives for a nation's labor force to work. If policy provides large incentives to quickly find a job, full-employment real GDP rises. If government gives tax incentives to invest in capital or technology, GDP_f rises.

Example:

In the 1990s, the U.S. economy saw dramatic increases in technology and investment in the capital stock. This period produced a significant increase in the real GDP at full employment, as shown in Figure 9.5.

Figure 9.5

- When the LRAS curve shifts to the right, this indicates economic growth, just as an outward shift in the production possibility curve does.

9.3 Macroeconomic Equilibrium

Main Topics: *Equilibrium Real GDP and Price Level, Recessionary and Inflationary Gaps, Shifting AD, The Multiplier Again, Shifting SRAS, Classical Adjustment from Short-Run to Long-Run Equilibrium*

We use supply and demand models to predict changes in the prices and quantities of microeconomic goods and services. Now that we have built a model of aggregate demand and aggregate supply, we use similar analysis to predict changes in real GDP and the average price level.

Equilibrium Real GDP and Price Level

When the quantity of real output demanded is equal to the quantity of real output supplied, the macroeconomy is said to be in equilibrium. Figure 9.6 illustrates **macroeconomic**

Figure 9.6

equilibrium at full employment Q_f and price level PL_f at the intersection of AD, SRAS, and LRAS.

Recessionary and Inflationary Gaps

When the economy is in equilibrium, but not at the level of GDP that corresponds to full employment (GDP_f), the economy is experiencing either a recessionary or an inflationary gap. As the name implies, a **recessionary gap** exists when the economy is operating below Q_f and the economy is likely experiencing a high unemployment rate. In Figure 9.7, the recessionary gap is the difference between GDP_f and GDP_r, or the amount that GDP must rise to reach GDP_f.

Figure 9.7

"Be able to locate these on a graph."
—AP teacher

An **inflationary gap** exists when the economy is operating above GDP_f. Because production is higher than GDP_f, a rising price level is the greatest danger to the economy. In Figure 9.8, the inflationary gap is the difference between GDP_i and GDP_f, or the amount that GDP must fall to reach GDP_f.

Figure 9.8

Shifting AD

Since you have mastered the microeconomic tools of supply and demand, you should have little trouble predicting how macroeconomic factors affect real GDP and the price level.

Shifts in AD

The economy is currently in equilibrium but at a very low recessionary level of real GDP. If AD increases from AD_0 to AD_1 in the nearly horizontal range of SRAS, the price level may only slightly increase, while real GDP significantly increases and the unemployment rate falls.

If AD continues to increase to AD_2 in the upward-sloping range of SRAS, the price level begins to rise and inflation is felt in the economy. This **demand-pull inflation** is the result of rising consumption from all sectors of AD.

If AD increases much beyond full employment to AD_3, inflation is quite significant and real GDP experiences minimal increases. Figures 9.9, 9.10, and 9.11 illustrate how rising AD has different effects on the price level and real GDP in the three stages of short-run AS.

Figure 9.9

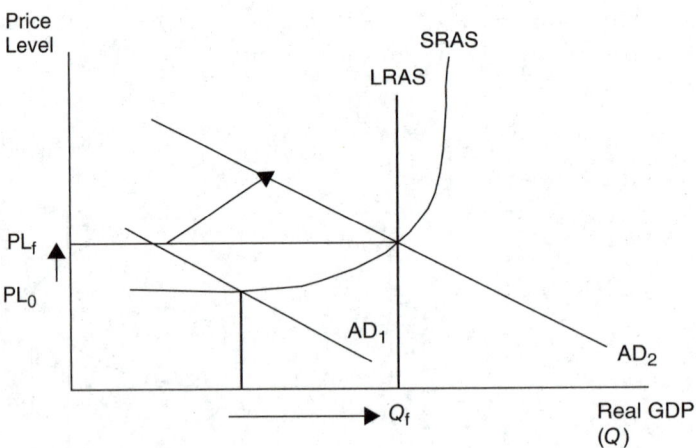

Figure 9.10

If aggregate demand weakens, we can expect the opposite effects on price level and real GDP. In fact, one of the most common causes of a recession is falling AD as it lowers real GDP and increases the unemployment rate. Inflation is not typically a problem with this kind of recession, as we expect the price level to fall, or **deflation**, with a severe decrease in AD. This is seen in Figure 9.12.

Figure 9.11

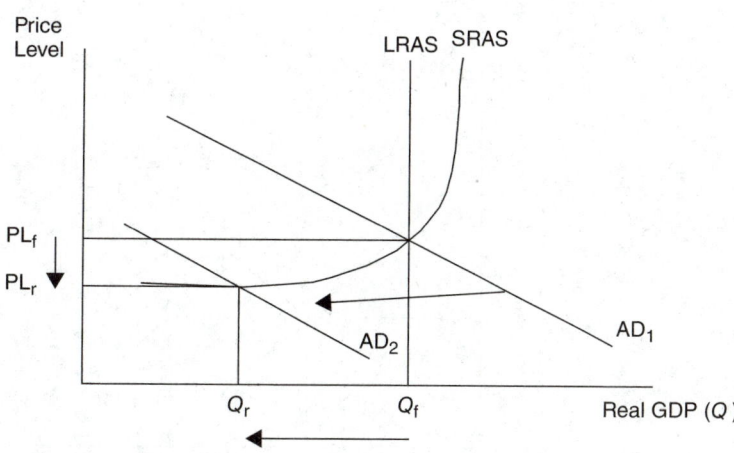

Figure 9.12

The Multiplier Again

One of the important topics of the previous chapter is the spending multiplier. When a component of autonomous spending increases by $1, real GDP increases by a magnitude of the multiplier. The full multiplier effect is only observed if the price level does not increase, and this only occurs if the economy is operating on the horizontal range of the SRAS curve. Figure 9.13 shows the full multiplier effect. (Note that the SRAS curve is likely a much smoother curve, but the multiplier effect can be illustrated more clearly with more linear segments.)

But what if the economy is operating in the upward-sloping range of SRAS? Figure 9.14 shows an identical rightward shift in AD. If there were no increase in the price level, the new equilibrium GDP would be at GDP_1, but with a rising price level, it is somewhat smaller at GDP_2. This means that the full multiplier effect is not felt because the rising price level weakens the impact of increased spending in the macroeconomy.

- The multiplier effect of an increase in AD is greater if there is no increase in the price level.
- The multiplier effect of an increase in AD is smaller if there is a larger increase in the price level.

Figure 9.13

Figure 9.14

Shifting SRAS

The macroeconomy is currently in equilibrium at full employment. In Figure 9.15, we simplify the short-run aggregate supply curve by drawing only the upward-sloping segment (and this is the usual treatment of SRAS in the AP curriculum). If nominal input prices were to fall, the SRAS curve shifts to the right. Assuming that the AD curve stays constant, the price level falls, real GDP increases, and the unemployment rate falls. This kind of **supply-side boom** would seemingly be the best of all situations, though it is likely to only be temporary. When the economy is producing beyond Q_f, eventually the high demand for production inputs will increase the prices of those inputs, shifting the SRAS curve back to the left and returning the economy to full employment.

If an increase in SRAS is the best of possible macroeconomic situations, a decrease in SRAS is one of the worst. Figure 9.16 shows that a decrease, or leftward shift, in SRAS creates inflation, lowers real GDP, and increases the unemployment rate. This **cost-push inflation**, or **stagflation**, creates very unpleasant economic conditions in the short run.

Figure 9.15

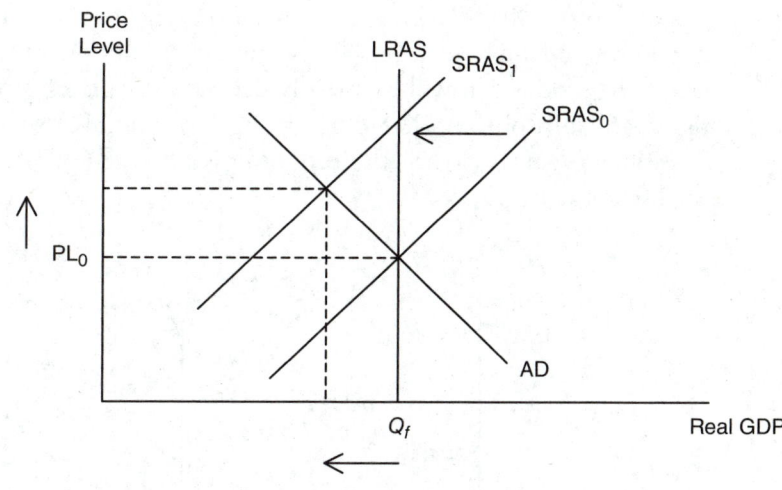

Figure 9.16

In the long run, however, the high unemployment should eventually relieve pressure on nominal input prices. When the input prices begin to fall, the SRAS shifts back to the right, returning the economy to full employment.

Supply Shocks

These shifts in SRAS are caused by events that are called **supply shocks**. A supply shock is an economy-wide phenomenon that affects the costs of firms, positively or negatively. Positive supply shocks might be the result of higher productivity or lower energy prices. Negative supply shocks usually occur when economy-wide input prices suddenly increase, like the OPEC oil embargoes of the 1970s or the Gulf War of 1990 to 1991.

> "Make it easier for the graders and use flow charts to answer free-response questions instead of long essays."
> —Justine, AP Student

- ↑ AD causes ↑ real GDP, ↓ unemployment and ↑ price level.
- ↓ AD causes ↓ real GDP, ↑ unemployment and ↓ price level.
- ↑ SRAS causes ↑ real GDP, ↓ unemployment and ↓ price level.
- ↓ SRAS causes ↓ real GDP, ↑ unemployment and ↑ price level.

Classical Adjustment from Short-Run to Long-Run Equilibrium

One of the toughest concepts for students to master is the way in which the AD/AS model presents both a short-run and a long-run equilibrium. Although some economists disagree, the prevailing treatment in the AP curriculum is that a recessionary or inflationary gap (a short-run equilibrium) will "self-correct" to a long-run equilibrium once enough time has passed for all prices to adjust. Let's see how this can happen.

Adjustment to a Recessionary Gap

Suppose the economy is currently operating at full employment, as shown in Figure 9.17 at the intersection of the AD, SRAS, and LRAS curves with a real GDP of Q_f. Now suppose that consumers and firms begin to lose confidence in the labor market and overall economy, causing AD to shift to the left. In the short run, this will cause a recessionary gap as real GDP falls to Q_r (unemployment rises), and the aggregate price level falls from PL_1 to PL_2. Ignoring any kind of fiscal or monetary policy intervention (which we will discuss in the next two chapters), this short-run recessionary gap can self-correct. How does this happen?

One of the hallmarks of a recession is a decreased demand for many factors of production, like labor, steel, oil, and other commodities. This decreased demand for critical factors of production will eventually decrease the prices of those factors, causing a gradual rightward shift of the SRAS curve to $SRAS_2$. The SRAS curve shifts to the right until the recessionary gap is closed, the economy is back at Q_f, and an even lower aggregate price level exists at PL_3.

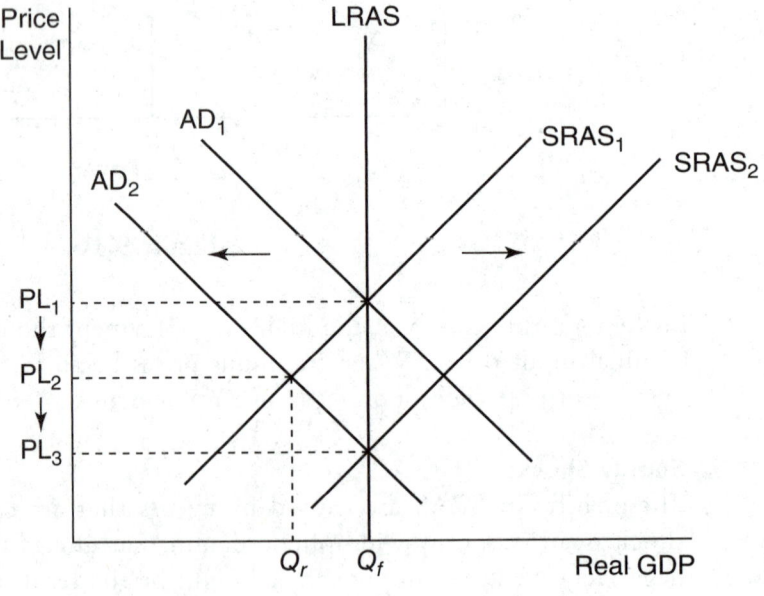

Figure 9.17

Adjustment to an Inflationary Gap

Let's begin again with long-run equilibrium at a real GDP of Q_f. When we incorporate an increase in the AD curve, we create an inflationary gap. Figure 9.18 shows that this increase to AD_2 causes an increase in real GDP to Q_i (a lower unemployment rate) and an increase in the aggregate price level to PL_2. How would this self-correct?

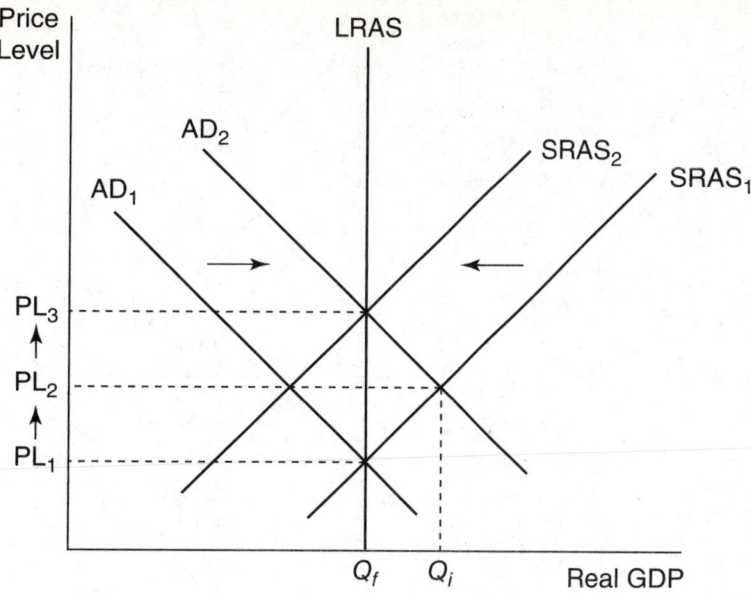

Figure 9.18

When the economy is really booming, there is stronger demand for labor and all of those other factors of production, and this causes factor prices to rise. As the factor prices rise, the SRAS curve begins to shift to the left to $SRAS_2$. Eventually, the inflationary gap is eliminated, and the economy is back in long-run equilibrium at Q_f, though at an even higher aggregate price level of PL_3.

- Using the AD/AS model to show the long-run adjustment to equilibrium after a short-run shift in AD is a very common FRQ on the AP Macroeconomics exam.

9.4 The Trade-Off Between Inflation and Unemployment

Main Topics: *Short-Run Changes in AD, The Phillips Curve, The Long-Run Phillips Curve, Expectations*

Changes in AD and AS create changes in our main macroeconomic indicators of inflation and unemployment. Many economists have studied the relationship between inflation and unemployment, and this section provides a very brief overview of one prominent theory, the Phillips curve. We also take another look at the effects of supply shocks and expectations.

Short-Run Changes in AD

In the upward-sloping range of the SRAS curve, there is a positive relationship between the price level and output. If AD is rising, the price level and real GDP are both rising. Since rising real GDP creates jobs and lowers unemployment, we connect these points of equilibrium and show an inverse relationship between inflation and the unemployment rate. See Figure 9.19.

Figure 9.19

The Phillips Curve

The inverse relationship between inflation and the unemployment rate has come to be known as the Phillips curve and in the short-run is downward sloping. The short-run Phillips curve is drawn in Figure 9.20. Though Figure 9.20 does not show it, the possibility of deflation at extremely high unemployment rates means that the Phillips curve may actually continue falling below the *x* axis.

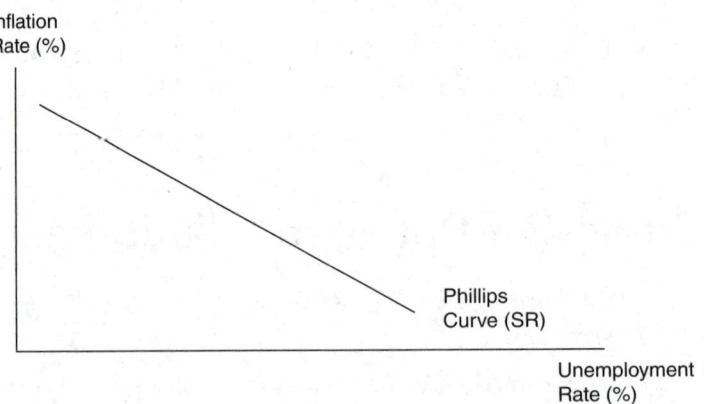

Figure 9.20

Supply Shocks and the Phillips Curve

We saw that when SRAS shifts to the right, holding AD constant, both the price level and unemployment rate fall. On the other hand, when SRAS shifts to the left, we get stagflation because inflation and unemployment rates are both rising. Figure 9.21 shows how supply shocks shift the Phillips curve inward when SRAS shifts to the right, and outward when SRAS shifts to the left.

Figure 9.21

The Long-Run Phillips Curve

The AD and AS model presumes that the long-run AS curve is vertical and located at full employment. As a result, the Phillips curve in the long run is also vertical at the natural rate of employment. You might recall that the natural rate of employment is the unemployment rate where cyclical unemployment is zero. Suppose this occurs at a measured unemployment rate of 4 percent. Figure 9.22 illustrates the long-run Phillips curve.

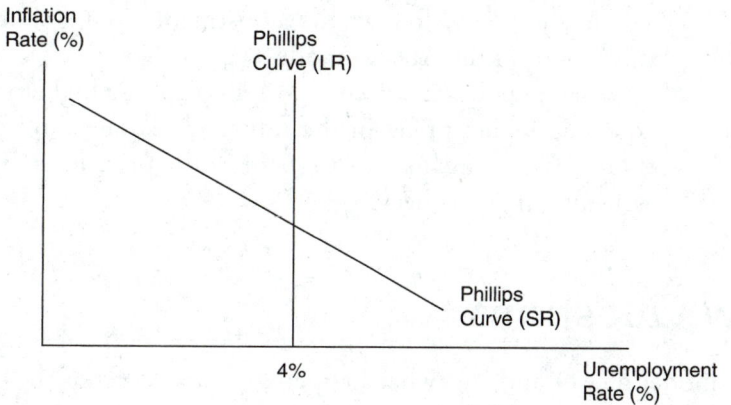

Figure 9.22

Expectations

The idea that there is, in the short term, an inverse relationship between inflation and unemployment, and in the long term, unemployment is always at the natural rate can be confusing. The reason is that sometimes a gap exists between the actual rate of inflation and the expected rate of inflation. Inflationary expectations play a role here in the derivation of the long-run Phillips curve. Figure 9.23 illustrates this concept with an example.

The expected inflation rate is 2 percent at a 4 percent natural rate of unemployment (point *a*). If AD unexpectedly rises, this drives up the rate of inflation to 5 percent, and as a result, firms are earning higher profits. Firms respond with more hiring, and this temporarily drops the unemployment rate to 2 percent (point *b*). This is seen as a movement along the short-run PC above from *a* to *b*.

Figure 9.23

The point at 5 percent inflation and 2 percent unemployment will not last. Workers realize that their real wages are falling and insist on a raise! As wages rise, the profits of firms begin to fall, and so too does employment back to the natural rate of 4 percent (point *c*). At this point both actual and expected inflation is 5 percent. Another short-run Phillips curve runs through this point. Points *a* and *c* must lie on one long-run Phillips curve, and that curve must be vertical. The process can repeat itself if AD continues to increase, or it can reverse itself if AD falls. You might notice that this adjustment from a point on the SRPC back to the LRPC follows the adjustment from a short-run equilibrium to the long-run equilibrium in the AD/AS model.

What happens if citizens and firms expect a higher rate of inflation than the actual rate? Expecting higher prices in the future, consumers and firms increase purchasing now and AD increases, which serves to increase the price level. The expectation in this case is really a self-fulfilling prophecy.

> Review Questions

1. Using the model of AD and AS, what happens in the short run to real GDP, the price level, and unemployment with more consumption spending (*C*)?

	REAL GDP	PRICE LEVEL	UNEMPLOYMENT
(A)	Increases	Decreases	Decreases
(B)	Decreases	Increases	Increases
(C)	Increases	Increases	Decreases
(D)	Decreases	Decreases	Decreases
(E)	Decreases	Decreases	Increases

2. Which is the best way to describe the AS curve in the long run?
   (A) Always vertical in the long run.
   (B) Always upward sloping because it follows the Law of Supply.
   (C) Always horizontal.
   (D) Always downward sloping.
   (E) Without more information we cannot predict how it looks in the long run.

3. Stagflation most likely results from
   (A) increasing AD with constant SRAS.
   (B) decreasing SRAS with constant AD.
   (C) decreasing AD with constant SRAS.
   (D) a decrease in both AD and SRAS.
   (E) an increase in both AD and SRAS.

4. Equilibrium real GDP is far below full employment, and the government lowers household taxes. Which is the likely result?
   (A) Unemployment falls with little inflation.
   (B) Unemployment rises with little inflation.
   (C) Unemployment falls with rampant inflation.
   (D) Unemployment rises with rampant inflation.
   (E) No change occurs in unemployment or inflation.

5. What is the main contrast between the short-run and long-run Phillips curve?
   (A) In the short run there is a positive relationship between inflation and unemployment, and in the long run the relationship is negative.
   (B) In the short run there is a positive relationship between inflation and unemployment, and in the long run the relationship is constant.
   (C) In the short run there is a negative relationship between inflation and unemployment, and in the long run the relationship is positive.
   (D) In the short run there is a negative relationship between inflation and unemployment, and in the long run the relationship is constant.
   (E) In the short run there is a constant relationship between inflation and unemployment, and in the long run the relationship is negative.

6. The effect of the spending multiplier is lessened if
   (A) the price level is constant with an increase in aggregate demand.
   (B) the price level falls with an increase in aggregate supply.
   (C) the price level is constant with an increase in long-run aggregate supply.
   (D) the price level falls with an increase in both aggregate demand and aggregate supply.
   (E) the price level rises with an increase in aggregate demand.

》 Answers and Explanations

1. **C**—An increase in consumption spending increases the AD curve, or shifts it to the right. Along the SRAS curve, we see increasing real GDP, a rising aggregate price level, and a lower unemployment rate.

2. **A**—All resources are employed at full employment in the long run, so firms cannot respond to an increase in the price level by increasing production. Thus, any increase in prices cannot increase production in the long run, and so AS is assumed to be vertical. Any short-run discrepancy in GDP, above or below, full employment adjusts back to GDP_f in the long run.

3. **B**—Stagflation is an increase in the price level and an increase in unemployment. This is most often the result of falling SRAS and a constant AD. Choice D is incorrect because a simultaneous decrease in AD puts downward pressure on the price level, which offsets the upward pressure from falling SRAS.

4. **A**—A deep recession describes macroeconomic equilibrium in the horizontal section of SRAS. Here, rising AD increases real GDP, and lowers unemployment, with little inflation.

5. **D**—The short-run Phillips curve is downward sloping but the long-run Phillips curve is vertical.

6. **E**—The full spending multiplier effect of an increase in AD is felt only if there is no rise in the price.

Rapid Review

Aggregate demand (AD): The inverse relationship between all spending on domestic output and the average price level of that output. AD measures the sum of consumption spending by households, investment spending by firms, government purchases of goods and services, and net exports (exports minus imports).

Foreign sector substitution effect: When the average price of U.S. output increases, consumers naturally begin to look for similar items produced elsewhere.

Interest rate effect: If the average price level rises, consumers and firms might need to borrow more money for spending and capital investment, which increases the interest rate and delays current consumption. This postponement reduces current consumption of domestic production as the price level rises.

Wealth effect: As the average price level rises, the purchasing power of wealth and savings begins to fall. Higher prices therefore tend to reduce the quantity of domestic output purchased.

Determinants of AD: AD is a function of the four components of domestic spending: C, I, G, and $(X - M)$. If any of these components increases (decreases), holding the others constant, AD increases (decreases), or shifts to the right (left).

Short-run aggregate supply (SRAS): The positive relationship between the level of domestic output produced and the average price level of that output.

Macroeconomic short run: A period of time during which the prices of goods and services are changing in their respective markets, but the input prices have not yet adjusted to those changes in the product markets. In the short run, the SRAS curve is typically drawn as upward sloping.

Macroeconomic long run: A period of time long enough for input prices to have fully adjusted to market forces. In this period, all product and input markets are in a state of equilibrium and the economy is operating at full employment (GDP_f). Once all markets in the economy have adjusted and there exists this long-run equilibrium, the LRAS curve is vertical at GDP_f.

Determinants of AS: AS is a function of many factors that impact the production capacity of the nation. If these factors make it easier, or less costly, for a nation to produce, AS shifts to the right. If these factors make it more difficult, or more costly, for a nation to produce, AS shifts to the left.

Macroeconomic equilibrium: Occurs when the quantity of real output demanded is equal to the quantity of real output supplied. Graphically this is at the intersection of AD and SRAS. Equilibrium can exist at, above, or below full employment.

Recessionary gap: The amount by which full-employment GDP exceeds equilibrium GDP.

Inflationary gap: The amount by which equilibrium GDP exceeds full-employment GDP.

Demand-pull inflation: This inflation is the result of stronger consumption from all sectors of AD as it continues to increase in the upward-sloping range of SRAS. The price level begins to rise, and inflation is felt in the economy.

Deflation: A sustained falling price level, usually due to severely weakened aggregate demand and a constant SRAS.

Recession: In the AD and AS model, a recession is typically described as falling AD with a constant SRAS curve. Real GDP falls far below full employment levels and the unemployment rate rises.

Supply-side boom: When the SRAS curve shifts outward and the AD curve stays constant, the price level falls, real GDP increases and the unemployment rate falls.

Stagflation: A situation in the macroeconomy when inflation and the unemployment rate are both increasing. This is most likely the cause of falling SRAS while AD stays constant.

Supply shocks: A supply shock is an economy-wide phenomenon that affects the costs of firms and the position of the SRAS curve, either positively or negatively.

Phillips curve: A graphical device that shows the relationship between inflation and the unemployment rate. In the short run it is downward sloping, and in the long run it is vertical at the natural rate of unemployment.

Fiscal Policy, Economic Growth, and Productivity

IN THIS CHAPTER

Summary: The model of AD and AS is a useful mechanism for looking at how the macroeconomy can be deliberately expanded, or contracted, by the government. **Fiscal policy** measures include government spending and tax collection to affect economic output, unemployment, and the price level. We use graphical analysis to show how fiscal policy attempts to move the economy to full employment and also discuss some of the ways in which fiscal policy is less effective than predicted by theory. This chapter concludes with a discussion of economic growth and productivity, and how policy might affect growth.

Key Ideas
- Fiscal Policy
- Budget Deficits and Crowding Out
- Economic Growth
- Productivity and Supply-Side Policy

10.1 Expansionary and Contractionary Fiscal Policy

Main Topics: *Expansionary Fiscal Policy, Contractionary Fiscal Policy, Deficits and Surpluses, Automatic Stabilizers*

This section of the chapter uses AD and AS to illustrate how fiscal policy can work in theory. Fiscal policy stresses the importance of a hands-on role for government in manipulating AD to "fix" the economy. Difficulties in fiscal policy and the supply-side perspective are addressed in the following section.

Expansionary Fiscal Policy

When the economy is suffering a recession, real GDP is low and unemployment is high. In the AD and AS model, a recessionary equilibrium is located below full employment, as shown in Figure 10.1. If the government increases its spending or lowers net taxes, the AD curve increases. Net taxes, if you recall, are tax revenues minus transfer payments. Of course, if the government is using tax cuts, rather than government spending, to expand the economy, the multiplier is smaller; so to get the same increase in real GDP, the size of the tax cut must be larger than an increase in government spending.

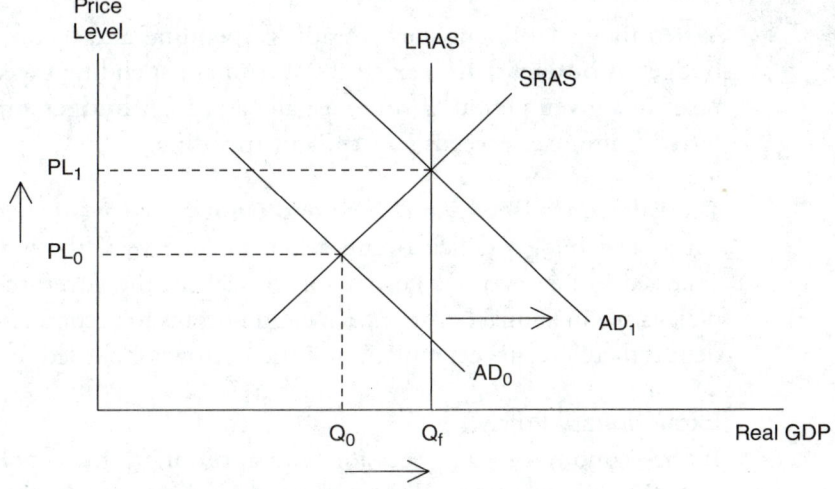

Figure 10.1

Contractionary Fiscal Policy

If the economy is operating beyond full employment, and inflation is becoming a problem, the government might need to contract the economy. This inflationary equilibrium is seen beyond full employment, as shown in Figure 10.2. This can be done by decreasing government spending or by increasing taxes, both of which cause a leftward shift in AD. The economy should see a little decrease in real GDP, but ideally a substantial decrease in the rate of inflation.

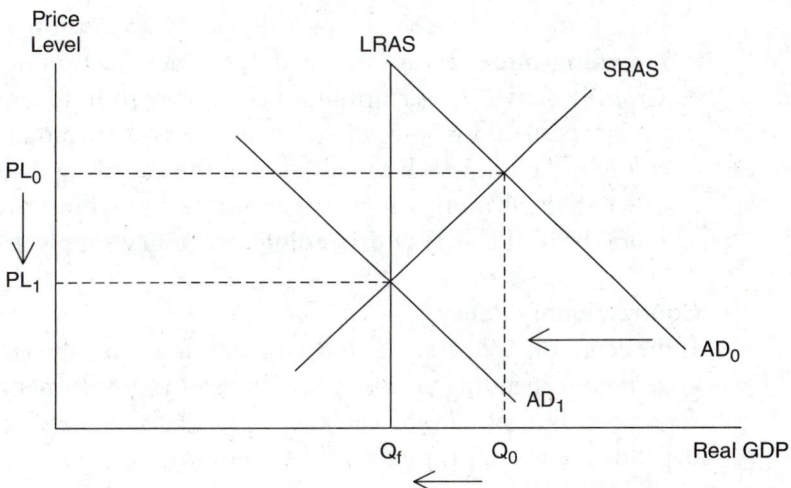

Figure 10.2

Are Prices Sticky?

Do prices fall, as Figure 10.2 seems to indicate? One of the points of contention is whether the price level can fall. Many economists (Keynesians) predict that prices are fairly inflexible, or "sticky" in the downward direction, so efforts to fight inflation are really efforts to slow inflation, not to actually lower the price level. Conversely, Classical school economists believe that the long-run economy naturally adjusts to full employment, and so they see the AS curve as vertical. This argument implies that prices are flexible and can rise and fall, as seen in Figure 10.2.

Deficits and Surpluses

When the government starts to adjust spending and/or taxation, there is an effect on the budget. A **budget deficit** exists if government spending exceeds the revenue collected from taxes in a given period of time, usually a year. A **budget surplus** exists if the revenue collected from taxes exceeds government spending.

The Difference Between Deficit and Debt

An annual budget deficit occurs when, in one year, the government spends more than is collected in tax revenue. To pay for the deficit, the government must borrow funds. When deficits are an annual occurrence, a nation begins to accumulate a **national debt**. The national debt is therefore an accumulation of the borrowing needed to cover past annual deficits.

Expansionary Policy

If the economy is in a recession, the appropriate fiscal policy is to increase government spending or lower taxes. When the government spends more, or collects less tax revenue, budget deficits are likely. There are two ways to finance the deficit, and each has the potential to weaken the expansionary policy.

- *Borrowing*. If a household wants to spend beyond its means, it enters the market for loanable funds as a borrower. The borrowed funds provide a short-term ability to purchase goods and services, but must be paid back, with interest, when the loan is due. The same is true when the government borrows, but when an entity as large as the federal government is borrowing from the banking system, the public, or foreign lenders, in the form of Treasury bonds, it increases the demand for loanable funds. This, in turn, increases the real rate of interest and reduces the quantity of funds available for private investment opportunities. So what? Well, if the goal is to expand the macroeconomy, then borrowing to finance the deficit slows down the expansion by increasing interest rates. This **crowding-out effect** is examined in the next section of this chapter.
- *Creating money*. The creation of new money to fund a deficit can avoid the higher interest rates caused by borrowing. The primary disadvantage of creating more money is the risk of inflation, which can also lessen the effectiveness of expansionary fiscal policy. The effect that inflation has on the multiplier was illustrated in the previous chapter, and more detailed effects of expanding the money supply are looked at in the next chapter.

Contractionary Policy

If the economy is operating above full employment, the appropriate fiscal policy is to lower government spending or raise taxes. When the government spends less, or collects more tax revenue, a budget surplus can occur. The effectiveness of the contractionary fiscal policy depends upon what is done with the surplus.

- *Pay down debt*. If the government pays down debt and retires bonds ahead of schedule, the demand for loanable funds decreases, decreasing interest rates. Lower interest rates

stimulate investment and consumption, which counters the contractionary fiscal policy and lessens the downward effects on the price level.
- *Do nothing.* By making regularly scheduled payments on Treasury bonds and retiring them on schedule, idle surplus funds are removed from the economy. By not allowing these funds to be recirculated through the economy, the anti-inflationary fiscal policy can be more effective.

Automatic Stabilizers

An **automatic stabilizer** is anything that increases a deficit during a recessionary period and increases a budget surplus during an inflationary period, without any discretionary change on the part of the government. There are some mechanisms built into the tax system that automatically regulate, or stabilize, the macroeconomy as it moves through the business cycle by changing net taxes collected by the government.

Progressive Taxes and Transfers

When the economy is booming and GDP is increasing, more and more households and firms begin to fall into higher and higher tax brackets. This means that a larger percentage of income is taken as income tax, which slows down the consumption of both households and firms. In addition, a strong economy reduces the need for such transfer payments as unemployment insurance and welfare. Thus, net taxes increase with GDP. Our progressive tax system is therefore contractionary when the economy is very strong. By automatically putting the brakes on spending, this reduces the threat of inflation and contributes to a budget surplus.

When the economy is suffering a recession and GDP is falling, households and firms find themselves in lower tax brackets. With a smaller percentage of income being taken as income tax, this provides a way for more consumption than would have been possible at the higher tax rate. Simultaneously, a weak economy increases the need for transfer payments like welfare payments. Thus, net taxes decrease with GDP. When the economy is sluggish, the progressive tax system is expansionary in nature. The lower tax brackets soften the effect of a recession and contribute to a deficit.

Figure 10.3 shows how, for a given level of government spending, net taxes rise and fall with GDP. These automatically reduce the threat of inflation when the economy is strong (GDP_i) and reduce the negative effects of a recession when the economy is weak (GDP_r). Ideally, at full employment (GDP_f), the budget should be balanced.

- Automatic stabilizers lessen, but do not eliminate, the business cycle swings.
- Automatic stabilizers lead to deficits during recession and surpluses during economic growth.

Figure 10.3

10.2 Difficulties of Fiscal Policy

Main Topics: *Crowding Out, Net Export Effect, State and Local Policies*

In theory, aggregate demand can be expanded or contracted, with government spending and/or taxes, to move the economy closer to full employment. In practice, there are some factors that lessen the effectiveness of fiscal policy. There are also some economists who disagree on fiscal policy targets.

Crowding Out

If the government must borrow funds to pay for expansionary fiscal policy, the government has an effect on the market for loanable funds. The market for loanable funds was introduced earlier in this text, and you might recall that public borrowing (in the form of a budget deficit) affects the demand for loanable funds. A government deficit increases the total demand for loanable funds but, by raising the real interest rate, reduces the quantity of loanable funds available to the private borrowers and investors. Less investment spending on capital goods is likely to reduce a nation's growth rate, a topic we'll explore at the end of this chapter.

"Crowding out is an important concept that may get asked more than once."
—AP Teacher

Figure 10.4 shows how a government budget deficit affects the demand for loanable funds and how we see crowding out. At the initial equilibrium, the real interest rate is 5%, the government has a balanced budget, and $100 billion is being saved by households and invested by firms.

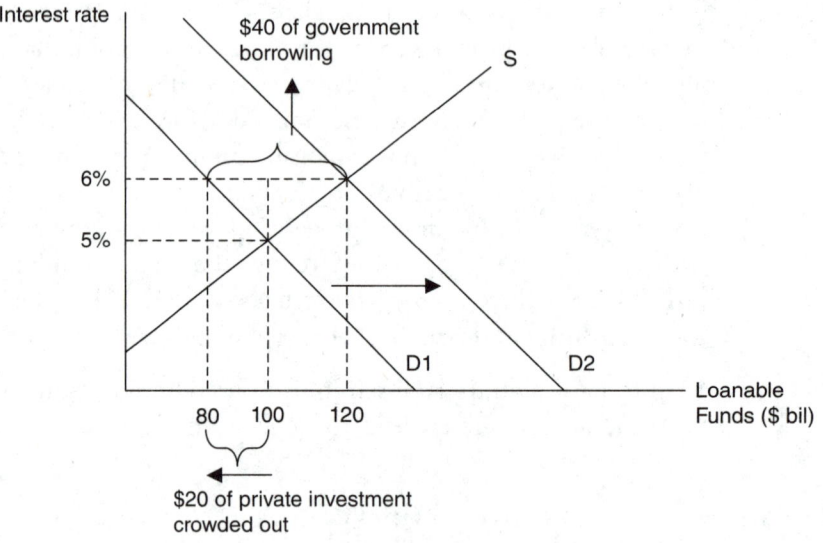

Figure 10.4

Now suppose that government fiscal policy creates a $40 billion budget deficit. To cover the deficit, the government must borrow $40 billion in the market for loanable funds. The new demand curve (D2) is simply the original demand curve, only it lays $40 billion to the right of D1. The new market equilibrium interest rate is 6%, and $120 billion is saved and invested. But remember that of this $120 billion, $40 billion is due to borrowing by the government. That leaves $80 billion in **private** borrowing and investment. So the government budget deficit caused **private** borrowing and investment to fall from $100 billion to $80 billion, and that is where we see the crowding out of $20 billion in private investment.

When the interest rate increases, households and firms are "**crowded out**" of the market for loanable funds. This decrease in C and I dampens the effect of expansionary fiscal policy. This is seen in Figure 10.5 as a movement from AD_1 to AD_2.

As we saw in Chapter 9, if increases in AD continue into the upward-sloping range of AS, some of the multiplier effect of the fiscal policy is consumed by inflation, and thus it is less effective.

When the government is fighting inflation with contractionary policy, we are likely to see the opposite of the crowding out problem. If a budget surplus is the result of the contractionary policy, and government debt is retired, the demand for loanable funds decreases, interest rates fall and private investment increases ("crowding in," perhaps), thus lessening the impact of contractionary fiscal policy.

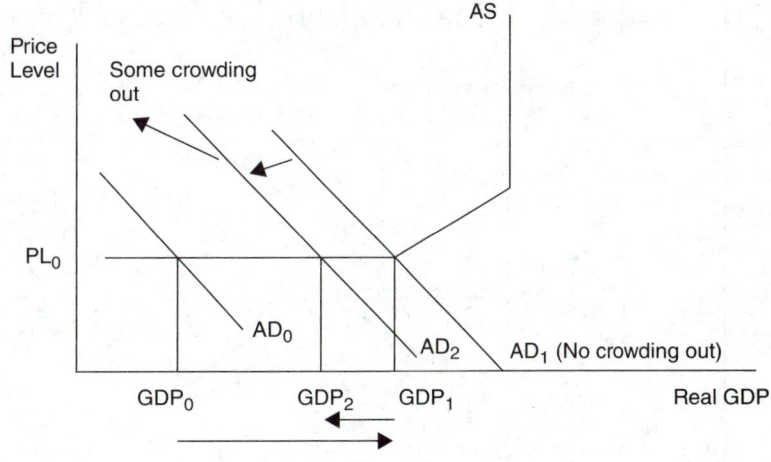

Figure 10.5

Another Way of Looking at Crowding Out

There are two different ways to show how a government budget deficit affects the market for loanable funds and crowds out private investment. I know that can be frustrating, but, hey, that's macro for you! Luckily, the outcomes are the same, and each approach is considered correct on the AP Macroeconomics exam.

The fundamental difference in these approaches is where the loanable funds model places the government. In the model presented, government borrowing (or saving, if there is a budget surplus) resides in the demand curve. Most textbooks use this approach. The demand curve represents the total of all of the private investing and borrowing (from firms) and public borrowing (from government). When the government has a budget deficit, the demand for loanable funds shifts to the right and the real interest rate rises. Private investment, the other source of the demand for loanable funds, decreases and is thus "crowded out."

Other popular macroeconomics textbooks, including the one that your teacher probably chose to use, place the government in the supply curve. The supply curve represents the sum of both private saving (from households) and public saving from the government. If the government has a budget deficit, public saving is negative and the supply of loanable funds shifts leftward. If the government has a budget surplus, public saving is positive and the supply of loanable funds shifts rightward.

Suppose the government is running a budget deficit and public saving is negative. Figure 10.6 shows that a leftward shift of the supply curve increases the interest rate in the market for loanable funds and decreases the quantity of loanable funds both invested and saved.

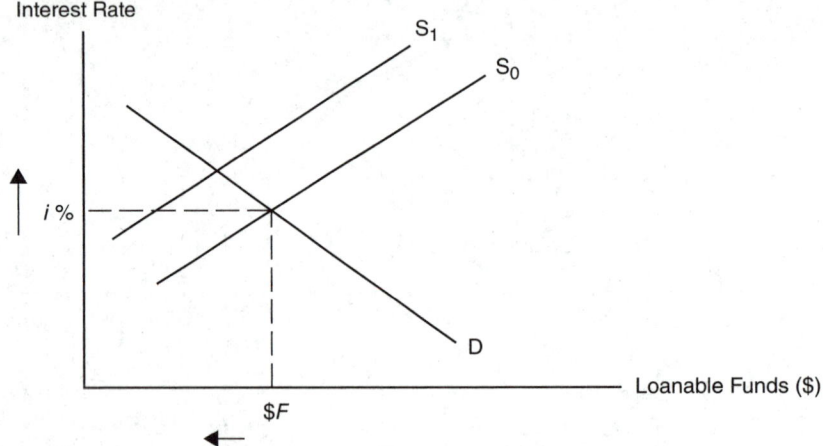

Figure 10.6

So it doesn't matter if your textbook (or teacher) treats crowding out as a leftward shift in supply of, or as a rightward shift in demand for, loanable funds. As long as you can see (or show) the impact of government budget deficits as a higher interest rate and lower private investment, you will score highly on those exam questions.

Net Export Effect

If the government is borrowing to conduct fiscal policy, the resulting increase in interest rates has a similar crowding out effect on net exports through foreign exchange rates. Again, this is a topic that is addressed in a later chapter, but the basics can be described here. If you are a German, a Malaysian, or a Brazilian and you see interest rates rising in the United States, this higher interest rate makes the United States an attractive place to invest your money and earn higher interest payments. However, you need dollars to purchase a U.S. security (e.g., a U.S. Treasury bond). The increased demand for dollars drives up the "price" of a dollar, which is measured in how many euros, ringgits, or reals it takes to buy a dollar on the currency market. The market for U.S. dollars is illustrated in Figure 10.7, where the price is measured in the number of euros it takes to acquire one dollar.

"Don't try to figure it out in your head. Draw the graphs and read your answers from them."
—Nate, AP Student

Figure 10.7

When the price of a dollar rises from E_0 to E_1, it now becomes more expensive for foreign citizens to buy goods made in the United States. All else equal, net exports in the United States fall when the dollar appreciates in value. Falling net exports decreases AD, which lessens the impact of the expansionary fiscal policy. This would be seen in much the same way as in Figure 10.5.

If the government is using contractionary fiscal policy to fight inflation, and interest rates begin to fall, the demand for dollars falls, depreciating the dollar and increasing net exports. This increase in net exports lessens the effectiveness of the contractionary fiscal policy.

- Expansionary fiscal policy is less effective if government borrowing crowds out private investment with higher interest rates.
- Expansionary fiscal policy is less effective if net exports fall because of an appreciating dollar.
- These effects also work in the opposite direction, making contractionary fiscal policy less effective when interest rates fall.

State and Local Policies

The U.S. Constitution does not require that the federal government balance the budget and most economists would agree that this is a good thing. After all, when the economy is in a recession, tax revenues are going to be low and deficits are likely to occur. Balancing the budget requires a combination of higher taxes and less spending, which only exacerbates the recession! Likewise, during a period of economic expansion, tax revenues are high and surpluses occur. Balancing the budget requires lower taxes or higher levels of spending to eliminate the surplus, which continues the expansion and risks higher inflation rates.

On the other hand, many state and local governments are required by law to balance their budgets. During recessions, tax revenue collected by these levels of government fall and elected officials are required to increase taxes and make difficult decisions on which state and local programs need to be cut.

So while the federal government is cutting taxes to increase your disposable income and spur economic growth, your state and local governments are increasing your taxes to make up for the budgetary shortfalls caused by the very recession the federal government is trying to fix. Argh! In my state of Indiana, since 2001 citizens have seen a 1 percent increase in the sales tax, increases in property taxes, and, in the history of my county, the first ever county income tax. Meanwhile, programs like education, law enforcement, and transportation have seen cutbacks to help offset lost federal funds.

So, in summary:

- State and local governments that are sometimes required by law to balance their budgets can thwart federal fiscal policy.

10.3 Economic Growth and Productivity

Main Topics: *Production Possibilities, Productivity, Determinants of Productivity, Supply-Side Policies*

Production Possibilities

Way back in Chapter 5, the topic of the PPF was introduced, and that chapter illustrated how the frontier can move outward over time. This simple graphical technique can be extremely useful and adaptable to seeing how growth can be impacted by government policy. Before we move on to policy, here is a quick refresher course in economic growth and productivity.

Figure 10.8

Figure 10.8 shows that this nation's production possibilities in CDs and digital cameras can grow over time if

1. the quantity of economic resources increases,
2. the quality of those resources improves, and/or
3. the nation's technology improves.

Productivity

The factors that shift a PPF outward over time make a lot of sense, but what they all have in common is that each has the potential to represent increased **productivity**. Productivity is typically described as measuring the quantity of output that can be produced per worker in a given amount of time. If a nation's labor force can produce more output per worker from one year to the next, we say that productivity has increased and the nation's PPF has shifted outward.

Determinants of Productivity

The determinants of productivity help to explain why some nations have grown at faster rates than other nations. This short list of determinants provides policy makers with a list of targets that can help to focus policy on factors that increase a nation's growth rate.

Stock of Physical Capital

Workers are more productive when they have tools at their disposal. Try painting a house without a brush, digging a hole without a shovel, or writing a term paper without a personal computer, and you'll find out how important tools can be to your productivity. The nice thing about increasing the quantity of physical capital in an economy is that, in many cases, the capital helps to increase the quantity of more capital. There should be policies that provide incentives to invest in physical capital. The supply-side policies described later in the chapter are examples of policies that can increase investment in physical capital.

Human Capital

Labor is a much more productive resource when it has more **human capital**. Human capital is the amount of knowledge and skills that labor can apply to the work that they do. An accountant who takes extra courses so that she can earn her stockbroker's license has increased her human capital. A nurse who studies to become a physician's assistant is increasing her human capital and becoming more productive. Human capital also includes the general health of the nation's labor force. A labor force that has been vaccinated against debilitating disease can bring more productivity to the nation's workplace than the labor force of a nation that has not received these vaccinations. There should be national policies that provide incentives to invest in human capital. How about subsidies to public education to decrease the price to households? Or low-interest federal student loans to help fund college? Or government agencies to research and promote the general physical and psychological health of the population?

Natural Resources

Productive resources provided by nature are called natural resources. A nation's stocks of minerals, fertile soil, timber, or navigable waterways contribute to productivity. **Nonrenewable** resources, such as oil and coal, have a finite supply and cannot replenish themselves. **Renewable** resources, such as timber and salmon, have the ability to repopulate themselves. Environmental protection laws are designed to maintain the quality of natural resources, so the productivity does not rapidly depreciate.

Technology

Technology is thought of as a nation's knowledge of how to produce goods in the best possible way. Imagine the technological leap that was made when humankind created fire, or the wheel, or the radio, or the assembly line, or the pizza crust with cheese in the middle. Amazing stuff! There should be policies that provide incentives to increase the rate of technological progress. The government's provision of research grants to university professors and laboratories helps to further our state of technology.

What Do All of These Productivity Determinants Have in Common?

They all require an investment, and funds for investment come from **saving**. Firms invest in physical capital and individuals invest in human capital. Nations invest in the conservation of their natural resources, and entrepreneurs invest in technological research.

"Productivity-friendly" policies should make it easier to invest, easier to save, or both. Some economists believe that supply-side policies have the potential to increase productivity, and therefore economic growth.

Supply-Side Policies

So far the discussion of fiscal policy is centered on changing government spending and/or taxing to expand or contract AD as a way to move the economy closer to full employment. Other economists believe that the government's fiscal policy should not be so proactive in manipulation of AD. These economists advocate a government that is more hands-off when it comes to fiscal policy. These economists believe that the economy generally moves to full employment without government intervention, but if the government does get involved, fiscal policy should focus on, or at least strongly consider, the AS half of the equation by providing incentives to increase saving and investment. The main idea behind **supply-side** fiscal policy is that tax reductions targeted to AS increase AS so that real GDP increases with very little inflation. This was our "best of all possible macroeconomic situations" from the previous chapter.

Saving and Investment

Supply-side proponents would suggest policies that lower, or remove, taxes on income earned from savings. This would encourage saving and increase the supply of loanable funds, decrease the real interest rate, and increase the amount of money that firms invest. Figure 10.9 shows an increase in the supply of loanable funds. These economists would also propose an **investment tax credit**, which reduces a firm's taxes if it invests in physical capital.

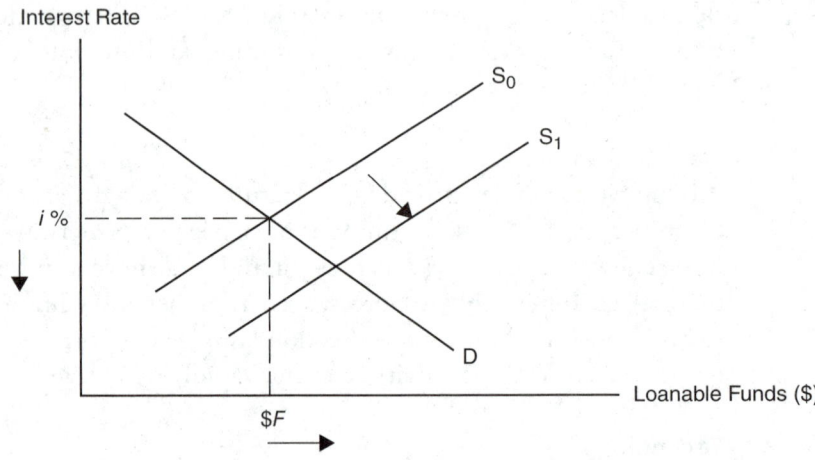

Figure 10.9

Lower income taxes increase disposable income for households, increase both consumption and savings from households, and increase the profitability of investment for firms. This increase in saving and investment allows for an increase in the productive capacity of a nation because more capital stock is accumulated. Ideally, this increase in investment increases the long-run AS curve. The increase in long-run AS is illustrated in Figure 10.10. Tax incentives to increase saving and investment on the supply side are likely to also increase AD. (Note: The price level is shown to remain constant, but this does not have to be, depending upon the magnitudes of the two curves' shifts.)

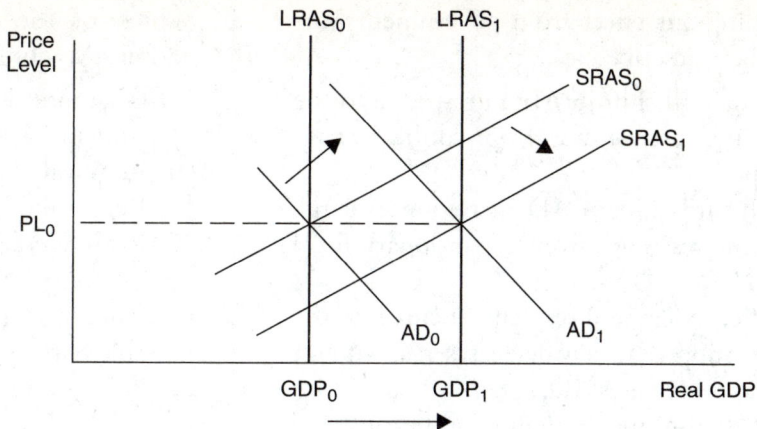

Figure 10.10

Though not all economists completely agree with their effectiveness, supply-side economists typically advocate other explanations for how lower taxes can increase AS as well as AD:

- *Productivity incentives.* Lower taxes mean workers take more of their pay home, which might prompt wage earners to work harder, take less time off, and be more productive. How hard would you work if 90 percent of your pay were lost to the taxman? People not currently in the workforce seek employment at lower tax rates. If the government has a large role in social programs, citizens learn to rely on the government and do less on their own.
- *Risk taking.* Entrepreneurs take big risks to start businesses and invest in new capital. Lowering the tax rate on profits increases the expected rate of return and encourages more investment.

> Review Questions

1. Which of the following would *not* be an example of contractionary fiscal policy?
   (A) Decreasing money spent on social programs
   (B) Increasing income taxes
   (C) Canceling the annual cost of living adjustments to the salaries of government employees
   (D) Increasing money spent to pay for government projects
   (E) Doing nothing with a temporary budget surplus

2. In a long period of economic expansion the tax revenue collected ____ and the amount spent on welfare programs ____ , creating a budget ____ .
   (A) increases, decreases, surplus
   (B) increases, decreases, deficit
   (C) decreases, decreases, surplus
   (D) decreases, increases, deficit
   (E) increases, increases, surplus

3. The crowding-out effect from government borrowing is best described as
   (A) the rightward shift in AD in response to the decreasing interest rates from contractionary fiscal policy.
   (B) the leftward shift in AD in response to the rising interest rates from expansionary fiscal policy.
   (C) the effect of the President increasing the money supply, which decreases real interest rates, and increases AD.
   (D) the effect on the economy of hearing the chairperson of the central bank say that he or she believes that the economy is in a recession.
   (E) the lower exports due to an appreciating dollar versus other currencies.

4. Which of the following fiscal policies is likely to be most effective when the economy is experiencing an inflationary gap?
   (A) The government decreases taxes and keeps spending unchanged.
   (B) The government increases spending and keeps taxes unchanged.
   (C) The government increases spending matched with an increase in taxes.
   (D) The government decreases spending and keeps taxes unchanged.
   (E) The government increases taxes and decreases spending.

5. Which of the following would likely slow a nation's economic growth?
   (A) Guaranteed low-interest loans for college students
   (B) Removal of a tax on income earned on saving
   (C) Removal of the investment tax credit
   (D) More research grants given to medical schools
   (E) Conservation policies to manage the renewable harvest of timber

6. The U.S. economy currently suffers a recessionary gap, and a budget deficit exists. If the government wishes to fix the recession, which of the following choices best describes the appropriate fiscal policy, the impact on the market for loanable funds, the interest rate, and the market for the U.S. dollar?

	FISCAL POLICY	LOANABLE FUNDS	INTEREST RATE	MARKET FOR $
(A)	Tax increase	Demand rises	Falling	Demand falls
(B)	Tax cut	Supply rises	rising	Demand rises
(C)	Tax cut	Demand rises	rising	Demand rises
(D)	Tax increase	Supply falls	Falling	Demand rises
(E)	Tax cut	Supply falls	Rising	Demand falls

> ## Answers and Explanations

1. **D**—This is expansionary policy, and the others either contract the economy or do nothing.

2. **A**—In an expansion, households should earn more income, which increases the taxes paid to the government. At the same time, people who needed welfare, or other government assistance, do not need it now because the unemployment level is low and wages are high. In this time of prosperity, the government should run a budget surplus.

3. **B**—If the government borrows to expand the economy, interest rates rise, thus crowding out private investors. This shifts AD leftward, weakening the fiscal policy impact.

4. **E**—Real GDP is at a level above full employment, so AD must be shifted leftward. Choice D shifts AD to the left and lessens the inflationary gap, but choice E couples higher taxes with lower spending and therefore is the most effective remedy. All other choices increase AD and worsen the inflationary gap.

5. **C**—An investment tax credit rewards firms that invest in physical assets. Removal of this tax credit slows investment, productivity, and growth. All other policies would increase the productivity of resources or increase technological innovation.

6. **C**—When a recessionary gap exists, the appropriate fiscal policy is to cut taxes and run an even larger budget deficit. The borrowing necessary to pay for a budget deficit increases the demand for loanable funds and increases the interest rate. Rising interest rates create a stronger demand for the U.S. dollar because U.S. Treasury bondholders are receiving more interest income. Knowing that the economy is in a recession allows you to quickly eliminate all tax increases.

❯ Rapid Review

Fiscal policy: Deliberate changes in government spending and net tax collection to affect economic output, unemployment, and the price level. Fiscal policy is typically designed to manipulate AD to "fix" the economy.

Expansionary fiscal policy: Increases in government spending or lower net taxes meant to shift the aggregate expenditure function upward and shift AD to the right.

Contractionary fiscal policy: Decreases in government spending or higher net taxes meant to shift the aggregate expenditure function downward and shift AD to the left.

Sticky prices: If price levels do not change, especially downward, with changes in AD, then prices are thought of as sticky or inflexible. Keynesians believe the price level does not usually fall with contractionary policy.

Budget deficit: Exists when government spending exceeds the revenue collected from taxes.

Budget surplus: Exists when the revenue collected from taxes exceeds government spending.

Automatic stabilizers: Mechanisms built into the tax system that automatically regulate, or stabilize, the macroeconomy as it moves through the business cycle by changing net taxes collected by the government. These stabilizers increase a deficit during a recessionary period and increase a budget surplus during an inflationary period, without any discretionary change on the part of the government.

Crowding-out effect: When the government borrows funds to cover a deficit, the interest rate increases and households and firms are crowded out of the market for loanable funds. The resulting decrease in C and I dampens the effect of expansionary fiscal policy.

Net export effect: A rising interest rate increases foreign demand for U.S. dollars. The dollar then appreciates in value, causing net exports from the United States to fall. Falling net exports decreases AD, which lessens the impact of the expansionary fiscal policy. This is a variation of crowding out.

Productivity: The quantity of output that can be produced per worker in a given amount of time.

Human capital: The amount of knowledge and skills that labor can apply to the work that they do and the general level of health that the labor force enjoys.

Nonrenewable resources: Natural resources that cannot replenish themselves. Coal is a good example.

Renewable resources: Natural resources that can replenish themselves if they are not overharvested. Lobster is a good example.

Technology: A nation's knowledge of how to produce goods in the best possible way.

Investment tax credit: A reduction in taxes for firms that invest in new capital like a factory or piece of equipment.

Supply-side fiscal policy: Fiscal policy centered on tax reductions targeted to AS so that real GDP increases with very little inflation. The main justification is that lower taxes on individuals and firms increase incentives to work, save, invest, and take risks.

CHAPTER 11

Money, Banking, and Monetary Policy

IN THIS CHAPTER

Summary: People often think that economics is the study of money. While you have already discovered that, strictly speaking, this is not the case, there is no denying the critical role of money in any economic system in the exchange of goods and services, employment of resources, and macroeconomic stability. This chapter first briefly defines money, the functions that it serves, and the market for it. Following a brief overview of the fractional reserve banking system, we discuss money creation. We then focus on the tools of monetary policy that the Federal Reserve uses to influence the macroeconomy. The chapter concludes with a discussion of fiscal and monetary policy coordination and how one school of economic thought sees the role of monetary policy.

Key Ideas
- Money as an Asset
- The Money Market
- The Money Multiplier
- Monetary Policy

11.1 Money and Financial Assets

Main Topics: *Financial Assets, Functions of Money, Present Value and Future Value, Supply of Money, Demand for Money, The Money Market, Changes in Money Supply*

The paper and coin currency that we carry around in our pockets is typically used for one thing: to buy stuff. Before we get into a more thorough discussion about money, let's briefly discuss financial assets other than the money in your pocket.

In general, money is anything that is used to facilitate exchange of goods between buyers and sellers. Human history has seen many things used as money, from shells and tobacco to gold and spices. These different forms of money have all performed certain functions.

Financial Assets

We have already discussed investment in physical (or capital) assets like machinery or new construction as components of GDP. The firm invests in a physical asset if the expected rate of return is at least as high as the real interest rate. Sometimes firms and households seek other forms of assets as a place for their money. Financial investments also yield a rate of return. We spend much more time discussing money as a short-term financial asset, but quickly address other financial assets like stocks and bonds.

Stocks

A share of stock represents a claim on the ownership of the firm and is exchanged in a stock market. Firms that wish to raise money for capital investment can issue, and sell, these partial shares of ownership. This form of **equity financing** avoids debt but relinquishes a small degree of control over the management, and profits, of the firm.

Bonds

A bond is a certificate of indebtedness. When a firm wants to raise money by borrowing, it can issue corporate bonds that promise the bondholders the principle amount, plus a specified rate of interest, with repayment on a specific maturity date. This form of **debt financing** commits the corporation to interest payments, but does not relinquish shares of ownership. Like stocks, bonds can be bought and sold in a secondary market. We shall see how the central bank can intervene in this market in a way that has profound effects on the economy.

Functions of Money

In general, money is anything that is used to facilitate an exchange of goods between buyers and sellers. Human history has seen many things used as money, from shells and tobacco to gold and spices. These different forms of money have all performed certain functions.

Today's paper and coin money is called **fiat money** because it has no intrinsic value (like gold) and no value as a commodity (like tobacco). It serves as money because the government declares it to be legal tender and, in doing so, the government assures us that it performs three general functions:

- *Medium of exchange.* Your employer exchanges dollars for an hour of your labor. You exchange those dollars for a grocer's pound of apples. The grocer exchanges those dollars for an orchard's apple crop, and on and on. If it weren't for money, we would still be engaging in the barter system, an extremely inconvenient way to exchange goods and services. If I were a cheese maker and I wanted apples, I would need to find an orchard that also needed cheese, and this would be a supremely difficult way to do my shopping.
- *Unit of account.* Units of currency (dollars, euro, yen, etc.) measure the relative worth of goods and services just as inches and meters measure relative distance between two points. Again, this is an improvement over the barter system where all goods are measured in terms of many other goods. The value of a pound of cheese in a barter economy is measured in a dozen eggs, or a half pound of sausage, or three pints of ale. With money, the value of cheese, and all other goods and services, is measured in terms of a monetary unit like dollars.
- *Store of value.* So long as prices are not rapidly increasing, money is a decent way to store value. You can put money under your mattress or in a checking account, and it is still

useful, with essentially the same value, a week or a month later. If I were the town cheese maker, I must quickly find merchants with whom to exchange my cheese, because if I wait too long, moldy cheese loses its value.

Time Value of Money

Money may serve as a store of value, but money does lose its value over time. Most of us prefer to receive money income as early as possible (the sooner we can begin to consume stuff) and pay our debts as late as possible. If you lend your best friend $100, would you rather be paid back tomorrow or five years from tomorrow? If you are not going to charge your best friend any interest on this loan, then you probably prefer your money as soon as possible. If your best friend paid you back in five years without interest, your $100 would certainly have lost value over time due to inflation. After all, not having $100 for such a long period of time means that you were unable to consume $100 worth of goods! Delaying your consumption of goods that would give you utility must surely come at a cost. The idea of a **time value of money** is perhaps the most important reason for paying interest on savings and charging interest on borrowing.

Present Value and Future Value

Many decisions in life involve paying upfront costs today with the promise of a payoff tomorrow or even years from now. Many of you are familiar with this trade-off because you were told by a parent that "If you finish eating your vegetables, you can watch TV before bedtime," or "If you wash the car, you can go to the movie with your friends." As you consider attending college, the same principle applies. The costs (tuition, books, etc.) are paid today, but the payoffs (marketable skills, useful knowledge, etc.) are received years from today. As the previous section illustrates, dollars today are worth more than future dollars; so there must be a way to convert present and future dollars to the same time period so that wise decisions can be made. The interest rate is the key.

Let's again assume that you are going to lend your friend $100 and that he is going to pay you back in one year. We'll also assume that there is no inflation, so a 10 percent nominal interest rate is equal to the real interest rate. The opportunity cost of lending your friend $100 is the interest you could have earned—$10, after a year had passed. So the interest rate measures the cost to you of forgoing the use of that $100. After all, you could have spent $100 on clothing right now that would have provided immediate benefit to you. To see the relationship between dollars today (present value, or PV) and dollars one year from now (future value, or FV), we can use a simple equation:

$$FV = PV \times (1 + r)$$

or, using our example:

$$FV = \$100 \times (1.10) = \$110$$

In other words, one year into the future, that $100 will be worth $110.

We can also rearrange our equation and solve for the present value PV:

$$PV = FV/(1 + r)$$

and, using our example again:

$$PV = \$110/(1.10) = \$100$$

This tells us that $110 a year from now is worth only $100 in today's dollars.

If you were lending the money for a period of two years,

$$FV = PV(1 + r)^2 = \$100 \times (1.10) \times (1.10) = \$121$$

What does this all mean? It means that your friend, as a borrower, must pay you $21 to compensate you for the fact that he has your $100 for a period of two years. It also says that had you, as a saver, put the $100 in the bank today, two years from now, you would have $121 to spend on goods and services. This implies that you would be completely indifferent to having $100 in your hand today or $121 two years from today. The differing sums are equivalent units of purchasing power, just measured at two different points in time, and it is the interest rate that equates the two.

So, to summarize:

- Money today is more valuable than the same amount of money in the future.
- The present value of $1 received one year from now is $1/(1 + r)$.
- The future value of $1 invested today, for a period of one year, is $1 \times (1 + r)$.
- Interest paid on savings and interest charged on borrowing is designed to equate the value of dollars today with the value of future dollars.

Supply of Money

At the core of monetary policy is regulation of the supply of money. Because our paper money is not backed by precious metals or crown jewels, we trust the government to keep the value of our money as stable as possible. This value is guaranteed by stabilizing the **money supply**, which is measured by the central bank as **M1 and M2** the latter being more broadly defined and less liquid than the former. **Liquidity** refers to how easily an asset can be converted to cash. A five-dollar bill, already being cash, is as liquid as it gets. A Van Gogh painting hidden in your attic is also an asset but not a very liquid one.

"There are a couple of questions on this. Know what is included in each category."
—Kristy, AP Student

We can say that:

- $M1$ = Cash + Coins + Checking deposits + Traveler's checks. $M1$ is the most liquid of money definitions.
- $M2$ = $M1$ + Savings deposits + Small (i.e., under $100,000 certificates of deposit) time deposits + Money market deposits + Money market mutual funds. $M2$ is slightly less liquid because the holders of these assets would likely incur a penalty if they wished to immediately convert the asset to cash.

At any given point in time, the supply of money is a constant. This implies that the current money supply curve is vertical. Because other measures of money supply are based upon the most liquid $M1$, when we discuss the money supply, we focus on $M1$. Insight gained from studying the expansion and contraction of $M1$ can be applied to $M2$.

Demand for Money

People demand goods like cheese because cheese helps satisfy wants. People demand money because it facilitates the purchase of cheese and other goods. In addition to this transaction demand for money, people also demand money as an asset, just as a government bond or a share of Intel stock is an asset. We quickly look at demand for money as the sum of money demand for transactions and money demand as an asset.

Transaction Demand. As nominal GDP increases, consumers demand more money to buy goods and services. For a given price level, if output increases, more money is demanded. Or for a given level of output, if the price level rises, more money is demanded. If nominal GDP is $1,000 and each dollar is spent an average of four times each year, money demand for transactions would be $1,000/4 = $250. If nominal GDP increases to $1,200, money demand for transactions increases to $1,200/4 = $300. We assume that the nominal rate of interest does not affect transaction demand for money, so when plotted on a graph with the nominal interest rate on the y axis, it is a constant.

Asset Demand. Money can be held as an asset at very little risk. If you put money under your mattress, there is the advantage of knowing that a crashing stock market or real estate market does not diminish the value of this asset. The main disadvantage of putting this asset under your mattress is that it cannot earn any interest as it would were you to invest that money in bonds, for example. As the interest rate on bonds rises, the opportunity cost of holding money under your mattress begins to rise, and so you are more likely to lessen your asset demand for money. At a lower interest rate on bonds, you are more likely to increase your asset demand for money.

Total Demand. Plotted against the nominal interest rate, the transaction demand for money is a constant MD_t. Adding this constant amount of money needed to make transactions to a downward-sloping asset demand for money (MD_a) provides us with the total money demand curve. This is seen in Figure 11.1

Figure 11.1

The Money Market

The central bank, having established a given level of money supply circulating in the economy, allows us to incorporate a vertical money supply (MS) curve with a downward-sloping money demand curve to complete the money market. John Maynard Keynes developed the *theory of liquidity preference*, which postulates that the equilibrium "price" of money is the interest rate where money supply intersects money demand. Just like any market, if the price is below equilibrium (a shortage), the price must rise, and if the price is above equilibrium (a surplus), the price must fall. Money demand can increase if more transactions are being made, but the real focus of the rest of this chapter is on changes in money supply. Equilibrium is shown in Figure 11.2.

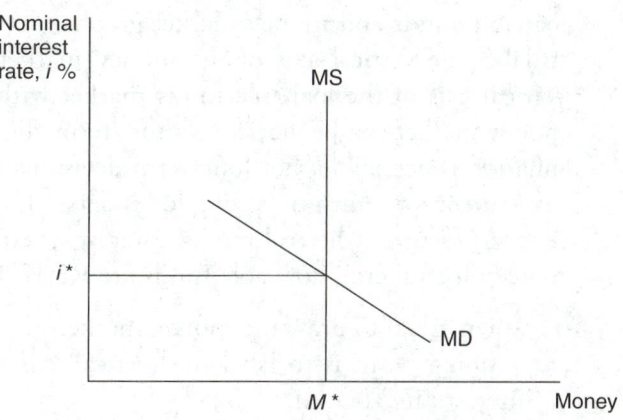

Figure 11.2

How Is the Money Market Different from the Market for Loanable Funds?

Understanding the difference between the money market and the loanable funds market can be tough, so we'll take it in two and a half parts. I'm sure the first is much more helpful, the second much more esoteric, and the half is going to earn you the graphing points.

> "This is an important question. Know the difference."
> —AP Teacher

1. *Breadth of scope.*

   The supply of loanable funds, which varies directly with the interest rate, comes from saving. The supply of money is more inclusive than just saving; it includes currency and checking deposits. A $100 bill in your wallet would fall into the money supply curve, but not into the supply of loanable funds. The demand for loanable funds comes from investment demand. The demand for money includes the money used for investment, but also for consumption (transaction demand) and for holding as an asset (asset demand). So basically the money market, both on the supply and the demand side, is broader, and more inclusive, than the market for loanable funds. The price (aka the interest rate) appears to be the same in both markets, and is the result of . . .

2. *Different philosophies.*

   We don't want to delve too much into the Keynesian versus Classical philosophical debates because they are quite unlikely to appear on your AP Macroeconomics exam. It can seem a little confusing to show the interest rate as the "price" in both the market for loanable funds and the market for money. The reason that both markets are presented here, and in your textbook, is that they represent fundamental differences in macroeconomic philosophies.

   - Classical economists believe that the price level is flexible and long-run GDP adjusts to the natural rate of employment. For any level of GDP, the interest rate adjusts to balance the supply and demand for loanable funds and the price level adjusts to keep the money market in equilibrium.

   - Keynesian economists believe that the price level is sticky. For any price level, the interest rate adjusts to balance the supply and demand for money, and this interest rate influences aggregate demand and thus the short-run level of GDP.

   - Bottom line here: The two different ways of looking at the interest rate are the result of two different ways of looking at the overall economy and the difference in the long-run (Classical) and short-run (Keynesian) views of the economy.

   . . . and ½. *Graphing.*

   While it *appears* that the same interest rate is graphed on the vertical axis of both the loanable funds and money market graphs, they are not in fact the same. It is correct to label the vertical axis of the money market with a nominal interest rate and the vertical axis of the loanable funds market with the real interest rate. Changes in the money market can be viewed as short-term changes, and therefore the role of expected inflation is negligible. For long-term decisions like investment and saving, the price of investment, or return on saving, does depend upon expected inflation, and so it makes sense to focus on the real rate of interest when making long-term plans. Here's a way to keep it straight: "Loanable funds are REAL-ly fun."

   - When asked to draw the money market, the best way to ensure that you receive the graphing point is to label the vertical axis in the money market as the "Nominal interest rate" or "n.i.r."

- If you simply label the vertical axis in the money market as "%" or "Interest rate" you may not earn all the graphing points.

Changes in Money Supply

When we talk about monetary policy, we are really talking about money supply policy. The tools used to expand or contract the money supply are discussed later in this chapter, but it's useful to see what is happening in the money market when the money supply increases or decreases.

An Increase in the Money Supply

Like the market for any commodity, when the supply increases, there exists a temporary surplus at the original equilibrium price. The money market is no different. At the original interest rate of 10 percent, the supply of money is $1,000. Now the Fed increases the money supply to $1,500. In Figure 11.3, you can see that at 10 percent, there is now a surplus of money.

With surplus money on their hands, people find other assets, like bonds, as places to put the extra money. As more people increase the demand for bonds, the bond price rises, and this lowers the effective interest rate paid on the bonds.

Figure 11.3

How does this work?

A bond is selling at a price of $100 and promises to pay $10 in interest. The interest rate = $10/$100 = 10 percent. But if the price of the bond is driven up to $125, the same $10 of interest actually yields only $10/$125 = 8.0 percent. With lower interest rates available in the bond market, the opportunity cost of holding cash falls and the quantity of money demanded increases along the downward-sloping MD curve until MD = $1,500. An increase in the money supply therefore decreases the interest rate.

A Decrease in the Money Supply

If the Fed decides to decrease the supply of money from $1,000 to $500, there is a shortage of money at the 10 percent interest rate. A shortage of money sends some bondholders to sell their bonds so that they have money for transactions. An increase in the supply of bonds in the bond market decreases the price and increases the rate of interest earned on those assets.

How does this work?

If the original price of the bond is $100, promising to pay $10 in interest, the interest rate is 10 percent. If the price falls to $90, the same $10 of interest now yields $10/$90 = 11.1 percent. Higher interest rates on bonds increase the opportunity cost of holding cash, and so the quantity of money demanded falls until the interest rate rises to the point where MD = $500. This adjustment is seen in Figure 11.4.

Figure 11.4

- Increasing the money supply lowers interest rates as surplus money moves into the bond market, increasing bond prices.
- Decreasing the money supply increases interest rates as a shortage of money creates a sell-off of bonds, decreasing bond prices.

11.2 Fractional Reserve Banking and Money Creation

Main Topics: *Fractional Reserve Banking, Money Creation, The Money Multiplier*

If you asked 10 bank tellers in your hometown, "Do you create money here?" I'm guessing that 9 or 10 of them would reply, "No way." They're wrong. The fractional reserve system of banking, plus the bank's profit motive, creates money and opens the door for the Fed to promote or inhibit such money creation.

Fractional Reserve Banking

Fractional reserve banking is a system in which only a fraction of the total money supply is held in reserve as currency. The short story that follows illustrates how fractional reserve banking might have evolved.

Eli's Community Bank (ECB) opens its doors and is now accepting deposits from citizens who want a safe place to put their money. Eli promises to always keep 100 percent of their money on hand so that if a person needs to buy groceries, he or she can simply withdraw some money and take it to the store.

One day, a citizen comes up to the bank asking to borrow some money to start a lemonade stand, but Eli has to turn her down because if any of his customers comes to withdraw money for groceries and finds that it was not in the vault, they would be extremely irritated.

After a month or so, Eli observes that on any given day, there are very few withdrawals and most of the time the deposited money just sits there in the vault, doing nothing.

Eli decides, just to be safe, to hold a small percentage of his total deposits in the vault to cover any daily withdrawals, and earn some interest income by lending out the rest to households or small businesses. He even realizes that he must offer a small rate of interest to his depositors to compensate them for that "whole time value of money thing." The fraction of total deposits kept on reserve is called the **reserve ratio**. Each time he receives a deposit, he puts that fraction in the vault and lends the rest. This process is the foundation for money creation and the Fed's ability to conduct monetary policy.

Money Creation

A specific example of how the fractional reserve system can multiply one new bank deposit into new created money illustrates the process of money creation.

The reserve ratio is 10 percent. In other words,

$$\text{Reserve ratio } (rr) = \text{Cash reserves/Total deposits} = .10$$

One way to see how checking deposits turn into loans and how loans turn into new money is to create a basic T-account, or **balance sheet**. The idea of a balance sheet is to show the assets and liabilities of a bank. In our example, total assets must equal total liabilities.

Asset. Anything owned by the bank or owed to the bank is an asset of the bank. Cash on reserve is an asset, and so are loans made to citizens.

Liability. Anything owned by depositors or lenders to the bank is a liability. Checking deposits of citizens or loans made to the bank are liabilities to the bank.

Let's look at an example:

Step 1. Katie takes $1,000 from under her mattress, deposits it at ECB, and opens a checking account. If the Federal Reserve, the central bank of the United States, tells the ECB that it must hold 10 percent of all deposits in reserve, then the ECB must comply and keep no less than $100 of Katie's deposit as "required" reserves. The remaining $900 of the deposit are excess reserves and can be kept on reserve in the bank or lent to another person.

Balance Sheet ECB (Step 1)

ASSETS		LIABILITIES	
Required Reserves	$ 100	Checking Deposits	$1,000
Excess Reserves	$ 900		
Total Assets	$1,000	Total Liabilities	$1,000

Step 2. ECB lends all $900 in excess reserves to Theo, a local farmer.

Balance Sheet ECB (Step 2)

ASSETS		LIABILITIES	
Required Reserves	$ 100	Checking Deposits	$1,000
Excess Reserves	$ 0		
Loans	$ 900		
Total Assets	$1,900	Total Liabilities	$1,000

Step 3. Theo uses his $900 at Tractor Supply, which has a checking account with ECB. Checking deposits have now increased by $900, and this is new money. ECB must keep $90 as required reserves, and excess reserves now total $810.

Balance Sheet ECB (Step 3)

ASSETS		LIABILITIES	
Required Reserves	$ 190	Checking Deposits	$1,900
Excess Reserves	$ 810		
Loans	$ 900		
Total Assets	$1,900	Total Liabilities	$1,900

Step 4. ECB makes an $810 loan to Max, who wants to buy some furniture. Max spends $810 at Furniture Factory, which also banks with ECB, increasing checking deposits by $810. ECB must keep $81 in required reserves, leaving $729 in excess reserves.

Balance Sheet ECB (Step 4)

ASSETS		LIABILITIES	
Required Reserves	$ 271	Checking Deposits	$2,710
Excess Reserves	$ 729		
Loans	$1,710		
Total Assets	$2,710	Total Liabilities	$2,710

The Money Multiplier

An initial deposit of $1,000 creates, after only two loans are made and redeposited, $2,710 of checking deposits. This process could continue until there are no more excess reserves to be loaned, ultimately creating $10,000 of deposits. Of this $10,000 of deposits, $1,000 was already in the money supply (cash under Katie's mattress) but $9,000 has been created as new money, seemingly out of thin air. This process is known as the money multiplier, which measures the maximum amount of new checking deposits that can be created by a single dollar of excess reserves. The idea of the money multiplier, not to mention the mathematics, is identical to our coverage of the spending multiplier.

$$M = 1/(\text{Reserve requirement}) = 1/rr \; (= 1/.10 = 10 \text{ in our example})$$

We had $900 in initial excess reserves and this would have multiplied into a maximum of $9,000 if (a) at every stage the banks kept only the required dollars in reserve, (b) at every stage borrowers redeposit funds into the bank and keep none as cash, and (c) borrowers are willing to take out excess reserves as loans.

- The maximum, or simple, money multiplier $M = 1/rr$.
- An initial amount of excess reserves multiplies by, at most, a factor of M.

This process works in reverse if, instead of an initial deposit, Katie makes a $1,000 withdrawal and puts the cash under her mattress. Rather than money creation, this could be called money destruction.

11.3 Monetary Policy

Main Topics: *Expansionary Monetary Policy, Contractionary Monetary Policy, Open Market Operations, Changing the Discount Rate, Changing the Required Reserve Ratio, Coordination of Fiscal and Monetary Policy, Quantity Theory of Money*

The Federal Reserve has three general tools of monetary policy at their disposal. The Fed can engage in open market operations, change the discount rate and change the required reserve ratio. Each of these can be used to expand or contract the money supply to stabilize prices and move the economy to full employment. We first look at the intended effects of expansionary and contractionary monetary policy and then investigate each of the tools in more detail.

Expansionary Monetary Policy

Unlike fiscal policy, which has a relatively direct impact on aggregate demand, real GDP, unemployment, and the price level, monetary policy takes a longer path to impact. Expansionary monetary policy is designed to fix a recession and increase aggregate demand, lower the unemployment rate, and increase real GDP. By increasing the money supply, the interest rate is lowered. A lower rate of interest increases private consumption and investment, which shifts the aggregate demand curve to the right. This process is illustrated in Figures 11.5 and 11.6.

Figure 11.5

Contractionary Monetary Policy

As you might imagine, contractionary monetary policy has the opposite effect as expansionary and is designed to avoid inflation by decreasing aggregate demand, which lowers the price level and decreases real GDP back to the full employment level. By decreasing the money supply, the interest rate is increased. A higher rate of interest decreases private consumption and investment, which shifts the aggregate demand to the left. This process is illustrated in Figures 11.7 and 11.8.

Figure 11.6

Figure 11.7

Figure 11.8

The chain of events for expansionary and contractionary monetary policy is as follows.

- *Unemployment is too high* →↑MS, ↓*i*%, ↑*I*, ↑AD, ↑real GDP, ↓unemployment
- *Inflation is too high* →↓MS, ↑*i*%, ↓*I*, ↓AD, ↓real GDP, ↓price level

Open Market Operations

Just like individuals and firms, the Federal Reserve, through the Federal Open Market Committee (FOMC), can buy and sell securities on the open market. Such an **open market operation (OMO)** typically involves the buying (or selling) of Treasury bonds from (or to) commercial banks and the general public. Of the three tools of monetary policy, conducting OMOs is by far the approach most frequently taken by the Fed.

Buying Securities. Commercial banks hold Treasury bonds as an asset rather than excess cash reserves. If the Fed offers to buy some of those securities, the banks would receive excess cash reserves and the Fed would get the bonds. When banks have excess reserves, the money creation process begins. The money supply increases and the interest rate falls.

"This is a great way to remember this!" —AP Teacher

- When the Fed buys securities, the money supply expands. If it helps to remember, use this: "**B**uying **B**onds = **B**igger **B**ucks" (a larger money supply).

Selling Securities. Commercial banks might be in the market to buy Treasury bonds as an asset rather than excess cash reserves. If the Fed offers to sell some of their securities, the banks would get the bonds and their excess cash reserves would fall. When banks have fewer excess reserves, the money destruction process begins. The money supply decreases and the interest rate rises.

- When the Fed sells securities, the money supply contracts. If it helps to remember, use this: "**S**elling **B**onds = "**S**maller **B**ucks" (a smaller money supply).

The Federal Funds Rate

The discussion of OMOs seems to indicate that the buying and selling of securities is the main policy tool. If the FOMC wants to lower the interest rate, it buys bonds. If the FOMC wants to increase the interest rate, it sells bonds. In reality, the federal funds rate is set as a target interest rate and the FOMC then proceeds to engage in OMOs to hit that target rate. The federal funds rate is the interest rate that banks charge other banks for short-term loans. One bank might need to borrow funds from other banks, primarily to cover an unexpected dip in reserves. The important thing to remember is that our analysis of monetary policy is the same whether we talk about changes in the money supply or changes in the target federal funds interest rate.

Changing the Discount Rate

There are times when commercial banks need a short-term loan from the Fed. When they borrow from the Fed, they pay an interest rate called the **discount rate**. When the Fed lowers the discount rate, it makes it more affordable for commercial banks to increase excess reserves by borrowing from the Fed. The entire amount of the loan goes into excess reserves and can be borrowed by customers of the bank, increasing the money supply. As a practical matter, the Fed tends to change the discount rate in lockstep with the federal funds target rate.

To summarize:

- Lowering the discount rate (or federal funds rate) increases excess reserves in commercial banks and expands the money supply.
- Raising the discount rate (or federal funds rate) decreases excess reserves in commercial banks and contracts the money supply.

Changing the Required Reserve Ratio

Though rarely used, if the Fed wants to increase excess reserves and expand the money supply, it could change the fraction of deposits that must be kept as required reserves. If the reserve ratio is .50, half of all deposits must be kept in the vault, leaving half to be loaned as excess reserves. The money multiplier in this case is two. But if the required reserve ratio were lowered to .10, 90 percent of all deposits could be lent as excess reserves. The money multiplier increases to 10.

So:

- Lowering the reserve ratio increases excess reserves in commercial banks and expands the money supply.
- Increasing the reserve ratio decreases excess reserves in commercial banks and contracts the money supply.

Table 11.1 summarizes how various tools of monetary policy can be used to target high unemployment or high inflation.

Table 11.1

	PROBLEM: HIGH UNEMPLOYMENT	PROBLEM: HIGH INFLATION
Monetary tool could be used to . . .	Buy bonds in an OMO.	Sell bonds in an OMO.
Or . . .	Lower the discount rate.	Raise the discount rate.
Or . . .	Lower the reserve ratio.	Raise the reserve ratio.
The effect would be . . .	↑MS, ↓i%, ↑I, ↑AD, ↑real GDP, ↓unemployment	↓MS, ↑i%, ↓I, ↓AD, ↓real GDP, ↓price level

Coordination of Fiscal and Monetary Policy

Congress and the President develop fiscal policy through the annual process of approving a spending budget and tax law. Chapter 10 showed how fiscal policy can be used to move the economy closer to full employment, but that it has some weakness, especially in the case when private investment is crowded out by government borrowing.

The central bank develops monetary policy and is independent of Congress and the President. This independence of monetary policy is believed to be a critical balance to fiscal policy that can be heavily politicized. After all, the creators of fiscal policy are elected by their constituents and might let an upcoming election taint the policy-making process. The central bank, free of election pressures, can develop monetary policy without this conflict of interest and perhaps work to counterbalance the downsides to fiscal policy. Let's look at three different scenarios where monetary and fiscal policy might be coordinated in Table 11.2.

> "Monetary policy does not affect government spending."
> —Elliot, AP Student

Table 11.2

THE PROBLEM:	FISCAL POLICY SOLUTION	BUDGET IMPACT	POTENTIAL CONSEQUENCE	MONETARY POLICY COMPLEMENT	KEEP AN EYE ON...
Deep recessionary gap and high unemployment	Tax cuts *and* increased spending to rapidly increase AD	Large Deficit	Higher interest rates, crowding out private investment, lower net exports and even weaker AD.	Expand MS to keep interest rates from rising. Increases AD to assist fiscal policy.	Higher Inflation
Mild recessionary gap and moderate unemployment	Tax cuts *or* increased spending to gradually increase AD and real GDP.	Moderate Deficit	Rising prices. Mild crowding out and lower net exports, weakening AD.	Contract MS to keep inflation from rising. Decreases AD, offsetting fiscal policy.	Rising Interest Rates
Inflationary gap	Tax hikes *and/or* decreased spending to rapidly decrease AD and real GDP.	Surplus	Lower interest rates "crowding in" private investment, higher net exports and even stronger AD.	Contract MS to keep interest rates from falling. Decreases AD to assist fiscal policy.	Higher Unemployment

- In a deep recessionary gap, expansionary monetary policy could be used to assist expansionary fiscal policy to quickly move to full employment. The risk then becomes a burst of inflation.
- In a mild recessionary gap, contractionary monetary policy could be used to offset expansionary fiscal policy to gradually move to full employment. The risk then becomes rising interest rates.
- In an inflationary gap, contractionary monetary policy could be used to assist contractionary fiscal policy to put downward pressure on the price level. The risk then becomes a rising unemployment rate.

Are There Critics of Monetary Policy?

Some economists disagree with the effectiveness of monetary policy, particularly the expansionary policies that are designed to eliminate a recessionary gap. One group of economists, which has come to be known as the "monetarists," argues against active open market purchases of Treasury securities on the grounds that such expansions of the money supply will not create more economic growth in the long run and will only create inflation. How would this happen?

Figure 11.9 shows an economy with a mild recessionary gap as real GDP (Q_r) falls below full employment output (Q_f). Suppose the central bank takes aggressive action and buys Treasury securities to expand the money supply. With a lower interest rate in the money market, aggregate demand increases to AD_2, increasing real GDP beyond full employment. While the unemployment rate falls in the short run, the aggregate price level

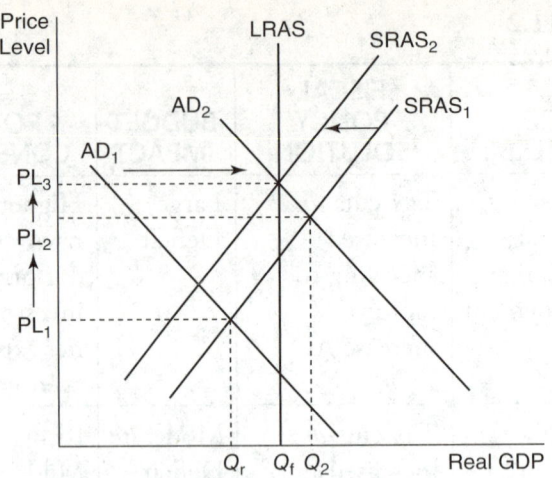

Figure 11.9

rises to PL$_2$ and inflation becomes a concern. As the economy, now with more money in circulation, adjusts to higher levels of spending, nominal wages and other factor prices rise, shifting the SRAS curve to the left to SRAS$_2$. When the economy fully adjusts, it is back at full employment, but the aggregate price level has now greatly risen to PL$_3$. Early monetarists such as Milton Friedman would therefore argue that such activist monetary policy doesn't "fix" the recession, it only creates inflation in the long run. The monetarists believe that the role of the central bank should be price stability, and the best way to accomplish this goal is to gradually and methodically increase the money supply by a fixed percentage each year.

Another way to see the monetarist view of monetary policy is to examine the equation of exchange, the topic we turn to next.

Quantity Theory of Money

Fiscal policy directly puts money into, or takes money out of, the pockets of households and firms, but monetary policy depends upon several cause-and-effect relationships. The critical link between monetary policy and real GDP is the relationship between changes in money supply, the real interest rate, and the level of private investment. After all, if the money supply increases and there is no increase in investment, expansionary monetary policy would have no effect on real GDP. As already noted, monetarists have become proponents of the **quantity theory of money**, which postulates that increasing the money supply has no effect on real GDP, but only serves to increase the price level.

One way to view this theory is to use the **equation of exchange**. The equation says that nominal GDP ($P \times Q$) is equal to the quantity of money (M) multiplied by the number of times each dollar is spent in a year (V), the **velocity of money**. For example, if in a given year the money supply is $100 and nominal GDP is $1,000, then each dollar must be spent 10 times; $V = 10$.

$$MV = PQ, \text{ or } V = PQ/M$$

If the money supply (M) increases, this increase must be reflected in the other three variables. To accommodate an increase in money supply, the velocity of money must fall, the price level must rise, or the economy's output of goods and services must increase.

Historically, the velocity of money in the United States has been fairly constant and stable, so the increase in M must result in changes in either P or Q. Economists believe that the quantity of output produced in a given year is a function of technology and the supply of resources, rather than the quantity of money circulating in the economy. Therefore, the increased money supply is going to only create a higher price level—inflation.

- The quantity theory of money predicts that any increase in the money supply only causes an increase in the price level.

» Review Questions

1. Which function of money best defines $1.25 as the price of a 20-ounce bottle of pop?

    (A) Medium of exchange
    (B) Unit of account
    (C) Store of value
    (D) Transfer of ownership
    (E) Fiat money

2. If a bank has $500 in checking deposits and the bank is required to reserve $50, what is the reserve ratio? How much does the bank have in excess reserves?

    (A) 10 percent, $450 in excess reserves
    (B) 90 percent, $50 in excess reserves
    (C) 90 percent, $450 in excess reserves
    (D) 10 percent, $50 in excess reserves
    (E) 10 percent, $500 in excess reserves

3. Which is *not* a way that the Fed can affect the money supply?

    (A) A change in discount rate
    (B) An open market operation
    (C) A change in reserve ratio
    (D) A change in tax rates
    (E) Buying Treasury securities from commercial banks

4. If the money supply increases, what happens in the money market (assuming money demand is downward sloping)?

    (A) The nominal interest rates rises.
    (B) The nominal interest rates falls.
    (C) The nominal interest rate does not change.
    (D) Transaction demand for money falls.
    (E) Transaction demand for money rises.

5. To move the economy closer to full employment, the central bank decides that the federal funds rate must be increased. The appropriate open market operation is to _____, which _____ the money supply, _____ aggregate demand, and fights _____.

	OMO	MONEY SUPPLY	AD	TO FIGHT
(A)	Buy bonds	Increases	Increase	Unemployment
(B)	Buy bonds	Increases	Increase	Inflation
(C)	Sell bonds	Decreases	Decrease	Unemployment
(D)	Sell bonds	Decreases	Increase	Inflation
(E)	Sell bonds	Decreases	Decrease	Inflation

6. Which of the following is a predictable advantage of expansionary monetary policy in a recession?

    (A) Decreases aggregate demand so that the price level falls.
    (B) Increases aggregate demand, which increases real GDP and increases employment.
    (C) Increases unemployment, but low prices negate this effect.
    (D) It keeps interest rates high, which attracts foreign investment.
    (E) It boosts the value of the dollar in foreign currency markets.

Answers and Explanations

1. **B**—The price in this case measures the relative price (value) of the pop.
2. **A**—The reserve ratio = Required reserves/checking deposits = .1 = 10%. Excess reserves = (Checking deposits – Required reserves) = ($500 – $50) = $450.
3. **D**—The Fed has no control of tax rates, which are an example of fiscal policy. All of the other choices are tools of monetary policy.
4. **B**—If the demand for money is downward sloping, the nominal interest rate falls because the money supply curve has shifted rightward.
5. **E**—If the central bank has decided that moving to full employment requires an increase in the federal funds rate, it must sell bonds to decrease the money supply. The resulting increase in interest rates decreases AD and puts downward pressure on the price level.
6. **B**—Expansionary monetary policies decrease the interest rate, causing AD to increase, which increases GDP at equilibrium and increases employment.

Rapid Review

Stock: A certificate that represents a claim to, or share of, the ownership of a firm.

Equity financing: The firm's method of raising funds for investment by issuing shares of stock to the public.

Bond: A certificate of indebtedness from the issuer to the bond holder.

Debt financing: A firm's way of raising investment funds by issuing bonds to the public.

Fiat money: Paper and coin money used to make transactions because the government declares it to be legal tender. Because it has no intrinsic value, it is backed by the public's trust that the government maintains its value.

Functions of money: Money serves three functions. It serves as a medium of exchange, a unit of account, and a store of value.

Present value: If r is the current interest rate, the present value of $1 received one year from now is $1/(1 + r)$.

Future value: If r is the current interest rate, the future value of $1 invested today for a period of one year is $1 \times (1 + r)$.

Money supply: The quantity of money in circulation as measured by the Federal Reserve (the Fed) as $M1$ and $M2$. Assumed to be fixed at a given point in time.

M1: The most liquid of money definitions and the basis for all other more broadly defined measures of money. $M1$ = Cash + Coins + Checking deposits + Traveler's checks.

Liquidity: A measure of how easily an asset can be converted to cash. The more easily it can be converted to cash, the more liquid the asset.

Transaction demand: The amount of money held in order to make transactions. This is not related to the interest rate, but it increases as nominal GDP increases.

Asset demand: The amount of money demanded as an asset. As nominal interest rates rise, the opportunity cost of holding money begins to rise and you are more likely to lessen your asset demand for money.

Money demand: The demand for money is the sum of money demanded for transactions and money demanded as an asset. It is inversely related to the nominal interest rate.

Theory of liquidity preference: Keynes' theory that the interest rate adjusts to bring the money market into equilibrium.

Fractional reserve banking: A system in which only a fraction of the total money deposited in banks is held in reserve as currency.

Reserve ratio (rr): The fraction of a bank's total deposits that are kept on reserve.

Reserve requirement: Regulation set by the Fed that states the minimum reserve ratio for banks.

Excess reserves: The cash reserves held by banks above and beyond the minimum reserve requirement.

Balance sheet or T-account: A tabular way to show the assets and liabilities of a bank. Total assets must equal liabilities.

Asset of a bank: Anything owned by the bank or owed to the bank is an asset of the bank. Cash on reserve is an asset and so are loans made to citizens.

Liability of a bank: Anything owned by depositors or lenders is a liability to the bank. Checking deposits of citizens or loans made to the bank are liabilities to the bank.

Money multiplier: This measures the maximum amount of new checking deposits that can be created by a single dollar of excess reserves. $M = 1/(\text{reserve ratio}) = 1/rr$. The money multiplier is smaller if (a) at any stage the banks keep more than the required dollars in reserve, (b) at any stage borrowers do not redeposit funds into the bank and keep some as cash, and (c) customers are not willing to borrow.

Expansionary monetary policy: Designed to fix a recession and increase aggregate demand, lower the unemployment rate, and increase real GDP, which may increase the price level.

Contractionary monetary policy: Designed to avoid inflation by decreasing aggregate demand, which lowers the price level and decreases real GDP back to full employment.

Open Market Operations (OMOs): A tool of monetary policy, it involves the Fed's buying (or selling) of securities from (or to) commercial banks and the general public.

Federal funds rate: The interest rate paid on short-term loans made from one bank to another. When this rate is a target for an OMO, bonds are bought or sold accordingly until the interest rate target has been met.

Discount rate: The interest rate commercial banks pay on short-term loans from the Fed.

Quantity Theory of Money: A theory that asserts that the quantity of money determines the price level and that the growth rate of money determines the rate of inflation.

Equation of Exchange: The equation says that nominal GDP ($P \times Q$) is equal to the quantity of money (M) multiplied by the number of times each dollar is spent in a year (V). $MV = PQ$.

Velocity of money: The average number of times that a dollar is spent in a year. V is defined as PQ/M.

International Trade

IN THIS CHAPTER

Summary: Economists agree on few things, but one of the few unifying themes in economics is that free and fair trade between two nations is mutually beneficial. Chapter 12 begins by reviewing the concept of comparative advantage and gains from trade, and the difference between the domestic and world price of a good. This chapter also revisits the currency exchange markets to illustrate how trade between nations requires the trade of currency and the connection of monetary policy to foreign exchange rates. Lastly, we look at the economic impact of trade barriers.

Key Ideas
- Absolute and Comparative Advantage
- Specialization and Gains from Trade
- Balance of Payments
- Foreign Exchange
- Trade Barriers

12.1 Comparative Advantage and Gains from Trade

Main Topics: *Comparative and Absolute Advantage; Gains from Trade; Exports, Imports, and the World Price*

Chapter 5 of this book introduces, albeit from the microeconomic perspective, the concept of production possibility curves. Comparative advantage and specialization at the microeconomic level explains why brain surgeons do not fly 747s and pilots do not analyze CAT scans. At the macroeconomic level, the **law of comparative advantage** says that nations can mutually benefit from trade so long as the relative production costs differ.

Comparative and Absolute Advantage

Our discussion of production possibilities illustrated the law of increasing costs. The more an economy produces of any one good, the more costly it becomes to produce the next unit. Rising costs of production lead to a search for less costly ways to produce and consume those goods. In many cases, this search leads to a potential trading partner who has **comparative advantage** in the production of a good. If Nation ABC can produce a good at lower opportunity cost than can Nation XYZ, it is said that Nation ABC has comparative advantage. An example can illustrate how this works between two states, but the same principle works between two nations.

> **Example:**
> Climate and topography have blessed Indiana with land extremely suitable for the cultivation of soybeans, but with very little harvestable timber. Oregon's timber production is unmatched, but farmers find it difficult to produce soybean crops that can compare to those grown in Indiana. Table 12.1 summarizes the production possibilities of these two isolated economies. Because Oregon can produce more timber than Indiana, Oregon is said to have an **absolute advantage** over Indiana in timber production. Indiana has an absolute advantage over Oregon in soybean production. Trade does not rely on absolute advantages, but on comparative advantages.

Table 12.1

INDIANA		OREGON	
Soybeans (tons)	Timber (tons)	Soybeans (tons)	Timber (tons)
0	6	0	10
9	3	5	5
18	0	10	0

Comparative Advantage and Specialization

In isolation, both states can produce soybeans and timber along their production possibility curves or frontiers (PPC or PPF), which are constrained by available technology and resources. Suppose that without trade, they enjoy consuming at the midpoint of the PPC. But if there are differences in production costs, they can each gain from specialization and trade. The opportunity costs of each good can be found from the table and can be illustrated in a production possibility curve for each state:

Oregon:
Opportunity cost of timber is 1 soybean.
Opportunity cost of soybeans is 1 timber.

Indiana:
Opportunity cost of timber is 3 soybeans.
Opportunity cost of soybeans is ⅓ timber.

Since Indiana can produce soybeans at a cost that is lower than Oregon's cost of soybeans, Indiana has a comparative advantage in soybeans. Oregon can produce timber at a lower cost than Indiana's cost of timber, so Oregon has a comparative advantage in timber production. With these differences in cost, Indiana should specialize in soybean production (zero timber), while Oregon should specialize in timber production (zero soybeans). Then the two should trade. These specialization points are labeled in Figure 12.1.

Figure 12.1

Gains from Trade

After each state specializes, suppose that each decides to keep half of its production and send the other half to the other state. See Figure 12.2.

Oregon:

Produce 10 timbers and send 5 to Indiana in exchange for 9 soybeans. Cost of a soybean before trade was 1 timber. Now we're getting 9 soybeans, but only giving up 5 timbers. The cost of giving up 1 timber is now is 5/9, which is less than 1 timber. Great deal!

Indiana:

Produce 18 soybeans, and send 9 to Oregon in exchange for 5 timbers. Cost of a timber before trade was 3 soybeans. Now we're getting 5 timbers and only giving up 9 soybeans. The cost now is 9/5, which is less than 3 soybeans. Great deal!

Another look at the production possibility curves after the trade shows that each state has actually moved *beyond* the constraints of their technology and resources.

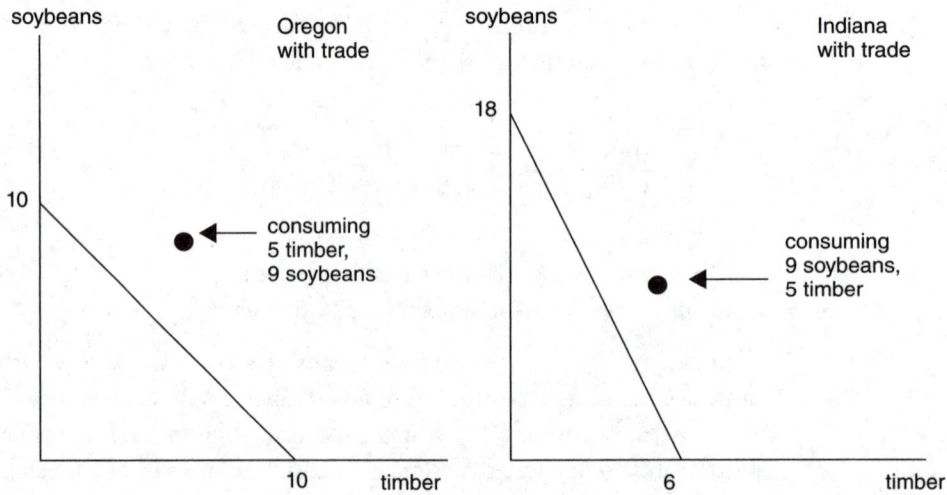

Figure 12.2

Consumption Frontier

There are many such trade possibilities. Figure 12.3 overlaps the two production possibility curves. The line that connects Indiana's specialization of soybeans to Oregon's specialization of timber is called the **consumption possibility frontier** because with trade, each state can consume along this line; without trade, these points are impossible to attain.

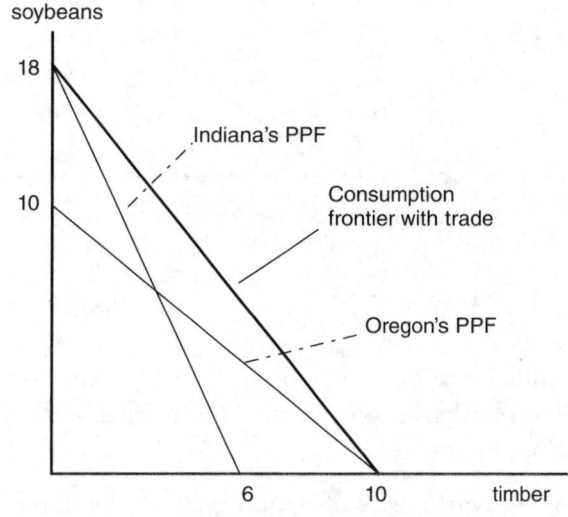

Figure 12.3

> "Make sure to draw your graphs BIG on the test so they're easier to read."
> —Sophia, AP Student

- If the opportunity costs of production are different, two economies find it mutually beneficial to specialize and trade.
- If you have comparative advantage in production of a good, specialize in production of that good and trade for the other.
- Specialization and trade allow nations to consume beyond the PPC.
- Free trade (i.e., without trade barriers) based on comparative advantage allows for a more efficient allocation of resources and greater prosperity for the trading partners than can be achieved without free trade.

Exports, Imports, and the World Price

In the market for a commodity like soybeans, many nations are both producers of soybeans and traders of soybeans. Whether or not a nation is a net exporter or a net importer of soybeans depends upon the difference between the **world price** with trade and the **domestic price** without trade.

Domestic Market Without Trade

Figure 12.4 illustrates the competitive U.S. market for soybeans without trade. The (admittedly hypothetical) competitive price of $10 per bushel is found at the intersection of domestic demand and supply. At this point six million bushels are produced.

World Market with Trade

If the United States begins to trade soybeans with other nations, the world price may rise above, or fall below, $10 per bushel. If the world price falls to $8, there exists a shortage of soybeans in the U.S. market. Domestic producers supply only four million bushels, but domestic consumers demand eight million bushels. The United States must then import

Figure 12.4

the difference of four million bushels. If the world price rises to $12, there exists a four-million bushel surplus in the U.S. market and the United States exports this surplus.

So, to reiterate:

- If the world price of a good is above the domestic price, the nation becomes an exporter of that good.
- If the world price of a good is below the domestic price, the nation becomes an importer of that good.

12.2 Balance of Payments

Main Topic: *Balance of Payments Accounts*

If Japanese citizens wish to purchase U.S. soybeans, the Japanese must pay in dollars. If U.S. citizens wish to buy Spanish olives, the Americans must pay in euros. Before goods can be exchanged between foreign trading partners, the currency of the importing nation must first be converted to the currency of the exporting nation.

Balance of Payments Accounts

When American citizens and firms exchange goods and services with foreign consumers and firms, payments are sent back and forth through major banks around the world. The Bureau of Economic Analysis tracks the flow of goods and currency in the **balance of payments statement**. This statement summarizes the payments received by the United States from foreign countries and the payments sent by the United States to foreign countries. Table 12.2 summarizes the main components of a hypothetical balance of trade for 2005.

Current Account

The current account shows current import and export payments of both goods and services. It also reflects investment income sent to foreign investors and investment income received by U.S. citizens who invest abroad. For example, if a Canadian is receiving dividends from an American corporation or interest from a U.S. Treasury bill, these dollars would be sent out of the country. After accounting for all of the payments sent to foreign countries and payments received from foreign countries, the balance on the current account in 2005 was –$26. A deficit balance such as this tells us that the United States sent more American dollars abroad than foreign currency received in current transactions.

Table 12.2

U.S. BALANCE OF PAYMENTS (HYPOTHETICAL)			
Current Account			
Goods exports	$30		
Goods imports	–$50		
Balance on goods (merchandise)		–$20	
Service exports	$18		
Service imports	–$12		
Balance on services		$6	
Balance on goods and service		–$14	Note: This negative balance indicates a trade deficit in goods and services.
Net investment income	–$5		
Net transfers	–$7		
Balance on current account		–$26	
Capital (or Financial) Account			
Inflow of foreign assets to U.S.	$35		
Outflow of U.S. assets abroad	–$20		
Balance on capital account		$15	
Official Reserves Account			
Official reserves		$11	
		$0	

Capital (or Financial) Account

When a nation buys a foreign firm, or real estate or financial assets of another nation, it appears in the capital account. For example, if a Swedish firm buys a manufacturing facility in Idaho, or if a Mexican citizen buys a U.S. Treasury bond, it is recorded as an inflow of foreign capital assets into the United States. If an American firm buys a ship-building company in Turkey, it would be an outflow of assets to foreign nations. A surplus balance of $11 tells us that there was more foreign capital investment in the United States than there was U.S. investment abroad.

Official Reserves Account

The Federal Reserve holds quantities of foreign currency called **official reserves**. When adding the current account and the capital account, if the United States has sent more dollars out than foreign currency has come in, as in the hypothetical example above, there exists a **balance of payments deficit**. In this case the Fed credits the account so that it balances. This is similar to taking money from your savings account to make up for an overdrafted checking account. If the current and capital account balances are positive, more foreign currency was coming into the United States than American dollars flowed abroad.

With this **balance of payments surplus**, the Fed transfers the surplus currency back into official reserves.

A Circular Flow of Dollars

With the exception of some statistical discrepancies, the U.S. dollars that Americans send to foreigners are equal to the U.S. dollars that foreigners send to Americans. It is helpful to think of the global circulation of dollars as another example of the circular-flow model. When you buy an imported jacket made in Honduras, this appears in the U.S. current account as a negative entry, because those dollars are leaving the country. However, what will a Honduran jacket producer do with those dollars? American dollars in Honduras are not very useful unless they are being spent on either American-made goods and services or American assets. One way or another, either through the purchase of an American good (like a Ford) or the purchase of an American financial asset (like a share of Ford stock), those dollars will return as a positive entry in either the current or capital account. And while the Federal Reserve will make short-term adjustments to the official reserves account to balance the difference between the current account balance and the capital account balance, in the long-term, dollars that leave the United States will eventually circle back into the United States. Thus, with all else equal, if Americans import more goods and services from abroad, the current account will move in the deficit direction but the capital/financial account will move in the surplus direction as those dollars return.

To summarize:

- U.S. imports require a demand for foreign currency and a supply of U.S. dollars.
- U.S. exports require a supply of foreign currency and a demand for U.S. dollars.
- If Current account balance + Capital account balance < 0, there is a balance of payments deficit.
- If Current account balance + Capital account balance > 0, there is a balance of payments surplus.

12.3 Foreign Exchange Rates

Main Topics: *Currency Markets, Appreciating and Depreciating Currency, Changes in Exchange Rates, Connection to Monetary Policy*

The previous section of the chapter discussed accounting for the flow of goods and services and currency between trading partners. The foreign exchange market, the topic of the following section, facilitates the importing and exporting of goods around the world.

Currency Markets

When nations trade goods and services, they are implicitly trading currency. The rate of exchange between two currencies is determined in the foreign currency market. Some nations fix their exchange rates, while others are allowed to "float" with the forces of demand and supply. For example, in the flexible exchange market for euros pictured in Figure 12.5, the equilibrium $2 dollar price of a euro is at the intersection of the supply of euros and the demand. Likewise, in the market for dollars seen in Figure 12.6, the equilibrium euro price of one dollar is .50 euros. This floating exchange rate has an impact on the balance of payments of both the United States and the European Union.

So:

- The **exchange rate** between two currencies tells you how much of one currency you must give up to get one unit of the second currency.
- For example, if $2 = 1 euro, $1 = .5 euro.
- For example, if $1 = 10 pesos, $.10 = 1 peso.

International Trade 167

Figure 12.5

Figure 12.6

 ## Appreciating and Depreciating Currency

If the U.S. economy is strong, Americans increase their demand for European goods and services. As American consumers increase their demand for the euro, they increase the supply of dollars in the foreign exchange market; the dollar price of a euro rises, and the euro price of a dollar falls. The euro as an asset is **appreciating** in value, and the dollar as an asset is **depreciating** in value. The changing value of euros and dollars is seen in Figures 12.7 and 12.8.

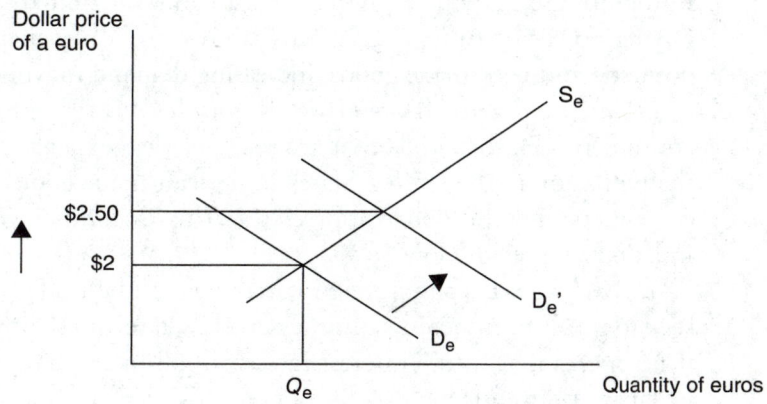

Figure 12.7

"Don't forget to label your axes." —Timot, AP Student

Figure 12.8

To summarize:

- When the price of a currency is rising, it is said to be appreciating, or "stronger." More dollars are needed to buy a euro.
- When the price of a currency is falling, it is said to be depreciating, or "weaker." Fewer euros are needed to buy a dollar.

It is *very* important to label the axes correctly in a FRQ that asks you to draw the market for a currency. If the market is for the dollar, the *x* axis should be labeled "Quantity of dollars." The label on the *y* axis depends on how the dollar is being priced. If we are pricing dollars in terms of the number of euros it takes to purchase $1, then the correct label is "Euros per dollar" or "Euro price of a dollar" or even "€/$." You will *not* earn a graphing point if you call it simply "Price," "P," or "$."

Changes in Exchange Rates

The preceding example illustrates that market forces and changing macroeconomic variables have an impact in the rate of exchange between the dollar and the euro. There are several determinants that affect currency appreciation and depreciation.

Consumer Tastes. When domestic consumers build a stronger preference for foreign-produced goods and services, the demand for those currencies increases and the dollar depreciates. On the other hand, if foreign consumers increase their demand for U.S.-made goods, the dollar appreciates.

Relative Incomes. When one nation's macroeconomy is strong and incomes are rising, all else equal, they increase their demand for all goods, including those produced abroad. So if Europeans are enjoying economic growth and the United States is in a recession, the relative buying power of European citizens is growing. They increase their consumption of both domestic and U.S.-made goods, increasing demand for the dollar and appreciating its value.

Relative Inflation. If one nation's price level is rising faster than that of another nation, consumers seek the goods that are relatively less expensive. If European inflation is higher than inflation in the United States, American-made goods are a relative bargain to German consumers and the dollar appreciates. This is another good reason for the Fed to keep inflationary pressure low.

Speculation. Because foreign currencies can be traded as assets, there are investors who seek to profit from buying currency at a low rate and selling it at a higher rate. For example, if it appears that future interest rates will fall in the United States relative to interest rates in Japan, the yen is looking like a good investment. Speculators would then increase their demand for Japanese assets, thus appreciating the yen and depreciating the dollar.

Connection to Monetary Policy

A final variable that affects the price of one currency relative to another is a difference in relative interest rates between nations. When the Fed increases the money supply, the interest rates on American financial assets begin to fall. If the interest rate is relatively lower in the United States, people around the world see U.S. financial assets as less attractive places to put their money. Demand for the dollar falls, and the dollar depreciates relative to other foreign currencies. A depreciating dollar makes goods in the United States less expensive to foreign consumers, so American net exports increase, which shifts the AD to the right.

Likewise, if the Fed decreases the money supply, American interest rates begin to rise and the dollar appreciates relative to foreign currencies. An appreciating dollar makes American goods more expensive to foreign consumers, decreasing American net exports, shifting AD to the left.

Be careful! When interest rates rise, we see a decrease in capital investments (machinery and other equipment) because it becomes more costly to borrow for those projects. But when interest rates rise, we see an increase in financial investments (bonds) because income earned on those bonds is rising.

Again:

- If the Fed ↑ MS, ↓i%, ↓D$, Depreciates the $, ↑ U.S. Net Exports, ↑ AD.
- If the Fed ↓ MS, ↑i%, ↑D$, Appreciates the $, ↓ U.S. Net Exports, ↓ AD.

Pay attention to the relationship between relative interest rates and exchange rates because it has made an appearance on several recent AP Macroeconomics exams.

All else equal, demand for the U.S. dollar increases and the dollar appreciates relative to the euro if:

- European taste for American-made goods is stronger.
- European relative incomes are rising, increasing demand for U.S. goods.
- The U.S. relative price level is falling, making U.S. goods relatively less expensive.
- Speculators are betting on the dollar to rise in value.
- The U.S. relative interest rate is higher, making the United States a relatively more attractive place for financial investments (i.e., bonds).

12.4 Trade Barriers

Main Topics: *Tariffs, Quotas*

The issue of free trade is hotly politicized. Proponents usually argue that free trade raises the standard of living in **both nations**, and most economists agree. Detractors argue that free trade, especially with nations that pay lower wages than those paid to domestic workers, costs domestic jobs in higher-wage nations. The evidence shows that in some industries, job losses have certainly occurred as free trade has become more prevalent. To protect domestic jobs, nations can impose trade barriers. Tariffs and quotas are among the most common of barriers.

Tariffs

In general, there are two types of tariffs. A **revenue tariff** is an excise tax levied on goods that are not produced in the domestic market. For example, the United States does not produce bananas. If a revenue tariff were levied on bananas, it would not be a serious impediment to trade, and it would raise a little revenue for the government. A **protective tariff** is an excise tax levied on a good that is produced in the domestic market. Though this tariff also raises revenue, the purpose of this tariff, as the name suggests, is to protect the domestic industry from global competition by increasing the price of foreign products.

Example:

The domestic supply and demand for steel is pictured in Figure 12.9. The domestic price is $100 per ton and the equilibrium quantity of domestic steel is 10 million tons. Maybe other nations can produce steel at lower cost. As a result, in the competitive world market, the price is $80 per ton. At that price, the United States would demand 12 million tons, but only produce eight million tons and so four million tons are **imported**. It is important to see that in the competitive (free trade) world market, consumer surplus is maximized and no deadweight loss exists. You can see the consumer surplus as the triangle below the demand curve and above the $80 world price.

If the steel industry is successful in getting a protective tariff passed through Congress, the world price rises by $10, increasing the quantity of domestic steel supplied, reducing the amount of steel imported from four million to two million tons. A higher price and lower consumption reduces the area of consumer surplus and creates deadweight loss.

Economic Effects of the Tariff

- *Consumers pay higher prices and consume less steel.* If you are building airplanes or door hinges, you have seen an increase in your costs.
- *Consumer surplus has been lost.*
- *Domestic producers increase output.* Domestic steel firms are not subject to the tariff, so they can sell more steel at the price of $90 than they could at $80.
- *Declining imports.* Fewer tons of imported steel arrive in the United States.
- *Tariff revenue.* The government collects $10 × 2 million = $20 million in tariff revenue, as seen in the shaded box in Figure 12.10 This is a transfer from consumers of steel to the government, not an increase in the total well-being of the nation.
- *Inefficiency.* There was a reason the world price was lower than the domestic price. It was more efficient to produce steel abroad and export it to the United States. By taxing this efficiency, the United States promotes the inefficient domestic industry and stunts the efficient foreign sector. As a result, resources are diverted from the efficient to the inefficient sector.
- *Deadweight loss now exists.*

Figure 12.9

Figure 12.10

Quotas

Quotas work in much the same way as a tariff. An **import quota** is a maximum amount of a good that can be imported into the domestic market. With a quota, the government only allows two million tons to be imported. Figure 12.11 looks much like Figure 12.10, only without revenue collected by government. So the impact of the quota, with the exception of the revenue, is the same: higher consumer price and inefficient resource allocation.

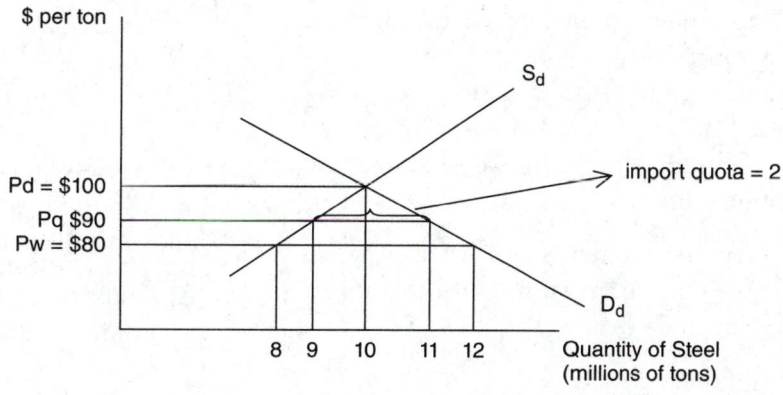

Figure 12.11

> "It is important to know the differences between tariffs and quotas."
> —Lucas, AP Student

Tariffs and quotas share many of the same economic effects.

- Both hurt consumers with artificially high prices and lower consumer surplus.
- Both protect inefficient domestic producers at the expense of efficient foreign firms, creating deadweight loss.
- Both reallocate economic resources toward inefficient producers.
- Tariffs collect revenue for the government, while quotas do not.

Review Questions

1. The United States produces rice in a competitive market. With free trade, the world price is lower than the domestic price. What must be true?

   (A) The United States begins to import rice to make up for a domestic shortage.
   (B) The United States begins to export rice to make up for a domestic shortage.
   (C) The United States begins to import rice to eliminate a domestic surplus.
   (D) The United States begins to export rice to eliminate a domestic surplus.
   (E) There is no incentive to import or export rice.

2. If the U.S. dollar and Chinese yuan are traded in flexible currency markets, which of the following causes an appreciation of the dollar relative to the Chinese yuan?

   (A) Lower interest rates in the United States relative to China
   (B) Lower price levels in China relative to the United States
   (C) Growing American preference to consume more Chinese-made goods
   (D) Rising per capita GDP in China, increasing imports from the United States
   (E) Speculation that the Chinese will decrease the money supply

3. You hear that the United States has a negative balance in the current account. With this information we conclude that

   (A) there is a trade deficit.
   (B) there is a capital account deficit.
   (C) there is a capital account surplus.
   (D) more U.S. dollars are being sent abroad than foreign currencies are being sent to the United States.
   (E) there is a trade surplus.

4. Which of the following is a consequence of a protective tariff on imported steel?

   (A) Net exports fall.
   (B) Income is transferred from domestic steel consumers to domestic steel producers.
   (C) Allocative efficiency is improved.
   (D) Income is transferred from domestic steel to foreign steel producers.
   (E) Aggregate supply increases.

5. If the Japanese economy suffers a deep, prolonged recession, in what ways would U.S. net exports and the values of the dollar and yen change?

	U.S. NET EXPORTS	VALUE OF DOLLAR	VALUE OF YEN
(A)	Decrease	Increase	Increase
(B)	Decrease	Decrease	Decrease
(C)	Decrease	Decrease	Increase
(D)	Increase	Decrease	Increase
(E)	Increase	Increase	Increase

6. When the United States places an import quota on imported sugar, we expect which of the following effects?

   (A) Consumers seek substitutes for sugar and products that use sugar.
   (B) Consumers consume more sugar and products that use sugar.
   (C) The supply of sugar increases.
   (D) Net exports in the United States fall.
   (E) The government collects revenue on every ton of imported sugar.

Answers and Explanations

1. **A**—If the world price is below the domestic price, a shortage exists in the domestic market. The importation of foreign rice fills this shortage.

2. **D**—Higher per capita income in trading nations increases demand for imported goods. The Chinese consumer increases demand for U.S. goods and services and for dollars.

3. **C**—When there is a negative balance in the current account, this does not always mean that there is a trade deficit. After all, there is more to the current account than the trade of goods and services. However, when there is a negative balance in the current account, there must be a positive balance (or surplus) in the capital account.

4. **B**—Protective tariffs increase the price of steel above the free-trade equilibrium. This higher price is a transfer of money from consumers to domestic producers of steel.

5. **C**—When the Japanese economy is suffering, demand for U.S. goods falls, decreasing U.S. net exports and demand for dollars. The dollar depreciates and the yen appreciates.

6. **A**—A quota increases the price of sugar so consumers seek substitutes. We may see rising demand for sugar-free gum or falling demand for rich desserts.

Rapid Review

Domestic price: The equilibrium price of a good in a nation without trade.

World price: The global equilibrium price of a good when nations engage in trade.

Balance of payments statement: A summary of the payments received by the United States from foreign countries and the payments sent by the United States to foreign countries.

Current account: This account shows current import and export payments of both goods and services and investment income sent to foreign investors of United States and investment income received by U.S. citizens who invest abroad.

Capital (or financial) account: This account shows the flow of investment on real or financial assets between a nation and foreigners.

Official reserves account: The Fed's adjustment of a deficit or surplus in the current and capital account by the addition or subtraction of foreign currencies so that the balance of payments is zero.

Exchange rate: The price of one currency in terms of a second currency.

Appreciating (depreciating) currency: When the value of a currency is rising (falling) relative to another currency, it is said to be appreciating (depreciating).

Determinants of exchange rates: External factors that increase the price of one currency relative to another.

Revenue tariff: An excise tax levied on goods not produced in the domestic market.

Protective tariff: An excise tax levied on a good that is produced in the domestic market so that it may be protected from foreign competition.

Import quota: A limitation on the amount of a good that can be imported into the domestic market.

Build Your Test-Taking Confidence

AP Macroeconomics Practice Exam 1
AP Macroeconomics Practice Exam 2

AP Macroeconomics Practice Exam 1
Section I: Multiple-Choice Questions

ANSWER SHEET

1. Ⓐ Ⓑ Ⓒ Ⓓ Ⓔ
2. Ⓐ Ⓑ Ⓒ Ⓓ Ⓔ
3. Ⓐ Ⓑ Ⓒ Ⓓ Ⓔ
4. Ⓐ Ⓑ Ⓒ Ⓓ Ⓔ
5. Ⓐ Ⓑ Ⓒ Ⓓ Ⓔ
6. Ⓐ Ⓑ Ⓒ Ⓓ Ⓔ
7. Ⓐ Ⓑ Ⓒ Ⓓ Ⓔ
8. Ⓐ Ⓑ Ⓒ Ⓓ Ⓔ
9. Ⓐ Ⓑ Ⓒ Ⓓ Ⓔ
10. Ⓐ Ⓑ Ⓒ Ⓓ Ⓔ
11. Ⓐ Ⓑ Ⓒ Ⓓ Ⓔ
12. Ⓐ Ⓑ Ⓒ Ⓓ Ⓔ
13. Ⓐ Ⓑ Ⓒ Ⓓ Ⓔ
14. Ⓐ Ⓑ Ⓒ Ⓓ Ⓔ
15. Ⓐ Ⓑ Ⓒ Ⓓ Ⓔ
16. Ⓐ Ⓑ Ⓒ Ⓓ Ⓔ
17. Ⓐ Ⓑ Ⓒ Ⓓ Ⓔ
18. Ⓐ Ⓑ Ⓒ Ⓓ Ⓔ
19. Ⓐ Ⓑ Ⓒ Ⓓ Ⓔ
20. Ⓐ Ⓑ Ⓒ Ⓓ Ⓔ
21. Ⓐ Ⓑ Ⓒ Ⓓ Ⓔ
22. Ⓐ Ⓑ Ⓒ Ⓓ Ⓔ
23. Ⓐ Ⓑ Ⓒ Ⓓ Ⓔ
24. Ⓐ Ⓑ Ⓒ Ⓓ Ⓔ
25. Ⓐ Ⓑ Ⓒ Ⓓ Ⓔ
26. Ⓐ Ⓑ Ⓒ Ⓓ Ⓔ
27. Ⓐ Ⓑ Ⓒ Ⓓ Ⓔ
28. Ⓐ Ⓑ Ⓒ Ⓓ Ⓔ
29. Ⓐ Ⓑ Ⓒ Ⓓ Ⓔ
30. Ⓐ Ⓑ Ⓒ Ⓓ Ⓔ
31. Ⓐ Ⓑ Ⓒ Ⓓ Ⓔ
32. Ⓐ Ⓑ Ⓒ Ⓓ Ⓔ
33. Ⓐ Ⓑ Ⓒ Ⓓ Ⓔ
34. Ⓐ Ⓑ Ⓒ Ⓓ Ⓔ
35. Ⓐ Ⓑ Ⓒ Ⓓ Ⓔ
36. Ⓐ Ⓑ Ⓒ Ⓓ Ⓔ
37. Ⓐ Ⓑ Ⓒ Ⓓ Ⓔ
38. Ⓐ Ⓑ Ⓒ Ⓓ Ⓔ
39. Ⓐ Ⓑ Ⓒ Ⓓ Ⓔ
40. Ⓐ Ⓑ Ⓒ Ⓓ Ⓔ
41. Ⓐ Ⓑ Ⓒ Ⓓ Ⓔ
42. Ⓐ Ⓑ Ⓒ Ⓓ Ⓔ
43. Ⓐ Ⓑ Ⓒ Ⓓ Ⓔ
44. Ⓐ Ⓑ Ⓒ Ⓓ Ⓔ
45. Ⓐ Ⓑ Ⓒ Ⓓ Ⓔ
46. Ⓐ Ⓑ Ⓒ Ⓓ Ⓔ
47. Ⓐ Ⓑ Ⓒ Ⓓ Ⓔ
48. Ⓐ Ⓑ Ⓒ Ⓓ Ⓔ
49. Ⓐ Ⓑ Ⓒ Ⓓ Ⓔ
50. Ⓐ Ⓑ Ⓒ Ⓓ Ⓔ
51. Ⓐ Ⓑ Ⓒ Ⓓ Ⓔ
52. Ⓐ Ⓑ Ⓒ Ⓓ Ⓔ
53. Ⓐ Ⓑ Ⓒ Ⓓ Ⓔ
54. Ⓐ Ⓑ Ⓒ Ⓓ Ⓔ
55. Ⓐ Ⓑ Ⓒ Ⓓ Ⓔ
56. Ⓐ Ⓑ Ⓒ Ⓓ Ⓔ
57. Ⓐ Ⓑ Ⓒ Ⓓ Ⓔ
58. Ⓐ Ⓑ Ⓒ Ⓓ Ⓔ
59. Ⓐ Ⓑ Ⓒ Ⓓ Ⓔ
60. Ⓐ Ⓑ Ⓒ Ⓓ Ⓔ

AP Macroeconomics Practice Exam 1, Section I

Multiple-Choice Questions

Time—1 hour and 10 minutes

60 questions

For the multiple-choice questions that follow, select the best answer and fill in the appropriate letter on the answer sheet.

1. Which of the following statements is true of production possibility curves and trade between nations?

    (A) Nations specialize and trade based on absolute advantage in production.
    (B) Free trade allows each nation to consume beyond the production possibility curve.
    (C) The flow of goods and services is based on the principle of absolute advantage.
    (D) Nations can consume at points beyond the production possibility curve by protecting domestic industries from free trade.
    (E) Tariffs and quotas divert resources from the inefficient producers of a good to the efficient producers of that good

2. A nation is producing at a point inside of its production possibility curve. Which of the following is a possible explanation for this outcome?

    (A) This nation has experienced a permanent decrease in its production capacity.
    (B) This nation has experienced slower than usual technological progress.
    (C) This nation has avoided free trade between other nations.
    (D) This nation is experiencing an economic recession.
    (E) This nation's economy is centrally planned.

3. How would fiscal and monetary policymakers combine spending, tax, and monetary policy to fight a recessionary gap, while avoiding large budget deficits?

	SPENDING POLICY	TAX POLICY	MONETARY POLICY
(A)	Higher spending	Lower taxes	Sell Treasury securities
(B)	Lower spending	Higher taxes	Buy Treasury securities
(C)	Lower spending	Lower taxes	Increasing the reserve ratio
(D)	Higher spending	Higher taxes	Lowering the discount rate
(E)	Higher spending	Higher taxes	Sell Treasury securities

4. Corn is exchanged in a competitive market. Which of the following definitely increases the equilibrium price of corn?

    (A) Both supply and demand shift rightward.
    (B) Both supply and demand shift leftward.
    (C) Supply shifts to the right; demand shifts to the left.
    (D) Supply shifts to the left; demand shifts to the right.
    (E) The government imposes an effective price ceiling in the corn market.

5. An increase in the consumer price index is commonly referred to as

    (A) economic growth.
    (B) inflation.
    (C) unemployment.
    (D) discouraged workers.
    (E) deflation.

6. Which of the following is characteristic of a centrally planned economic system?

    (A) Resources are allocated based on relative prices.
    (B) The circular flow of goods and services minimizes the role of the federal government.
    (C) Private ownership of resources is fundamental to economic growth.
    (D) Government planners decide how best to produce goods and services.
    (E) Efficiency is superior to the market economic system.

7. The government has just lowered personal income taxes. Which of the following best describes the effects that this policy has on the economy?

    (A) Higher disposable income, higher consumption, higher real GDP, lower unemployment
    (B) Higher disposable income, lower consumption, higher real GDP, lower unemployment
    (C) Lower disposable income, higher consumption, higher real GDP, lower unemployment
    (D) Lower disposable income, lower consumption, lower real GDP, higher unemployment
    (E) Higher disposable income, higher consumption, higher real GDP, higher unemployment

8. Which of the following are harmed by unexpectedly high rates of inflation?

    (A) Borrowers repaying a long-term loan at a fixed interest rate.
    (B) Savers who have put their money in long-term assets that pay a fixed interest rate.
    (C) Workers who have negotiated cost-of-living raises into their contracts.
    (D) Renters of apartments who have signed a lease that holds rent constant for two years.
    (E) Employers paying workers the minimum wage.

9. Which of the following statements is true?

    (A) The velocity of money is equal to real GDP divided by the money supply.
    (B) Dollars earned today have more purchasing power than dollars earned a year from today.
    (C) The supply of loanable funds consists of investors.
    (D) The demand for loanable funds consists of savers.
    (E) Expansionary fiscal policy shifts the money supply curve to the right, lowering interest rates.

10. If your nominal income rises 4 percent and your real income falls 1 percent, by how much did the price level change?

    (A) 5 percent decrease
    (B) ¼ percent increase
    (C) 3 percent increase
    (D) 3 percent decrease
    (E) 5 percent increase

11. Which of the following best measures changes in the price level of national product?

    (A) The consumer price index
    (B) The real interest rate
    (C) The unemployment rate
    (D) The producer price index
    (E) The GDP deflator

12. Which of the following lessens the impact of expansionary fiscal policy?

    (A) An increase in the marginal propensity to consume.
    (B) Lower interest rates that cause a decrease in net exports.
    (C) Higher interest rates that cause an increase in net exports.
    (D) Higher interest rates that decrease private investment.
    (E) Falling price levels.

13. Suppose that the unemployment rate falls from 6 percent to 5 percent and the inflation rate falls from 3 percent to 2 percent. Which of the following best explains these trends?

    (A) An increase in aggregate demand.
    (B) A decrease in both aggregate demand and aggregate supply.
    (C) An increase in both aggregate demand and aggregate supply.
    (D) An increase in aggregate supply.
    (E) An increase in aggregate demand and a decrease in aggregate supply.

14. A nation's economic growth can be seen as a(n)

    (A) increase in the SRAS curve.
    (B) increase in the AD curve.
    (C) increase in the LRAS curve.
    (D) decrease in the production possibility curve.
    (E) increase in the short-run Phillips curve.

15. Some economists believe that when aggregate demand declines, prices are inflexible or "sticky" in the downward direction. This implies that the short-run aggregate supply curve is

    (A) upward sloping at full employment.
    (B) horizontal below full employment.
    (C) vertical at full employment.
    (D) vertical below full employment.
    (E) vertical above full employment.

16. Which of the following policies best describes supply-side fiscal policy?

    (A) An increase in the money supply
    (B) Increased government spending
    (C) Lower taxes on research and development of new technology
    (D) Higher taxes on household income
    (E) More extensive government social welfare programs

17. A likely cause of falling Treasury bond prices might be

    (A) expansionary monetary policy.
    (B) contractionary monetary policy.
    (C) a depreciating dollar.
    (D) fiscal policy designed to reduce the budget deficit.
    (E) a decrease in the money demand.

18. The economy is currently operating at full employment. Assuming flexible wages and prices, how would a decline in aggregate demand affect GDP and the price level in the short run, and GDP and the price level in the long run?

	SHORT-RUN GDP	SHORT-RUN PRICE LEVEL	LONG-RUN GDP	LONG-RUN PRICE LEVEL
(A)	Falls	Falls	No change	Falls
(B)	Falls	Falls	Falls	Falls
(C)	No change	Falls	No change	No change
(D)	Falls	Falls	No change	No change
(E)	Falls	Falls	Falls	Falls

19. In the long run, aggregate supply is

    (A) upward sloping at full employment.
    (B) horizontal below full employment.
    (C) vertical at full employment.
    (D) vertical below full employment.
    (E) vertical above full employment.

20. What does the presence of discouraged workers do to the measurement of the unemployment rate?

    (A) Discouraged workers are counted as "out of the labor force," thus the unemployment rate is understated, making the economy look stronger than it is.
    (B) Discouraged workers are counted as "out of the labor force," thus the unemployment rate is understated, making the economy look weaker than it is.
    (C) Discouraged workers are not surveyed, so there is no impact on the unemployment rate.
    (D) Discouraged workers are counted as "unemployed," thus the unemployment rate is understated, making the economy look stronger than it is.
    (E) Discouraged workers are counted as "unemployed," thus the unemployment rate is overstated, making the economy look weaker than it is.

21. Which of the following is true of the complete circular flow model of an open economy?

    (A) All goods and services flow through the government in exchange for resource payments.
    (B) There is no role for the foreign sector.
    (C) Households supply resources to producers in exchange for goods and services.
    (D) Producers provide goods and services to households in exchange for the costs of production.
    (E) The government collects taxes from firms and households in exchange for goods and services.

22. Which of the following most likely increases aggregate demand in the United States?

    (A) An American entrepreneur founds and locates a software company in London.
    (B) The U.S. military closes a military base in California.
    (C) The Chinese government makes it increasingly difficult for American firms to export goods to China.
    (D) A Mexican entrepreneur founds and locates a software company in St. Louis.
    (E) The Canadian government cancels an order for airliners from a firm located in Seattle.

23. When both short-run aggregate supply and aggregate demand increase, which of the following can be said for certain?

    (A) The price level rises, but real GDP falls.
    (B) Both the price level and real GDP rise.
    (C) The price level rises, but the change in real GDP is uncertain.
    (D) The price level falls, but real GDP rises.
    (E) Real GDP rises, but the change in the price level is uncertain.

24. When nominal GDP is rising, we would expect money demand to

    (A) increase as consumers demand more money as a financial asset, increasing the interest rate.
    (B) increase as consumers demand more money for transactions, increasing the interest rate.
    (C) decrease as the purchasing power of the dollar is falling, decreasing the interest rate.
    (D) decrease as consumers demand more money for transactions, increasing the interest rate.
    (E) increase as consumers demand more money as a financial asset, decreasing the interest rate.

25. Which of the following tends to increase the spending multiplier?

    (A) An increase in the marginal propensity to consume
    (B) A decreased velocity of money
    (C) An increase in the marginal propensity to save
    (D) An increase in the real interest rate
    (E) An increase in the price level

26. Households demand more money as an asset when

    (A) nominal GDP falls.
    (B) the nominal interest rate falls.
    (C) bond prices fall.
    (D) the supply of money falls.
    (E) nominal GDP increases.

27. Which of the following represents a combination of contractionary fiscal and expansionary monetary policy?

	FISCAL POLICY	MONETARY POLICY
(A)	Higher taxes	Selling Treasury securities
(B)	Lower taxes	Buying Treasury securities
(C)	Lower government spending	Increasing the reserve ratio
(D)	Lower government spending	Increasing the discount rate
(E)	Higher taxes	Buying Treasury securities

28. Higher levels of consumer wealth and optimism would likely have which of the following changes in the market for loanable funds?

	MARKET FOR LOANABLE FUNDS	INTEREST RATE
(A)	Increase in supply	Rising
(B)	Increase in demand	Rising
(C)	Decrease in demand	Falling
(D)	Decrease in supply	Falling
(E)	Decrease in supply	Rising

29. Investment demand most likely increases when
    (A) real GDP decreases.
    (B) the cost of acquiring and maintaining capital equipment rises.
    (C) investor optimism improves.
    (D) the real rate of interest rises.
    (E) taxes on business investment rise.

30. At the peak of a typical business cycle, which of the following is likely the greatest threat to the macroeconomy?
    (A) Unemployment
    (B) Bankruptcy
    (C) Declining labor productivity
    (D) Falling real household income
    (E) Inflation

31. Suppose that households increase the demand for U.S. Treasury bonds as financial assets. Which of the following accurately describes changes in the money market, the interest rate, and the value of the dollar in foreign currency markets?

	MONEY MARKET	INTEREST RATE	DOLLAR
(A)	Increased supply	Rising	Appreciates
(B)	Increased demand	Rising	Appreciates
(C)	Decreased demand	Falling	Appreciates
(D)	Decreased supply	Falling	Depreciates
(E)	Decreased demand	Falling	Depreciates

32. If households are more optimistic about the future, how would the consumption function be affected?
    (A) The marginal propensity to consume would increase, increasing the slope of the consumption function.
    (B) The entire consumption function would shift downward.
    (C) The entire consumption function would shift upward.
    (D) The marginal propensity to consume would decrease, increasing the slope of the consumption function.
    (E) The marginal propensity to consume would increase, decreasing the slope of the consumption function.

33. U.S. real GDP most likely falls when
    (A) tariffs and quotas are removed.
    (B) investment in human capital is high.
    (C) the money supply is increased.
    (D) there is a trade surplus in goods and services.
    (E) the value of the dollar, relative to foreign currencies, is high.

34. If current real GDP is $5,000 and full employment real GDP is at $4,000, which of the following combinations of policies is the most likely to have brought the economy to this point?
    (A) A decrease in taxes and a lower discount rate
    (B) An increase in government spending and an increase in taxes
    (C) A decrease in taxes and selling bonds in an open market operation
    (D) An increase in government spending and an increase in the discount rate
    (E) A decrease in taxes and a decrease in government spending

35. If a nation is operating at full employment, and the central bank engages in contractionary monetary policy, the nation can expect the interest rate, the purchases of new homes, and the unemployment rate to change in which of the following ways?

	INTEREST RATES	NEW HOMES	UNEMPLOYMENT RATE
(A)	Decrease	Increase	Increase
(B)	Decrease	Decrease	Decrease
(C)	Increase	Decrease	Decrease
(D)	Increase	Decrease	Increase
(E)	Increase	Increase	Increase

36. Expansionary monetary policy is designed to

    (A) decrease the interest rate, increase private investment, increase aggregate demand, and increase domestic output.
    (B) decrease the interest rate, increase private investment, increase aggregate demand, and increase the unemployment rate.
    (C) increase the interest rate, increase private investment, increase aggregate demand, and increase domestic output.
    (D) increase the interest rate, decrease private investment, increase aggregate demand, and increase domestic output.
    (E) increase the interest rate, decrease private investment, decrease aggregate demand, and decrease the price level.

37. If the economy is operating at full employment, which of the following policies will create the most inflation in the short run?

    (A) An increase in government spending matched by an equal increase in taxes
    (B) An increase in government spending with no change in taxes
    (C) A decrease in government spending and a matching increase in taxes
    (D) A decrease in taxes with no change in government spending
    (E) A decrease in government spending matched by an equal decrease in taxes

38. Which of the following is a component of the $M1$ measure of money supply?

    (A) Savings deposits
    (B) Gold bullion
    (C) Cash and coins
    (D) 30-year Treasury certificates
    (E) 18-month certificates of deposits

39. Assuming that households save a proportion of disposable income, which of the following relationships between multipliers is correct?

    (A) Tax multiplier > Spending multiplier > Balanced budget multiplier
    (B) Spending multiplier = Tax multiplier > Balanced budget multiplier
    (C) Spending multiplier > Tax multiplier = Balanced budget multiplier
    (D) Spending multiplier > Tax multiplier > Balanced budget multiplier
    (E) Tax multiplier > Spending multiplier = Balanced budget multiplier

40. The fractional reserve banking system's ability to create money is lessened if

    (A) households that borrow redeposit the entire loan amounts back into the banks.
    (B) banks hold excess reserves.
    (C) banks lend all excess reserves to borrowing customers.
    (D) households increase checking deposits in banks.
    (E) the Federal Reserve lowers the reserve ratio.

41. All else equal, when the United States exports more goods and services,

    (A) the value of the dollar falls as the supply of dollars increases.
    (B) the value of the dollar rises as demand for dollars increases.
    (C) the value of the dollar falls as demand for dollars decreases.
    (D) the value of the dollar rises as the supply of dollars increases.
    (E) the value of the dollar falls as demand for dollars increases.

42. If the reserve ratio is 10 percent and a new customer deposits $500, what is the maximum amount of money created?

    (A) $500
    (B) $4,500
    (C) $5,000
    (D) $50
    (E) $5,500

43. Suppose today's headline is that private investment has decreased as a result of an action by the Federal Reserve. Which of the following choices is the most likely cause?

    (A) Selling Treasury securities to commercial banks
    (B) Lowering of the discount rate
    (C) Decreasing the reserve ratio
    (D) Elimination of a corporate tax credit on investment
    (E) A stronger stock market has increased investor optimism

44. If $1,000 is deposited into a checking account and excess reserves increase by $700, the reserve ratio must be:

    (A) 70%.
    (B) 30%.
    (C) 40%.
    (D) 90%.
    (E) 75%.

45. Suppose a nation is experiencing an annual budget surplus and uses some of this surplus to pay down part of the national debt. One potential side effect of this policy would be

    (A) increase interest rates and throw the economy into a recession.
    (B) increase interest rates and depreciate the nation's currency.
    (C) decrease interest rates and risk an inflationary period.
    (D) decrease interest rates and throw the economy into a recession.
    (E) decrease interest rates and appreciate the nation's currency.

46. Which of the following best describes a key difference between the short-run and long-run aggregate supply curve?

    (A) Short-run aggregate supply is upward sloping as nominal wages quickly respond to price level changes.
    (B) Long-run aggregate supply is upward sloping as nominal wages quickly respond to price level changes.
    (C) Short-run aggregate supply is vertical as nominal wages quickly respond to price level changes.
    (D) Short-run aggregate supply is upward sloping as nominal wages do not quickly respond to price level changes.
    (E) Long-run aggregate supply is vertical as nominal wages do not quickly respond to price level changes.

47. The "crowding-out" effect refers to which of the following?

    (A) Lower interest rates that result from borrowing to conduct expansionary monetary policy
    (B) Higher interest rates that result from borrowing to conduct contractionary fiscal policy
    (C) Higher interest rates that result from borrowing to conduct expansionary fiscal policy
    (D) Higher interest rates due to borrowing to conduct contractionary monetary policy
    (E) Lower interest rates due to borrowing to conduct expansionary fiscal policy

48. Which of the following is a predictable consequence of import quotas?

    (A) Increased competition and lower consumer prices
    (B) Increased government tax revenue from imported goods
    (C) Rising net exports and a rightward shift in aggregate supply
    (D) An improved allocation of resources away from inefficient producers and lower consumer prices
    (E) Higher consumer prices and a misallocation of resources away from efficient producers

49. If the Federal Reserve was concerned about the "crowding-out" effect, they could engage in

    (A) expansionary monetary policy by lowering the discount rate.
    (B) expansionary monetary policy by selling Treasury securities.
    (C) contractionary monetary policy by raising the discount rate.
    (D) contractionary monetary policy by lowering the discount rate.
    (E) expansionary monetary policy by raising the reserve ratio.

50. Which of the following would likely contribute to faster rates of economic growth?

    (A) A more restrictive immigration policy
    (B) Negative net investment
    (C) Higher taxes on households and firms
    (D) Higher government funding of research on clean energy supplies
    (E) Protective trade policies

51. A nation that must consistently borrow to cover annual budget deficits risks

    (A) a depreciation of the nation's currency as foreigners increase investment in the nation.
    (B) a decline in net exports as the nation's goods become more expensive to foreign consumers.
    (C) lower interest rates that discourage foreign investment in the nation.
    (D) an appreciation of the nation's currency as foreigners decrease investment in the nation.
    (E) lower interest rates that reduce private investment in productive capital.

52. Economic growth is best described as

    (A) an increase in the production possibility curve and an increase in the natural rate of unemployment.
    (B) an increase in the production possibility curve and a leftward shift in long-run aggregate supply.
    (C) a decrease in the production possibility curve and a rightward shift in long-run aggregate supply.
    (D) a decrease in the production possibility curve and a leftward shift in long-run aggregate supply.
    (E) an increase in the production possibility curve and a rightward shift in long-run aggregate supply.

53. Which of the following is true of automatic fiscal policy stabilizers?

    (A) For a given level of government spending, they produce a deficit during a recession and a surplus during an expansion.
    (B) They serve to prolong recessionary and inflationary periods.
    (C) The regressive tax system is a fundamental component of automatic stabilizers.
    (D) For a given level of government spending, they produce a surplus during a recession and a surplus during an expansion.
    (E) They lengthen the business cycle.

54. Which of the following is an example of expansionary monetary policy for the Federal Reserve?

    (A) Increasing the discount rate
    (B) Increasing the reserve ratio
    (C) Buying Treasury securities from commercial banks
    (D) Lowering income taxes
    (E) Removal of import quotas

55. Labor productivity and economic growth increase if

    (A) a nation subsidizes education for all citizens.
    (B) a nation imposes tariffs and quotas on imported goods.
    (C) a nation removes penalties for firms that pollute natural resources.
    (D) a nation ignores societal barriers like discrimination.
    (E) a nation taxes income from interest on saving.

56. The short-run Phillips curve depicts the ____ relationship between ____ and ____.

    (A) positive, price level, interest rate
    (B) negative, interest rate, private investment
    (C) negative, the inflation rate, the unemployment rate
    (D) positive, price level, real GDP
    (E) negative, interest rate, money demand

57. A negative, or contractionary, supply shock will

    (A) shift the Phillips curve to the left.
    (B) shift the investment demand curve to the right.
    (C) shift the money demand curve to the right.
    (D) shift the money supply curve to the left.
    (E) shift the Phillips curve to the right.

58. When a nation is operating at the natural rate of unemployment,

    (A) there is no cyclical unemployment.
    (B) the inflation rate is zero.
    (C) there is no structural unemployment.
    (D) the nation is experiencing a recession.
    (E) the unemployment rate is zero.

59. Which of the following likely results in a permanent increase in a nation's productive capacity?

    (A) A decline in the birth rate
    (B) Declining adult literacy rates
    (C) Widespread relocation of manufacturing firms to low-wage nations
    (D) National program of child immunization
    (E) A global increase in the price of crude oil

60. Lower interest rates in the United States cause the value of the dollar and exports to change in which of the following ways?

	VALUE OF THE DOLLAR	U.S. EXPORTS
(A)	Increasing	Increasing
(B)	Increasing	Decreasing
(C)	Decreasing	Increasing
(D)	Decreasing	Unchanged
(E)	Increasing	Increasing

Answers and Explanations

1. **B**—The gains from free trade are based on the principles of comparative, not absolute, advantage and specialization. Free trade allows nations to consume at points beyond their own PPC. In this way, free trade improves the economic well-being of trading nations. Tariffs inhibit the flow of free trade and promote inefficiency.

2. **D**—Points within the PPC imply unemployed resources, and this is indicative of a recession.

3. **D**—Balanced budget fiscal policy to eliminate a recession could increase spending and pay for that spending with higher taxes. Coordination of monetary policy requires some expansion of the money supply.

4. **D**—Combining a leftward supply shift with a rightward demand shift unambiguously raises the price.

5. **B**—Computing the change in the CPI is the most common way to measure price inflation.

6. **D**—A centrally planned economy decides which goods are needed and how best to provide them to the population. Resources are allocated and goods are distributed by the government, not the price system.

7. **A**—Lower taxes increase disposable income. Consumers spend most of this disposable income, which increases real GDP and lowers the unemployment rate.

8. **C**—Savers receive interest payments in "cheap" dollars and lose the purchasing power of their interest income due to rapid inflation.

9. **B**—Choice (A) is incorrect because the equation of exchange defines the velocity of money as nominal GDP divided by money supply. The supply of loanable funds includes savers, not investors. Fiscal policy shifts the AD curve, not the money supply curve.

10. **E**—The %Δ in real income is equal to the %Δ in nominal income less the rate of inflation.

11. **E**—The GDP deflator is a price index for all goods and services that go into national product. It is more inclusive than the CPI (consumer goods) and the PPI (producer inputs).

12. **D**—Expansionary fiscal policy can be weakened if government borrowing drives up interest rates and diminishes private investment.

13. **D**—If the unemployment rate and inflation rate are both falling, they are likely the result of an increase in AS (either SRAS or LRAS).

14. **C**—An increase (or rightward shift) in the LRAS curve represents economic growth because this shows an increase in full employment real GDP.

15. **B**—If AD is falling and prices are not also falling, the AS curve must be horizontal. Keynesians believe that prices are sticky in the downward direction, but Classical economists believe prices are flexible. It is no surprise that the classical AS curve is vertical.

16. **C**—Supply-side fiscal policy tries to boost investment and productivity to increase LRAS and foster economic growth over time.

17. **B**—Falling bond prices correspond to rising interest rates, so look for the choice that increases interest rates. Lower money demand, one financial asset, creates rising demand for bonds, an alternative financial asset. Choice E therefore increases bond prices and lowers interest rates.

18. **A**—If prices and wages are flexible, the long-run economy readjusts to full employment. Falling AD lowers the price level and real GDP in the short run, but eventually lower wages shift the short-run AS curve to the right, further lowering the price level and moving long-run production back to full employment.

19. **C**—The short-run AS curve is upward sloping; the long-run AS is vertical at full employment.

20. **A**—The BLS only counts a worker as "unemployed" if he or she is actively seeking work. A discouraged worker is, by definition, not seeking work and so the worker's omission from the unemployment rate understates this measure of economic health, making the economy look better than it is.

21. **E**—In the full circular flow model, the role of government is to collect taxes from firms and households in exchange for goods and services. Choice C is tempting, but households supply resources in exchange for wages, which they then use to purchase goods and services.

22. **D**—All production done in the United States is counted in U.S. GDP, regardless of the nationality of the entrepreneur.

23. **E**—Increased SRAS lowers the price level, but increased AD increases the price level. The change in the price level is uncertain, but real GDP rises.

24. **B**—The transaction demand for money rises with higher levels of nominal GDP. With a fixed supply of money, increased demand for money increases the interest rate as consumers sell financial assets (e.g., bonds), lowering the bond price and increasing the interest rate.

25. **A**—The spending multiplier $M = 1/(1 - \text{MPC}) = 1/\text{MPS}$, so an increase in the marginal propensity to consume increases the multiplier.

26. **B**—Asset demand for money is negatively related to the interest rate. Lower interest rates decrease the opportunity cost of holding money.

27. **E**—This is the only choice that combines contractionary fiscal and expansionary monetary policy.

28. **E**—Increased consumer wealth shifts the saving function downward. Less saving decreases the supply of loanable funds, raising the interest rate.

29. **C**—Increased optimism shifts investment demand to the right.

30. **E**—At the peak of the business cycle, the economy is very strong. Real GDP and incomes are high, unemployment is low, and the threat is a rapid increase in the price level.

31. **E**—An increase in demand for bonds as a financial asset decreases the demand for money and lowers the interest rate. A lower interest rate in the U.S. money market makes the United States a less attractive place for foreign investors to place their money. This decreased demand for dollars depreciates the value of the dollar relative to foreign currencies.

32. **C**—Greater optimism shifts the consumption function upward. The MPC is unchanged.

33. **E**—If the value of the dollar is high, it makes American goods more expensive to foreign consumers. This decreases net exports and lowers U.S. real GDP. All other choices likely increase real GDP.

34. **A**—With the economy operating beyond full employment, look for a combination of expansionary policies. All of the other choices include a contractionary policy with an expansionary policy, thus making A the most likely culprit.

35. **D**—Contractionary monetary policy increases interest rates. Higher interest rates decrease new home demand, investment spending, and AD, and increase the unemployment rate.

36. **A**—Expanding the money supply decreases the interest rate, increases investment, and stimulates AD.

37. **B**—Because the spending multiplier is larger than the tax multiplier, AD shifts farther to the right when spending is increased with no change in taxes. With the economy currently at full employment, this largest of rightward shifts in AD will be the most inflationary policy.

38. **C**—Because $M1$ is the most liquid measure of money, it begins with cash and coins.

39. **D**—For a given MPC, the spending multiplier exceeds the tax multiplier, which exceeds the balanced budget multiplier, which is always 1.

40. **B**—Money creation slows if banks do not lend all excess reserves.

41. **B**—More exports means an increased demand for the dollar. Stronger demand for the dollar increases the value of the dollar.

42. **B**—The money multiplier is $1/rr = 10$. So a $500 deposit creates $450 of new excess reserves, which can multiply to $4,500 of newly created money.

43. **A**—Lower levels of investment are the result of higher interest rates so look for the choice that describes a decrease in the money supply.

44. **B**—If $700 of a $1,000 deposit is in excess reserves, $300 or 30 percent must have been reserved.

45. **C**—Reducing debt lowers interest rates, which increases private investment and risks inflation. Lower interest rates decrease foreign investment in the United States. Weaker demand for dollars depreciates the value of the dollar.

46. **D**—The short-run AS curve is upward sloping because when AD increases, the prices of goods and services rise faster than wages. This results in a profit opportunity for producers to increase output. In the long run, wages have time to fully respond to changes in the price level.

47. **C**—High levels of government borrowing increase the interest rate and squeeze private investors out of the investment market.

48. **E**—Quotas do not raise money for the domestic government, but they do increase prices and protect inefficient domestic producers, drawing resources away from efficient foreign producers.

49. **A**—To avoid crowding out, the Fed should increase the money supply, and a lower discount rate does that.

50. **D**—Long-term investment in human capital and new technologies increases economic growth rates. Protection of a nation's natural resources and health of the citizens increases labor productivity.

51. **B**—Extensive borrowing increases the interest rate on U.S. securities. Foreign investors seek to buy dollars so that they can invest in these securities, but when the dollar appreciates, American exports become more expensive to foreign consumers, and so net exports fall.

52. **E**—When a nation's productive capacity increases, the PPC and long-run AS curves both shift rightward.

53. **A**—This choice describes exactly what automatic stabilizers do. By providing automatic fiscal stimulus during a recession, they also lessen the impact of a recession by shortening the business cycle.

54. **C**—Buying securities from commercial banks puts excess reserves in the banks, which begins the money creation process.

55. **A**—Subsidized public education is an investment in human capital and greatly increases labor productivity over time. This is one of the determinants of economic growth.

56. **C**—This choice describes the negative-sloping Phillips curve with the inflation rate on the y axis and the unemployment rate on the x axis.

57. **E**—If SRAS shifts to the left, both inflation and unemployment rise, and results in a Phillips curve that is further to the right than before the supply shock.

58. **A**—At the natural rate of unemployment, there is frictional and structural unemployment, but no cyclical job loss.

59. **D**—If more children are immunized against disease, the size of the adult workforce increases and higher levels of human capital and productivity are seen over time.

60. **C**—Lower interest rates decrease the demand for the dollar, which makes U.S.-made goods more affordable to foreign consumers, so exports from the United States increase.

AP Macroeconomics Practice Exam 1, Section II

Free-Response Questions

Planning time—10 minutes

Writing time—50 minutes

At the conclusion of the planning time, you have 50 minutes to respond to the following three questions. Approximately half of your time should be given to the first question, and the second half should be divided evenly between the remaining two questions. Be careful to clearly explain your reasoning and to provide clear labels to all graph axes and curves.

1. It is January 1, 2010, and the U.S. economy is operating at the level of real GDP that corresponds to full employment. The U.S. government is operating with a balanced budget and net exports are equal to zero.
    (A) Using a correctly labeled aggregate demand and aggregate supply graph, identify each of the following:
        i. The current level of real GDP
        ii. The current price level
    (B) Suppose that by the end of 2010, Americans are importing more goods and services from other nations than they are exporting to other nations (a trade deficit) and there exists a deficit balance in the current account.
        i. How will this affect the balance of the capital/financial account? Explain.
        ii. In the AD/AS graph above, show how the trade deficit will affect the U.S. economy, the level of real GDP, and the equilibrium price level.
    (C) Consider again the deficit balance in the current account.
        i. How will the deficit balance in the current account affect the demand for the dollar in the market for dollars?
        ii. Will the dollar appreciate or depreciate against other major foreign currencies?
    (D) Given your response to (B)(ii), how could the U.S. government engage in discretionary fiscal policy to return the economy to full employment GDP? Explain.

2. Suppose that political upheaval in Argentina has sparked rampant inflation.
    (A) Explain how this unexpected inflation would impact the following groups:
        i. Retirees living on fixed monthly pensions
        ii. Banks with many outstanding loans that are being repaid at fixed interest rates
    (B) Assume that the central bank of Argentina has the same tools of monetary policy as the Fed in the United States. Explain one monetary policy that the central bank could use to lessen the inflation.
    (C) State one fiscal policy that the government could use to lessen the inflation.
    (D) Suppose that the inflation in Argentina is still a problem in the long run. Using a correctly labeled graph, show how the inflation would affect the value of the Argentine peso in the foreign exchange markets.

3. Assume that the U.S. economy is currently operating at the full employment level of real gross domestic product.

   (A) Suppose that full employment occurs at an unemployment rate of 4 percent and an annual inflation rate of 3 percent. Based upon this information, show the short-run and long-run Phillips curves in a correctly labeled graph.

   (B) Assume the U.S. economy is still at full employment, with an unemployment rate of 4 percent and an annual inflation rate of 3 percent. The government now decides to increase personal income taxes.
   i. State how this will impact the equilibrium price level and real GDP in the U.S. economy.
   ii. Show the impact of this increase in personal income taxes on your graph in part B.

› Free-Response Grading Rubric

Note: Based on my experience, these point allocations roughly approximate the weighting on similar questions on the AP examinations. Be aware that every year the point allocations differ and partial credit is awarded differently.

Question 1 (11 points)

Part (A): 3 points

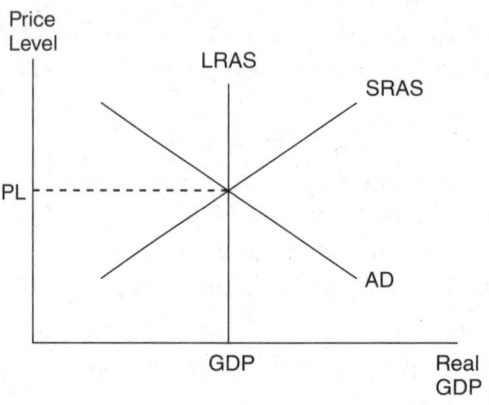

1 point is given for a downward-sloping AD, an upward-sloping SRAS, and a vertical LRAS all intersecting at the same point.

   i. 1 point is given for labeling real GDP on the horizontal axis at the intersection of all three curves.
   ii. 1 point is given for labeling the price level on the vertical axis at the intersection of all three curves.

TIP 1: On graphing problems, you can lose a point for not indicating which variables lie on each graphical axis. In this case, it would be as simple as a PL and rGDP.

TIP 2: When asked to identify equilibrium price and quantity, do these in some way. Dashed lines from the intersection to the axes are enough.

TIP 3: Draw your graphs large enough for you to clearly identify the important components of the graph. If your graph is the size of a postage stamp, it becomes more difficult for you to identify all the relevant parts. It is also very tough for the reader to find all of the points.

Part (B): 4 points
i. 2 points. 1 point is given for identifying "surplus" or "moves toward surplus" and 1 point for explaining that the existence of excess dollars from the trade deficit in the hands of foreign citizens leads to an increase in the purchase of U.S. financial assets by foreigners.
ii. 2 points. 1 point is given for a leftward shift in the AD curve and 1 point for showing the new intersection with SRAS and indicating the decreased level of real GDP and the decreased price level.

Part (C): 2 points
i. 1 point is given for stating that there will be a decrease in the demand for dollars.
ii. 1 point is given for indicating the dollar will depreciate in value relative to other foreign currencies.

Part (D): 2 points
i. 1 point is given for stating either that the government could decrease taxes or increase government spending.
ii. 1 point is given for indicating that this policy would shift AD to the right, increasing real GDP.

What About Partial Credit?
Partial credit differs from year to year, so you do not want to bet your perfect 5 on the generosity of unknown readers. However, it is possible that you might receive some points for being consistent with an incorrect response. For example, suppose in (C)(i) you said that the demand for the dollar would increase. You would not receive the first point. However, if you said that the dollar would then appreciate, you could receive the second point for being consistent. Another opportunity for partial credit exists in (D). Suppose that in (B)(ii) you had shown the AD curve shift to the right. You would not receive any points in (B)(ii). However, in (D) you could describe a contractionary fiscal policy such as increasing taxes or decreasing government spending and you could receive both points in (D).

Question 2 (6 points)

Part (A): 2 points
i. 1 point: High unexpected inflation decreases the purchasing power of pensioners.

ii. 1 point: Banks collect loan repayments that have lost value with high inflation.

Part (B): 1 point
1 point is given for contractionary monetary policy—either raising the discount rate, raising the reserve ratio, or selling securities in an open market operation. The explanation must describe how higher rates will decrease investment, AD, and the price level.

Part (C): 1 point
1 point given for a contractionary fiscal policy. Raise taxes or lower government spending.

Part (D): 2 points
These are graphing points.
1 point is given for a graph with correctly labeled axes and an initial equilibrium identified at the intersection of the supply of pesos and the demand for pesos, and 1 point is given for showing a leftward shift of the demand curve and clearly showing that the value of the peso has fallen; it is depreciating.

Note: To receive all graphing points in the market for a currency, graph axes *must* be correctly labeled!

Question 3 (6 points)

Part (A): 3 points

These are graphing points, but to get all points, you need to explicitly incorporate all of the given information in the Phillips curve graph.

1 point: Graph axes that show the unemployment rate on the horizontal axis and the inflation rate on the vertical axis.

1 point: Show the downward-sloping SRPC intersecting the vertical LRPC.

1 point: At the intersection of SRPC and LRPC, identify an unemployment rate of 4 percent on the horizontal axis and an inflation rate of 3 percent on the vertical axis.

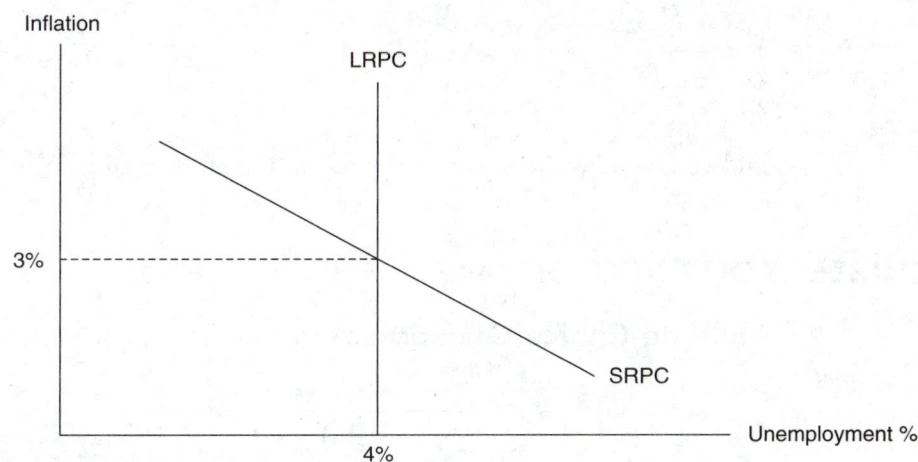

Part (B): 3 points

i. 2 points. A short sentence will suffice as long as you state that there will be a decrease in real GDP and a decrease in the price level.

ii. 1 point. A change in AD does not shift either Phillips curve; it causes a movement along the SRPC. The reason is that shifting AD does not cause the level of full employment, and thus the natural rate of unemployment, to change. Because unemployment is rising and the price level is falling, you would show a movement downward and to the right on the SRPC.

Scoring and Interpretation

AP Macroeconomics Practice Exam 1

Multiple-Choice Questions:

Number of correct answers: _____
Number of incorrect answers: _____
Number of blank answers: _____
Did you complete this part of the test in the allotted time? Yes/No

Free-Response Questions:

1. _____/11
2. _____/6
3. _____/6

Did you complete this part of the test in the allotted time? Yes/No

Calculate Your Score:

Multiple-Choice Questions:

$$\frac{}{(\# \text{ right})} = \frac{}{\text{MC raw score}}$$

Free-Response Questions:

Free-response raw score = $(1.3636 \times \text{Score \#1}) + (1.25 \times \text{Score \#2}) + (1.25 \times \text{Score \#3}) =$ _____

Add the raw scores from the multiple-choice and free-response sections to obtain your total raw score for the practice exam. Use the table that follows to determine your grade, remembering these are rough estimates using questions that are not actually from AP exams, so do not read too much into this conversion from raw score to AP score.

MACROECONOMICS #1	
RAW SCORE	APPROXIMATE AP GRADE
71–90	5
53–70	4
43–52	3
31–42	2
0–30	1

AP Macroeconomics Practice Exam 2
Section I: Multiple-Choice Questions

ANSWER SHEET

AP Macroeconomics Practice Exam 2, Section I

Multiple-Choice

Time—1 hour and 10 minutes

60 questions

For the multiple-choice questions that follow, select the best answer and fill in the appropriate letter on the answer sheet.

Questions 1 and 2 refer to the figure below.

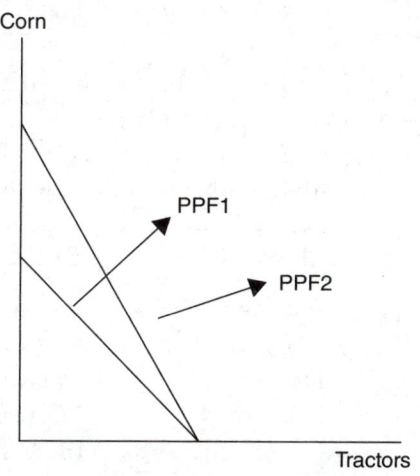

1. Suppose that the production possibility frontier (PPF) of this nation moves from PPF1 to PPF2. Which of the following could be the cause of this movement?
   (A) Technological improvements in the production of tractors
   (B) A long-lasting and destructive drought
   (C) A more efficient use of steel, an important raw material in the production of tractors
   (D) An economy-wide improvement in the productivity of the labor force
   (E) More effective pesticides used to protect crops from insect damage

2. Now that the economy is operating on PPF2, what has happened to the opportunity cost of producing these goods?
   (A) The opportunity cost of producing tractors has decreased, while the opportunity cost of producing corn has increased.
   (B) The opportunity cost of producing tractors has increased, while the opportunity cost of producing corn has decreased.
   (C) The opportunity costs of producing tractors and corn have both decreased.
   (D) There has been no change in the opportunity cost of producing tractors and corn.
   (E) The opportunity costs of producing tractors and corn have both increased.

3. The price of gasoline has recently increased, while at the same time gasoline consumption has also increased. What is happening in the gasoline market?
   (A) This is evidence that contradicts the law of demand.
   (B) The price of crude oil has fallen, shifting the supply of gasoline to the right.
   (C) A price ceiling has been imposed in the market for gasoline.
   (D) The price of automobiles has increased, shifting the demand for gasoline to the left.
   (E) Consumers prefer larger automobiles, shifting the demand for gasoline to the right.

4. If Nation A can produce a good at lower opportunity cost than Nation B can produce the same good, it is said that
   (A) Nation A has comparative advantage in the production of that good.
   (B) Nation B has comparative advantage in the production of that good.
   (C) Nation A has absolute advantage in the production of that good.
   (D) Nation B has absolute advantage in the production of that good.
   (E) Nation A has economic growth in the production of that good.

5. Which of the following is a consequence of removal of a protective tariff on imported steel?
   (A) Imports fall.
   (B) Income is transferred from steel consumers to domestic steel producers.
   (C) Income is transferred from foreign steel producers to domestic steel producers.
   (D) Allocative efficiency is improved.
   (E) Aggregate supply is decreased.

6. In the last 20 years, firms that produce cameras have begun to produce fewer 35-mm cameras and more digital cameras. This trend is an example of

   (A) how central planners dictate which cameras are produced.
   (B) the market system answering the question of "how" cameras should be produced.
   (C) the market system answering the question of "what" cameras should be produced.
   (D) the market system answering the question of "who" should consume the cameras that are produced.
   (E) how firms fail to respond to improvements in technology and changes in consumer tastes.

7. Which of the following transactions would be included in the official computation of gross domestic product?

   (A) Josh buys a new pair of running shoes.
   (B) Nancy offers to babysit her granddaughter.
   (C) Max buys his dad's used car.
   (D) Eli cannot go to a concert, so he resells his ticket to a friend.
   (E) Melanie rakes the leaves in her own yard.

8. Theo loses his job at the public swimming pool when the pool closes for the winter. This is an example of

   (A) cyclical unemployment.
   (B) discouraged worker.
   (C) seasonal unemployment.
   (D) frictional unemployment.
   (E) structural unemployment.

9. Which of the following is not a scarce economic resource?

   (A) Labor
   (B) Capital
   (C) Human wants
   (D) Land
   (E) Natural resources

10. How does an increasing national debt impact the market for U.S. dollars and the value of the dollar with respect to other currencies?

	MARKET FOR THE DOLLAR	VALUE OF THE DOLLAR
(A)	Increased demand	Appreciating
(B)	Increased supply	Appreciating
(C)	Decreased supply	Depreciating
(D)	Decreased demand	Depreciating
(E)	Increased demand	Depreciating

11. Suppose the price level in the United States has risen in the past year, but production of goods and services has remained constant. Based on this information, which of the following is true?

	NOMINAL GDP	REAL GDP
(A)	Increased	Increased
(B)	No change	Decreased
(C)	Decreased	Decreased
(D)	Increased	Decreased
(E)	Decreased	Increased

12. Which of the following is not an addition to national income?

    (A) Wages
    (B) Salaries
    (C) Interest
    (D) Depreciation of physical capital
    (E) Profits

13. Which choice produces a faster rate of economic growth for the United States?

    (A) Institution of higher tariffs on imported goods
    (B) More investment in capital infrastructure and less consumption of nondurable goods and services
    (C) Elimination of mandatory school attendance laws
    (D) Annual limits on the number of foreigners immigrating into the United States
    (E) More investment in the military and less investment in higher education

YEAR	ADULT POPULATION	EMPLOYED	UN-EMPLOYED
2003	1000	600	200
2004	1200	800	200

14. The table above summarizes the local labor market. Based on this information, which of the following is an accurate statement?

    (A) The number of discouraged workers has fallen from 2003 to 2004.
    (B) Although the population has grown, the labor force has remained constant from 2003 to 2004.
    (C) The unemployment rate fell from 33 percent in 2003 to 25 percent in 2004.
    (D) The economic recession in 2003 worsened in 2004.
    (E) The unemployment rate fell from 25 percent in 2003 to 20 percent in 2004.

15. Which of the following is true of money and financial markets?

    (A) As the demand for bonds increases, the interest rate increases.
    (B) For a given money supply, if nominal GDP increases, the velocity of money decreases.
    (C) When demand for stocks and bonds increases, the asset demand for money falls.
    (D) A macroeconomic recession increases the demand for loanable funds.
    (E) Equilibrium in the money market occurs where the transaction demand for money equals the supply of money.

16. Which of the following would increase the aggregate demand function?

    (A) Higher levels of imported goods
    (B) Lower levels of consumer wealth
    (C) A higher real interest rate
    (D) Lower taxes on personal income
    (E) Lower levels of exported goods

17. The figure above shows aggregate demand (AD) and supply (AS) for the economy. Assuming that aggregate demand remains constant, which of the following best predicts the short-run price level, the long-run price level, and the long-run level of output?

	SHORT-RUN PRICE LEVEL	LONG-RUN PRICE LEVEL	LONG-RUN OUTPUT
(A)	P2	P1	Q4
(B)	P2	P2	Q1
(C)	P2	P3	Q1
(D)	P1	P2	Q3
(E)	P3	P2	Q2

18. Which of the following is not included in the U.S. GDP?

    (A) The U.S. military opens a new base in a foreign country with 1,000 U.S. personnel.
    (B) Japanese consumers buy thousands of CDs produced in the United States.
    (C) An American pop singer performs a sold-out concert in Paris.
    (D) A French theatrical production tours dozens of American cities.
    (E) American construction companies build thousands of new homes all across the United States and Canada.

19. A policy supported by supply-side economists would be

    (A) higher taxes on corporate profits.
    (B) lower tax rates on interest earned from savings.
    (C) removal of investment tax credits.
    (D) a longer duration of unemployment benefits.
    (E) higher marginal income tax rates to fund social welfare programs.

20. According to the quantity theory of money, increasing the money supply serves to

    (A) stimulate short-run production and employment with very little long-run inflation.
    (B) increase short-run output, but it is the source of long-run inflation.
    (C) lower the unemployment rate while also lowering the rate of inflation.
    (D) increase the nation's long-run capacity to produce.
    (E) decrease short-run real GDP but increase real GDP in the long run.

21. Of the following choices, the most direct exchange in the circular flow model of a private closed economy is when

    (A) households provide goods to firms in exchange for wage payments.
    (B) households provide resources to firms in exchange for goods.
    (C) households provide revenues to firms in exchange for wage payments.
    (D) firms supply goods to households in exchange for revenues.
    (E) firms supply resources to households in exchange for costs of production.

22. Suppose that the federal government reclassified the purchase of a new home as consumption spending rather than investment spending. This decision would

    (A) increase aggregate demand and decrease real GDP.
    (B) decrease aggregate demand and decrease real GDP.
    (C) decrease aggregate demand and increase real GDP.
    (D) increase aggregate demand and increase real GDP.
    (E) have no impact on aggregate demand and real GDP.

23. Suppose that current disposable income is $10,000 and consumption spending is $8,000. For every $100 increase in disposable income, saving increases $10. Given this information,

    (A) the marginal propensity to consume is .80.
    (B) the marginal propensity to save is .20.
    (C) the marginal propensity to save is .10.
    (D) the marginal propensity to save is .90.
    (E) the marginal propensity to consume is .10.

24. When we observe an unplanned decrease in inventories, we can expect

    (A) prices to begin to fall.
    (B) output to begin to rise.
    (C) saving to begin to fall.
    (D) output to begin to fall.
    (E) planned investment to begin to rise.

25. Stagflation is the result of

    (A) a leftward shift in the aggregate supply curve.
    (B) a leftward shift in the aggregate demand curve.
    (C) a leftward shift in both the aggregate supply and aggregate demand curves.
    (D) a rightward shift in the aggregate supply curve.
    (E) a rightward shift in the aggregate demand curve.

26. If the short-run aggregate supply curve is horizontal, it is because

    (A) there exist many unemployed resources so that output can be increased without increasing wages and prices.
    (B) any increase in output requires a corresponding increase in wages and prices.
    (C) increases in output cause prices to increase, but wages adjust much less quickly.
    (D) falling interest rates increase the demand for goods and services, putting upward pressure on prices.
    (E) resources are fully employed so that output can be increased but only if the price level also increases.

27. In a private closed economy, which of the following statements is true?

    (A) Household saving can never be negative.
    (B) Investment is always greater than savings.
    (C) The economy is in equilibrium when consumption equals saving.
    (D) Saving is equal to zero when consumption equals disposable income.
    (E) Government is the only source of spending and investment.

28. Which of the following is true of a typical contraction of the business cycle?

    (A) Consumption is falling, but household wealth is rising.
    (B) Consumption is increasing.
    (C) Private investment is rising.
    (D) Employment and inflation are low.
    (E) Private saving rates are rising.

29. Which of the following is most likely to produce stronger economic growth over time?

    (A) More rapid consumption of natural resources.
    (B) Higher adult illiteracy rates.
    (C) A falling stock of capital goods.
    (D) Investment tax credits.
    (E) Higher taxes on foreign capital investment.

30. If $100 of new autonomous private investment were added to an economy with a marginal propensity to consume of .90, by how much would aggregate demand shift to the right?

    (A) $190
    (B) $900
    (C) $1,000
    (D) $1,900
    (E) $90

31. Which of the following is true about the relationship between the $M1$ and $M2$ measures of money?

    (A) $M1$ minus $M2$ equals 0.
    (B) $M1$ includes checking deposits, while $M2$ includes checking and saving deposits.
    (C) $M2$ includes coin and paper money, but $M1$ does not.
    (D) $M2$ is more liquid than $M1$.
    (E) $M1$ is greater than $M2$.

32. Which of the following increases the size of the tax multiplier?

    (A) An increase in the marginal propensity to consume.
    (B) An increase in the reserve ratio.
    (C) An increase in the marginal propensity to save.
    (D) A decrease in the spending multiplier.
    (E) A decrease in the velocity of money.

33. Which of the following might worsen a nation's trade deficit?

    (A) Lower wages relative to other nations.
    (B) Lower taxes on corporate profits relative to other nations.
    (C) A higher interest rate on financial assets relative to other nations.
    (D) A higher rate of inflation relative to other nations.
    (E) Other nations remove tariffs and quotas on foreign imports.

34. If the economy is suffering from extremely high rates of inflation, which of the following fiscal policies would be an appropriate strategy for the economy?

    (A) Increase government spending and decrease taxes.
    (B) Decrease government spending and increase taxes.
    (C) Increase government spending with no change in taxes.
    (D) The Federal Reserve increases the discount rate.
    (E) Decrease taxes with no change in government spending.

35. Which of the following is an example of an expansionary supply shock?

    (A) Rapid increasing wages
    (B) A greatly depreciated currency
    (C) Declining labor productivity
    (D) Lower than expected agricultural harvests
    (E) Lower factor prices in major industries

36. Which of the following fiscal policy combinations would be most likely to slowly increase real GDP without putting tremendous upward pressure on the price level?

    (A) Increase government spending with a matching decrease in taxes.
    (B) Decrease government spending with a matching increase in taxes.
    (C) Increase government spending with no change in taxes.
    (D) The Federal Reserve lowers the reserve ratio.
    (E) Increase taxes with a matching increase in government spending.

37. Which of the following is an example of contractionary monetary policy?

    (A) The Fed lowers the reserve ratio.
    (B) The Fed lowers the discount rate.
    (C) The Fed increases taxes on household income.
    (D) The Fed decreases spending on welfare programs.
    (E) The Fed sells Treasury securities to commercial banks.

38. The economy is in a deep recession. Given this economic situation, which of the following statements about monetary policy is accurate?

    (A) Expansionary policy would only worsen the recession.
    (B) Expansionary policy greatly increases aggregate demand if investment is sensitive to changes in the interest rate.
    (C) Contractionary policy is the appropriate stimulus for investment and consumption.
    (D) If the demand for money is perfectly elastic, expansionary monetary policy might be quite effective.
    (E) An open market operation that sells government securities is the only realistic way to improve the economy.

39. Daddy Morebucks withdraws $1 million from his savings account and puts the cash in his refrigerator. This affects $M1$ and $M2$ in which of the following ways?

	M1	M2
(A)	Rises	Rises
(B)	No change	No change
(C)	Falls	Falls
(D)	Rises	Falls
(E)	Rises	No change

40. What is the main difference between the short-run and long-run Phillips curve?

    (A) The short-run Phillips curve is downward sloping and the long-run Phillips curve is upward sloping.
    (B) The short-run Phillips curve is upward sloping and the long-run Phillips curve is vertical.
    (C) The short-run Phillips curve is horizontal and the long-run Phillips curve is upward sloping.
    (D) The short-run Phillips curve is downward sloping and the long-run Phillips curve is vertical.
    (E) The short-run Phillips curve is vertical and the long-run Phillips curve is upward sloping.

41. Which of the following insures the value of the U.S. dollar?

    (A) The euro and other foreign currencies held by the Federal Reserve
    (B) Gold bars in secure locations like Fort Knox
    (C) The promise of the U.S. government to maintain its value
    (D) The value of the actual paper on which it is printed.
    (E) An equal amount of physical capital, land, and natural resources

42. The reserve ratio is .10 and Mommy Morebucks withdraws $1 million from her checking account and keeps it as cash in her refrigerator. How does this withdrawal potentially impact money in circulation?

    (A) Decreases it by $9 million
    (B) Decreases it by $1 million
    (C) Decreases it by $100,000
    (D) Increases it by $1 million
    (E) Decreases it by $10 million

43. If the economy were experiencing a recessionary gap, choose the option below that would be an appropriate fiscal policy to eliminate the gap, and the predicted impact of the policy on real GDP and unemployment.

	FISCAL POLICY	REAL GDP	UNEMPLOYMENT
(A)	Increase taxes.	Increase	Decrease
(B)	Decrease spending.	Decrease	Increase
(C)	Decrease taxes.	Increase	Increase
(D)	Increase money supply.	Increase	Decrease
(E)	Decrease taxes.	Increase	Decrease

44. Monetary tools of the Federal Reserve do *not* include which of the following choices?

    (A) Buying Treasury securities from commercial banks
    (B) Changing tariffs and quotas on imported goods
    (C) Changing the reserve ratio
    (D) Changing the discount rate
    (E) Selling Treasury securities to commercial banks

45. Of the following choices, which combination of fiscal and monetary policy would most likely reduce a recessionary gap?

	FISCAL POLICY	MONETARY POLICY
(A)	Increase taxes.	Increase the reserve ratio.
(B)	Decrease spending.	Sell Treasury securities.
(C)	Decrease taxes.	Buy Treasury securities.
(D)	Increase spending.	Increase the reserve ratio.
(E)	Decrease taxes.	Increase the discount rate.

46. For a given level of government spending, the federal government usually experiences a budget ____ during economic ____ and a budget _____ during economic _____.

    (A) deficit, recession, surplus, expansion
    (B) surplus, recession, deficit, expansion
    (C) deficit, expansion, surplus, recession
    (D) surplus, recession, surplus, expansion
    (E) deficit, recession, deficit, expansion

47. Suppose that elected officials and the central bank agree to combine fiscal and monetary policies to lessen the threat of inflation. Which of the following combinations would likely accomplish this goal?

	FISCAL POLICY	MONETARY POLICY
(A)	Decrease taxes	Increase the reserve ratio
(B)	Decrease spending	Buy government securities
(C)	Decrease taxes	Sell government securities
(D)	Decrease spending	Decrease the reserve ratio
(E)	Increase taxes	Increase the discount rate

48. Congress has embarked on another round of expansionary fiscal policy to boost employment and get reelected. As chair of the central bank, how would you reduce the "crowding-out" effect and what macroeconomic problem might your policy exacerbate?

    (A) Increase the reserve ratio, risking the devaluation of the dollar
    (B) Sell government securities, risking inflation
    (C) Buy government securities, risking a recessionary gap
    (D) Lower the discount rate, risking inflation
    (E) Lower the discount rate, risking cyclical unemployment

49. Which of the following is likely to shift the long-run aggregate supply curve to the right?

    (A) A nation that devotes more resources to nondurable consumption goods, rather than durable capital goods
    (B) Research that improves the productivity of labor and capital
    (C) More restrictive trade policies
    (D) Annual limits to immigration of foreign citizens
    (E) A permanent increase in the price of energy

50. Holding all else equal, which of the following monetary policies would be used to boost U.S. exports?

    (A) Increasing the discount rate
    (B) Increasing the reserve ratio
    (C) Buying government securities
    (D) Lowering tariffs
    (E) Removing import quotas

51. Which of the following could limit the ability of a central bank to conduct expansionary monetary policy?

    (A) Money demand is nearly perfectly elastic.
    (B) Investment demand is nearly perfectly elastic.
    (C) Banks make loans with all excess reserves.
    (D) Households carry very little cash, holding their money in checking and saving deposits.
    (E) Money supply is nearly perfectly inelastic.

52. Which of the following is a predictable advantage of expansionary monetary policy in a recession?

    (A) It decreases aggregate demand so that the price level falls, which increases demand for the dollar.
    (B) It increases investment, which increases aggregate demand and increases employment.
    (C) It increases aggregate demand, which increases real GDP and increases the unemployment rate.
    (D) It keeps interest rates high, which attracts foreign investment.
    (E) It decreases the interest rate, which attracts foreign investment in U.S. financial assets.

53. Suppose the economy is in long-run equilibrium when a temporary expansionary supply shock is felt in the economy. This changes the short-run Phillips curve, the short-run unemployment rate, and the long-run unemployment rate in which of the following ways?

	SHORT-RUN PHILLIPS CURVE	SHORT-RUN UN-EMPLOYMENT	LONG-RUN UN-EMPLOYMENT
(A)	Shifts down	Falls	Rises
(B)	Shifts up	Rises	Falls
(C)	Shifts down	Falls	Falls
(D)	Shifts up	Rises	Rises
(E)	Shifts down	Rises	Falls

54. As the Japanese economy expands, in what ways do U.S. net exports, the values of the dollar and the yen change?

	U.S. NET EXPORTS	VALUE OF DOLLAR	VALUE OF YEN
(A)	Decrease	Increase	Increase
(B)	Increase	Decrease	Increase
(C)	Decrease	Decrease	Increase
(D)	Increase	Increase	Decrease
(E)	Increase	Increase	Increase

55. Suppose the President plans to cut taxes for consumers and also plans to increase spending on the military. How does this affect real GDP and the price level?

    (A) GDP increases and the price level decreases.
    (B) GDP decreases and the price level increases.
    (C) GDP stays the same and the price level increases.
    (D) GDP decreases and the price level decreases.
    (E) GDP increases and the price level increases.

56. U.S. dollars and the European Union's (EU's) euro are exchanged in global currency markets. Which of the following is true?

    (A) If inflation is high in the EU and the price level in the United States is stable, the value of the dollar appreciates.
    (B) If the Fed decreases the money supply, the value of the dollar depreciates.
    (C) If EU consumers are less inclined to purchase American goods, the dollar appreciates.
    (D) If U.S. income levels are rising relative to incomes in the EU, the euro depreciates.
    (E) If the European central bank expands the money supply, the euro appreciates.

57. If in a given year the government collects more money in net taxes than it spends, there would exist

    (A) a current account deficit.
    (B) a budget surplus.
    (C) a trade surplus.
    (D) a budget deficit.
    (E) a trade deficit.

58. Which component of a nation's balance of payments recognizes the purchase and sale of real and financial assets between nations?

    (A) The capital account
    (B) The official reserves account
    (C) The current account
    (D) The trade deficit account
    (E) The trade surplus account

59. An import quota on foreign automobiles is expected to

    (A) increase domestic efficiency and protect domestic producers at the expense of foreign producers.
    (B) decrease the price of automobiles and protect domestic consumers at the expense of foreign producers.
    (C) increase the price of automobiles and protect domestic producers at the expense of consumers.
    (D) increase the price of automobiles and protect domestic consumers at the expense of domestic producers.
    (E) decrease domestic efficiency and protect domestic producers at the expense of domestic autoworkers.

60. When a large increase in aggregate demand has an even greater increase in real GDP, economists refer to this as

    (A) the balanced budget multiplier.
    (B) the money multiplier.
    (C) the foreign substitution effect.
    (D) the wealth effect.
    (E) the spending multiplier.

Answers and Explanations

1. **E**—The capacity to produce corn has increased, but the capacity for tractor production is the same. More effective pesticides do not improve the ability to produce tractors but improve the ability to harvest corn.
2. **B**—When the slope of the PPF increases, the opportunity cost of producing the x axis good rises.
3. **E**—Rising prices and rising quantities does not disprove the law of demand; it simply reflects a rightward shift in demand with a constant supply curve.
4. **A**—Defines comparative advantage.
5. **D**—Tariffs create inefficiency in the world steel market.
6. **C**—The free market responds to changes in consumer tastes, technology, and prices to produce "what" is most wanted by society.
7. **A**—Household production is not included in GDP calculations. Second-hand sales are counted the first time the good was produced.
8. **C**—Know the difference between types of unemployment.
9. **C**—Human wants are neither scarce nor are they economic resources.
10. **A**—Rising national debt increases interest rates and attracts foreign investment in U.S. financial assets. Greater demand for dollars appreciates the dollar.
11. **D**—Nominal GDP rises with the price level. If output increases at a slower rate than increases in the price level, real GDP falls.
12. **D**—National income includes all sources of income and depreciation is not a source of income.
13. **B**—Know the factors critical to long-term economic growth.
14. **E**—UR = U/LF and LF = (E + U).
15. **C**—Stocks, bonds, and money are all financial assets. All else equal, rising demand for stocks and bonds lowers the asset demand for money.
16. **D**—Lower taxes on personal income increase consumption and AD.
17. **C**—Short-run equilibrium is where short-run AS intersects AD, in this case, above full employment. In the long run, wages increase, shifting SRAS leftward until settling at full employment Q_1 and higher price P_3.
18. **C**—GDP includes all production or spending done in the United States, regardless of nationality. A singer's production of a concert is counted in French GDP.
19. **B**—Supply-side economists prefer lower taxes on saving to encourage saving. More saving increases investment and increases AS.
20. **B**—The equation of exchange says MV = PQ, and it is assumed that Q and V are fairly constant. Any increase in money supply (M) might initially boost output, but it eventually results in a higher price level (P).
21. **D**—Know the circular flow model.
22. **E**—This reclassification would not affect AD or tabulation of GDP.
23. **C**—If income increases $100 and saving increases by $10, the MPS = .10 and the MPC = .90.
24. **B**—If inventories unexpectedly fall, consumption exceeds production, so expect production to begin rising.
25. **A**—Stagflation is inflation with high unemployment, and this occurs when AS shifts to the left.
26. **A**—The horizontal range of SRAS occurs when resources are unemployed. If output rises, wages do not rise and prices are constant.
27. **D**—Consumption spending is equal to disposable income minus saving: $C = DI - S$.
28. **D**—Weak AD (contraction) causes job loss and low inflation rates.
29. **D**—Investment tax credits provide incentives for firms to invest in capital equipment and new factory construction. This policy stimulates economic growth and productivity.
30. **C**—With an MPC = .90, $M = 10$, so increased investment shifts AD $1,000 to the right.

31. **B**—Remember, *M*2 includes *M*1 but also includes less liquid forms of money like savings accounts. If you added *M*1 and *M*2, you would be adding *M*1 twice.

32. **A**—Tm = *M* × MPC. A larger MPC increases the size of Tm.

33. **D**—Higher inflation to other nations causes goods to be more expensive relative to those produced abroad, causing a drop in net exports.

34. **B**—High inflation rates require a decrease in AD, and this is the only contractionary fiscal policy. Fed policy is not fiscal; it is monetary.

35. **E**—Lower factor prices in major industries represent decreased costs of production, and this creates an increased SRAS.

36. **E**—This balanced budget policy increases real GDP at a slower rate than the other expansionary options.

37. **E**—Selling securities pulls excess reserves out of the banking system, decreasing the money supply.

38. **B**—Expansionary policy lowers interest rates and is more effective if investment increases greatly. If money demand is perfectly elastic, increased money supply does not lower interest rates, thus failing to stimulate investment.

39. **E**—Moving money from savings to cash increases *M*1, but both savings and cash are already included in *M*2, so it has no effect on these two larger measures of money.

40. **D**—The short-run Phillips curve portrays the inverse relationship between inflation and unemployment rates. In the long run, it is vertical at the natural rate of unemployment.

41. **C**—The U.S. dollar is not "backed" by any physical asset or commodity.

42. **A**—The money multiplier is 10, so withdrawing $1 million leads you to conclude that money in circulation falls by $10 million, but the original $1 million is still in circulation, so money falls by $9 million.

43. **E**—Know how fiscal policy affects real GDP and unemployment.

44. **B**—The Fed does not make changes in tariff and quota policy.

45. **C**—Have a strong knowledge of fiscal and monetary policies.

46. **A**—Budget deficits emerge during recessions because net taxes fall when incomes fall. The trend is reversed during expansion.

47. **E**—Know all combinations of fiscal and monetary policy.

48. **D**—The central bank wants to increase the money supply to lower interest rates. Combine the expansionary fiscal with the expansionary monetary policy, and the bank risks inflation.

49. **B**—Long-run AS rises if the productive capacity of the economy rises and more productive labor and capital resources have this effect.

50. **C**—Lower interest rates decrease foreign demand for U.S. securities, depreciating the dollar. "Cheap" dollars make U.S. exports more affordable to foreigners, increasing exports.

51. **A**—A horizontal money demand curve implies that increasing the money supply does not lower the interest rate. Investment is constant, and AD does not increase.

52. **B**—Know how monetary policy affects investment, AD, and employment.

53. **A**—If short-run AS shifts rightward, the short-run Phillips curve shifts down, or leftward. The short-run unemployment rate falls below the natural rate but eventually rises back to the natural rate and a lower rate of inflation, as expectations readjust to the new AS.

54. **D**—Higher Japanese incomes increase net exports in the United States, increasing the value of the dollar versus the yen, decreasing the value of the yen versus the dollar.

55. **E**—Know how fiscal policy affects AD, real GDP, and the price level.

56. **A**—A difference in relative prices affects the exchange rate between the dollar and the euro. European customers will see U.S. goods as relatively less expensive and increase their purchases from the United States, thus appreciating the dollar and depreciating the euro.

57. **B**—This defines a budget surplus.

58. **A**—In the balance of payments statement, the capital account shows the flow of currency in physical and financial assets.

59. **C**—Import quotas protect domestic producers at the expense of the higher price paid by consumers.

60. **E**—Because an injection of dollars into the circular flow goes through the economy several times, the impact on real GDP is multiplied.

AP Macroeconomics Practice Exam 2, Section II

Free-Response Questions

Planning time—10 minutes

Writing time—50 minutes

At the conclusion of the planning time, you have 50 minutes to respond to the following three questions. Approximately half of your time should be given to the first question, and the second half should be divided evenly between the remaining two questions. Be careful to clearly explain your reasoning and to provide clear labels to all graph axes and curves.

1. The U.S. economy is experiencing a severe recession, and the budget is currently balanced.

   (A) One policy analyst advocates expansionary tax cuts, while another advocates expansionary government spending. Which of these policies will have the greatest impact on real domestic output? Explain how you know.

   (B) Choose one of the two proposed policies in part (A).
      i. Based on this policy, will the federal budget be in a deficit, in a surplus, or balanced?
      ii. Based on your response to (B)(i), state what happens to interest rates in the market for loanable funds. Explain.

   (C) Assuming that the economy has still not recovered from the recession, identify one tool of the Federal Reserve that might stimulate the economy.

   (D) Using a correctly labeled graph of the money market, show how the Fed policy identified in part (C) would affect interest rates.

   (E) Explain one factor that might lessen the effectiveness of the Fed's monetary policy.

2. Assume that the European Union (EU) has experienced lower interest rates, while interest rates in the United States have remained relatively high. Explain how these lower real interest rates will affect each of the following:

   (A) The purchase of EU financial assets by American investors
   (B) The international value of the euro (EU currency)
   (C) EU exports of goods and services to the United States
   (D) EU imports of goods and services from the United States

3. The nation of Melania produces only two goods: melons and cupcakes. The production possibility frontier in Melania is concave (bowed outward), and the nation is currently operating at full employment.

   (A) In a correctly labeled graph, show the production possibility frontier in Melania.
      i. Identify a combination of melons and cupcakes that corresponds to full employment with the point F.
      ii. Does the concave production possibility frontier exhibit constant, increasing, or decreasing opportunity costs? Explain.

   (B) Suppose that the economy of Melania falls into recession. Identify a combination of melons and cupcakes that corresponds to a recession with the point R. Add this point to the graph.

   (C) Suppose that Melania experiences an improvement in production technology in growing melons, but this technology has no impact on the ability to produce cupcakes. In the graph from part (A), show how this better technology will affect the production possibility frontier.

Free-Response Grading Rubric

Note: Based on my experience, these point allocations roughly approximate the weighting on similar questions on the AP examinations. Be aware that every year the point allocations differ and partial credit is awarded differently.

Question 1 (10 points)

Part (A): 2 points
1 point: Given for stating that the spending policy will increase real GDP more than the tax cut policy.

1 point: Given for stating that the spending multiplier is greater than the tax multiplier. Tax cuts increase disposable income and some of that is saved, not spent, so the multiplier effect is smaller.

Part (B): 3 points
  i. 1 point: Given for stating that regardless of policy, the budget will be in deficit.
  ii. 1 point: Given for stating that interest rates will rise.
     An additional 1 point is given for the explanation that the government borrowing causes demand for loanable funds to shift to the right (or the supply of loanable funds to shift to the left).

Part (C): 1 point
1 point: Given for providing an expansionary monetary policy. Either lowering the discount rate, lowering the reserve ratio, or buying Treasury securities in an open market operation.

Part (D): 3 points
These are graphing points.

1 point: Given for a correctly drawn money market graph with the vertical axis labeled as nominal interest rate and the horizontal axis labeled as quantity of money.

1 point: Given for showing a vertical money supply curve and a downward-sloping money demand curve with the equilibrium interest rate on the vertical axis.

1 point: Given for showing an increased money supply and a decreased interest rate.

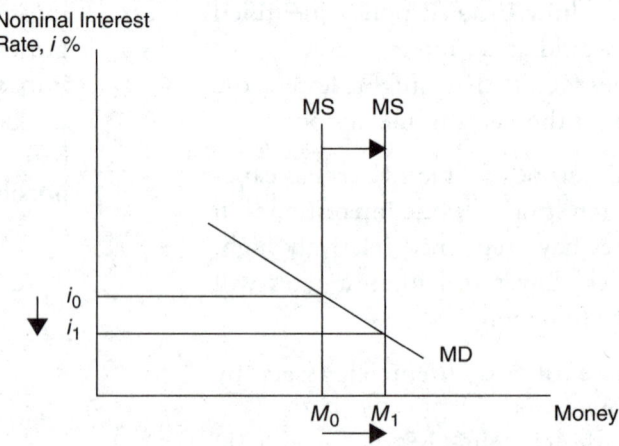

Part (E): 1 point
Identify a reason why greater money supply might not result in a large boost to real GDP.

- Money demand is very elastic.
- Investment demand is very inelastic.

- Banks hold excess reserves rather than making loans.
- Borrowers do not redeposit their loans, but hold some as cash.

Question 2 (4 points)

Part (A): 1 point: Given for stating that lower interest rates make EU financial assets less attractive to American investors, so fewer EU financial assets will be purchased.

Part (B): 1 point: Given for stating that decreased demand for the euro depreciates the euro versus the dollar and appreciates the dollar against the euro.

Part (C): 1 point: Given for stating that a depreciating euro makes EU goods look like a bargain to American consumers, increasing the demand for EU goods and services. The EU exports more goods to the United States.

Part (D): 1 point: Given for stating that an appreciating dollar makes American goods look more expensive to EU consumers, decreasing demand for U.S. goods and services. The EU imports fewer U.S. goods.

Question 3: (6 points)

Part (A): 4 points
1 point: Given for showing a concave production possibility curve (PPC) with melons and cupcakes labeled on the axes.

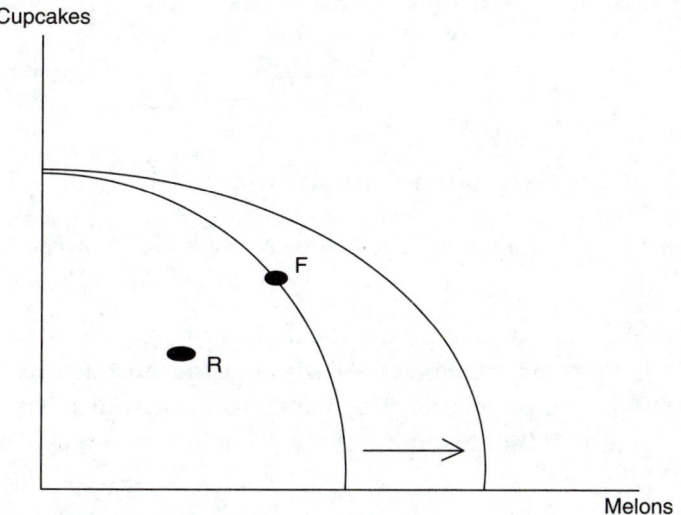

i. 1 point: Given for identifying point F at some point on the PPC.

ii. 1 point: Given for stating that the PPC exhibits increasing opportunity costs. 1 point for explaining that the concave shape means that increasing production of melons (or cupcakes) requires giving up more and more units of cupcakes (or melons) because the resources are not equally productive in producing melon and cupcakes. Some resources are better suited to producing melons than they are at producing cupcakes.

Part (B): 1 point
1 point: Given for showing point R somewhere inside the PPC.

Part (C): 1 point
1 point: Given for showing the PPC increasing along the melons axis but not changing on the cupcakes axis.

Scoring and Interpretation

AP Macroeconomics Practice Exam 2

Multiple-Choice Questions:
Number of correct answers: _____
Number of incorrect answers: _____
Number of blank answers: _____

Did you complete this part of the test in the allotted time? Yes/No

Free-Response Questions:

1. _____/10
2. _____/4
3. _____/6

Did you complete this part of the test in the allotted time? Yes/No

Calculate Your Score:

Multiple-Choice Questions:

$$\frac{}{(\text{\# right})} = \frac{}{\text{MC raw score}}$$

Free-Response Questions:

Free-Response Raw Score = $(1.5 \times \text{Score \#1}) + (1.875 \times \text{Score \#2}) + (1.25 \times \text{Score \#3})$ = _____

Add the raw scores from the multiple-choice and free-response sections to obtain your total raw score for the practice exam. Use the table that follows to determine your grade, remembering these are rough estimates using questions that are not actually from AP exams, so do not read too much into this conversion from raw score to AP score.

MACROECONOMICS #2	
RAW SCORE	APPROXIMATE AP GRADE
71–90	5
53–70	4
43–52	3
31–42	2
0–30	1

90 AP Macroeconomics Activities and Questions in

5 Minutes a Day

INTRODUCTION

Welcome to *5 Minutes to a 5: 180 Questions and Activities*! This bonus section is another tool for you to use as you work toward your goal of achieving a 5 on the AP exam(s) in May. Since AP Macroeconomics and AP Microeconomics courses are typically taught in concurrent semesters, students often find themselves preparing for these exams in the span of one school year. As such, in this section you will find 90 questions and activities that pertain to the AP Macroeconomics course and 90 questions and activities that pertain to the AP Microeconomics course. These questions cover the most essential material in each course and will guide you in preparation for either one or both exams.

One of the secrets to excelling in your AP class is spending a bit of time *each day* studying the subject(s). The questions and activities offered here are designed to be done one per day, and each should take 5 minutes or so to complete. (Although there might be exceptions. Depending on the exam—some exercises may take a little longer, some a little less.) You will encounter stimulating questions to make you think about a topic in a big way, and some very subject-specific activities, which cover the main book's chapters; some science subjects will offer at-home labs, and some humanities subjects will offer ample chunks of text to be read on one day, with questions and activities for follow-up on the following day(s). There will also be suggestions for relevant videos for you to watch, websites to visit, or both. Most questions and activities are linked to the specific chapters of your book, so you are constantly fortifying your knowledge.

Remember, approaching this section for 5 minutes a day is much more effective than bingeing a week's worth in one sitting! So if you practice all the extra exercises in this section and reinforce the main content of this book, we are certain you will build the skills and confidence needed to succeed on your exam. Good luck!

—Editors of McGraw-Hill Education

Check off each activity as it is completed.

1.	❑	24.	❑	47.	❑	70.	❑
2.	❑	25.	❑	48.	❑	71.	❑
3.	❑	26.	❑	49.	❑	72.	❑
4.	❑	27.	❑	50.	❑	73.	❑
5.	❑	28.	❑	51.	❑	74.	❑
6.	❑	29.	❑	52.	❑	75.	❑
7.	❑	30.	❑	53.	❑	76.	❑
8.	❑	31.	❑	54.	❑	77.	❑
9.	❑	32.	❑	55.	❑	78.	❑
10.	❑	33.	❑	56.	❑	79.	❑
11.	❑	34.	❑	57.	❑	80.	❑
12.	❑	35.	❑	58.	❑	81.	❑
13.	❑	36.	❑	59.	❑	82.	❑
14.	❑	37.	❑	60.	❑	83.	❑
15.	❑	38.	❑	61.	❑	84.	❑
16.	❑	39.	❑	62.	❑	85.	❑
17.	❑	40.	❑	63.	❑	86.	❑
18.	❑	41.	❑	64.	❑	87.	❑
19.	❑	42.	❑	65.	❑	88.	❑
20.	❑	43.	❑	66.	❑	89.	❑
21.	❑	44.	❑	67.	❑	90.	❑
22.	❑	45.	❑	68.	❑		
23.	❑	46.	❑	69.	❑		

CHAPTER 5 – USING THE FOUR ECONOMIC RESOURCES IN WRITING A RESEARCH PAPER

> Suppose you are assigned a 10-page research paper on the Great Depression. List the four economic resources that you would use to complete the research assignment. Be as specific as possible.

THE OPPORTUNITY COST OF GOING ON A DATE

You're going to go on a date with a significant other. What is the opportunity cost of this activity?

You will need to do a little research on all of the costs involved. First determine what you plan to do on the date. For example, if you are going to go see a movie, you should search the cinema's website to investigate ticket prices. If you plan to go out to dinner, check out the restaurant's menu to estimate your share of the final bill, including tax and tip.

1. Figure out what you plan to do on your date.

2. Do you need to buy a ticket, food and drink, or anything else?

3. Will you require transportation? If you are using a car, estimate the amount of gasoline you will require and the local price of that gasoline.

4. Determine how much time, including the transportation time, you will need for the date. What is the value of your time as measured by an hourly wage you could receive if you had worked instead?

5. Use all of this information to determine the total opportunity cost of going on the date.

Day 3

HOW MANY TACOS WILL YOU EAT?

Imagine a day when you've skipped lunch, and you're very hungry for dinner. You know a taco truck that sells tacos at $1 each. In this hypothetical situation, how many tacos do you think you would purchase and eat?

Now, with this number in mind, draw a graph of marginal benefit and marginal cost curves that shows your decision to stop buying tacos.

Day 4

YOUR PRODUCTION POSSIBILITIES

Suppose that each day you have 16 waking hours to divide between studying (measured in pages read) and socializing (measured in text messages sent).

a. Assuming constant opportunity costs, draw your production possibility curve (PPC) with pages read on the *x*-axis and text messaging on the *y*-axis.

b. Now suppose your wireless Internet speed is cut in half, reducing the speed at which text messages are received and sent. Adjust your PPC from part (a).

c. How has the opportunity cost of studying changed? Can you explain *why* it has changed?

Day 5

COMPARATIVE ADVANTAGE AROUND THE HOUSE

Let's say that there are two tasks that need to be performed around the house: folding clean towels in the laundry and washing dirty plates in the sink. The following table summarizes how many towels could be folded and how many plates could be washed by two kids in the household.

Hourly Output for Eli: 16 towels and 0 plates, or 0 towels and 8 plates
Hourly Output for Theodore: 6 towels and 0 plates, or 0 towels and 6 plates

a. Does either kid have an absolute advantage in these two tasks? How do you know?

b. If Eli and Theodore each split their time equally between folding towels and washing plates, what is their combined output in 1 hour?

c. If Eli and Theodore specialized their tasks based on comparative advantage, what is their combined output in 1 hour?

ALLOCATIVE EFFICIENCY, PRODUCTIVE EFFICIENCY, AND EQUITY

Suppose you were going to bake a dozen cookies for yourself and 3 friends. When the cookies are done, you will also determine how many cookies each person receives.

1. How would these cookies be baked if you were productively efficient in the kitchen? Hint: It might be easier to think of a situation where the cookies were produced inefficiently.

2. How might the dozen cookies be distributed if your goal was an equitable distribution?

3. Suppose your goal was an allocatively efficient distribution of the dozen cookies. How might you change your equitable distribution from part 2 to reflect this new goal?

Day 7

GROWTH

Imagine an economy that produces only two items: automobiles (representing the manufacturing sector) and wheat (representing the agricultural sector). For the sake of simplicity, we will assume that there are constant opportunity costs along the production possibility curve (PPC). Our initial PPC has been drawn as follows.

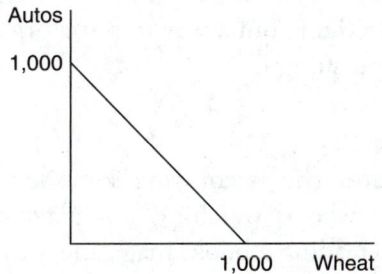

a. Adjust the PPC to reflect new technology that increases maximum automobile production by 25% but has no impact on wheat production. How does this affect the opportunity cost of wheat?

b. Adjust the PPC to reflect new seeds that produce drought-resistance wheat that increases maximum wheat production by 50% but has no impact on automobile production. How does this affect the opportunity cost of automobiles?

c. Adjust the PPC to reflect new technology that increases maximum automobile production by 50% and also increases maximum wheat production by 50%. How does this affect the opportunity cost of wheat?

Day 8

ARE FREE THINGS REALLY FREE?

We often find ourselves enjoying some "free" leisure time by watching a television show, texting with friends, or just reading. We do these things because they are enjoyable, but are they really free? Economists know that nothing is truly free, because there is always a second activity that was sacrificed to pursue the first activity.

In this exercise we will try to figure out a way to put a price on both the enjoyment of an activity and the cost of pursuing it.

Measuring Benefit.

Your task is to find someone who is enjoying some leisure. Maybe you can locate a family member or friend who is watching TV, playing a video game, texting or chatting on their phone, or reading a book, magazine, or newspaper.

Suppose you find someone watching a TV show. Your economic brain tells you that this person is choosing to watch TV because he or she believes the benefit exceeds the cost. How can we measure the benefit?

Measuring Cost.

Let's return to our person watching TV. Ask him or her, "If our cable/satellite connection suddenly stopped, what would you do instead?" Make sure that the person provides you with his or her *next best* choice for the use of this time. How can we measure the cost of skipping that second-best activity?

HAVE YOU EXPERIENCED MORE PRODUCTIVITY?

The production possibilities curve can increase (shift to the right) if the resources become more productive. The same is true for an individual. Watch this short video from the Bureau of Labor Statistics, "What Is Productivity?":

http://www.bls.gov/lpc/

When you're done with the video, think about tasks that you now perform more quickly or better than when you first started doing those things. Are there things that you have learned to do around the house, or at school, that have made you more productive over time?

CHAPTER 6 – DEMAND DETERMINANTS (CURVE SHIFTERS)

Even though you are studying for a macroeconomics exam, it is critical that you have a solid grasp of the factors that shift demand curves to the left or to the right.

For each of the following, describe how the demand for coffee will be affected. Be sure to determine which, if any, of the demand shifters is at work.

a. The American Medical Association reports that drinking coffee will lower your risk of cancer, increase your IQ, and improve your love life.

b. The price of coffee increases.

c. The state of the economy is rapidly improving, and coffee is a normal good.

d. The price of energy drinks, another caffeinated beverage, is rising.

e. The price of coffee-making machines is increasing.

Day 11

SUPPLY DETERMINANTS (SUPPLY SHIFTERS)

It is also very important that you have a solid grasp of the determinants of supply.

For each of the following, describe how the supply of oak tables will be affected. Be sure to determine which, if any, of the supply shifters is at work.

a. Producers have developed a faster way of constructing the oak tables.

b. The price of oak lumber has decreased.

c. A boom in the market for maple tables has increased the price that consumers are willing to pay for maple tables.

d. New manufacturers of oak tables have recently begun production and sale of oak tables.

e. The price of oak tables has fallen.

Day 12

SHORTAGES AND SURPLUSES

The table below shows the quantity of Cheezbows that are demanded (Qd) and supplied (Qs) at several prices.

PRICE	Q_d	Q_s	
$10	15	30	
$9	18	28	
$8	21	26	
$7	24	24	
$6	27	22	
$5	30	20	
$4	33	18	
$3	36	16	
$2	39	14	
$1	42	12	

At each price, determine whether there exists a shortage or a surplus of Cheezbows, and calculate the size of the shortage or surplus.

Day 13

CHANGES TO MARKET EQUILIBRIUM 1

Suppose the competitive market for oranges is in equilibrium. Given the following scenarios, you must (1) identify the specific shifter that is happening, (2) state which direction a curve is shifting, and (3) predict changes to the equilibrium price and quantity of oranges.

Note: A diagram is not required to answer these questions, but might be useful to you.

a. All else equal, the cost of labor used in picking oranges has increased.

b. All else equal, the *New York Times* reports that eating oranges increases your life span.

c. All else equal, the price of pears has decreased.

d. All else equal, combine the effects of parts (a) and (b).

Day 14

CHANGES TO MARKET EQUILIBRIUM 2

Suppose the competitive market for peanut butter is in equilibrium. Given the following scenarios, predict changes to the equilibrium price and quantity of peanut butter. Be sure to determine which of the market shifters is at work. A diagram is not required, but might be useful to you.

a. All else equal, the government places a per-unit tax on each jar of peanut butter produced.

b. All else equal, the price of strawberry jelly has decreased.

c. All else equal, the wholesale price of raw peanuts has decreased

d. All else equal, combine the events from parts (b) and (c).

Day 15

CALCULATING CONSUMER SURPLUS

Suppose the demand curve for Snabbles is given by the following equation:

$$P = 215 - 3Q_d$$

The current price of a Snabble is $125. Draw this demand curve, and calculate consumer surplus at the current price.

Day 16

CALCULATING PRODUCER SURPLUS

Suppose the supply curve of Draggnits is given by the following equation:

$$P = 60 + \tfrac{1}{2}Q_s$$

The current price of a Draggnits is $140. Draw this supply curve, and calculate producer surplus at the current price.

Day 17

CALCULATING EQUILIBRIUM AND CONSUMER AND PRODUCER SURPLUS

Let's say that the market for Snabbles has demand and supply equations that look like this:

Demand
$$P = 25 - Q_d$$

Supply
$$P = 1 + 2Q_s$$

a. Solve for market equilibrium price and quantity.

b. In equilibrium, calculate consumer and producer surplus. Note: It may help to draw the market, including the vertical intercepts.

CHAPTER 7 – LOCATING GROSS DOMESTIC PRODUCT DATA

> Today you will need to do a little bit of searching on the Internet to find answers to the following:
>
> - Can you find the government agency that calculates the GDP in the United States?
> - Can you find annual data for real (also called "chained dollar") GDP for the 5 most recent years? Hint: Look for a downloadable Excel spreadsheet.
> - Can you calculate the percentage change in real GDP between the most recent year available and the year prior to that year?

Day 19

VALUING PRODUCTION IN A SIMPLE ECONOMY

Suppose a very simple pizza-based economy produces only three items: pizza, breadsticks, and sodas. The following table shows the quantity of each item produced in the last 2 years and the prices that prevailed for those items. Complete the table by computing the value of the production of each item and the GDP in each year.

2014	QUANTITY	PRICE	VALUE OF PRODUCTION
Pizzas	200	$10	
Breadsticks	150	$2	
Sodas	400	$1	
Totals		N/A	
2015	**QUANTITY**	**PRICE**	**VALUE OF PRODUCTION**
Pizzas	300	$10	
Breadsticks	150	$2	
Sodas	300	$1	
Totals		N/A	

Day 20

A SIMPLE CIRCULAR FLOW DIAGRAM

The following is a very simple version of the circular flow diagram. In this economy there is no role for the government and there is no connection to foreign countries. Draw arrows that reflect the flow of resources (or factors of production), goods/services, and the payments for those factors and for those goods/services. Make sure your arrows are correctly labeled. Hint: There should be four arrows connecting the households and the firms.

Day 21

THE COMPONENTS OF GDP

If one were to compute GDP by adding up the four sectors of spending, you would have the familiar:

$$GDP = C + I + G + (X - M)$$

Your job is to go back to the government agency that collects GDP data and find each of these spending components for the most recent quarter. Hint: Look for a recent news release and links to a "Full Release and Tables" PDF file.

Make note of how large each of the four sectors is as a percentage of the total.

Day 22

CREATING A HYPOTHETICAL PRICE INDEX

The most commonly used price index in the United States is the Consumer Price Index (CPI), but we can create a price index for anything. All we need are a few prices over a few time periods and a decision on what time period is going to be our base year. The price index in the current year is computed by:

100 × (Price in current year)/(Price in the base year)

The following table provides some hypothetical prices for a hypothetical product, a Whizzling. Use this as practice in creating a price index, the WPI. Use 2012 as your base year and complete the table.

YEAR	PRICE	WPI
2011	$5	
2012	$10	
2013	$6	
2014	$8	
2015	$10	
2016	$12	

Day 23

FIND THE CONSUMER PRICE INDEX

Today you will need to do a little bit more searching on the Internet to find answers to the following:

- Can you find the government agency that calculates the rate of inflation in the United States?
- Can you find monthly data for the Consumer Price Index (CPI-U) for a few recent years? Hint: Look for databases.
- Can you calculate the percentage change in the CPI-U between the most recent month available and the previous month? This is the monthly inflation rate.
- Can you find monthly data for the inflation rate for a few recent years? This is also available in a downloadable form.

DEFLATING NOMINAL VALUES TO REAL VALUES

If we want to track the monetary value of anything, including a nation's output over time, we need to fix the prices that we use to a base year and then measure nominal dollars in a given year by using the prices that existed in that base year. This process of adjusting nominal values into inflation-adjusted, or real, values is called "deflation."

To adjust a nominal value into a real value, we make the following computation:

Real value in a year = 100 × (Nominal value in that year)/(Price index in that year)

The following table shows a person's nominal salary over a period of a few years and the average monthly CPI that existed in those years. Looking at the nominal salaries, we see that this person appears to be earning more money in 2016 than in 2012. Use the CPI to adjust those nominal salary values into real values. The current base year for the CPI is 1984. Once this table is completed, we will be able to determine if this person's salary has *really* risen once inflation has been accounted for.

YEAR	NOMINAL SALARY	CPI (1984 = 100)	REAL SALARY
2011	$50,000	129.453	
2012	$52,500	131.976	
2013	$53,000	133.592	
2014	$55,000	135.524	
2015	$58,000	135.362	

Day 25

WHO DATES THE BUSINESS CYCLE

You have learned that there is something called a business cycle that shows the expansion and contraction of economic activity over time. Do some more searching on the Internet to discover the organization that determines when expansions and recessions in the United States start and stop. Then find a list of recessions in the history of the U.S. economy. Look at the length of the most recent recession, and compare it to the average length of a recession in the years since 1945. What does this tell you about the most recent recession?

PERSONAL STORIES FROM THE GREAT RECESSION

> The Great Recession of 2007–2009 was long in its duration and painful in its consequences. If you are in high school now, you might not recall many details about that time in U.S. history. Your task is to find someone who does have clear memories of that time. Ask a few people if they have any stories about the impact of the recession on their lives, on the lives of people that they know, or on the company in which they were employed at the time. Take a little time to learn about this Great Recession from the stories and anecdotes that these people have to share.

Day 27

INFLATION RATES OVER TIME

> The Federal Reserve Bank of St. Louis has an excellent source of data called "FRED." Go to their website at:
>
> https://fred.stlouisfed.org/
>
> Search for "inflation, consumer prices for the United States." You should find at least one graph that shows inflation rates in the United States over a period of a few decades.
>
> - What is the worst period of inflation in this period of time, and when did it occur?
> - Looking at your graph, does it appear that inflation rates have become more erratic or more stable as the graph gets closer to the present day?
> - Vertical bars in the graph show periods of recession. What usually happens to inflation rates during recessions? Why do you think that happens?

Day 28

CALCULATING UNEMPLOYMENT RATES

A country has the following labor statistics for the civilian population:

Population under 16 years old .... 2.5 million

Population over 16 years old who are working part time .... 4 million

Population over 16 years old who are working full time .... 14 million

Those without jobs and who are actively seeking jobs .... 2.5 million

Those without jobs and not actively seeking jobs .... 1.5 million

a. Calculate the size of the civilian labor force and the unemployment rate.

b. Suppose that 1 million of those who were without jobs but seeking work become "discouraged" and drop out of the labor force. Recalculate the unemployment rate. Why does this happen?

EMPLOYED, UNEMPLOYED, OR OUT OF THE LABOR FORCE?

Read the following document that the Bureau of Labor Statistics provides.

https://www.bls.gov/cps/cps_htgm.pdf

Once you think you have a good grasp of how the government classifies people as either employed, unemployed, or out of the labor force, see if you can correctly classify the following six people.

1. Theo is a 14-year-old student who mows lawns in the neighborhood on the weekends at $7 per hour.

2. Eli is a 23-year-old graduate student working on his Ph.D. in Economics. He was offered a job 6 months ago, but decided he would rather focus on his courses and declined the offer.

3. Melanie is a 33-year-old college professor who has an annual salary of about $60,000.

4. Max is a 20-year-old college student who waits tables for 16 hours on the weekend and usually earns about $400 in tips.

5. Tommy used to work on the dock, but the union has been on strike, and he feels down on his luck. He doesn't know when the strike will end, so he's trying to find a job playing his six-string guitar, but so far he has not found any work.

6. Gina used to work in the diner all day, but she was recently fired. Since then, she has applied for several job openings and is waiting to hear whether she got the job or not. Until then, she dreams of running away.

UNEMPLOYMENT RATES OVER TIME

Once again it's time to consult the FRED to look at unemployment rates in the past. Search for something like "Civilian Unemployment Rate" and find a good graph over time.

- In the graph that you find, what is the highest unemployment rate, and in what year did it occur?
- Does the unemployment rate appear to be more erratic or more stable as the graph gets closer to the present day?
- Looking at the vertical gray bars that identify recessions, what happens to the unemployment rate during recessions? Why do you suppose that happens?

Day 31

THE DIFFERENT UNEMPLOYMENT RATES

The official unemployment rate reported by the U.S. Bureau of Labor Statistics (BLS) is referred to as "U-3" but there are other, more broadly defined, measures of unemployment and underemployment. Find the most recent Current Population Survey (CPS) report. This is the monthly report that summarizes the state of the labor market. Begin your search here:

https://www.bls.gov/cps/

When you find the most recent CPS report, go to the bottom for additional tables of data. Look for Table A-15 "Alternative Measures of Unemployment." Acquaint yourself with the measures of U-4, U-5, and U-6. Get a sense of what is meant by a "marginally attached worker" and a "discouraged worker." What do you think it means to be "employed part time for economic reasons," and why might it be important to track the number of people who fall into this category. You might dig around the BLS website and try to find definitions of these important labor force categories.

CHAPTER 8 – CONSUMPTION AND SAVINGS SCHEDULES

We have seen that consumption spending in the United States amounts to nearly 70% of GDP, so it is very important to have a grasp of how changes to consumption can greatly impact the economy. For now we will assume that there are no taxes or transfers in the economy, so household disposable income (DI) is equal to consumption spending (C) plus saving (S).

Suppose that Pam is a typical consumer. For every additional $1,000 of disposable income, Pam will consume $900 of it and save $100. If she had no income at all, she would still consume $100 by drawing down her accumulated savings by the same amount.

Complete the following table so that we have a complete schedule of her consumption and savings at several levels of disposable income.

DISPOSABLE INCOME (DI)	CONSUMPTION (C)	SAVINGS (S)
$0	$100	–$100
$1,000		
$2,000		
$3,000		
$4,000		
$5,000		
$6,000		

Day 33

DERIVING A CONSUMPTION FUNCTION

We have already completed the consumption and saving schedules for Pam, our typical consumer. We will now introduce Pam's grandmother, Gram. Let's try to create an equation for Pam's consumption function, and then we'll do the same for Gram.

PAM			GRAM		
DISPOSABLE INCOME (DI)	CONSUMPTION (C)	SAVING (S)	DISPOSABLE INCOME (DI)	CONSUMPTION (C)	SAVING (S)
$0	$100	−$100	$0	$100	−$100
$1,000	$1,000	$0	$1,000	$700	$300
$2,000	$1,900	$100	$2,000	$1,300	$700
$3,000	$2,800	$200	$3,000	$1,900	$1,100
$4,000	$3,700	$300	$4,000	$2,500	$1,500
$5,000	$4,600	$400	$5,000	$3,100	$1,900
$6,000	$5,500	$500	$6,000	$3,700	$2,300

These functions are straight lines, and the equation of a line is typically described as: $y = mx + b$.

For the consumption function, we plot consumption on the vertical axis and disposable income on the horizontal.

With this information, derive the consumption equations for Pam and Gram.

↓ 5 Minutes to a 5

Day 34

DERIVING A SAVINGS FUNCTION

Once again here are the consumption and savings schedules for our consumers, Pam and Gram.

PAM			GRAM		
DISPOSABLE INCOME (DI)	CONSUMPTION (C)	SAVING (S)	DISPOSABLE INCOME (DI)	CONSUMPTION (C)	SAVING (S)
$0	$100	–$100	$0	$100	–$100
$1,000	$1,000	$0	$1,000	$700	$300
$2,000	$1,900	$100	$2,000	$1,300	$700
$3,000	$2,800	$200	$3,000	$1,900	$1,100
$4,000	$3,700	$300	$4,000	$2,500	$1,500
$5,000	$4,600	$400	$5,000	$3,100	$1,900
$6,000	$5,500	$500	$6,000	$3,700	$2,300

Use the same techniques for building a consumption function to build the savings functions.

For the savings function, we plot savings on the vertical and disposable income on the horizontal.

Day 35

THE ROLE OF INVESTMENT

In the overall economy, consumption spending amounts to nearly 70% of all spending. While investment spending is a much smaller percentage of the total, it can be much more volatile and critical to shaping the business cycle.

Return to the website for the St. Louis Federal Reserve:

>https://fred.stlouisfed.org/search?st=corn+production

Search for "real gross private domestic investment," and see what you can find. Once you find a good graph of this important component of spending, try to identify any long-term trends. Now look more closely at the vertical gray bars that identify recessions. Do you notice anything about changes in investment around those recessions? What about the *timing* of change in investment?

Day 36

THE MARKET FOR LOANABLE FUNDS 1

In a correctly labeled graph of the loanable funds market, show how a general feeling of business optimism would affect the market and the equilibrium real interest rate.

THE MARKET FOR LOANABLE FUNDS 2

In a correctly labeled graph of the American loanable funds market, show how the market would change if foreign households and firms decided to put their money in American banks, rather than their own domestic banks. Show how this will affect the equilibrium real interest rate.

THE SPENDING MULTIPLIER

We will assume that people spend 90% of all income and save the rest. Complete the following table. To get you started, the first two rounds have been completed. In round one, Person A takes $1,000 out from under her mattress and spends it at person B's store. In round 2, person B has spent $900 at person C's business. After 12 rounds have been completed, add up the total spending generated by the initial $1,000.

TRANSACTION	SPENDING	SAVING
A to B	$1,000	N/A
B to C	$900	$100
C to D		
D to E		
E to F		
F to G		
G to H		
H to I		
I to J		
J to K		
K to L		
L to M		
Totals =		

Day 39

A TABLE FULL OF SPENDING MULTIPLIERS

The size of the simple spending multiplier (M) is directly related to the marginal propensity to consume (MPC) and inversely related to the marginal propensity to save (MPS).

$$M = \frac{1}{(1-MPC)} = \frac{1}{MPS}$$

Complete the table below to see how this works.

MPC	MPS	M
1	0	
0.90	0.10	
0.80	0.20	
0.75	0.25	
0.67	0.33	
0.60	0.40	
0.50	0.50	
0.40	0.60	
0.33	0.67	
0.20	0.80	
0.10	0.90	
0	1	

SOME MULTIPLIER SCENARIOS

For each of the following four scenarios, use the spending multiplier (*M*) to estimate the eventual impact on GDP in the economy.

- A nation with an *MPC* = 0.80 experiences an increase in autonomous investment spending of $10 billion.
- A nation with an *MPC* = 0.75 experiences a decrease in autonomous next exports of $6.5 billion.
- A nation with an *MPC* = 0.50 experiences an increase in autonomous government spending of $15 billion.
- A nation with an *MPC* = 0.90 experiences a decrease in autonomous consumption spending of $5 billion.

THE TAX MULTIPLIER

Suppose the government has sent person A $1,000 in tax rebates. We assume that people spend 90% of all income and save the rest. Complete the following table. To get you started, the first two rounds have been completed. In round 1, person A takes her $1,000 tax rebate and spends $900 at person B's store. In round 2, person B has spent $810 at person C's business. After 12 rounds have been completed, add up the total spending generated by the initial $1,000 tax rebate.

TRANSACTION	SPENDING	SAVING
A to B	$900	$100
B to C	$810	$90
C to D		
D to E		
E to F		
F to G		
G to H		
H to I		
I to J		
J to K		
K to L		
L to M		
Totals =		

A TABLE FULL OF TAX MULTIPLIERS

The size of the tax multiplier (T_m) is directly related to the marginal propensity to consume (*MPC*) and inversely related to the marginal propensity to save (*MPS*). There are a couple of different ways to compute the tax multiplier, but it will always be smaller than the spending multiplier (*M*).

$$T_m = (MPC) \times \frac{1}{(1 - MPC)} = \frac{MPC}{MPS} = MPC \times M$$

Complete the table below to see how this works.

MPC	MPS	M	T_M
1	0	∞	
0.90	0.10	10	
0.80	0.20	5	
0.75	0.25	4	
0.67	0.33	3	
0.60	0.40	2.5	
0.50	0.50	2	
0.40	0.60	1.67	
0.33	0.67	1.5	
0.20	0.80	1.25	
0.10	0.90	1.11	
0	1	1	

SOME TAX MULTIPLIER SCENARIOS

For each of the following four scenarios, use the tax multiplier (T_m) to estimate the eventual impact on GDP in the economy.

- A nation with an $MPC = 0.80$ experiences an increase in transfer payments of $10 billion.
- A nation with an $MPC = 0.75$ experiences a decrease in taxes of $6.5 billion.
- A nation with an $MPC = 0.50$ experiences an increase in taxes of $15 billion.
- A nation with an $MPC = 0.90$ experiences a decrease in transfer payments of $5 billion.

Day 44

BALANCED BUDGET MULTIPLIER

The nation of Theodorea has a marginal propensity to consume of 0.75. The government wishes to spend $3 billion on some new infrastructure, but legislators insist that taxes be increased by $3 billion to pay for the projects.

a. Use the spending multiplier to compute how much GDP will change due to the increased government spending.

b. Use the tax multiplier to compute how much GDP will change due to the increased taxes.

c. Based on your results, what is the eventual impact of this balanced-budget project on the Theodorean economy?

CHAPTER 9 – THE AD CURVE

> Without looking at your text or class notes, can you explain why the AD curve is downward sloping from these three effects?
>
> - Foreign sector substitution effect
> - Interest rate effect
> - Wealth effect

CHANGES IN THE AD CURVE

For each of the following, determine how the AD curve will increase or decrease. What component(s) of AD is changing?

a. Households are pessimistic about the state of the economy and their immediate job security.

b. Interest rates are at historically low levels.

c. The government has passed legislation that increases military spending.

d. Large economies in Asia are experiencing recessions.

Day 47

MORE CHANGES IN THE AD CURVE

Once again, for each of the following, determine how the AD curve will increase or decrease. What component(s) of AD is changing?

a. Firms are becoming more optimistic about the profitability of expansion projects.

b. The stock market is growing and households have experienced increased wealth.

c. The government has decided to increase taxes on household income.

d. Products made in the domestic economy are becoming more popular for foreign consumers.

THE SHAPE OF THE SHORT-RUN AS CURVE

The SRAS is usually drawn with an upward slope. Without looking at your textbook or notes, can you explain why?

Day 49

SHIFTS IN THE SRAS CURVE

For each of the following, determine how the SRAS curve will increase or decrease.

a. A new tax system is legislated that offers tax rebates on new research and development.

b. The economy is experiencing widespread increases in input prices.

c. Unnecessary and redundant business regulation is removed.

d. A nation is hit with a crippling drought and water shortages that require enormous sacrifice.

Day 50

DRAWING A RECESSIONARY GAP

Use a graph of the AD/AS model to show a recessionary gap. In your graph, make sure that you distinguish between the SRAS and LRAS curves. Label current price level as PL_r, current output as GDP_r and full-employment output as GDP_f.

DRAWING AN INFLATIONARY GAP

Use a graph of the AD/AS model to show an inflationary gap. In your graph, make sure that you distinguish between the SRAS and LRAS curves. Label current price level as PL_i, current output as GDP_i and full-employment output as GDP_f.

Day 52

PREDICTING CHANGES IN REAL GDP AND THE PRICE LEVEL

> Assume the economy is operating at full employment. In each of the following, predict the impact on AD or SRAS and how the event will likely change the price level and real GDP.
>
> **a.** Firms are less optimistic about future profitability.
>
> **b.** Foreign consumers are experiencing higher household incomes.
>
> **c.** Household wealth is increasing due to a strong real estate market.
>
> **d.** Input prices are steadily rising.
>
> **e.** The government has created tax incentives designed to increase productivity.

HISTORICAL DIFFERENCES BETWEEN REAL GDP AND POTENTIAL GDP

Find the following graph at the FRED website:

https://fred.stlouisfed.org/series/GDPPOT

This graph shows the real potential GDP in the United States since the late 1940s. We want to compare potential real GDP to actual real GDP. At the top right of the window, select "Edit Graph" and then select "Add Line." Now type something like "real GDP," and you should get several options. Make sure you choose actual dollars, not the percentage change in real GDP. Once you have found it, select "Add Data Series" and now your graph should have two lines on it.

Try zooming in on a recession from U.S. economic history (vertical gray bars). What do you notice about your graph during those times? Are there times when actual real GDP was above potential? Are there times when real GDP was below potential but the economy was not in a recession?

DRAWING THE PHILLIPS CURVE

Suppose that the full employment in the economy occurs at 5% unemployment and 2.5% inflation. This is also called the NAIRU, or "non-accelerating inflation rate of unemployment." In a correctly labeled graph, draw the long-run and short-run Phillips curves that reflect this information.

Now suppose that the actual unemployment rate rises to 6% and the inflation rate falls to 2%. Show this in the graph as point U. In the AD/AS model, what would explain a movement to point U?

Day 55

BILL PHILLIPS' MONIAC

Originally built in 1949 by New Zealand economist Dr. Bill Phillips, the MONIAC (Monetary National Income Analogue Computer) is one of the coolest models of the macroeconomy you will ever see. Powered by water, this device shows the circulation of money through the economy and how policy changes (like monetary policy) can affect all aspects of the economy. Take a look at some of the Reserve Bank of New Zealand's explanatory video, then investigate the virtual MONIAC, and you'll be impressed by the ingenuity of this device and you'll have another insight into the complexity of the circular flow model in the real world.

https://www.youtube.com/watch?v=FeFwyWcIHts

http://www.rbnzmuseum.govt.nz/activities/moniac/introduction.aspx

CHAPTER 10 – FISCAL POLICY PRESCRIPTION

You are the lead economist for the president, and you know that the economy is currently in the situation depicted by the following graph. What are the fiscal policy options that you might prescribe to the president? How would these policies alter the graph? Are there any downsides to your policies?

MORE FISCAL POLICY PRESCRIPTIONS

You are the lead economist for the president, and you know that the economy is currently in the situation depicted by the following graph. What are the fiscal policy options that you might prescribe to the president? How would these policies alter the graph? Are there any downsides to your policies?

Day 58

WHAT IS CROWDING OUT?

One criticism of expansionary fiscal policy is that it can lead to "crowding out." Without looking at your textbook or notes, can you explain what this means?

Day 59

CROWDING OUT IN THE LOANABLE FUNDS MARKET

Suppose the government has a balanced budget when the economy enters a recession. To combat the recession with fiscal policy, the government cuts taxes and increases spending. The resulting deficit requires the government to borrow by issuing Treasury bonds.

In a correctly labeled graph, show the following:

- Initial equilibrium interest rate r_1 and quantity of loanable funds F_1
- The impact that borrowing has on the market (we can assume that borrowing is included in the demand side of the market)
- The new equilibrium interest rate r_2 and quantity of loanable funds F_2
- The new quantity of private investment PF_1 and the quantity of government borrowing B

NATIONAL DEBT AS A SHARE OF THE ECONOMY

The U.S. national debt has grown quite a bit since the 1940s, but then again so has the size of the overall economy. One of the better measures of how much debt the nation has accumulated is to measure it as a percentage of the GDP in that year. Go back to the St. Louis FRED and search for such a graph. Make note of any trends that you see.

Each year the Office of Management and Budget (OMB) prepares a report on the nation's budget surplus and/or deficit. They also compute this as a percentage of GDP, and of course prices change over time, so to keep these measurements in "constant" dollars, we should correct for inflation. The OMB has such a table. Go to the following website, look for Table 1.3, and download the Excel file. The key column is the very last one, which shows the size of the annual surplus (positive numbers) or deficit (negative), as a percentage of the GDP in that year, using constant 2009 dollars. Make note of any trends that you see here.

https://obamawhitehouse.archives.gov/omb/budget/Historicals

Day 61

MORE CROWDING OUT

Another type of crowding out due to government borrowing centers on net exports. Without looking at your textbook or notes, can you explain this "net export effect"?

A HANDS-OFF CLASSICAL APPROACH TO RECESSIONS

The following graph shows a short-run equilibrium with a recessionary gap. Rather than use fiscal policy to try to return the economy to full employment GDP, describe the "Classical" adjustment to long-run equilibrium. Adjust the graph accordingly.

A HANDS-OFF CLASSICAL APPROACH TO INFLATION

The following graph shows a short-run equilibrium with an inflationary gap. Rather than use fiscal policy to try to return the economy to full employment GDP, describe the "Classical" adjustment to long-run equilibrium. Adjust the graph accordingly.

MORE GROWTH AND PRODUCTIVITY

Economic growth can be represented by an outward shift in a nation's production possibility curve. In an earlier activity you watched a video about productivity from the BLS website. Head back to the BLS website and their section on productivity:

https://www.bls.gov/lpc/

Find a Commissioner's Corner blog entry titled, "Why This Counts: Productivity and Its Impact on Our Lives" dated August 9, 2016. Give this short essay a careful read. How has productivity changed in the United States since 1947? How is productivity changing since 2007, the beginning of the Great Recession? Are labor productivity and real wages correlated?

CHANGES IN HUMAN CAPITAL

An important factor in greater labor productivity is higher levels of education. The percentage of a nation that has completed a certain level of education is called educational attainment and this data is collected by the Census Bureau. The following report describes how educational attainment has changed in the United States over time, and how it differs for men and women and whites and non-whites:

http://www.census.gov/prod/2012pubs/p20-566.pdf

After reading the document, describe how educational attainment has changed since the 1940s. Can you summarize differences between men and women, and between whites and non-whites? Can you find data in the report that illustrates how more educational attainment is associated with higher earnings?

SHOWING ECONOMIC GROWTH IN THE AD/AS MODEL

We have seen that economic growth can be shown as an outward shift of the PPC, but how is economic growth shown in the AD/AS model? The following is a graph that shows the economy in long-run equilibrium. Adjust the graph to show long-run growth, perhaps due to policies that encourage productivity gains of all kinds.

Day 67

WHAT WE CAN LEARN FROM BABYSITTING CO-OPS AND POW CAMPS

> Watch this video in which economist Tim Harford describes two situations that fostered a different type of money and how each system slipped into a recession. He also compares the two recessions and how the "government" in each case could, or could not, act to fix the recessions.
>
> https://www.youtube.com/watch?v=AOljR_tKlBk
>
> Do you see the active role of government stimulus in the babysitting co-op story? How does it relate to the fiscal policy tools that you have learned?
>
> What does Dr. Harford mean when he describes the POW camp as being hit by a recessionary "shock"? How is this different from the babysitting co-op recession?

CHAPTER 11 – STOCKS VS. BONDS

A firm can use stocks and/or bonds as ways of raising money. These are both forms of financial assets for those that possess them. Without looking at your textbook or your notes, can you describe the difference between a stock and a bond?

Day 69

HISTORY OF MONEY

The paper currency and coins (a.k.a. fiat money) that you might have nearby is the result of thousands of years of experimentation with different forms of money. Here are links to a couple of amusing short videos about the history of money. Once you have watched them, can you explain why we use money rather than barter to acquire the goods and services we desire? And how does our current fiat money satisfy the three functions of money better than eggs would?

https://www.youtube.com/watch?v=ADaY6THQp3Y

https://www.youtube.com/watch?v=AjTwcQYgISA

SOME TIME VALUE OF MONEY CALCULATIONS

Let's get out the calculators and work on some problems.

a. You are borrowing $50 from a friend and promise to repay her in 1 year. If you agree to a 4% interest rate, how much will you return to your friend 1 year from today?

b. Your grandpa agrees to send you $100 in a year. If the interest rate you can receive in a bank is 5%, what is the present value of Grandpa's promised gift?

c. You have won a raffle that promises to pay you $5,000 in 2 years or you can take $4,500 now. Banks are paying 10% interest rates today. Which of these two offers should you accept?

Day 71

THE MONEY SUPPLY

How much money is out there in circulation? The measure $M1$ is the basis for counting up all of the money circulating. Return to the St. Louis FRED website and search for "$M1$ Money Stock." Do you see any trends in $M1$? What might explain any trends?

https://fred.stlouisfed.org/

MULTIPLE DEPOSIT MONEY CREATION

The system of fractional reserve banking has been around for a long time and allows for new deposits to multiply and expand the money supply. It is also fundamental to the success of any monetary policy. Let's see how this works with a simple example. Assume that the bank is required to keep 10% of all checking deposits in reserve and lends out the rest. Borrowers immediately deposit all of their borrowed cash into their own checking accounts.

Keep track of all new checking deposits in the following table. We begin with person A taking $1,000 from his sock drawer and depositing it into the First Bank of Madville (FBM). The FBM holds $100 of his deposit in reserve and lends $900 to person B, who deposits the money into her checking account. These first two rounds are done for you. The arrow shows you the connection between a new loan and a new checking deposit. Stop with the deposit in round 7.

ROUND	DEPOSIT	CASH IN RESERVE	A LOAN IS MADE
1	$1,000 from person A	$100	$900 to person B
2	$900 from person B	$90	$810 to person C
3			
4			
5			
6			
7			
	Total = $		Total = $

Day 73

THE MONEY DEMAND CURVE

> Without looking at your textbook or your class notes, can you explain why the demand for money is drawn downward sloping?

THE RELATIONSHIP BETWEEN BOND PRICES AND INTEREST RATES

Remember a bond is like an IOU, or a promise that the issuer makes to repay the purchaser, plus interest. There is an inverse relationship between the price of a bond and the interest rate bondholders receive at maturity. Let's try to figure out how this works.

Suppose you buy a Treasury bond for $900 and you are promised repayment of $1,000 when it matures. What is the interest rate on this bond?

Now suppose that the demand for bonds rises and the same bond is now selling for a price of $950, with the same repayment of $1,000 upon maturity. What is the interest rate now?

Why would the demand for bonds increase in the first place? Can you speculate a couple of reasons why this might happen?

A SHIFT IN MONEY DEMAND

In a correctly labeled graph of the money market, show the current equilibrium nominal interest rate. Suppose the economy gets some momentum and nominal GDP is rising this year. Adjust your graph to reflect this change. How does this affect the nominal interest rate?

THE MONEY MULTIPLIER

The Federal Reserve sets the reserve requirement (*rr*) for banks in the United States. This is the minimum fraction of checking deposits that must be kept on reserve in the bank. We have seen how a deposit can create even more new money within the fractional banking system. This money multiplier effect is critically dependent on the reserve requirement:

$$M = 1/rr$$

Complete the table with several different values of *rr*.

RESERVE REQUIREMENT (RR)	MONEY MULTIPLIER
0.01	
0.05	
0.10	
0.20	
0.25	
0.50	

Day 77

THE TOOLS OF THE FED

Without looking at your textbook or class notes, can you list the three tools of the Federal Reserve in conducting monetary policy? How would each be changed if the Fed wanted to increase the money supply?

Day 78

MONETARY POLICY 1

Economic indicators have told you, an economist at the Fed, that real GDP has significantly slipped below potential GDP and that the unemployment rate has been rising for several months in a row. If you were to propose an OMO to the Chair, what would it be? In a graph of the money market, show how your proposal would affect interest rates. In an AD/AS graph of the economy, show how your proposal should affect the economy.

MONETARY POLICY 2

Economic indicators have told you, an economist at the Fed, that real GDP has significantly increased above potential GDP and that the unemployment rate has fallen below the NAIRU. While this might appear to be good news, the inflation rate has steadily been increasing to unacceptable levels. If you were to propose an OMO to the Chair, what would it be? In a graph of the money market, show how your proposal would affect interest rates. In an AD/AS graph of the economy, show how your proposal should affect the economy.

MONETARY POLICY IN THE GREAT RECESSION

You have learned that the Fed should expand the money supply and lower interest rates to stimulate the economy in a recession. But what happens when a *really big* recession hits? The following link is an essay that describes the Fed's reaction to the Great Recession of 2007–2009. One of the difficulties that the Fed faced is what is known as a "liquidity trap." Do a little background reading, maybe from your textbook, on what is meant by a liquidity trap. Try to find mention of this problem in the Fed's essay. When faced with the liquidity trap, what other measures did the Fed pursue during this very challenging time for the U.S. economy?

http://www.federalreservehistory.org/Events/DetailView/58

A good video describing the financial aspects of the Great Recession can be found here:

https://www.youtube.com/watch?v=dI6HNi5I8d4

KEYNES VS. HAYEK

The macroeconomic debates surrounding fiscal and monetary policy is whether or not each is actually useful, and if not, whether it should be abandoned. The proactive approach, where the government has a strong hand in steering the economy, has come to be called the Keynesian approach after John Maynard Keynes. The Keynesians believe that a stagnant economy needs to be boosted by government spending or lower interest rates from Fed action. They think that the economy will take too long to self-correct, thus creating a lot of long-term pain.

The alternative to an active government role is no role at all; let the economy come to long-run equilibrium without interference. This belief is strongly cemented in the philosophy of F. A. Hayek, a strong champion of how unfettered markets can cure economic downturns and that expansionary monetary policy (and the low interest rates that accompany it) will only lead to inflation.

For an entertaining take on these competing philosophies, watch this video and see if you can find some logical points in each of the arguments:

https://www.youtube.com/watch?v=d0nERTFo-Sk

https://www.youtube.com/watch?v=GTQnarzmTOc

CHAPTER 12 – COMPARATIVE ADVANTAGE AND TRADE

These two countries are producing textiles and wheat using equal amounts of resources. Use the following table to answer the following questions.

	COUNTRY A		COUNTRY B	
Bushels of wheat	15	0	10	0
Units of textiles	0	60	0	60

a. Which nation has comparative advantage in wheat production, and which nation has comparative advantage in textile production? Show your work.

b. If trade is done based on comparative advantage and specialization, create a specific trade agreement that would allow both nations to consume beyond their production possibility curves.

Day 83

DEMAND FOR THE U.S. DOLLAR

For each of the following scenarios, determine if the European demand for the dollar would increase or decrease and explain your reasoning.

a. Interest rates in the United States are lower than in Europe.

b. Products made in the United States are more popular among European consumers.

c. European nations are experiencing a significant recession.

d. The price level in the United States is very stable, while European price levels are rapidly rising.

5 Minutes to a 5

Day 84

CONNECTING MONETARY POLICY TO FOREIGN EXCHANGE

> Suppose the U.S. economy is experiencing a recession.
>
> **a.** How will the Fed move to combat the recession, and how will this action affect interest rates in the U.S. economy?
>
> **b.** How will the Fed's action affect the value of the U.S. dollar and net exports in the United States? Explain.

Day 85

A HOTEL ROOM ABROAD

Search the Internet for a hotel room in the European Union (EU), and find the price of a room in euros. Hint: You might have to go directly to the hotel's website (rather than Travelocity) to get the prices in euros. Now go to a website like the one that follows, and find the exchange rate between the U.S. dollar and the euro. Find how many dollars it costs to buy 1 euro. Now use this exchange rate to determine how many dollars it would cost you to book that hotel room. Use the same currency exchange website to determine the exchange rate a year ago; then use it to compute the price of that room 1 year ago. If you were to take a vacation to Europe now, would it be more or less expensive than it was a year ago?

http://www.xe.com/

GRAPHING THE CURRENCY MARKET

Create a correctly labeled graph of the market for the euro, priced in U.S. dollars. If interest rates in the European Union were higher than they were in the United States, how would the market for the euro be affected? Add this to your graph and show whether the euro would appreciate or depreciate against the dollar.

Day 87

THE OTHER SIDE OF THE PREVIOUS MARKET

In the previous exercise, we were looking at what happened to the market for the euro, but something was also happening in the market for the dollar. Can you draw the changes in the market for the dollar? The dollar is priced in euros.

THE BENEFITS OF INTERNATIONAL TRADE

> Watch the following video that describes how international trade has benefited the U.S. economy in many quantitative ways.
>
> https://www.youtube.com/watch?v=uuYuYax04Vk
>
> There is a lot of data presented here. See if you can extract some of the important conclusions about how more trade is associated with a stronger U.S. economy.

Day 89

THE U.S. BALANCE OF PAYMENTS

Go to the Bureau of Economic Analysis at the following website, and find the most current news release of the "International Transactions."

https://www.bea.gov/

One important part of the balance of payments is the current account. The current account describes the flow of exports and imports of goods and services, and income payments to and from the United States. The current account is where we find whether a nation had a trade surplus (exports exceed imports) or a trade deficit (imports exceed exports). Take a look at the news release; there should also be summary tables near the end. Did the United States have a trade surplus or a deficit? How big was it?

ANOTHER GAINS FROM TRADE EXERCISE

Take a look at the following PPCs for two nations, Theodoria and Elijastan. Based on only these two graphs, determine how these two nations could specialize and gain from trade. You will need to determine which nation exports steel and which nation exports food. Finally, find an acceptable terms of trade that would benefit both nations.

Answers

Day 1

1. Labor: Your efforts in doing the research and typing the paper

2. Capital: The library or Internet site in which you found research, the computer on which you typed the paper

3. Natural resources: The electricity used to operate the computer and printer, the paper on which you printed the research paper

4. Entrepreneurial ability: Your know-how and creativity in bringing all of the other resources together to create a high-quality final product

Day 2

Note: the following numbers are hypothetical but give you an idea of how to compute *your actual* opportunity cost.

1. I selected a movie and a pizza, and I would offer to pay for the entire date. The local price of a movie ticket is $10 and a pizza for two people is $15.

2. I will buy two drinks during the movie, and this will cost about another $6.

3. The nearest cinema is 6 miles away, the pizza place is another 1 mile away, and my date lives ½ mile from my house, so I would drive 15 total miles. My car gets about 30 miles per gallon, so I would use ½ gallon of gas. Local prices are about $2.50 per gallon so my driving costs are about $1.25.

4. The movie lasts 122 minutes, eating a pizza takes another 60 minutes, and the drive is estimated to be 15 minutes each way, for a total of 212 minutes, or 3.53 hours. If I could make a wage of $10 per hour, I could have earned $35.33 (ignoring taxes) during the movie.

5. Total opportunity cost of this movie = ($10 × 2) + $15 + $6 + $1.25 + $35.33 = $77.58.

Day 3

Since each taco costs $1, the marginal cost curve should be drawn horizontal at $1. The marginal benefit curve is drawn downward sloping because the next taco provides less additional benefit. After all, your hunger is partially satisfied with each taco, so the next taco isn't quite as great as the one that came before.

So if your hypothetical number of tacos was 5, the graph should look something like this:

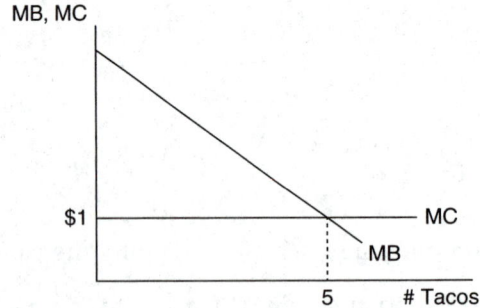

Day 4

a. A PPC with constant opportunity costs should be drawn as a straight line.

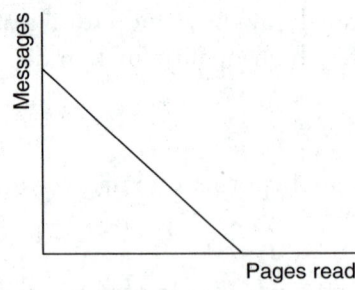

b. Since the Internet speed is cut in half, the PPC should move inward along the *y*-axis but not along the *x*-axis.

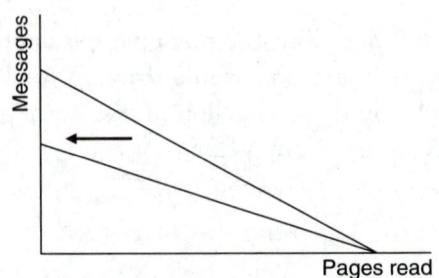

c. The opportunity cost of studying has now decreased. Remember that the opportunity cost of an activity, studying in this case, is what you have given up to engage in that activity. Now that your Internet speed has been cut in half, every hour spent studying comes at a smaller sacrifice in the number of messages you could have been sending and reading.

Day 5

a. Yes. Eli has an absolute advantage in both tasks because he can outproduce Theodore in both folding towels and washing plates.

b. If Eli splits his time equally, he can fold 8 towels and wash 4 plates.

If Theodore does the same, he can fold 3 towels and wash 3 plates.

Total output: 11 towels + 7 plates = 18

c. A person is said to have a comparative advantage in a task if he or she can perform that task at a lower opportunity cost.

For every plate that Eli washes, he gives up 2 towels folded, so that is his opportunity cost of washing plates. On the other hand, for every towel that he folds, he gives up washing half of a plate.

For every plate that Theodore washes, he gives up 1 towel folded. And for every towel he folds, he gives up 1 washed plate.

So we can see that Theodore has a lower opportunity cost of washing plates (1 towel) when compared to Eli's opportunity cost of washing plates (2 towels). Theodore has a comparative advantage in washing plates. On the other hand, Eli has the comparative advantage in folding towels because he gives up ½ washed plate while Theodore gives up 1 washed plate.

If they specialize based on comparative advantage, Eli should spend all of his time folding towels, and Theodore should spend all of his time washing plates.

Total output with specialization: 16 towels + 6 plates = 22.

Day 6

1. Productive efficiency is achieved when you produce the maximum amount of output for a given level of technology and resources. If you were inefficient in the kitchen, you might use the correct quantity of ingredients but produce only 10 cookies. Another way of being productively inefficient would be to produce a dozen cookies but waste some of the ingredients in the process (like dropping an egg on the floor or spilling some flour).

2. Most people, if equity were the goal, would give each person 3 cookies. Of course this outcome depends upon how you define "equitable." Rather than this egalitarian outcome, another might define equitable by giving the most cookies to the person with the highest GPA or other arbitrary measure of merit. This is similar to saying that the highest wages should be paid to those who are most productive.

3. Allocative efficiency would be achieved if the cookies were distributed to maximize the happiness of the 4 people eating them. One way to do this would be to give the most

cookies to the person who most desired them (or was the hungriest) and the fewest cookies to the person who had the least desire for cookies. Alternatively, you could give each person 3 cookies and then allow them to trade cookies among themselves. When there are no more trades to be made, it's likely you have found an efficient allocation.

Day 7

a.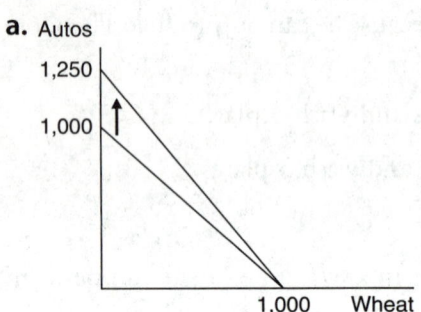

A 25% increase in maximum automobile production moves the vertical intercept up to 1,250 autos. Remember that the slope of the PPC gives us the opportunity cost of wheat. Prior to the technology, 1 unit of wheat cost 1 automobile, but now 1 unit of wheat costs 1.25 automobiles. Because automobile-producing technology has improved, devoting resources to wheat costs society more automobiles that could have been produced.

b.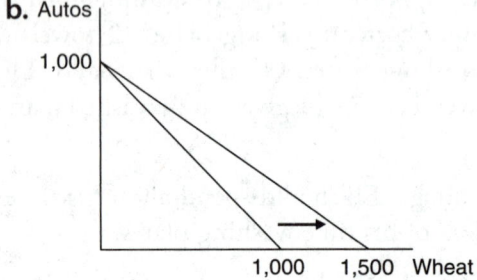

A 50% increase in maximum wheat production moves the horizontal intercept out to 1,500 units of wheat. Remember that the inverse of the slope of the PPC gives us the opportunity cost of automobiles. Prior to the drought-resistant seeds, 1 automobile cost 1 unit of wheat, but now 1 automobile costs 1.5 units of wheat. Because of the improved wheat production, devoting resources to automobiles costs society more units of wheat that could have been produced.

c.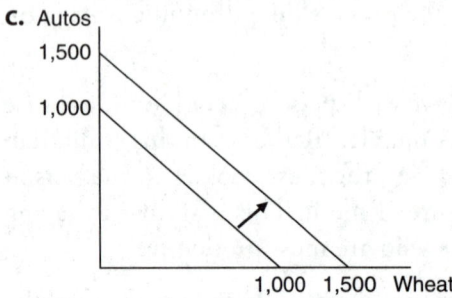

Better technology has improved production of both goods by the same degree. The new opportunity cost of wheat is still 1 auto, and the opportunity cost of 1 auto is still 1 unit of wheat.

Day 8

To measure the benefit of an activity that has no price tag, economists can try to create a hypothetical auction.

Ask this person, "How much money would I need to pay you to stop watching TV and forgo the enjoyment (utility) you are receiving from it? Would you take $1, $5, $10?" Keep increasing the bid until this person accepts a hypothetical compensation to give up doing something he or she enjoys: watching TV. Once you reach this number, you know how much economic value (money) this person places on watching TV. After all, if the person would accept $20 to turn off the TV, watching the TV must be worth $20 to them.

We can do a similar exercise to try to measure the opportunity cost of not doing a second-best use of our time. You have asked a person to tell you what he or she would be doing if the TV signal suddenly ended and he or she could not watch TV during this time. Of course, this person could give you any of dozens of possible activities, but suppose the person tells you that he or she would be playing a game on his or her phone. Now ask this person, "If you were playing a game on your phone, how much money would I need to pay you to stop?" Begin the auction at $1 and gradually raise the hypothetical price until the person accepts a value that would compensate for turning off the game.

If the person would need to be paid $10 to turn off the game, this is the value the person places on playing the game. Because the person is watching TV at the moment, and not playing the game, then missing the game means the person is sacrificing $10 of potential enjoyment. This is the opportunity cost of watching TV.

If your friend or family member is acting like economists predict, the dollar value they give you for the benefit of watching TV should exceed the dollar value they give you for giving up the second-best activity. If they do not, it opens the door for an interesting conversation about why they would choose to watch TV if the costs exceed the benefit.

Day 9

In the video, Beth sees an increase in her productivity when she learns how to make better birdhouses more quickly. Her productivity is measured as an increase in her output for the same number of inputs. We can also see productivity if she makes the same number of birdhouses with fewer inputs.

If you can think of a task around the house or at school that you can complete now more quickly than when you first attempted it, then you have increased your productivity.

Day 10

a. This is an increase in tastes and preferences, so demand for coffee shifts to the right.

b. This will not cause a shift in the demand for coffee; it will cause the quantity of coffee to increase downward along the demand curve.

c. This is an increase in income; so because coffee is a normal good, demand shifts to the right.

d. This is an increase in the price of a substitute good, so demand for coffee shifts to the right.

e. This is an increase in the price of a complementary good, so the demand for coffee shifts to the left.

Day 11

a. Faster-production technology will increase the supply (shift it to the right) of oak tables.

b. Oak lumber is a critical input, so a lower price of the lumber will shift the supply of oak tables to the right.

c. Tables made of maple are production substitutes for tables made of oak. If the price of maple tables is rising, producers will decrease the supply of oak tables (shift to the left).

d. As more producers of oak tables enter the market, the supply of oak tables will shift to the right.

e. Tricky one! This is not a shift in the supply of oak tables, it is a movement downward along the supply curve. A lower price decreases the quantity of tables supplied, but does not shift the curve.

Day 12

A surplus exists when quantity supplied exceeds quantity demanded, and these are seen at all prices above $7. The size of the surplus is equal to Q_s minus Q_d.

A shortage exists when quantity demanded exceeds quantity supplied, and these are seen at all prices below $7. The size of the shortage is equal to Q_d minus Q_s.

The only price where there is neither a shortage nor a surplus is $7, and this is the market equilibrium price.

PRICE	Q_d	Q_s	SHORTAGE OR SURPLUS
$10	15	30	Surplus = 15
$9	18	28	Surplus = 10
$8	21	26	Surplus = 5
$7	24	24	Equilibrium, $Q_d = Q_s$
$6	27	22	Shortage = 5
$5	30	20	Shortage = 10
$4	33	18	Shortage = 15
$3	36	16	Shortage = 20
$2	39	14	Shortage = 25
$1	42	12	Shortage = 30

Day 13

a. The price of a key input is rising, so this would shift the supply of oranges to the left, causing a decrease in the quantity and increase in price.

b. A health benefit (longer life span) would increase tastes and preferences for oranges, causing an increase in the demand and eventual increase in both price and quantity.

c. The price of a substitute good is decreasing, so demand for oranges will decrease, causing a decrease in both price and quantity.

d. When we combine a decrease in the supply with an increase in the demand for oranges, the price will certainly rise, but the change in market quantity will depend on which shift is larger. If the supply shift is larger, quantity will fall. If the demand shift is larger, quantity will rise.

Day 14

a. A tax on the production of peanut butter will act like a higher input cost and decrease the supply. A decrease in the supply will increase the price of peanut butter and decrease equilibrium quantity.

b. Strawberry jelly is likely a complementary product, so a lower price will increase the demand for peanut butter, increasing both the price and quantity in the market.

c. A lower price of raw peanuts is a lower input price for making peanut butter. The supply of peanut butter will increase, causing a lower market price and higher market quantity.

d. When we combine an increase in demand with an increase in supply, we know for certain that equilibrium quantity will increase. However, the change in the equilibrium price is uncertain and depends on which shift is larger. If the demand shift is larger, the price will increase. If the supply shift is larger, the price will decrease.

Day 15

Consumer surplus is the area below the demand curve and above the price. When the demand curve is a straight line, we can calculate consumer surplus as the area of a triangle; we just need to know the dimensions (height and width) of the triangle. To get the height, we need the vertical intercept and the price. The vertical intercept, the price when quantity is zero, is $215, and the current price is given to you as $125. To get the width, we need the quantity of Snabbles demanded. Using a price of $125 in the demand equation, we solve for a quantity of 30 units.

Calculate $CS = \frac{1}{2} \times (\$90)(30) = \$1,350$

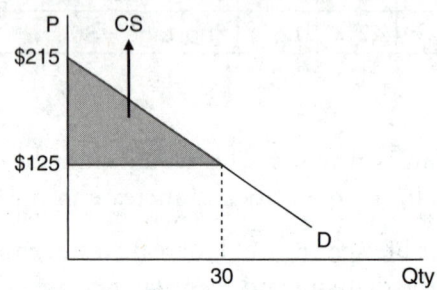

Day 16

Producer surplus is the area above the supply curve and below the price. When the supply curve is a straight line, we can calculate producer surplus as the area of a triangle; we just need to know the dimensions (height and width) of the triangle. To get the height, we need the vertical intercept and the price. The vertical intercept, the price when quantity is zero, is $60, and the current price is given to you as $140. To get the width, we need the quantity of Draggnits supplied. Using a price of $140 in the supply equation, we solve for a quantity of 160 units.

Calculate $PS = \frac{1}{2} \times (\$80)(160) = \$6,400$

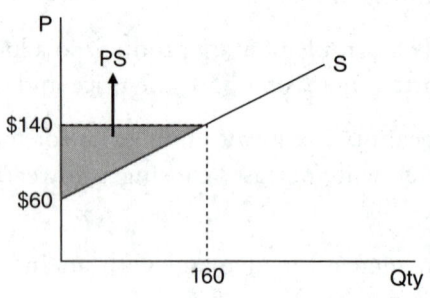

Day 17

a. Set the price from the demand curve equal to the price from the supply curve.

$$25 - Q = 1 + 2Q$$
$$24 = 3Q$$
$$Q = 8 \text{ and } P = \$17$$

b.

$$CS = \tfrac{1}{2}(\$8)(8) = \$32 \text{ (area below demand and above price)}$$
$$PS = \tfrac{1}{2}(\$16)(8) = \$64 \text{ (area below price and above supply)}$$

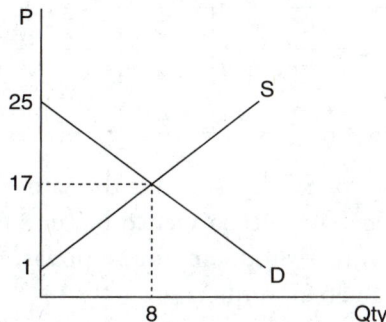

Day 18

- The Bureau of Economic Analysis, an office within the Department of Commerce, produces the GDP numbers in the United States. Website: http://www.bea.gov/
- Under the heading of "U.S. National Accounts," you should be able to find downloadable data for real GDP. Website: https://www.bea.gov/national/index.htm#gdp
  The following table shows annual real GDP from 2011 to 2015. Notice that the dollars are presented in billions of 2009 dollars. That means that the base year being used is 2009, so the output in each of these years was valued using prices that existed in 2009.

YEAR	REAL GDP (BILLIONS OF 2009 DOLLARS)
2011	$15,020.6
2012	$15,354.6
2013	$15,612.2
2014	$15,982.3
2015	$16,397.2

The percentage change between the two most recent years in this table is calculated by:

$$\%\Delta\text{real GDP} = 100 \times (2015 \text{ real GDP} - 2014 \text{ real GDP})/(2014 \text{ real GDP})$$
$$= 100 \times (\$16{,}397.2 - \$15{,}982.3)/(\$15{,}982{,}3) = 2.60\%$$

Day 19

To compute the value of production, multiply the quantity produced by the price. Then sum up the quantity column and the value of production column.

2014	QUANTITY	PRICE	VALUE OF PRODUCTION
Pizzas	200	$10	$2,000
Breadsticks	150	$2	$300
Sodas	400	$1	$400
Totals	Total = 750	N/A	Total = $2,700
2015	**QUANTITY**	**PRICE**	**VALUE OF PRODUCTION**
Pizzas	300	$10	$3,000
Breadsticks	150	$2	$300
Sodas	300	$1	$300
Totals	Total = 750	N/A	Total = $3,600

Notice that the total number of products sold is the same in each year (750), but the value of production has risen. This has happened because the *mix* of the products has changed and now the economy is producing more pizzas, the most valuable product, and fewer sodas, the least valuable product.

Day 20

Households and firms are connected in two ways:

- Households supply factors of production (e.g., labor) in exchange for payments (e.g., wages).
- Firms supply goods and services to households in exchange for expenditures.

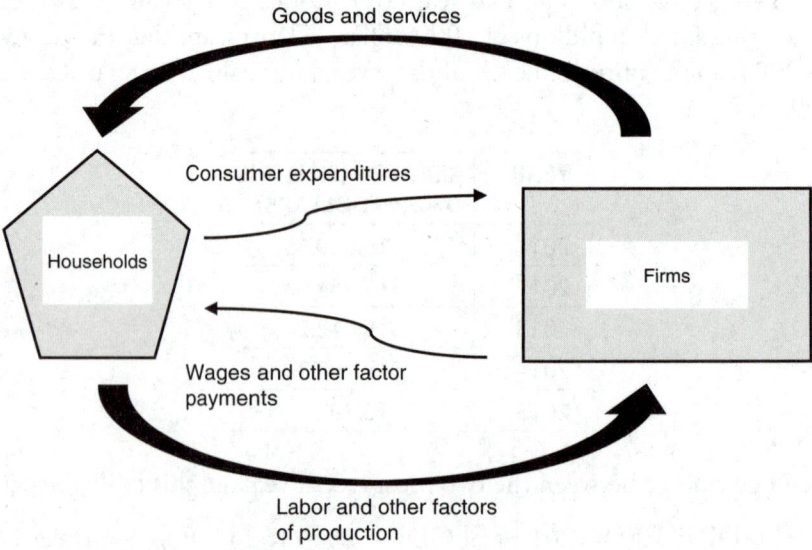

Day 21

At this writing, the most recent quarterly release was the third quarter of 2016. You will find these released reports here:

http://www.bea.gov/national/index.htm#gdp

Here is the link to the full release and tables from November 2016:

http://www.bea.gov/newsreleases/national/gdp/2016/pdf/gdp3q16_2nd.pdf

Table 3 of this report has the relevant information.

In the column for the third quarter of 2016, GDP (in billions of seasonally adjusted dollars) is broken down into the components. If you add the four components, the total is likely going to be slightly different due to rounding.

Third Quarter 2016

$$GDP = \$18{,}657.9$$
$$C = \$12{,}825.3 \text{ (68.7\% of the total)}$$
$$I = \$3{,}010.0 \text{ (16.1\%)}$$
$$G = \$3{,}281.5 \text{ (17.6\%)}$$
$$X - M = -\$459.0 \text{ (}-2.5\%\text{)}$$

While your numbers will be different than these, you will probably find that consumption spending is nearly 70% of all spending in the economy.

Day 22

Using the following formula for the WPI, the table should look like this.

$$\text{WPI} = 100 \times (\text{Price in current year})/(\text{Price in the base year})$$

A price index is always equal to 100 in the base year.

YEAR	PRICE	WPI
2011	$5	= 100 × ($5/$10) = 50
2012	$10	= 100
2013	$6	= 60
2014	$8	= 80
2015	$10	= 100
2016	$12	= 120

Day 23

- The Bureau of Labor Statistics (BLS) computes and reports the CPI every month. The BLS website is found here: https://www.bls.gov/
- Near the top of the page you will find a drop-down menu for "Subjects" and you should see "Consumer Price Index." There are several ways to find recent values of the CPI. One way is to explore the section of "CPI Databases." Look for the option of "All Urban Consumers" and "Top Picks" here: https://www.bls.gov/cpi/data.htm
Check the top box that says "U.S. All items, 1982–1984 = 100," and then select the button for "Retrieve data." You should now see about 10 years of monthly data for the CPI that uses the period of 1982–1984 as the base year.
- To calculate the monthly inflation rate between two consecutive months (October to November 2016 as an example), we do this:

$$\text{Monthly inflation} = 100 \times (\text{CPI November} - \text{CPI October})/(\text{CPI October})$$

$$= 100 \times (241.353 - 241.729)/241.729 = -0.16\%$$

You might see along the right-hand side of the main page some little subheadings for inflation and the CPI. These should be accompanied by a little icon that looks like a graph. Look for something that says "CPI-U, U.S. City Average, All Items," as this is the broadest measurement of inflation. You might find a page similar to this:

https://data.bls.gov/timeseries/CUUR0000SA0?output_view=pct_12mths

Day 24

To deflate nominal salaries into real salaries, we use this formula:

Real salary in a year = 100 × (Nominal salary in that year)/(CPI in that year)

YEAR	NOMINAL SALARY	CPI (1984 = 100)	REAL SALARY
2011	$50,000	129.453	=100 × ($50,000)/(129.453) = $38,624
2012	$52,500	131.976	$39,780
2013	$53,000	133.592	$39,673
2014	$55,000	135.524	$40,583
2015	$58,000	135.362	$42,848

We can now see that this person's salary, after adjusting for inflation, did gradually rise from 2011 to 2015, but actually took a small decrease between 2012 and 2013.

Day 25

The National Bureau of Economic Research (NBER) is a professional organization of economists that does empirical research across many fields in economics. One aspect of the NBER is the Business Cycle Dating Committee. This is the group of economists that determines when recessions begin and end. Here is the website:

http://www.nber.org/cycles/cyclesmain.html

The most recent recession began in December 2007 (the peak of the cycle) and ended in June 2009 (the trough of the cycle). This duration of 18 months is much longer than the average of 11.1 months in the business cycles since 1945, which tells us that the "Great Recession" was noteworthy for how long it lasted.

Day 26

Clearly there are no correct answers for this exercise. If you speak with enough people, you might hear stories that involve:

- A lost job
- Wages and/or benefits either declined, or pay raises that were canceled
- A lost home due to foreclosure
- A nearby business that closed
- Personal savings that were exhausted
- A vacation or other large purchase that was given up

Day 27

With a little bit of searching on the FRED, you probably found a graph like this one:

https://fred.stlouisfed.org/series/FPCPITOTLZGUSA

- The highest rate of inflation in this graph was 13.5% in 1980.
- The ups and downs of the inflation graph appears to be more stable as we get into the 1990s and 2000s. You can see this in fewer dramatic spikes and valleys in the graph. Yes, there are ups and downs in the last 15 years, but they aren't as high or as low.
- The inflation rate almost always declines in the recessionary period. You can really see this in the most recent Great Recession. In fact the inflation rate in 2009 was actually negative 0.36% in 2009. The logical explanation is that recessions are associated with less spending throughout the economy. When there is less spending on goods and services, there is little pressure on prices to rise; in fact they usually fall.

Day 28

a. Nobody below the age of 16 is considered part of the labor force. The labor force consists of all those above the age of 16 who are employed (working at least 1 hour a week) plus those who are unemployed (without work but seeking a job). If a person does not have a job and has chosen to not seek a job, they are out of the labor force.

$$\text{Employed } (E) = 4 + 14 = 18 \text{ million}$$

$$\text{Unemployed } (U) = 2.5 \text{ million}$$

$$\text{Labor Force } (E + U) = 18 + 2.5 = 20.5 \text{ million}$$

The unemployment rate (UR) is the ratio of the number of unemployed (U) divided by the labor force (LF).

$$UR = 100 \times (U/LF) = 100 \times (2.5/20.5) = 12.2\%$$

b. When 1 million of the unemployed stop looking for work, the ranks of the unemployed *and* the total labor force is 1 million people smaller. The new unemployment rate is:

$$UR = 100 \times (U/LF) = 100 \times (1.5/19.5) = 7.7\%$$

The unemployment rate has significantly fallen because the "discouraged" workers are no longer counted amongst the unemployed; they are considered out of the labor force.

Day 29

1. Theo is younger than 16, so he is not counted as a member of the labor force, even though he is actually working as a lawn mower in the neighborhood.

2. Eli does not have a job right now, but he is not in the labor force because he is not actively seeking a job.

3. Melanie is employed and is working full-time.

4. Max is employed and is working part-time.

5. Tommy is considered employed. He has a job, but has not been working due to a labor dispute. Although he is not working and is actively searching for work as a guitar player, his status as employed (although on strike) supersedes what would normally qualify him as unemployed.

6. Gina is considered unemployed. She has lost her job and is actively seeking a new job. We can only presume that she is living on a prayer.

Day 30

You probably found a graph similar to this one:

https://fred.stlouisfed.org/series/UNRATE

- The highest unemployment rate was 10.8% in December 1982.
- It might be a little difficult to see, but the unemployment rate has become slightly more stable since the early 1980s. Before about 1980 there were wider increases and decreases, and after 1980 there were fewer and they were not rising as high or dropping as low. The exception, of course, is the most recent recession when unemployment rates increased steeply.
- In all of the recessionary periods, unemployment was rising. The explanation is simple and relates to the circular flow diagram. When it feels like the economy is weakening, people reduce their spending. When households spend less on goods and services, firms employ fewer factors of production, and this reduces household income. And when household income falls, households spend less, and the downward cycle continues.

Day 31

At the time of this writing, the most recent CPS was the November 2016 report. A portion of the table of unemployment measures is replicated as follows.

MEASURE	NOV. 2016
U-3 Total unemployed, as a percent of the civilian labor force (official unemployment rate)	4.6
U-4 Total unemployed plus discouraged workers, as a percent of the civilian labor force plus discouraged workers	5
U-5 Total unemployed, plus discouraged workers, plus all other persons marginally attached to the labor force, as a percent of the civilian labor force plus all persons marginally attached to the labor force	5.8
U-6 Total unemployed, plus all persons marginally attached to the labor force, plus total employed part time for economic reasons, as a percent of the civilian labor force plus all persons marginally attached to the labor force	9.3

If you have done a little digging and read the fine print in the footnotes of Table A-15, you might have discovered the following:

Marginally attached: This refers to a person who is currently not working and was not searching for work last month, but indicates that he or she would like to work and had searched for work at some point in the last year.

The official rate of U-3 would not include these people, because they were not currently looking for work. However, they are interested in working and have searched for work in the last year, so they have not completely given up and permanently left the labor force.

Discouraged worker: This is a subset of the marginally attached people. They have not been searching for work because they don't believe there is anything available to them. They might feel like they don't have sufficient skills, or that they are too young/old for any work, or that they are discriminated against for any number of reasons.

We can see that in November 2016 that the inclusion of discouraged workers would increase the unemployment rate from the official 4.6% to 5% (U-4).

If we included all of the marginally attached workers, the unemployment rate would rise again to 5.8% (U-5).

Working part-time for economic reasons: This definition describes people working 1–34 hours per week (part time) but would rather be working more than 35 hours a week (full time). They are working part time because they cannot find a full-time position or their employer has cut back their hours due to weak demand for the firm's products. Since these people are not unemployed, we might think of them as underemployed.

In November 2016 if this final group of the underemployed is added, the unemployment rate rises to 9.3%.

In any month that you choose, you will find the same pattern of an increasing rate of unemployment as we move from U-3 to U-6. This is simply a result of how the BLS for many decades has decided to draw the line on what constitutes an unemployed person. If you have been searching for work in the last month, you're unemployed; if not, you're out of the labor force.

Day 32

Since Pam consumes $900 for every additional $1,000 of disposable income, the column of C rises by $900 each time. In a similar way, the column for S rises by $100 every time DI increases by $1000.

DISPOSABLE INCOME (DI)	CONSUMPTION (C)	SAVINGS (S)
$0	$100	−$100
$1,000	$1,000	0
$2,000	$1,900	$100
$3,000	$2,800	$200
$4,000	$3,700	$300
$5,000	$4,600	$400
$6,000	$5,500	$500

Day 33

Once again, the equation of a line is $y = mx + b$.

In the consumption equation, the vertical intercept (b) is the value of consumption when disposable income is zero. This is called autonomous consumption. The slope (m) is the change in consumption divided by the change in disposable income. This is called the marginal propensity to consume (MPC).

We can see from the tables that both Pam's and Gram's autonomous consumptions are $100.

Pam's consumption rises by $900 when her disposable income rises by $1000, so her MPC is 0.90.

On the other hand, Gram's consumption rises by only $600 when her disposable income rises by $1,000, so her MPC is 0.60.

This gives us enough information to construct the consumption equations.

$$\text{Pam: } C = 100 + (0.90 \times DI)$$
$$\text{Gram: } C = 100 + (0.60 \times DI)$$

Day 34

In the savings equation, the vertical intercept (b) is the value of savings when disposable income is zero. This is called autonomous savings. The slope (m) is the change in savings divided by the change in disposable income. This is called the marginal propensity to save (*MPS*).

We can see from the tables that both Pam's and Gram's autonomous savings are –$100.

Pam's savings rises by $100 when her disposable income rises by $1,000, so her MPS is 0.10.

On the other hand, Gram's savings rises by $400 when her disposable income rises by $1,000, so her MPS is 0.40.

This gives us enough information to construct the savings equations.

$$\text{Pam: } S = -100 + (0.10 \times DI)$$
$$\text{Gram: } S = -100 + (0.40 \times DI)$$

Day 35

You might have found a graph like this one:

https://fred.stlouisfed.org/series/GPDIC1

Even after holding prices constant (2009 dollars), it is clear that investment spending has dramatically increased since the 1950s. A closer look at the actual numbers shows that real investment spending in 2016 is more than 10 times greater than it was in 1947.

It is also clear that investment spending drops during economic recessions. This isn't surprising, because recessions are associated with less spending across the board. However, if you take a look at *when* investment spending begins to decline, it is usually at least two quarters before the recession officially begins. Because of this, economists use changes in investment spending as an important "economic indicator" of a potential change in the business cycle.

Day 36

The market for loanable funds has a downward sloping demand and an upward sloping supply curve. The real interest rate is on the vertical axis. Hint: Make sure that you label your vertical axis as the real rate (or $r\%$).

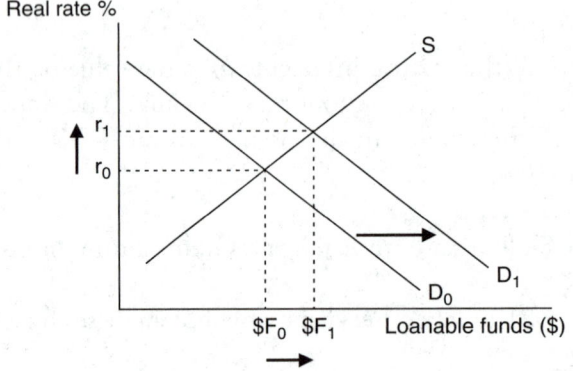

Increased business optimism would likely mean more capital investment and an increase in the demand for loanable funds. A shift to the right would increase the equilibrium interest rate and the quantity of funds borrowed and lent.

Day 37

Once again, you should draw the market for loanable funds with a downward sloping demand and an upward sloping supply curve. The real interest rate is on the vertical axis.

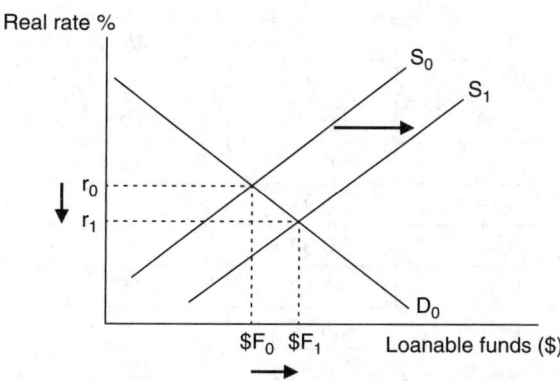

When households and firms show increased saving in American banks, the supply of loanable funds shifts to the right. A supply shift to the right would decrease the equilibrium interest rate and increase the quantity of funds borrowed and lent.

Day 38

After 10 more rounds of spending the initial $1,000 has generated a total of $7,175.70. In other words, it has multiplied by more than seven times the initial amount of spending. This is the spending multiplier at work.

TRANSACTION	SPENDING	SAVING
A to B	$1,000	N/A
B to C	$900	$100
C to D	$810	$90
D to E	$729	$81
E to F	$656.10	$72.90
F to G	$590.49	$65.61
G to H	$531.44	$59.05
H to I	$478.30	$53.14
I to J	$430.47	$47.83
J to K	$387.42	$43.05
K to L	$348.68	$38.74
L to M	$313.81	$34.87
Totals =	$7,175.70	$686.19

Day 39

Technically you cannot compute M when the MPC is 1 and the MPS is zero, but if you imagine dividing by something very close to zero, we would get a spending multiplier that is very, very big.

MPC	MPS	M
1	0	∞
0.90	0.10	10
0.80	0.20	5
0.75	0.25	4
0.67	0.33	3
0.60	0.40	2.5
0.50	0.50	2
0.40	0.60	1.67
0.33	0.67	1.5
0.20	0.80	1.25
0.10	0.90	1.11
0	1	1

The table makes it clear that if the MPC is quite high (or MPS quite low), an injection of spending from any sector will eventually multiply to a much greater amount.

Day 40

For each scenario you must first compute the spending multiplier and then determine whether GDP would increase or decrease by a magnitude equal to that of the multiplier.

- A nation with an $MPC = 0.80$ experiences an increase in autonomous investment spending of $10 billion.

$M = 1/0.20 = 5$. If I increases by $10 billion, this should eventually cause an increase of $50 billion in GDP.

- A nation with an $MPC = 0.75$ experiences a decrease in autonomous next exports of $6.5 billion.

$M = 1/0.25 = 4$. If $(X–M)$ decreases by $6.5 billion, this should eventually cause a decrease of $26 billion in GDP.

- A nation with an $MPC = 0.50$ experiences an increase in autonomous government spending of $15 billion.

$M = 1/0.5 = 2$. If G increases by $15 billion, this should eventually cause an increase of $30 billion in GDP.

- A nation with an $MPC = 0.90$ experiences a decrease in autonomous consumption spending of $5 billion.

$M = 1/0.9 = 10$. If C decreases by $5 billion, this should eventually cause a decrease of $50 billion in GDP.

Day 41

After 12 rounds of spending, the $1,000 tax rebate created $6,458.13 of new spending. The tax rebate generated more than 6 times the amount of money circulating in the economy than the initial rebate. This is the tax multiplier at work.

TRANSACTION	SPENDING	SAVING
A to B	$900.00	$100.00
B to C	$810.00	$90.00
C to D	$729.00	$81.00
D to E	$656.10	$72.90
E to F	$590.49	$65.61
F to G	$531.44	$59.05
G to H	$478.30	$53.14
H to I	$430.47	$47.83
I to J	$387.42	$43.05
J to K	$348.68	$38.74
K to L	$313.81	$34.87
L to M	$282.43	$31.38
Totals =	$6,458.13	$717.57

Day 42

Again, we see that the tax multiplier falls as the MPC falls. The T_m is always smaller than the spending multiplier because a change in autonomous spending (G) immediately impacts the circular flow of spending, while a change in taxes (or transfer payments) must first go through a consumer's consumption function, and in that function a fraction will be saved, not spent.

MPC	MPS	M	T_m
1	0	∞	∞
0.90	0.10	10	9.00
0.80	0.20	5	4.00
0.75	0.25	4	3.00
0.67	0.33	3	2.00
0.60	0.40	2.5	1.50
0.50	0.50	2	1.00
0.40	0.60	1.67	0.67
0.33	0.67	1.5	0.50
0.20	0.80	1.25	0.25
0.10	0.90	1.11	0.11
0	1	1	0.00

Notice that if the MPC is quite small in an economy, a change in taxes or transfers will have a negligible multiplied impact on GDP.

Day 43

For each scenario you must first compute the tax multiplier and then determine the eventual impact of the tax or transfer change on GDP.

- A nation with an *MPC* = 0.80 experiences an increase in transfer payments of $10 billion.

$T_m = 0.8/0.2 = 4$, so an increase in transfer payments of $10 billion will multiply to a $40 billion increase in GDP.

- A nation with an *MPC* = 0.75 experiences a decrease in taxes of $6.5 billion.

$T_m = 0.75/0.25 = 3$, so a decrease in taxes of $6.5 billion will multiply to a $19.5 billion increase in GDP.

- A nation with an *MPC* = 0.50 experiences an increase in taxes of $15 billion.

$T_m = 0.5/0.5 = 1$, so an increase in taxes of $15 billion will multiply to a $15 billion decrease in GDP.

- A nation with an *MPC* = 0.90 experiences a decrease in transfer payments of $5 billion.

$T_m = 0.9/0.1 = 9$, so a decrease in transfer payments of $5 billion will multiply to a $45 billion decrease in GDP.

Day 44

a. The spending multiplier $M = 1/0.25 = 4$, so an increase in $G = \$3$ billion will multiply to a $12 billion *increase* in GDP.

b. The tax multiplier $T_m = 0.75/0.25 = 3$, so an increase in taxes of $3 billion will multiply to a $9 billion *decrease* in GDP.

c. Net impact of this balanced-budget project = $12 billion − $9 billion = $3 billion

Day 45

- Foreign sector substitution effect

    If the aggregate price level in the United States is falling relative to that of other nations, consumers in other nations will wish to purchase more goods from the United States. At the same time, American consumers would wish fewer products from foreign nations. As a result, net exports would rise and GDP increases downward along the AD curve.

- Interest rate effect

    If the aggregate price level is falling in the United States, there will need to be less borrowing to afford big-ticket items. This puts downward pressure on interest rates and with lower interest rates current spending increases. This creates a downward movement along the AD curve.

- Wealth effect

  If the aggregate price level falls in the United States, the purchasing power of accumulated wealth will rise, and current spending rises. This also creates a downward movement along the AD curve.

Day 46

a. Pessimistic households will decrease consumption (C) and decrease AD (shift to the left).

b. Low interest rates will increase investment (I) and also consumption (C) and increase AD (shift to the right).

c. More military spending is an increase in government spending (G) and increases AD.

d. Recessions in Asia make it more difficult to export to those nations, so net exports (X – M) decreases and decreases AD.

Day 47

a. When firms are more optimistic about profitability, investment rises (I) and AD increases.

b. More household wealth increases consumption (C) and increases AD.

c. Higher income taxes decreases consumption (C) and decreases AD.

d. Stronger foreign preference of domestic products increases net exports (X – M) and increases AD.

Day 48

The reason the SRAS is believed to be upward sloping is that input prices are thought to rise more slowly than the aggregate price level. So when the price level rises, firms can increase output, and with input prices lagging behind, firms are more profitable in the short run.

Day 49

a. Policies like tax rebates for research and development allow companies to increase production and increases SRAS. Note: This kind of policy can also increase the long-run AS (LRAS) curve over a longer time period.

b. Widespread increases in input (or factor) prices causes the SRAS to shift to the left.

c. The elimination of redundant business regulation should increase the SRAS.

d. An environmental disaster, like a drought, would decrease the SRAS. Note: If a short-term lack of water turns into a permanent situation, the LRAS might also shift to the left.

Day 50

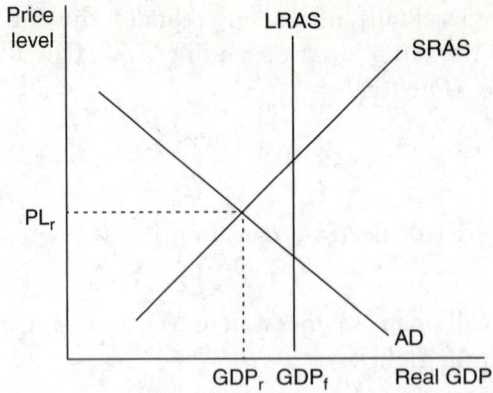

A recessionary gap means that current GDP falls below full-employment (or potential) GDP so you want to draw your intersection of AD and SRAS to the left of the vertical LRAS line.

Day 51

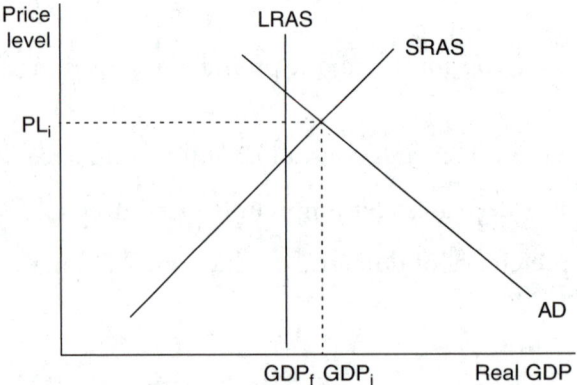

An inflationary gap means that current GDP lies above full-employment (or potential) GDP so you want to draw your intersection of AD and SRAS to the right of the vertical LRAS line.

Day 52

a. Firms with less optimistic expectations will decrease investment spending, and AD decreases. The price level and real GDP will both fall.

b. When foreign consumers have more income, they will buy more domestic-made products, increasing next exports. The increase in AD will increase both price level and real GDP.

c. More household wealth causes consumption spending to rise, increasing AD. The increased AD causes both the price level and real GDP to increase.

d. Input prices that are rising will cause the SRAS to decrease, causing the price level to rise and real GDP to fall.

e. Policies designed to increase productivity should increase the SRAS, causing the price level to fall and real GDP to rise.

Day 53

If you were successful in combining both data series in one graph, it probably looks a lot like this.

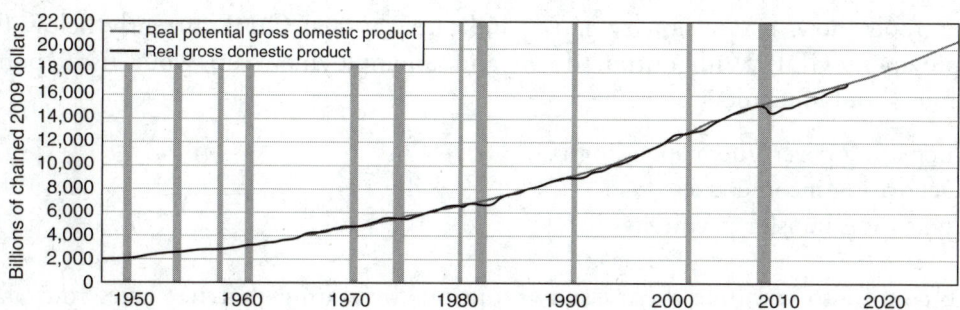

When you zoom in on recessionary periods, the real GDP dips significantly below potential GDP. This is a classic recessionary gap that we see in the AD/AS model as a decrease in AD. There are some periods where actual real GDP exceeds the potential GDP, the most recent being the quarters between 2005 and 2007, right before the Great Recession. If you look back, there are several instances where a period like this (actual exceeding potential) ended with a recession. There are many years when the economy is not officially in a recession, yet real GDP is below potential GDP. This illustrates the difference between simply producing below potential and *really* producing below potential. The recovery that began in the middle of 2009 caused the economy to emerge from the Great Recession, but real GDP has not yet caught up to potential GDP.

Day 54

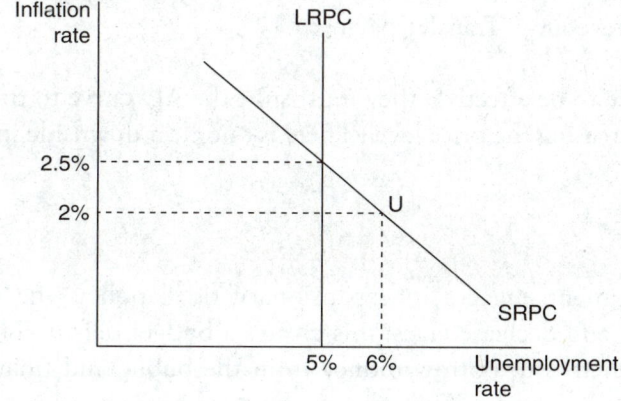

The LRPC is always drawn as a vertical line at the NAIRU, and the SRPC is downward sloping to reflect the trade-off between lower unemployment rates and higher inflation rates.

In the AD/AS model, this is explained by a decrease in the AD curve. Such a shift would decrease real GDP, increasing the unemployment rate, and decrease the price level, reducing inflation.

Day 55

There are no answers for this activity. ☺

Day 56

The graph shows a recessionary gap as indicated by real GDP currently below full employment GDP. With output down and unemployment up, your fiscal policy options should include:

- Increasing government spending (G)
- Decreasing income taxes
- Increasing transfer payments

One could also combine these last two options by stating that net taxes must fall: Net taxes = (Tax revenue − Transfer payments)

If these policies are to be effective, they must shift the AD curve to the right, increasing real GDP and decreasing the unemployment rate. There are two potential downsides: a higher price level and a larger budget deficit.

Day 57

The graph shows an inflationary gap as indicated by real GDP currently above full employment GDP. While output is quite high, so is inflation, so your fiscal policy options should include:

- Decreasing government spending (*G*)
- Increasing income taxes
- Decreasing transfer payments

Again, you could also combine these last two options by stating that net taxes must rise: Net taxes = (Tax revenue − Transfer payments)

If these policies are to be effective, they must shift the AD curve to the left, decreasing real GDP and decreasing the price level. There is one clear downside in that unemployment will rise.

Day 58

When the government engages in expansionary fiscal policy, the usual plan is to increase spending and decrease taxes; this creates a budget deficit. The typical way of paying for the deficit is to borrow money from the public and financial institutions in the form of issuing bonds. When the government borrows a lot of money, there is pressure on interest rates to rise. Higher interest rates reduce private investment that would have, if interest rates had remained lower, otherwise been done. In other words, the government borrowing "crowds out" private investment.

Day 59

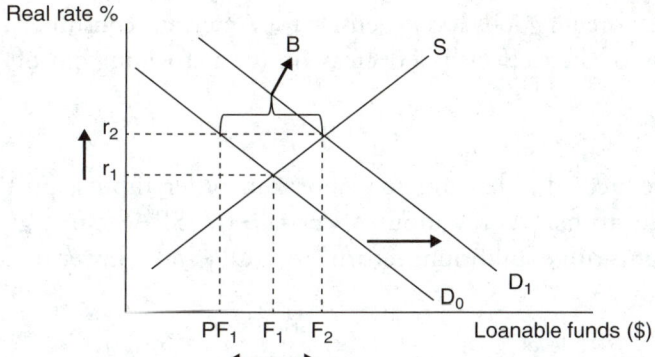

The borrowing increases the demand curve to D_1 and this increases equilibrium interest rates. However, the quantity of private borrowing/investment falls from F_1 (no deficit) to PF_1 (deficit spending). The difference between the private borrowing/investing and the total is the amount of government borrowing (B). The decrease from F_1 to PF_1 is the crowding out of private investment.

Day 60

Searching around the FRED you might have found a graph that looks like this.

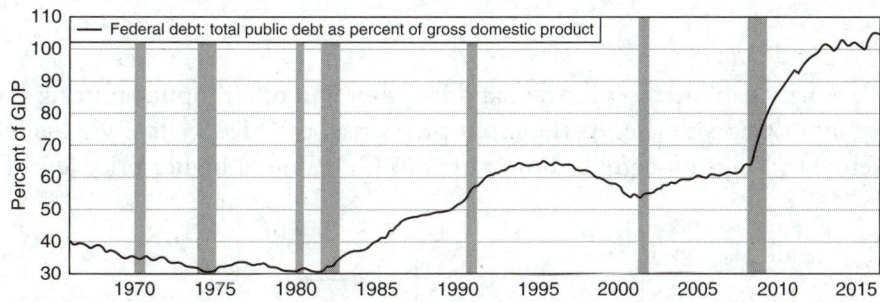

This graph clearly shows that the national debt, as a percentage of the GDP has been rising since about 1980. Although this graph doesn't go back as far as World War II, this ratio was about 120% in 1946 as the government spending was ramped up to support the military. More recently, we can see there was a steady increase in the 1980s, then a modest decline in the late 1990s, a slow increase in the early 2000s, and then a precipitous increase during and after the Great Recession.

On an annual basis, the OMB table tells us that the annual deficit, as a size of the GDP, was largest during the WWII years. Since the end of WWII, this ratio has dropped and stayed under 10% of GDP. During and immediately after the Great Recession, this ratio was almost 10% due to the dramatic decrease in tax revenue and sizable spending in an attempt to put the brakes on the worst recession since 1929.

Day 61

More government borrowing increases interest rates in the United States. When foreign citizens and firms see that they can earn higher interest in the United States, they deposit more of their currency in American banks. This increases the demand for the U.S. dollar, which increases the value of the dollar in currency markets. Finally, a more expensive dollar makes American-made goods more expensive to foreign consumers, so exports fall. It also makes foreign goods less expensive for American consumers, so imports rise. The combination of these effects is a decrease in (or a crowding out of) net exports.

Day 62

The recession reduces the demand for labor and other inputs, putting pressure on those input prices to fall. As the input prices fall, the SRAS curve gradually shifts to the right. The long-run equilibrium returns to GDP_f and a lower price level PL_f.

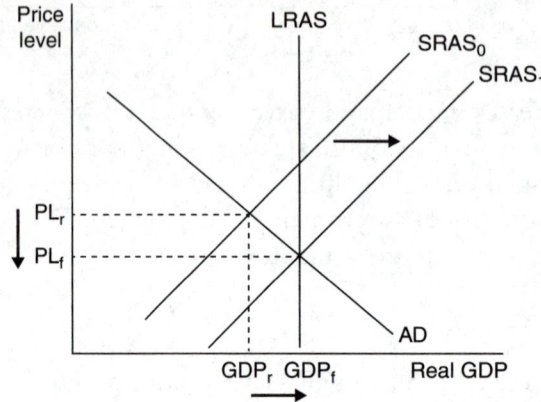

Day 63

The inflationary gap increases the demand for labor and other inputs, putting pressure on those input prices to rise. As the input prices rise, the SRAS curve gradually shifts to the left. The long-run equilibrium returns to GDP_f and a higher price level PL_f.

Day 64

Productivity has certainly risen since 1947. According to the blog post, "Compared to 1947, we now produce 330 percent more goods and services per hour of work. On average, thanks to advances in technology, education, management, and so on, you can do in 15 minutes what your grandparents or great grandparents needed more than an hour to do in 1947."

Since 2007, productivity has risen only 1% each year, which is much lower than the long-term average of 2.2% each year.

The graph that compares productivity to real hourly wages shows almost a perfect match before about 1970. Since then, the productivity line has risen at a faster rate than the real hourly wage line, creating a widening gap.

Day 65

According to data presented in the Census report (and Figure 1 in the report), in 1940 only about 25% of people above the age of 25 had completed high school, but by 2009 that had increased to 85%. In 1940 about 5% of people had a bachelor's degree or more, but in 2009 that number was up to 30%. Clearly the American workforce has more educational attainment today than it did after World War II.

Table 1 in the report provides data that shows that a greater percentage of women have completed a high school degree or more (85.9% to 84.5%), but a greater percentage of men have completed a bachelor's degree or higher (28.4% to 27.4%).

There are also some differences in educational attainment across the races. For example Asians have the highest percentage of having a bachelor's degree or higher (49.7%), while Hispanics had the lowest rate at (12.6%).

The report also identifies clear financial advantages to higher levels of education. According to one section, "Median earnings for a worker with a bachelor's degree were 77 percent higher than median earnings for a worker with a regular high school diploma, and median earnings for an advanced degree were 31 percent higher than earnings for a bachelor's degree."

Day 66

Long-run growth is shown as a rightward shift of the LRAS curve. When the economy comes to a new long-run equilibrium, the new level of full employment GDP will be higher. The new price level could be higher or lower, or the same, depending upon the magnitude of the AD and SRAS shifts that will eventually accompany the LRAS shift.

Day 67

When the babysitting co-op was floundering and members were not spending often enough, the committee running it pumped more money (tokens) into the system. This is akin to a tax cut or rebate in our study of fiscal policy. When the members had more tokens in their accounts, they spent them and the co-op flourished.

Dr. Harford describes the "shock" as an unexpected hit to the economic system from something outside the system. Unlike the early struggles of the babysitting co-op, the POW camp's economy was running smoothly, with sophisticated features like a futures market for bread and coffee exports to Germans on the outside of the fence. The external shock was that the Red Cross shipments were prevented from delivering the goods. This caused the economy to collapse. In the babysitting co-op, there was no external shock, the economy just needed a stimulus to accelerate the rate of spending.

Day 68

A share of stock represents a claim on the ownership of a firm. A firm issues shares of stock to raise money (equity financing), but in exchange relinquishes a small degree of control over management and profits of the firm.

A bond is a certificate of indebtedness (an IOU). A firm issues a bond to raise money (debt financing), but in exchange commits the firm to repaying the principle of the bond, plus interest.

Day 69

The big difficulty with the barter system is the "double coincidence of wants." If I am an egg farmer, and I want to go shopping, I must find other merchants who want my eggs in exchange for the goods they produce. This is a pretty inefficient way to conduct commerce.

The three functions of any kind of money are:

- Medium of exchange
- Unit of account
- Store of value

Fiat money (cash) is a good medium of exchange because it circumvents the double coincidence of wants. If I need horseshoes, I don't need to find a blacksmith who also wants eggs. I sell my eggs to those who want eggs and collect the money. Then I take the money to the blacksmith and pay him for the horseshoes. This is far superior to using eggs as money.

Fiat money is also a good unit of account. We simply measure the value of all things, like horseshoes and eggs, in a unit everyone understands, money. And if there was a price of 0.50 units of money, we could divide our money and pay that price. If we tried to use eggs as our money, all things would be measured in how many eggs it would cost to purchase them. Since not all people want eggs, and since 0.50 eggs isn't going to work very well, this isn't going to be a good pricing system.

Fiat money is a good store of value as it can last a long time. Eggs will go bad in a few days, making them worthless as money. Fiat money does lose value if inflation is rampant, so it is important for the central bank to maintain the value of the money.

Day 70

To solve these problems we must use the present value formula:

$$PV = \frac{FV}{(1+r)^t}$$

where FV is some dollar amount received or paid t years into the future, and r is the interest rate (or discount rate). Or we can solve the equation for future value and we have:

$$FV = PV(1+r)^t$$

a. The present value of your loan is $50, the interest rate is 4% and you agree to repay the loan in 1 year.

$$FV = PV(1+r)^t = 50(1.04) = \$52$$

b. The future value of the gift is $100, the interest rate is 5%, and you have to wait 1 year to receive it.

$$PV = \frac{FV}{(1+r)^t} = \frac{\$100}{10.5} = \$95.24$$

c. There are two ways to make this comparison. The first is to compute the present value of $5,000 received in two years.

$$PV = \frac{FV}{(1+r)^t} = \frac{5,000}{(1.10)^2} = \$4,132.23$$

Since the present value of these winnings is less than $4,500, you should take the $4,500 now.

The second way to make the comparison is to compute the future value of $4,500 today, if you put it in the bank for 2 years.

$$FV = PV(1+r)^t = 4,500(1.10)^2 = \$5,445$$

Since this future value is greater than the winnings of $5,000, you should still take the $4,500 now and put it in the bank for two years.

Day 71

You probably found a graph that looks like this.

The stock of *M*1 has risen slowly since the 1980s, was fairly constant in the late 1990s and early 2000s, and then increased more rapidly since the Great Recession. Of course, the reason for the rapid increase was to combat, along with the government's aggressive fiscal policy, this very deep recession and the slow recovery from it.

Day 72

The completed table is below.

ROUND	DEPOSIT	CASH IN RESERVE	A LOAN IS MADE
1	$1,000 from person A	$100	$900 to person B
2	$900 from person B	$90	$810 to person C
3	$810 from person C	$81	$729 to person D
4	$729 from person D	$72.90	$656.10 to person E
5	$656.10 from person E	$65.61	$590.49 to person F
6	$590.49 from person F	$59.05	$531.44 to person G
7	$531.44 from person G		
	Total = $5,217.03		Total = $4,217.03

The table shows how money is created by simply holding a fraction in reserve (10%) and lending the rest to new borrowing customers. If we subtract the initial $1,000 deposit (because it was already in circulation), the loans and deposits from persons B through G amount to $4,217.03 that did not previously exist. Think of this as *new money* circulating in the economy.

Day 73

The money market graph has the nominal interest rate on the vertical axis, and the quantity of money demanded rises as the nominal interest rate falls. The reason is that money is another type of financial asset. When it is held (demanded) in your pocket, it is very useful for making transactions, but it doesn't earn any interest as an asset. As the interest rate rises, you could earn more interest income, so you will put that money back into another financial asset, like the purchase of a Treasury bond, and demand less of it in your pocket. The nominal interest rate is simply the opportunity cost of holding money in your pocket, and as we already know, when opportunity cost of something rises, we demand less of it.

Day 74

In the first case, you will earn $100 when the bond matures ($1000 − $900) and since you paid $900 for the bond, you have earned an interest rate of 11.1% ($100/$900). In the second case, you will earn $50 when the bond matures ($1,000 − $950), so the interest rate is now 5.26% ($50/$950). As you can see from this quick example, when the price of a bond rises, the effective interest rate is going to fall.

The demand for bonds can rise for many different reasons. One reason might be that the rate of return on other financial assets is not very high. For example, if the stock market is slumping, people might put more money into bonds, thus increasing the demand for bonds and their prices. Another reason for an increase in demand for bonds is uncertainty. The U.S. Treasury bond is deemed one of the safest, if not *the* safest, financial asset available. Relative to other parts of the world, the U.S. government is stable and always repays the bonds that have been issued. So if financial markets in Europe or Asia are in turmoil, or if there is widespread geopolitical unrest, investors might return to U.S. Treasury bonds, increasing their demand. Another reason for higher demand for bonds is that there is a surplus of money in the money market. With a surplus of money in circulation, households and firms are going to look for a place to put this money, and the market for U.S. Treasury bonds is one such place.

Day 75

Be sure to draw your money supply curve as vertical and money demand as downward sloping. Also be sure to label the vertical axis as the nominal interest rate (or "nir").

The initial equilibrium in the money market is at an interest rate of i_1. A stronger economy and increased nominal GDP will increase the demand for money, as people are making more transactions. The shift to the right of MD creates a shortage of money at the original interest rate. With not enough money in circulation, people will sell their bonds and this increases the supply of bonds, decreasing the price, and increasing interest rates.

Day 76

Use the formula for the money multiplier:

$$M = 1/rr$$

The completed table follows.

RESERVE REQUIREMENT (rr)	MONEY MULTIPLIER
0.01	100
0.05	20
0.10	10
0.20	5
0.25	4
0.50	2

If (a big IF) the reserve requirement was 0.01, banks would need to hold only 1% of deposits in reserve and could lend out the remaining 99%. This could dramatically increase the multiplication of any deposits but would also put the bank at risk. What if many depositors showed up and wanted to withdraw all of their money (a.k.a. a bank run) on the same day? With only 1% of all deposits being held, this could wipe out the bank. To lessen this risk, the Fed has chosen an $rr = 10\%$ and allows banks that find their reserves to be insufficient on any given day to borrow from either other banks or the Fed itself.

Day 77

1. Change the reserve requirement. If the Fed wanted to increase the money supply, they could decrease the reserve requirement, allowing banks to lend a larger percentage of all deposits and increasing the money multiplier.

2. Change the discount rate. The discount rate is the rate the Fed charges banks that wish to borrow money. To increase the money supply, the Fed could lower the discount rate, making these loans more affordable to the banks. Banks borrow from the Fed, increasing excess reserves, and increasing lending to customers, thus increasing the supply of money.

3. Execute open market operations (OMO). The Fed buys and sells Treasury securities in the open market to affect the amount of money banks have in reserve. If the Fed wanted to increase the money supply, they would buy bonds from large banks. These banks would now have more money in excess reserves, they would start the lending process, and more money would be created.

Day 78

To fight a recessionary gap, you should propose an OMO whereupon you are buying securities from banks. These purchases will inject money into the banks and the money multiplier effect will increase the money supply.

The graph should show the vertical money supply curve shifting to the right, decreasing the nominal interest rate.

The AD/AS graph should show AD shifting to the right as lower interest rates will boost investment spending (I) and consumption spending (C). This increase in AD should get real GDP closer to potential GDP and reduce the unemployment rate.

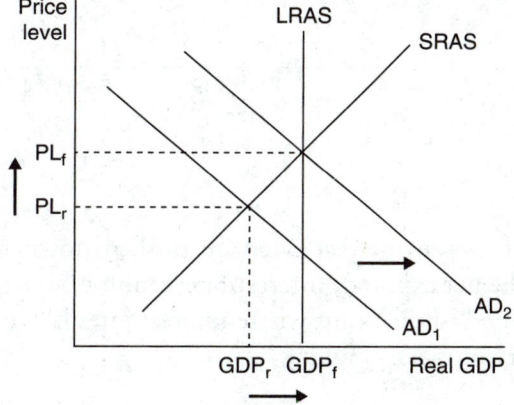

Day 79

To fight an inflationary gap, you should propose an OMO whereupon you are selling securities to banks. These sales will withdraw money from the banks, and the money multiplier effect will decrease the money supply.

The graph should show the vertical money supply curve shifting to the left, increasing the nominal interest rate.

The AD/AS graph should show AD shifting to the left as higher interest rates will reduce investment spending (*I*) and consumption spending (C). This decrease in AD should get real GDP closer to potential GDP and reduce the price level and inflation.

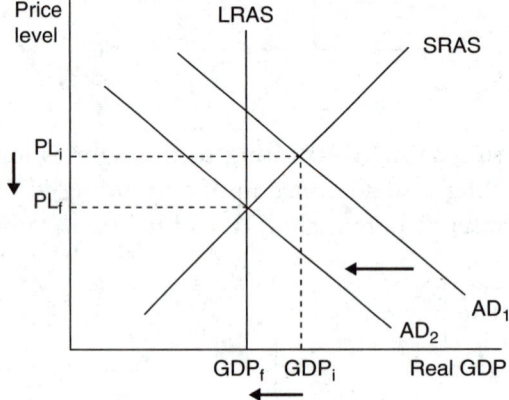

Day 80

A liquidity trap occurs when interest rates are pushed down to zero. Unlike other economic variables (like net exports), interest rates cannot be negative values. So if the money supply is increased to the point where interest rates hit zero, there is no further benefit to expansionary monetary policy.

In the essay from the Fed, when the author refers to the "effective lower bound" of interest rates, he is describing the liquidity trap. With the economy continuing to languish, the Fed was forced to look for nontraditional methods of sparking the economy.

The first thing that is discussed in the article is the Fed's use of key language in their reports to the banking industry and general public. The Fed wanted to reassure banks that the nearly zero percent interest rates were going to last for a while. They hoped that this would allow banks to begin lending again and plan for a more certain future.

The Fed also began to purchase certain financial assets from banks and financial institutions. Part of the reason that banks were not lending was because they were saddled with billions of dollars of nearly worthless mortgages and a popular investment called "mortgage backed securities." The thinking was that if the Fed took those nearly worthless investments out of the banks, it would free them to return to normal business.

Of course we know now that recovery from the Great Recession, despite the combined efforts of fiscal and monetary policy, continues to be slow.

Day 81

There really are no solutions to this activity, but it does provide food for thought and some hard-to-answer questions. Is a weak economy like a dead car battery that just needs a spark of spending? Should the government bail out firms that are failing? What would we do with the people who are unemployed if we waited for the economy to self-correct?

Many economists agree that there are valid points to be made by both sides of this philosophical divide. And all economists agree that the real-world is much more complex than the theoretical models presented in textbooks. However, these models, imperfect as they are, provide us with a baseline for understanding how the economy works and how policies *might* have effective impacts on it.

Day 82

a. To find comparative advantage, we must compute the opportunity cost of producing each commodity.

Nation A:

Producing $1W$ costs $4T$

Producing $1T$ costs $1/4W$

Nation B:

Producing $1W$ costs $6T$

Producing $1T$ costs $1/6W$

Nation A produces wheat at a lower cost than can nation B, so nation A has comparative advantage in W. Nation B produces textiles at a lower cost than can nation A, so nation B has comparative advantage in T.

b. Nation B is going to specialize in T, but they want some W. If they produced their own W, it would cost $6T$, so they need a lower price for W from a trading partner. Maybe they try to get $1W$ for a price of $5T$.

Would nation A go for this?

They are specializing in W. If they gave up $1W$ on their own, they would gain $4T$, but nation B is offering them $5T$.

So both nations would agree to a deal that involves $1W$ exchanging for $5T$, or $1T$ exchanging for $0.20W$.

Day 83

a. Low interest rates will deter savers from depositing money in American banks, and they will keep their money in European banks where the return is higher. This will decrease the demand for the dollar.

b. If American products are more popular, demand for those products rises and the demand for the dollar rises with it.

c. A recession in Europe decreases the demand for imported goods from the United States, so demand for the dollar falls.

d. If European prices are rising and prices in the United States are not, American products are going to be more affordable and demand for the dollar will rise.

Day 84

a. The Fed should increase the money supply, probably with an open market purchase of bonds from large banks. An increase in the money supply will cause interest rates to fall, boosting AD and lessening the recessionary gap.

b. Lower interest rates make foreign saving in U.S. financial institutions less attractive, so the demand for the dollar will decrease, causing the value of the dollar to fall. Another way to say this is that the dollar is depreciating (or weakening) against other currencies. If the dollar is less expensive to foreigners, it makes American-made products less expensive to foreign consumers, so the United States will export more products. At the same time, a weaker dollar means that Americans find foreign goods to be more expensive, so imports in the U.S. economy fall. With exports rising and imports falling, net exports ($X - M$) increase.

Day 85

I found a Hilton Doubletree hotel in Madrid, Spain, that had a room in April 2017 priced at 209 euros. At the date of this writing, $1 could get you 1.05415 euros, or 1 euro could get you $0.94863 so to pay for the room in euros, I would need:

$$209 \text{ euros} \times (0.94863 \text{ \$/euro}) = \$198.26$$

One year ago, the exchange rate was on euro equal to $0.94829, so the room a year ago would have cost:

$$209 \text{ euros} \times (0.94829 \text{ \$/euro}) = \$198.19$$

Since this hotel room is basically the same price (in U.S. dollars), I will assume that my European vacation today would cost about the same as it would have cost a year ago.

Day 86

The tricky part of drawing currency markets is getting the vertical axis labeled correctly. We are drawing the market for the euro (€), so the vertical axis needs to be labeled as the price of a euro. Since we are going to price it in U.S. dollars, we should label the vertical axis as "dollars per euro" or the "dollar price of a euro" or simply "$/€".

Higher interest rates in Europe will attract savers from the United States, and this increases the demand for the euro, causing the euro to appreciate in value. It would now cost more dollars to acquire more euros or products made in the European Union.

Day 87

We are drawing the market for the U.S. dollar, and so the vertical axis needs to be labeled as the price of a dollar. Since we are going to price it in euros, we should label the vertical axis as "euros per dollar" or the "euro price of a dollar" or simply "€/$".

Higher interest rates in Europe will attract savers from the United States, and this increases the demand for the euro, causing the euro to appreciate in value. At the same time, the supply of dollars is increasing. Think of it this way: If Americans are demanding more euros, they must offer more dollars in exchange. The graph shows that the price of a dollar is falling; the dollar is depreciating. It would now cost fewer euros to acquire more dollars or products made in the United States.

Day 88

There are several trends that support the assertion that trade benefits the U.S. economy. For example, the very first chart shows that U.S. exports have risen sharply over the same period of time that U.S. real GDP has risen gradually. Trade in the U.S. economy is now about 30% of total GDP. The video also describes how the "made in America" slogan is no longer true, as firms often import raw materials to produce a final product. The video also discusses the fact that trade does reduce employment in some sectors and some regions of the country, but that trade creates other jobs. In fact, labor-saving technology (like robotics) is the primary cause of lost manufacturing job losses, not trade.

Day 89

At this writing, the most recent news release from the BEA was for the third quarter of 2016. From the report, we see that:

Exports of goods and services = $564.1 billion

Imports of goods and services = $680.5 billion

So there was a trade deficit in goods and services of $116.4 billion

Day 90

We need to determine opportunity costs to figure out which nation has comparative advantage in steel and food.

Theodoria:

The opportunity cost of 1 food is 1 steel.

The opportunity cost of 1 steel is 1 food.

Elijastan:

The opportunity cost of 1 food is .25 steel.

The opportunity cost of 1 steel is 4 food.

Comparative Advantage and Specialization:

Since Theodoria can produce steel at a lower cost than Elijastan (1 food compared to 4 food), Theodoria should specialize in steel production. Likewise, Elijastan should specialize in food production because they produce it at a lower cost (0.25 steel compared to 1 steel) than Theodoria.

Terms of Trade:

One possibility that would benefit both nations is if they exchanged 1 steel for 2 food. To see how this would work, suppose Elijastan sent 40 food to Theodoria in exchange for 20 steel.

Would Elijastan find this acceptable? Without trade, if Elijastan wanted 20 steel they would need to sacrifice 80 food. With trade, they need to give up only 40 food. So definitely Elijastan is happy with this arrangement.

Would Theodoria benefit from this trade? Without trade, if Theodoria wanted 40 food they would need to sacrifice 40 steel. With trade, they have to give up only 20 steel. Theodoria is also pleased with this arrangement.

5 Minutes to a 5

90 AP Microeconomics Activities and Questions in

5 Minutes a Day

Check off each activity as it is completed.

1.	❏	24.	❏	47.	❏	70.	❏
2.	❏	25.	❏	48.	❏	71.	❏
3.	❏	26.	❏	49.	❏	72.	❏
4.	❏	27.	❏	50.	❏	73.	❏
5.	❏	28.	❏	51.	❏	74.	❏
6.	❏	29.	❏	52.	❏	75.	❏
7.	❏	30.	❏	53.	❏	76.	❏
8.	❏	31.	❏	54.	❏	77.	❏
9.	❏	32.	❏	55.	❏	78.	❏
10.	❏	33.	❏	56.	❏	79.	❏
11.	❏	34.	❏	57.	❏	80.	❏
12.	❏	35.	❏	58.	❏	81.	❏
13.	❏	36.	❏	59.	❏	82.	❏
14.	❏	37.	❏	60.	❏	83.	❏
15.	❏	38.	❏	61.	❏	84.	❏
16.	❏	39.	❏	62.	❏	85.	❏
17.	❏	40.	❏	63.	❏	86.	❏
18.	❏	41.	❏	64.	❏	87.	❏
19.	❏	42.	❏	65.	❏	88.	❏
20.	❏	43.	❏	66.	❏	89.	❏
21.	❏	44.	❏	67.	❏	90.	❏
22.	❏	45.	❏	68.	❏		
23.	❏	46.	❏	69.	❏		

CHAPTER 5 – USING THE FOUR ECONOMIC RESOURCES IN THE KITCHEN

> Suppose you are going to make dinner for a friend. List the four economic resources that you would use to complete the dinner. Be as specific as possible.

THE OPPORTUNITY COST OF GOING TO THE MOVIES

You're going to go see a movie at a nearby cinema. What is the opportunity cost of this activity?

You will need to do a little research on all of the costs involved. This might be done by searching the cinema's website or visiting it in person to record the necessary information.

1. Select a movie and determine the price of a ticket.
2. Will you buy snacks or drinks? Record those prices.
3. Will you require transportation to get to the cinema? If you are using a car, estimate the amount of gasoline you will require and the local price of that gasoline.
4. Determine how much time, including the transportation time, you will need to watch the movie. What is the value of your time as measured by an hourly wage you could receive if you had worked instead?
5. Use all of this information to determine the total opportunity cost of going to the movie.

Day 3

HOW MANY SLICES OF PIZZA WILL YOU EAT?

Imagine a day when you've skipped lunch, and you're very hungry for dinner. You know a pizza place that sells pizza by the slice at $2 each. In this hypothetical situation, how many slices of pizza do you think you would purchase and eat?

Now with this number in mind, draw a graph of marginal benefit and marginal cost curves that shows your decision to stop buying pizza.

YOUR PRODUCTION POSSIBILITIES

Suppose that each day you have 16 waking hours to divide between studying (measured in pages read) and socializing (measured in text messages sent).

a. Assuming constant opportunity costs, draw your production possibility curve (PPC) with pages read on the *x*-axis and text messaging on the *y*-axis.
b. Now suppose you complete a speed-reading course that increases the number of pages you can read in an hour. Adjust your PPC from part (a).
c. How has the opportunity cost of socializing changed? Can you explain *why* it has changed?

COMPARATIVE ADVANTAGE AROUND THE HOUSE

Let's say that there are two tasks that need to be performed around the house: folding clean towels in the laundry and washing dirty plates in the sink. The following table summarizes how many towels could be folded and how many plates could be washed by two kids in the household.

Hourly Output for Eli: 20 towels and 0 plates, or 0 towels and 10 plates
Hourly Output for Theodore: 6 towels and 0 plates, or 0 towels and 6 plates

a. If Eli and Theodore each split their time equally between folding towels and washing plates, what is their combined output in 1 hour?
b. If Eli and Theodore specialized their tasks based on comparative advantage, what is their combined output in 1 hour?

ALLOCATIVE EFFICIENCY, PRODUCTIVE EFFICIENCY, AND EQUITY

> Suppose you were going to bake a dozen cookies for yourself and 3 friends. When the cookies are done, you will also determine how many cookies each person receives.
>
> 1. How would these cookies be baked if you were productively efficient in the kitchen? Hint: It might be easier to think of a situation where the cookies were produced inefficiently.
>
> 2. How might the dozen cookies be distributed if your goal was an equitable distribution?
>
> 3. Suppose your goal was an allocatively efficient distribution of the dozen cookies. How might you change your equitable distribution from part 2 to reflect this new goal?

Day 7

CONSTANT, INCREASING, AND DECREASING OPPORTUNITY COSTS

> In the production possibilities model, there is more than one way to draw the PPC. Assume that we can use economic resources in our economy to produce only shoes and pizza. In each of the following scenarios, sketch a graph of the PPC. In each case, what must we assume about the substitutability of our resources? Which graph more accurately depicts the trade-offs we face when producing more output?
>   a. The opportunity cost of producing more pizza is a constant number of shoes.
>   b. The opportunity cost of producing more pizza is an increasing number of shoes.
>   c. The opportunity cost of producing more pizza is a decreasing number of shoes.

GROWTH

Imagine an economy that produces only two items: automobiles (representing the manufacturing sector) and wheat (representing the agricultural sector). For the sake of simplicity, we will assume there are constant opportunity costs along the production possibility curve. Our initial PPC has been drawn as follows.

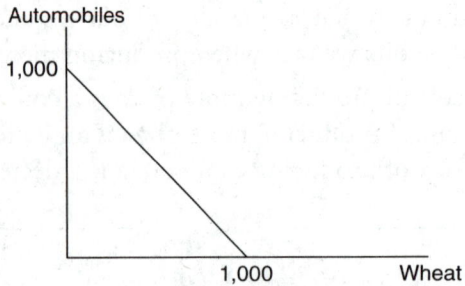

a. Adjust the PPC to reflect new technology that increases maximum automobile production by 20% but has no impact on wheat production. How does this affect the opportunity cost of wheat?
b. Adjust the PPC to reflect a crippling drought that decreases maximum wheat production by 25% but has no impact on automobile production. How does this affect the opportunity cost of automobiles?
c. Adjust the PPC to reflect new technology that increases maximum auto production by 20% and also increases maximum wheat production by 50%. How does this affect the opportunity cost of wheat?

A CHANGING PPC OVER TIME

When a nation's stock of economic resources increases, the PPC shifts outward. To get a sense of how this has happened in the United States, you will need to find some data.

A. Labor Force

The civilian labor force is measured as the total number of people (over the age of 16) working plus the number of people not working but trying to find work. The size of the labor force can be found at the following website:

http://www.bls.gov/cps/lfcharacteristics.htm#laborforce

Look for links to "Database: Retrieve historical data series" and "Top Series," and ultimately find the seasonally adjusted civilian labor force. Try to find data going back as far as it exists. Calculate the percentage change in the labor force over this time period. Note: If you're pretty good with using Excel, create a graph that shows the change over time.

B. Capital Stock

A nation's stock of capital (equipment and buildings) is also very important in producing goods and services. If a nation invests in new capital, and replaces the capital that wears out (depreciation), then the stock of capital increases, and the PPC shifts outward.

The Federal Reserve Bank of St. Louis, or the FRED, has a website with lots of data, and there are many ways to access it. You'll begin exploring the FRED's site here: https://fred.stlouisfed.org/

Search for "capital stock" and you'll get many results, but you should focus on data that is measured in "constant dollars." This simply means that the data have been adjusted for inflation over time. Once you find your data, the FRED will also likely produce a graph for you. Again, calculate the percentage change in the nation's capital stock.

CHAPTER 6 – ARE FREE THINGS REALLY FREE?

We often find ourselves enjoying some "free" leisure time by watching a television show, texting with friends, or just reading. We do these things because they are enjoyable, but are they really free? Economists know that nothing is truly free, because there is always a second activity that was sacrificed in order to pursue the first activity.

In this exercise we will try to figure out a way to put a price on both the enjoyment of an activity and the cost of pursuing it.

Measuring Benefit

Your task is to find someone who is enjoying some leisure. Maybe you can locate a family member or friend who is watching TV, playing a video game, texting or chatting on his or her phone, or reading a book, magazine, or newspaper.

Suppose you find someone watching a TV show. Your economic brain tells you that this person is choosing to watch TV because he or she believes the benefit exceeds the cost. How can we measure the benefit?

Measuring Cost

Let's return to our person watching TV. Ask the person, "If our cable/satellite connection suddenly stopped, what would you do instead?" Make sure that the person provides you with his or her *next best* choice for the use of this time. How can we measure the cost of skipping that second-best activity?

Day 11

BUILDING A FRIENDLY DEMAND CURVE

Think of a good or a service that you and your friends buy on a regular basis. For the sake of this example, let's say that this good is a ticket to a movie. Each individual has an individual demand curve for movie tickets, and this demand curve shows us the relationship between a variety of prices and the quantity of movie tickets a person would demand in a period of time, say, a month.

Use a table like the following to collect data from yourself and at least five friends. You might begin by asking each friend, "If the price of a movie ticket were $10, how many tickets would you be willing and able to buy in a month?" Record their responses, and repeat with higher and lower prices.

Use the data to construct a demand curve for the product you have chosen.

PRICE PER MOVIE TICKET	QUANTITY DEMANDED BY YOU	QUANTITY DEMANDED FOR FRIEND 1	QUANTITY DEMANDED FOR FRIEND 2	QUANTITY DEMANDED FOR FRIEND 3	QUANTITY DEMANDED FOR FRIEND 4	QUANTITY DEMANDED FOR FRIEND 5
$6						
$8						
$10						
$12						
$14						

Day 12

DEMAND DETERMINANTS (CURVE SHIFTERS)

It is critical that you have a solid grasp of the factors that shift demand curves to the left or to the right.

For each of the following, describe how the demand for orange juice will be affected. Be sure to determine which, if any, of the demand shifters is at work.

a. The *New York Times* reports that drinking orange juice will lower your risk of cancer, increase your IQ, and increase your life expectancy.
b. The price of apple juice increases.
c. The economy goes into a recession, and orange juice is a normal good.
d. Consumers expect the price of orange juice to rise in the future because a hurricane damaged the orange crop in Florida.
e. The price of orange juice drops.

Day 13

MORE DEMAND DETERMINANTS

For each of the following, how will the United States demand for 1-pound blocks of cheddar cheese be affected? Your response must include (1) which, if any, of the demand shifters is at work and (2) which direction, if any, the demand for cheddar cheese is shifting.

a. The price of 1-pound blocks of Swiss cheese is rising.
b. The price of 1-pound blocks of cheddar cheese is falling.
c. The average household income in the United States is rising.
d. An outbreak of "mad cow" disease creates a widespread fear of eating dairy products.
e. The price of crackers is rising.

Day 14

A FRIENDLY SUPPLY CURVE

With the help of several friends, your goal is to construct a supply of labor curve. Each individual worker makes a decision on how many hours (e.g., in a week) of work to supply at different hourly wages. When we combine all of these individual supply decisions, we have a market supply of labor.

Use a table like this one to collect data from yourself and at least five friends. Begin by asking each friend, "If you could receive an hourly wage of $10, how many hours of work would you supply in a week?" Record their response and repeat with higher and lower wages.

Use the data to construct a labor supply curve for the market.

HOURLY WAGE	QUANTITY OF HOURS SUPPLIED BY YOU	QUANTITY OF HOURS SUPPLIED BY FRIEND 1	QUANTITY OF HOURS SUPPLIED BY FRIEND 2	QUANTITY OF HOURS SUPPLIED BY FRIEND 3	QUANTITY OF HOURS SUPPLIED BY FRIEND 4	QUANTITY OF HOURS SUPPLIED BY FRIEND 5
$6						
$8						
$10						
$12						
$14						

Day 15

SUPPLY DETERMINANTS

It is very important that you have a solid grasp of the determinants of supply.

For each of the following, describe how the supply of academic textbooks will be affected. Be sure to determine which, if any, of the supply shifters is at work.

a. Publishers have developed a more efficient way of mass-producing textbooks.
b. The price of paper has increased.
c. A boom in the market for self-help books has increased the price consumers are willing to pay for self-help books.
d. Several publishing companies have failed and have left the industry.
e. The government provides a $5 subsidy to every new textbook produced.

Day 16

MORE SUPPLY DETERMINANTS

Here's even more practice with your supply determinants.

For each of the following, describe how the *supply* of pumpkin pie will be affected. Be sure to identify which, if any, of the supply shifters is at work.

a. All else equal, the price of pumpkins is falling.
b. All else equal, the price of apple pies is increasing.
c. All else equal, bakeries are able to bake more pies each day in larger ovens.
d. All else equal, the price of pumpkin pies is falling.
e. All else equal, several new pumpkin pie bakeries have just begun to operate.

Day 17

SHORTAGES AND SURPLUSES

The following table shows the quantity of Cheezbows that are demanded (Q_d) and supplied (Q_s) at several prices.

PRICE	Q_d	Q_s	
$10	20	110	
9	25	100	
8	30	90	
7	35	80	
6	40	70	
5	45	60	
4	50	50	
3	55	40	
2	60	30	
1	65	20	

At each price, determine whether there exists a shortage or a surplus of Cheezbows, and calculate the size of the shortage or surplus.

WHAT DOES THE DEMAND CURVE TELL US?

It's easy to learn the law of demand and understand that higher prices, all else equal, are associated with lower quantities demanded. You also know that shifts of the demand curve are the result of a change in one of those other variables, but it's instructive to gain a little more understanding of what these demand curves are telling us.

Let's use a simple linear demand equation to demonstrate what this is all about.

Demand equation:

$$P = 50 - 2Q_d$$

a. In a correctly labeled graph, draw this demand curve, being careful to label the vertical and horizontal intercepts.
b. At any price, the demand curve tells us how many units of the product consumers are willing and able to purchase. If the current price is $30, how many units will be demanded? Add this point to the graph.
c. At any quantity, the demand curve tells us the highest price consumers would be willing to pay for this product. If the current quantity is 15 units, what is the highest price consumers would pay? Add this point to the graph.
d. Now suppose the demand for this product increases and the new demand equation is:

$$P = 100 - 2Q_d$$

Add the new demand curve to the graph, again being sure to label the intercepts.
e. Redo part (b). How does your new quantity demanded reflect the shift in demand?
f. Redo part (c). How does your new price reflect the shift in demand?

Day 19

CHANGES TO MARKET EQUILIBRIUM

Suppose the competitive market for apples is in equilibrium. Given the following scenarios, you must: (1) identify the specific shifter that is happening, (2) state which direction a curve is shifting, and (3) predict changes to the equilibrium price and quantity of apples.

   Note: A diagram is not required to answer these questions, but might be useful to you.

   a. All else equal, the cost of labor used in picking apples has decreased.
   b. All else equal, the *New York Times* reports that eating apples increases the likelihood of contracting Ebola.
   c. All else equal, the price of oranges has increased.
   d. All else equal, combine the effects of parts (a) and (b).

Day 20

MORE CHANGES TO MARKET EQUILIBRIUM

Suppose the competitive market for pumpkin pie is in equilibrium. Given the following scenarios, predict changes to the equilibrium price and quantity of pumpkin pie. Be sure to determine which of the market shifters is at work. A diagram is not required but might be useful to you.

a. All else equal, the economy is robust and consumer purchasing power has increased.
b. All else equal, the price of apple pies has decreased.
c. All else equal, five small pumpkin pie bakeries merge into one bakery.
d. All else equal, combine the events from parts (a) and (c).

CONSUMER SURPLUS FROM GROCERY RECEIPTS

Consumer surplus is the difference between that maximum price you would have paid for an item (this is called willingness to pay) and the actual price you paid for an item. Your task here is to compute a friend's or family member's consumer surplus from a recent shopping trip that person made. Complete a table like the following. Find a person who has recently gone to the grocery store (or any store or restaurant for that matter), purchased a few items, and has the receipt. With the receipt as your guide, try to elicit from this person how much he or she would have paid for each item.

ITEM PURCHASED	HIGHEST PRICE SHOPPER WOULD HAVE PAID (WTP)	ACTUAL PRICE PAID (P)	CONSUMER SURPLUS EARNED (CS = WTP − P)
			Σ CS =

Day 22

CALCULATING CONSUMER SURPLUS

Suppose the demand curve for Gizmos is given by the following equation:

$$P = 250 - 3Q_d$$

The current price of a Gizmo is $100.

Draw this demand curve, and calculate consumer surplus at the current price.

Day 23

CALCULATING PRODUCER SURPLUS

Suppose the supply curve of Whodats is given by the following equation:

$$P = 100 + \tfrac{1}{2}Q_s$$

The current price of a Whodat is $200.

Draw this supply curve, and calculate producer surplus at the current price.

Day 24

CALCULATING MARKET EQUILIBRIUM

It's a useful exercise to employ a little bit of algebra to calculate equilibrium price and quantity, and it can be useful in seeing how a demand or supply shift affects price and quantity.

Suppose that the market for Snarrs is given by the following demand and supply equations:

Demand

$$P = 700 - 2Q_d$$

Supply

$$P = 100 + Q_s$$

a. Calculate equilibrium quantity and price in the Snarr market.
b. Now suppose the supply curve shifts to the left so that the new supply curve is:

$$P = 160 + Q_s$$

First predict the change in price and quantity after a decrease in supply; then calculate the new price and new quantity in the market for Snarrs.

c. Let's assume the supply of Snarrs has returned to the original equation. Now the demand has shifted to the right, so that the new demand curve is:

$$P = 760 - 2Q_d$$

First predict the change in price and quantity after an increase in demand; then calculate the new price and new quantity in the market for Snarrs.

Day 25

CALCULATING CONSUMER AND PRODUCER SURPLUS IN EQUILIBRIUM

Let's say that the market for Whoopsidoos has demand and supply equations that look like this:

<u>Demand</u>

$$P = 12 - \tfrac{1}{4} Q_d$$

<u>Supply</u>

$$P = 3 + \tfrac{1}{2} Q_s$$

a. Solve for market equilibrium price and quantity.
b. In equilibrium, calculate consumer and producer surplus. Note: It may help to draw the market, including the vertical intercepts.

EFFICIENCY AND INEFFICIENCY IN THE MARKET

Competitive markets are said to be efficient because the equilibrium outcome maximizes the sum of consumer and producer surplus. Your task is to show this in a neatly drawn graph.

a. Draw market equilibrium and label the equilibrium price P_e and equilibrium quantity Q_e.
b. Shade the areas of consumer and producer surplus.
c. Now suppose a law limited the quantity of this product to about half of Q_e. Add this regulated quantity to the graph and label it Q_r.
d. At quantity Q_r, show the area of consumer and producer surplus that would *not* be earned if this law were in place.

Day 27

CHAPTER 7 – BASIC ELASTICITY OF DEMAND

For each of the following scenarios, calculate the price elasticity of demand and determine whether demand for the product is elastic, inelastic, or unit elastic.

a. The price of gasoline increases by 5%, and the gallons of gasoline demanded falls by 3%.
b. The price of broccoli decreases by 6%, and the quantity of broccoli demanded rises by 9%.
c. The price of wool socks increases by 7.5%, and the quantity of wool socks demanded falls by 7.5%.

Day 28

PRICE ELASTICITY OF DEMAND AROUND THE HOUSE

> Think of something that your family purchases on a regular basis. Ask someone (maybe a parent) in the house how many of these products are purchased in a typical month. Then ask the same person how many would be purchased if the price increased by 50%. Use this person's responses to calculate the price elasticity of demand for this product, at least in your household.
>
> Tip: if the person you are interviewing finds it difficult to answer the second question, you might have to give that person a specific price increase of 50% to make it more real, and less hypothetical, for them. For example, you might say, "Movie tickets usually cost us $12, so a 50% increase would make the new price of a movie ticket $18."

Day 29

DRAWING DEMAND CURVES WITH VARYING ELASTICITIES

Without consulting your textbook or class notes, draw four demand curves in one graph.

    a. A perfectly inelastic demand curve, labeled D_{PI}
    b. A perfectly elastic demand curve, labeled D_{PE}
    c. A relatively elastic, but not perfectly elastic, demand curve, labeled D_E
    d. A relatively inelastic, but not perfectly inelastic, demand curve, labeled D_I

Day 30

USING THE MIDPOINT FORMULA

Suppose the demand curve for a hoozit is given by the following equation:

$$P = 100 - 2Q_d$$

The current price of a hoozit is $40, but management is considering lowering the price to $20.

a. Use the midpoint formula to calculate the price elasticity of demand between these two prices on the demand curve.
b. Interpret your result from part (a).

DEMAND, TOTAL REVENUE, AND ELASTICITY

The following table shows a demand schedule for a hypothetical product. Your task is to complete the table. When it comes to computing the price elasticity of demand, use the midpoint formula between two adjacent prices. For example, at a price of $7, use the midpoint between $8 and $7. For this reason, there is a shaded cell of the table at $8.

PRICE PER UNIT	QUANTITY OF THE GOOD DEMANDED	TOTAL REVENUE = $P \times Q_d$	PRICE ELASTICITY OF DEMAND
$8	0		
$7	1		
$6	2		
$5	3		
$4	4		
$3	5		
$2	6		
$1	7		
$0	8		

Day 32

THE TOTAL REVENUE TEST

We start with the completed table from the previous day. Can you explain, in your own words, why the total revenue initially rises when the price falls, but eventually total revenue begins to fall with further decreases in the price? Hint: It has everything to do with what is happening with price elasticity of demand when the price falls.

PRICE PER UNIT	QUANTITY OF THE GOOD DEMANDED	TOTAL REVENUE = $P \times Q_d$	PRICE ELASTICITY OF DEMAND
$8	0	$0	
$7	1	$7	15.00
$6	2	$12	4.33
$5	3	$15	2.20
$4	4	$16	1.29
$3	5	$15	0.78
$2	6	$12	0.45
$1	7	$7	0.23
$0	8	$0	0.07

Day 33

ELASTICITY AND REVENUE

Dr. Susan DeBeers, the president of a local college, is facing a shortfall of total revenue from student tuition at the college. She believes that if the college lowers tuition by 5%, that total revenues will increase. She has asked you for your economic advice. You know, from your research, that the price elasticity of demand for similar colleges is approximately equal to 0.50. In a short paragraph, report to Dr. DeBeers on how her plan will or will not achieve her goal of increasing total revenue to the college. She has never had a class in microeconomics, so be sure to explain your reasoning, and include any specific estimates that might help her understand the analysis.

Day 34

INCOME ELASTICITY

For each of the following goods, determine whether the good is normal or inferior, and interpret what each income elasticity actually tells us.

GOOD OR SERVICE	INCOME ELASTICITY OF DEMAND (E_I)	NORMAL OR INFERIOR?
Eggs	0.35	
Flour	−0.37	
Margarine	−0.21	
Furniture	1.47	

Day 35

SUBSTITUTES OR COMPLEMENTS?

For each pair of goods, identify which goods are substitutes for each other and which are complements of each other. Then interpret each cross-price elasticity of demand.

GOOD	CROSS ELASTICITY WITH RESPECT TO A CHANGE IN THE PRICE OF:	CROSS ELASTICITY	SUBSTITUTES OR COMPLEMENTS?
Beef	Pork	0.27	
Cereal	Milk	−0.90	
Butter	Margarine	0.67	
Potatoes	Meat	−0.50	

INCOME ELASTICITY OF DEMAND AROUND THE HOUSE

Once again, it's time to think of something that your family purchases on a regular basis. Ask someone (maybe a parent) in the house how many of these products are purchased in a typical month. Then ask the same person how many would be purchased if household income increased by 50%. Use this person's responses to calculate the income elasticity of demand, at least in your household, for this product.

Note: Alternatively you could ask how this person would respond if household income were decreased by 50% (or cut in half).

Day 37

COMBINING PRICE AND CROSS-PRICE ELASTICITY OF DEMAND

> Suppose that the cross-price elasticity of breakfast cereal with respect to a change in the price of milk is equal to –0.80. Suppose also that the price elasticity of demand for cereal is 0.45 and the price elasticity of demand for milk is 0.20.
>
> Assume that conditions in the market for milk have resulted in a decrease in milk supply, and the price of milk has risen by 10%.
>
>   a. Calculate how this will affect the quantity of milk demanded.
>   b. Calculate how this will affect the quantity of cereal demanded.
>   c. Calculate how much the price of cereal needs to be changed to offset the impact of the higher milk prices.

5 Minutes to a 5

ELASTICITY OF FARM SUPPLY

Farmer Liz raises turkeys, and each young turkey requires about nine months to mature to the point where it is ready to be sold. Suppose you tell Liz that you've heard that turkey prices have significantly risen, and you think she should take advantage of these high prices and sell a lot more turkeys. Liz thinks about it for a moment and then replies, "I can't right now, but I will certainly take your advice in nine months."

Draw a supply curve that reflects Liz's comment about her ability to supply more turkeys now and label it S_{SR}. In the same graph, draw a supply curve that reflects Liz's comment about her willingness to supply more turkeys in nine months and label it S_{LR}. How do these supply curves relate to the price elasticity of supply for Liz's turkeys?

DRAWING AN EFFECTIVE PRICE CEILING

The market for gazjabs is in equilibrium, and the government decides to create a price ceiling for this product.

a. In a correctly labeled graph of the gazjab market, show the equilibrium price (P_e) and quantity (Q_e).
b. Add an effective price ceiling in the market and label the price P_c.
c. Does this create a shortage or a surplus of gazjabs? Show this in your graph.

DRAWING AN EFFECTIVE PRICE FLOOR

The market for doozles is in equilibrium, and the government decides to create a price floor for this product.

a. In a correctly labeled graph of the doozle market, show the equilibrium price (P_e) and quantity (Q_e).
b. Add an effective price floor in the market and label the price P_f.
c. Does this create a shortage or a surplus of doozles? Show this in your graph.

DEADWEIGHT LOSS OF A PRICE CEILING

The following graph shows a price ceiling (P_c) in a competitive market. The graph also shows the areas of consumer and producer surplus if the market did *not* have a price ceiling and came to equilibrium.

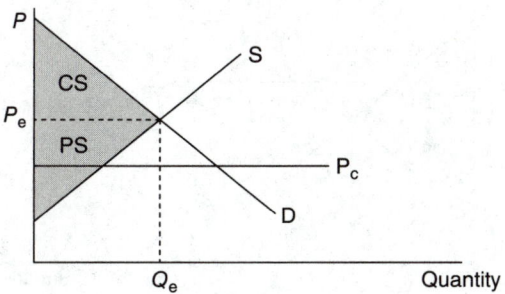

After the price ceiling is in place, identify the new areas of consumer surplus (CS), producer surplus (PS), and deadweight loss (DWL).

DEADWEIGHT LOSS OF A PRICE FLOOR

The following graph shows a price ceiling (P_f) in a competitive market. The graph also shows the areas of consumer and producer surplus if the market did *not* have a price floor and came to equilibrium.

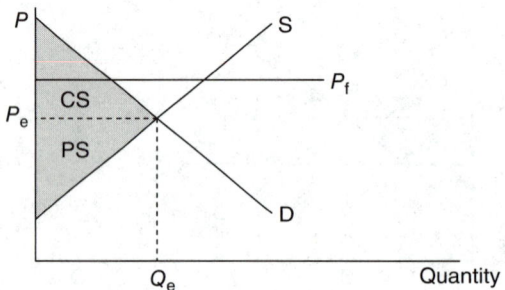

After the price floor is in place, identify the new areas of consumer surplus (CS), producer surplus (PS), and deadweight loss (DWL). Assume that the surplus units will *not* be purchased by the government.

SHOWING THE IMPACT OF AN EXCISE TAX

The market for snaghozzles is competitive, has come to equilibrium, and is shown as follows. The consumer and producer surplus in the market is also shown.

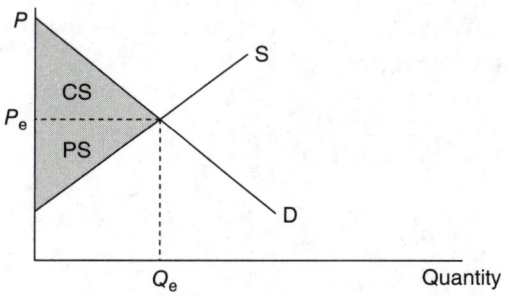

Now suppose the government has levied an excise tax of $\$T$ on the supply of snaghozzles. In a new graph of the market, show the following:

- The new supply curve that reflects the tax of $\$T$ (S_t)
- The new quantity of snaghozzles exchanged in the market (Q_t)
- The new price paid by buyers (P_b) of snaghozzles
- The new price sellers receive after paying the tax (P_s)
- Consumer surplus (CS) and producer surplus (PS)
- Tax revenue collected by the government (G)
- Deadweight loss (DWL)

INFERRING THE INCIDENCE OF A TAX

One product that has an excise tax levied on it is tobacco. Suppose you hear that a tax sufficient to increase the price of cigarettes by 10% reduces adult consumption of cigarettes by about 4%. What does this information say about the likely incidence of the tax between consumers and producers?

Day 45

THE INCIDENCE OF A TAX ON ELECTRICITY PRODUCTION

> Some economists argue that a tax should be levied on electricity production, especially if it is generated by fossil fuels (i.e., coal) to reduce pollution and greenhouse gas emissions. Suppose you read in the newspaper that the president of an electricity provider claims that any tax on electricity production "will simply be passed on to the consumers." If this is true, what must be true of the demand for electricity? Do you think the president of the company is correct in this assertion?

SHOWING THE IMPACT OF A PER-UNIT SUBSIDY

The market for snaghozzles is competitive, has come to equilibrium, and is shown as follows. A subsidy on each snaghozzle produced is being proposed. This subsidy of $S would allow for production and consumption of Q_s snaghozzles. Your job is to analyze the social welfare of such a program. Complete the following table. The competitive market outcome has been completed for you.

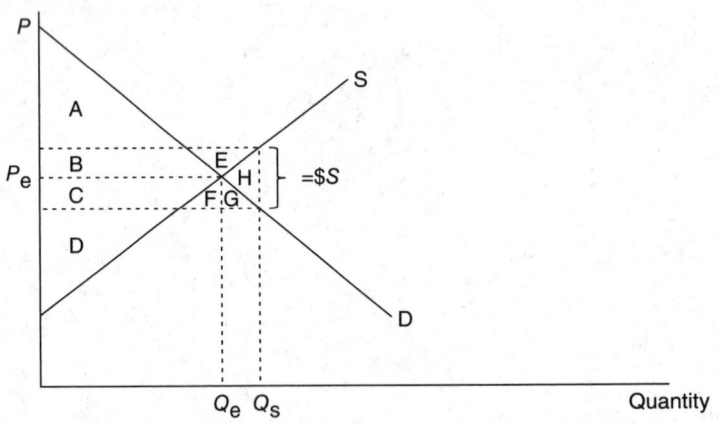

	BEFORE THE SUBSIDY	AFTER THE SUBSIDY
Consumer surplus	A + B	
Producer surplus	C + D	
Government spending	0	
Total surplus	A + B + C + D	
Deadweight loss	0	

400

THE IMPACT OF INTERNATIONAL TRADE IN A MARKET

The domestic market for jaggnods is shown as follows. Because international trade is prohibited, the domestic price is P_d, and the quantity exchanged in the domestic market is Q_d.

Suppose that the world price of jaggnods is P_w, and it is significantly lower than P_d. If international trade in jaggnods is allowed, identify the units demanded in the domestic market (Q_1), identify the units supplied by domestic producers (Q_2), and the total amount of jaggnods imported from foreign producers (I).

Day 48

SHOWING THE IMPACT OF A TARIFF

The domestic market for quizbogs is shown as follows. If international trade is prohibited, the domestic price is P_d, and the quantity exchanged in the domestic market is Q_d.

Suppose that the world price of quizbogs is P_w, and it is significantly lower than P_d. When international trade in quizbogs is allowed, the units demanded in the domestic market (Q_1) exceeds the units supplied by domestic producers (Q_2), and the total amount of quizbogs imported from foreign producers (I) is the difference.

Now the domestic government is planning to impose an import tariff on each quizbog imported into the domestic market. The new domestic price (P_T) would be approximately halfway between P_d and P_w.

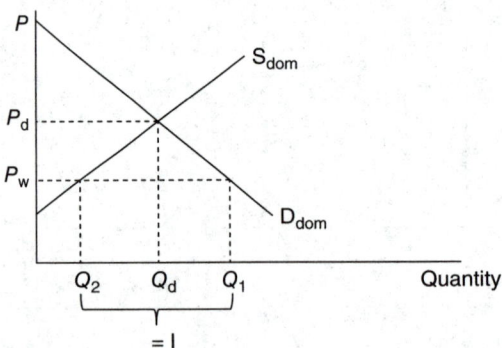

In a new graph, use arrows to show how the tariff impacts domestic consumption and domestic production and the impact on the domestic price. Label the new quantity of quizbogs imported, and government tariff revenue (G). Finally, identify the deadweight loss (DWL) from the tariff.

Day 49

WINNERS AND LOSERS FROM TRADE RESTRICTIONS

If you want to see real-world examples of import tariffs, go to the website for the U.S. International Trade Commission and their Harmonized Tariff Schedule:

https://usitc.gov/tata/hts/bychapter/index.htm

You will see many different product categories and can select any of them to see how much of an import tariff is levied by the U.S. government. For example, if you select Chapter 9, you will discover that there is no tariff levied on imported coffee, but there is a 6.4% tariff on imported green tea.

Make a short list of who you think benefits from an import tariff on a product like green tea and who is harmed by such tariffs.

TOTAL AND MARGINAL UTILITY

Max likes chocolate, but his utility rises at a decreasing rate as more chocolate is eaten. If he eats more than 7 pieces of chocolate, he knows that he will get sick.

Draw two graphs. The first is Max's total utility from eating chocolate, and the second is his marginal utility from eating chocolate. Be sure to show in each graph the point at which he stops eating chocolate.

Day 51

THE DISUTILITY FROM CONSUMPTION

Interview a friend or family member, and try to find a good or service that this person would absolutely not consume, even if it was free, because he or she really, *really* does not enjoy it. You might try asking, "Are there any foods that you just cannot or will not eat?" or "Is there a type of music or a specific singer/band that you just cannot stand?" Once you have found something that this person detests so much that he or she wouldn't consume even 1 unit at a price of zero, try to draw this person's total utility curve for this product.

UTILITY MAXIMIZATION 1

Suppose that Mary spends her entire income of $250 on goods X and Y. The price of X is $10 and the price of Y is $30. The table shows how Mary's marginal utility changes as she increases her consumption of each good.

a. The combination of 1X and 8Y is affordable. How much total utility is Mary enjoying at this combination of X and Y? Use the utility maximization rule to explain why this could not be the preferred combination of these two goods. How would Mary adjust her consumption?

# OF UNITS OF GOOD X CONSUMED	MARGINAL UTILITY OF GOOD X	# OF UNITS OF GOOD Y CONSUMED	MARGINAL UTILITY OF GOOD Y
1	10	1	30
2	7	2	28
3	6	3	24
4	5	4	21
5	4	5	18
6	3	6	16
7	2	7	15
8	1	8	14

b. Assuming she maximizes her utility, how many units of each good should she purchase? How much total utility is Mary enjoying at this combination?

UTILITY MAXIMIZATION 2

Theo has $50 to spend on jellybeans (B) and crackers (C). The price of jellybeans is $10 per bag and the price of crackers is $5 per box.

Refer to the following table of utility that Theo would receive from various combinations of crackers and jellybeans.

QTY OF CRACKERS	TOTAL UTILITY FROM CRACKERS	QTY OF JELLYBEANS	UTILITY FROM JELLYBEANS
0	0	0	0
2	70	1	80
4	130	2	150
6	180	3	210
8	220	4	260
10	250	5	300

a. Focusing only on the combinations that use all of his income, complete the following table to find the combination that maximizes Theo's total utility.

# CRACKERS	# JELLYBEANS	TOTAL UTILITY
0	5	
2	4	
4	3	
6	2	
8	1	
10	0	

b. Now maximize Theo's utility by finding the marginal utility of each product and then finding the marginal utility per dollar spent on each product. Note: Theo's consumption of crackers is rising by two boxes at a time.

QTY OF CRACKERS	UTILITY FROM CRACKERS	MU_C	MU_C/P_C	QTY OF JELLYBEANS	UTILITY FROM JELLYBEANS	MU_B	MU_B/P_B
0	0			0	0		
2	70			1	80		
4	130			2	150		
6	180			3	210		
8	220			4	260		
10	250			5	300		

Using this approach, what is the utility maximizing combination of crackers and jellybeans? How much utility is he enjoying?

CHAPTER 8 – ECONOMIC AND ACCOUNTING PROFIT

> You own and operate a skateboard shop. Each year, you receive revenue of $250,000 from your skateboard sales, and it costs you $130,000 to obtain the skateboards. In addition, you pay $40,000 for electricity, taxes, and other expenses each year. Instead of running the skateboard shop, you could become an accountant and receive a yearly salary of $50,000. A large clothing retail chain wants to expand and offers to rent the shop from you for $40,000 per year. How do you explain to your friends that despite making a profit, it is too costly for you to continue running your shop? Support your explanation with necessary computations.

FIXED AND VARIABLE COSTS OF DRIVING

Let's consider the ownership of a car and the output of car ownership measured as miles driven in a month. Make a list of variable costs of producing miles driven and another list of fixed costs.

Day 56

FIXED AND VARIABLE COSTS OF LIVING

Let's consider living in a house or apartment and the output of living in the residence measured as nights slept in the residence. Make a list of variable costs of producing nights slept in the residence and another list of fixed costs.

TOTAL, MARGINAL, AND AVERAGE PRODUCTS OF LABOR

A local cabinet maker can employ carpenters, and a fixed amount of capital equipment, to assist him in building cabinets for kitchens and bathrooms. The following table gives some information on his monthly short-run production function.

# OF CARPENTERS	TOTAL PRODUCT (# OF CABINETS PER MONTH)	MARGINAL PRODUCT	AVERAGE PRODUCT
0	0	X	X
1			8
2	18		
3		8	
4	32		
5			7.2
6	38		
7		-2	

a. Complete the table.
b. Ignoring for now the cost of employing carpenters, how many carpenters should this owner hire? Explain.

Day 58

EXPLAINING DIMINISHING MARGINAL RETURNS IN PRODUCTION

> Without looking at your class notes or a textbook, can you explain why economists think that the marginal product of labor diminishes as more labor is hired in the short run?

THE RELATIONSHIP BETWEEN TOTAL PRODUCT AND MARGINAL PRODUCT OF LABOR CURVES

The following three graphs show three different short-run total product of labor curves.

Using the shapes of these TP_L curves, draw the MP_L curve that would be derived from each of them. Which of these TP_L curves makes the most economic sense?

Graph A

Graph B

Graph C

Day 60

SHORT-RUN COSTS OF PRODUCTION

Melanie's apparel shop makes women's accessories in a perfectly competitive market.

Some of the production costs for Melanie's shop are given as follows. You will need to complete the table.

PRODUCTION (Q)	TFC	TVC	TC	MC
0	$5			N/A
1		$6		
2			14	
3		13		
4			23	
5				7
6		34		
7		45		
8			63	

GRAPHING THE SHORT-RUN TOTAL AND MARGINAL COSTS

PRODUCTION (Q)	TFC	TVC	TC	MC
0	$5	$0	$5	N/a
1	5	6	11	6
2	5	9	14	3
3	5	13	18	4
4	5	18	23	5
5	5	25	30	7
6	5	34	39	9
7	5	45	50	11
8	5	58	63	13

In one graph, plot the TFC, TVC, and TC curves.

In another graph, plot the MC curve.

Day 62

AVERAGE COSTS IN THE SHORT RUN

Hint: If you're good at using Excel, you can do these quickly. If not, maybe try using a calculator.

Complete the following table.

PRODUCTION (Q)	TFC	TVC	TC	MC	AFC	AVC	ATC
0	$5	$0	$5		XX	XX	XX
1	5	6	11	$6			
2	5	9	14	$3			
3	5	13	18	$4			
4	5	18	23	$5			
5	5	25	30	$7			
6	5	34	39	$9			
7	5	45	50	$11			
8	5	58	63	$13			

GRAPHING THE SHORT-RUN AVERAGE COSTS CURVES

PRODUCTION (Q)	MC	AFC	AVC	ATC
0		XX	XX	XX
1	$6	$5.00	$6.00	$11.00
2	$3	$2.50	$4.50	$7.00
3	$4	$1.67	$4.33	$6.00
4	$5	$1.25	$4.50	$5.75
5	$7	$1.00	$5.00	$6.00
6	$9	$0.83	$5.67	$6.50
7	$11	$0.71	$6.43	$7.14
8	$13	$0.63	$7.25	$7.88

In one graph, plot the AFC, AVC, ATC, and MC curves.

Hint: If you're good at using Excel, you can do these quickly. If not, maybe try using graph paper.

NAME THAT CURVE!

The following short-run cost curves are unnamed. Your job is to correctly identify them, without the use of your books and/or class notes.

CHAPTER 9 – THE CHARACTERISTICS OF PERFECT COMPETITION

Quick! Can you list the characteristics of perfect competition? Ready, set, go!

MAXIMIZING PROFIT IN THE SHORT RUN IN PERFECT COMPETITION

Suppose grapes are grown in a perfectly competitive market. Short-run costs for a grape farmer are given in the following table.

OUTPUT (Q)	TFC	TVC	TC
0	$500	$0	$500
1	$500	$150	$650
2	$500	$200	$700
3	$500	$260	$760
4	$500	$340	$840
5	$500	$450	$950
6	$500	$590	$1,090
7	$500	$770	$1,270
8	$500	$1,000	$1,500
9	$500	$1,290	$1,790
10	$500	$1,650	$2,150

If the price of a bushel of grapes is $230, find the profit maximizing level of output. If there are two output levels that provide the same maximum profit, we choose the greater of the two outputs. Compute the level of profit each producer would earn.

OUTPUT (Q)	TOTAL REVENUE = P × Q	PROFIT (+) OR LOSS (−) = TR − TC
0		
1		
2		
3		
4		
5		
6		
7		
8		
9		
10		

Suppose the price of grapes drops to $180. How much would the firm produce, and how much short-run profit would be earned?

THE PROFIT-MAXIMIZATION RULE

Suppose grapes are grown in a perfectly competitive market. Short-run costs for a grape farmer are given in the following table.

OUTPUT (Q)	TFC	TVC	TC
0	$500	$0	$500
1	$500	$150	$650
2	$500	$200	$700
3	$500	$260	$760
4	$500	$340	$840
5	$500	$450	$950
6	$500	$590	$1,090
7	$500	$770	$1,270
8	$500	$1,000	$1,500
9	$500	$1,290	$1,790
10	$500	$1,650	$2,150

If the price of a bushel of grapes is $290, use the profit-maximization rule to find the profit maximizing level of output. Compute the level of profit each producer would earn.

If the price of grapes fell to $80 per bushel, determine how many bushels the farmer should supply in the short run and compute profit.

THE SIDE-BY-SIDE GRAPHS OF PERFECT COMPETITION PROFIT

There will come a time when you will need to throw down your high-level ninja graphing skills, and there is nothing more ninja-like than a perfect side-by-side representation of perfect competition in the short run.

Here's the situation. A market is perfectly competitive in the short run, and the typical firm is earning positive economic profit. In the side-by-side graphs, show equilibrium in the market, output for the typical firm, and the area of economic profit. Everything must be perfectly labeled.

THE SIDE-BY-SIDE GRAPHS OF PERFECT COMPETITION LOSSES

Again, you must have these graphing skills down.

Here's the situation. A market is perfectly competitive in the short run, and the typical firm is earning negative economic profit (losses), but is not in a shutdown situation. In the side-by-side graphs, show equilibrium in the market, output for the typical firm, and the area of economic losses. Everything must be perfectly labeled.

LONG-RUN ADJUSTMENT TO EQUILIBRIUM IN PERFECT COMPETITION

> a. A perfectly competitive market is in short-run equilibrium, and firms are earning positive economic profit. Describe how this market and the typical firm will adjust in the long run.
> b. A perfectly competitive market is in short-run equilibrium, and firms are earning negative economic profit. Describe how this market and the typical firm will adjust in the long run.
> c. In the side-by-side graphs of perfect competition, show long-run equilibrium in the market, price, and output for the typical firm. Everything must be perfectly labeled.

THE CHARACTERISTICS OF MONOPOLY

> Quick! Can you list the characteristics of monopoly? Ready, set, go!

MONOPOLY PROFIT MAXIMIZATION

A monopolist has the following total cost data and demand schedule:

OUTPUT (UNITS)	PRICE ($)	TOTAL COST ($)
0	12	5
1	11	10
2	10	15
3	9	20
4	8	25
5	7	30
6	6	35
7	5	40
8	4	45
9	3	50
10	2	55
11	1	60
12	0	65

a. If this monopolist is unregulated, find the profit-maximizing quantity, price, and profit.
b. Suppose that the government imposes a lump-sum tax of $1 that increases total fixed cost by $1. Find the new profit-maximizing quantity, price, and profit.
c. Now suppose the lump-sum tax from part (b) is eliminated, but the government wishes to regulate this monopolist to produce at the level of output where there is zero deadweight loss. How will this affect the output, price, and profit realized by the monopolist? Be specific.

DRAWING MONOPOLY

Eli is a profitable monopolist seller of doodads. In a correctly labeled graph, draw Eli's profit-maximizing level of output, the price he would charge, and his area of monopoly profit.

Day 74

CHARACTERISTICS OF MONOPOLISTIC COMPETITION

> Quick! Can you list the characteristics of monopolistic competition? Ready, set, go!

Day 75

LONG-RUN ADJUSTMENTS IN MONOPOLISTIC COMPETITION

a. A monopolistically competitive market is in short-run equilibrium, and firms are earning positive economic profit. Describe how this market and the typical firm will adjust in the long run.
b. A monopolistically competitive market is in short-run equilibrium, and firms are earning negative economic profit. Describe how this market and the typical firm will adjust in the long run.
c. In a graph of one firm in monopolistic competition, show long-run equilibrium price and output. Everything must be perfectly labeled.

Day 76

A GAME THEORY PROBLEM

Hamm and Rye are two oligopolistic widget manufacturers engaged in bitter competition with one another. Each firm is deciding whether to build a new factory in a neighboring state. The following table shows profit payoffs for the firms (Hamm, Rye) under various scenarios:

		RYE	
		BUILD	DON'T BUILD
Hamm	Build	5, 5	3, 7
	Don't build	6, 1	4, 2

a. Does either firm have a dominant strategy? Explain why or why not.
b. What is the Nash equilibrium of this game? Explain how you came to this conclusion.
c. Is this a prisoner's dilemma? Explain how you came to this conclusion.

Day 77

ONLINE PRISONER'S DILEMMA

Your assignment is to play a game against a computer-simulated opponent. The following three links should take you to different simulated prisoner's dilemma games. Play the games a few times, experiment with strategies, and try to beat your opponent. What seems to work, and what does not?

http://www.gametheory.net/web/pdilemma/

http://serendip.brynmawr.edu/bb/pd.html

http://www.iterated-prisoners-dilemma.net/

CHAPTER 10 – THE MRP$_L$ AND HIRING DECISION

Hamilton's Pizza Parlor has the production function per hour shown in the following table. The hourly wage rate for each worker is $8, and each pizza sells for $2.

QUANTITY OF LABOR (WORKERS)	QUANTITY OF PIZZA	
0	0	
1	9	
2	15	
3	20	
4	24	
5	27	
6	29	
7	30	

a. Hamilton is an economics major and describes herself as a "price taker and a wage taker." What does this mean?
b. Calculate the value of the marginal revenue product of labor (MRP$_L$), and add this to the table.
c. How many units of labor should Hamilton employ? Illustrate this hiring decision in a correctly labeled graph.
d. Now suppose that the price of pizza rises to $4. How does this affect Hamilton's hiring decision? Show this in the graph from part (c).

Day 79

CHANGES IN FACTOR MARKETS

Let's assume that the markets for labor, land, and capital are all perfectly competitive. For each of the following scenarios, predict what would happen in the factor market, and predict changes in equilibrium price and quantity of that factor.

a. The factor market: semitruck drivers

The event: the price of diesel fuel falls

b. The factor market: elementary school teachers

The event: the government requires two more years of education before a person can become a teacher

c. The factor market: capital equipment

The event: interest rates are rising

d. The factor market: beachfront property

The event: the sea level continues to rise

Day 80

DOING SOME RESEARCH ON AN OCCUPATION

Go to the following link for the *Occupational Outlook Handbook* (OOH):

http://www.bls.gov/ooh/

Browse the many different occupations, or search for something specific, and read about the occupation. Report on the following:

- What do these people do?
- What kind of education or training would you need?
- What are current pay levels?
- What is the growth outlook (jobs and percentage change) from 2014–2024?

Investigate several different occupations that might interest you, and see if there are qualities that are encouraging or maybe discouraging your interest in that occupation.

Day 81

LEAST-COST AND PROFIT-MAXIMIZING COMBINATION OF INPUTS

In the following table are the marginal product schedules for two resources, labor and capital. Both resources are variable and are employed in purely competitive resources markets. The price of the output, which is sold in a perfectly competitive output market, is $0.50. The price of labor is $1 and the price of capital is $2.

QTY OF LABOR EMPLOYED	MARGINAL PRODUCT OF LABOR	MRP OF LABOR	QUANTITY OF CAPITAL EMPLOYED	MARGINAL PRODUCT OF CAPITAL	MRP OF CAPITAL
1	20		1	20	
2	16		2	18	
3	12		3	16	
4	10		4	12	
5	8		5	8	
6	4		6	6	
7	2		7	4	
8	1		8	2	

a. Complete the table by computing the MRP for each resource.
b. What is the least-cost combination of labor and capital that would enable the firm to produce 144 units of output?
c. What is the profit-maximizing combination of labor and capital?
d. What is the total output and profit when the firm is employing the profit-maximizing combinations of labor and capital?

Day 82

CHAPTER 11 – PRIVATE AND PUBLIC GOODS

Review the concepts of excludability and rivalry that identify the difference between private and public goods. Use these concepts to classify the following goods and services.

   a. A gallon of milk
   b. Streetlamps along a highway
   c. An hour of legal advice from an attorney
   d. Lobsters in the Atlantic Ocean

A TRAGEDY OF THE COMMONS

A special kind of environmental and economic problem is when a common resource is overexploited, often to the point of ruin, because of the nonexcludable and rival characteristics of it. There are many examples of this tragedy of the commons," but one of the best known cases is that of overfishing the world's oceans. To see how this happens, go to the following website and play the Tragedy of the Bunnies game. http://bunnies.learnliberty.org/

Read the instructions, and play both rounds of the game. When you're done, read the "moral of the story." Why do you think that common resources (like fish in the ocean) are so commonly overexploited?

Day 84

GRAPHING A POSITIVE EXTERNALITY

Suppose that snaghorns are exchanged in a perfectly competitive market, and the consumption of snaghorns provides utility to third parties who are not consuming this fine product. In a correctly labeled graph, show the following:

- The quantity produced by the market (Q_m) and the market price (P_m)
- The spillover benefit received by the third parties on each snaghorn consumed
- The socially efficient quantity (Q_e) and the efficient price (P_e)
- The area of deadweight loss to society from not producing the efficient quantity of snaghorns

Day 85

BEES AND APPLES

Quinton is a beekeeper who has several beehives, and he makes a living selling honey at the farmers' market. Quinton's neighbor is Payton, and she owns an apple orchard and makes a living selling apples at the same farmers' market. One day at the farmers' market, an economist named Fernando is buying both apples and honey. He tells Payton that she should really send Quinton some money so he can install more beehives. Why would an economist make such a suggestion? Or is he just delirious from grading papers and should be completely ignored? Explain.

Day 86

GRAPHING A NEGATIVE EXTERNALITY

Suppose that goosedumples are exchanged in a perfectly competitive market, and the production of goosedumples imposes costs on third parties who are not involved in the exchange of this product. In a correctly labeled graph, show the following:

- The quantity produced by the market (Q_m) and the market price (P_m).
- The spillover cost imposed on the third parties on each goosedumple produced.
- The socially efficient quantity (Q_e) and the efficient price (P_e).
- The area of deadweight loss to society from not producing the efficient quantity of goosedumples.

PROGRESSIVE INCOME TAX BRACKETS

In the United States, personal income is taxed with a system of progressive tax rates, or tax brackets. As your taxable income rises, so does the marginal tax rate that you pay. Go to the following link to see tax brackets for 2016. https://www.irs.com/articles/projected-us-tax-rates-2016

Use these tax brackets to compute the amount of taxes a single person would pay if she had a taxable income of $60,000.

Day 88

YOUR LOCAL ENVIRONMENT

Pollution is a perfect example of a negative externality. Do you know how much pollution is in your zip code? What chemicals are ending up in your water? Where is it coming from? The Environmental Protection Agency has a great way of answering these questions.

Go to the following website:

https://www.epa.gov/communities

Enter the zip code of your choice, and explore the environmental quality of this area. Find the following information. Include either links or screen shots of the results. (1 point for each of the following bullet items)

- Find the current air quality index (AQI) at the nearest air quality monitoring station to your zip code. Is it safe to go outside?
  You can find more specific AQI information here:
  https://www.airnow.gov/index.cfm?action=aqibasics.aqi#underaqi
- Under the water quality menu, look for "Water Quality Assessment." Is there a body of water that is listed as impaired in any way? How so? What's wrong with it?
- Find the link for My WATERS Mapper. You might have to enter your zip code again. On the right side look for "Water Impairments." Select one or all of the three options and report what you find. You might have to adjust the zoom of the map. Any streams, rivers, or lakes that are impaired?
- Now select the "My Land" menu. Another map will pop up. On the right side, select the Hazardous Waste box. You will probably see several locations show up in your map. Select one of those locations. What type of business is this? What can you discover about their toxic waste? Are there any concerns about specific chemicals or compounds?
- Go to the "My Health" menu. What kind of cancer risk exists in this community? What is the main cause of this cancer risk? How does infant mortality compare in your chosen zip code to the state average and national average? Do the same comparison for low birth weight.

Day 89

A REGRESSIVE SALES TAX

Most U.S. states have legislated a sales tax on most purchases. Some cities have also created higher sales taxes than other parts of the state. For example, the 2016 sales tax in Illinois is 6.25%, but the state grants counties and cities the flexibility to increase the local sales tax. In Chicago, the sales tax in 2016 was 10.25%.

A sales tax is considered a regressive tax because the tax payment is a smaller share of income as income rises. Let's see how this works.

Melanie earns $2,000 per week, and Eric earns $1,000 per week. Suppose each of these consumers is shopping for $100 of clothing in Indiana, a state with a sales tax rate of 7%.

Compute the amount of sales tax each shopper will pay, and then compute what fraction of weekly income this sales tax amounts to.

INCOME DISTRIBUTION

The Census Bureau of the United States collects data on many things, including how income is distributed across households. The distribution is divided into fifths, or quintiles, so that the households that earn less than 80% of all households fall into the bottom quintile, and the households that earn more than 80% of all households fall into the top quintile. Select the following link provided, and then choose table H-2 "All races." This will download a file in Excel, and you can see data going back to the late 1960s.

http://www.census.gov/data/tables/time-series/demo/income-poverty/historical-income-households.html

From the same page above, you can download table H-4 to see a Gini index for the United States for the same period of time. The Gini ratio is a measure of how equally income is distributed across a nation's households. The closer the Gini ratio is to zero, the more equally income is distributed. The closer it is to 1 (or 100 if you multiply the index by 100), the more unequally it is distributed.

The United Nations produces a "Human Development Report," and part of that report is a statistic called a "Human Development Index." Values close to 1 indicate a highly developed nation with strong institutions, health, and prosperity for the citizens. Part of this HDI is the Gini coefficient measure of income equality. The following link allows you to see estimates of a Gini coefficient for many nations. You will find it if you scroll down to Table 3 of this report. Notice that the report shows both the HDI and the "inequality adjusted HDI" that accounts for several measures of inequality within the nation.

http://hdr.undp.org/sites/default/files/hdr_2015_statistical_annex.pdf

Questions

- What has happened to income equality in the United States since the late 1960s? Are there any possible explanations for what you see in the data?
- How does the United States compare to other nations in the Gini coefficient, and how is this reflected in the inequality adjusted HDI?

Answers

Day 1

1. Labor: Your efforts in buying the groceries, preparing and cooking the food, serving the meal
2. Capital: The knives, pans, oven, or any other equipment you would need to cook the meal
3. Natural resources: The raw ingredients (meat, vegetables, spices, etc.)
4. Entrepreneurial ability: Your know-how and creativity in bringing all of the other resources together to make the meal

Day 2

Note: The following numbers are hypothetical but give you an idea of how to compute your *actual* opportunity cost.

1. I selected *Star Trek Beyond*, and the local price of a ticket is $10.
2. Yes, I will buy popcorn and a drink, and this will cost about another $10.
3. The nearest cinema is 6 miles away, so I would drive 12 total miles. My car gets about 24 miles per gallon, so I would use ½ gallon of gas. Local prices are about $2 per gallon, so my driving costs are about $1.
4. The movie lasts 122 minutes, and the drive is estimated to be 9 minutes each way, for a total of 140 minutes, or 2.33 hours. If I could receive a wage of $10 per hour, I could have earned $23.33 (ignoring taxes) during the movie.
5. Total opportunity cost of this movie = $10 + $10 + $1 + $23.33 = $44.33

Day 3

Since each slice of pizza costs $2, the marginal cost curve should be drawn horizontal at $2. The marginal benefit curve is drawn downward sloping because the next slice of pizza provides less additional benefit. After all, your hunger is partially satisfied with each slice, so the next slice isn't quite as great as the one that came before.

So if your hypothetical number of pizza slices was 4, the graph should look something like this:

Day 4

a. A PPC with constant opportunity costs should be drawn as a straight line.

b. Since the speed-reading course allows you to read more pages in an hour, the PPC should move outward along the *x*-axis but not along the *y*-axis.

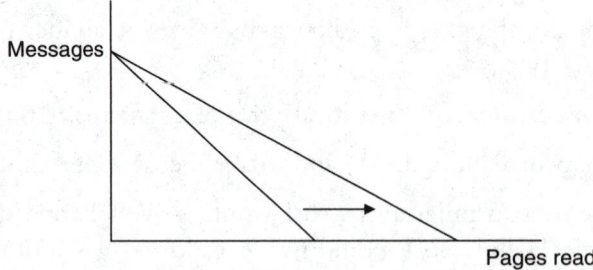

c. The opportunity cost of socializing has now increased. Remember that opportunity cost of an activity, socializing in this case, is what you have given up to engage in that activity. Now that you are a speed-reader, every hour spent socializing comes at a greater sacrifice in the number of pages you could have been reading.

Day 5

a. If Eli splits his time equally, he can fold 10 towels and wash 5 plates.

If Theodore does the same, he can fold 3 towels and wash 3 plates.

Total output: 13 towels + 8 plates = 21

b. A person is said to have comparative advantage in a task if he or she can perform that task at a lower opportunity cost.

For every plate that Eli washes, he gives up 2 towels folded, so that is his opportunity cost of washing plates. On the other hand, for every towel that he folds, he gives up washing ½ plate.

For every plate that Theodore washes, he gives up 1 towel folded. And for every towel he folds, he gives up 1 washed plate.

So we can see that Theodore has a lower opportunity cost of washing plates (1 towel) when compared to Eli's opportunity cost of washing plates (2 towels). Theodore has comparative advantage in washing plates. On the other hand, Eli has the comparative advantage in folding towels because he gives up ½ washed plate while Theodore gives up 1 washed plate.

If they specialize based on comparative advantage, Eli should spend all of his time folding towels and Theodore should spend all of his time washing plates.

Total output with specialization: 20 towels + 6 plates = 26

Day 6

1. Productive efficiency is achieved when you produce the maximum amount of output for a given level of technology and resources. If you were inefficient in the kitchen, you might use the correct quantity of ingredients but produce only 10 cookies. Another way of being productively inefficient would be to produce a dozen cookies, but waste some of the ingredients in the process (like dropping an egg on the floor or spilling some flour).

2. Most people, if equity were the goal, would give each person 3 cookies. Of course, this outcome depends upon how you define "equitable." Rather than this egalitarian outcome, another might define equitable by giving the most cookies to the person with the highest GPA or other arbitrary measure of merit. This is similar to saying that the highest wages should be paid to those who are most productive.

3. Allocative efficiency would be achieved if the cookies were distributed to maximize the happiness of the four people eating them. One way to do this would be to give the most cookies to the person who most desired them (or was the hungriest) and the fewest cookies to the person who had the least desire for cookies. Alternatively, you could give each person 3 cookies and then allow them to trade cookies among themselves. When there are no more trades to be made, it's likely you have found an efficient allocation.

Day 7

For all three graphs I will put units of pizza on the horizontal axis and units of shoes on the vertical axis. The slope of the PPC always gives you the opportunity cost of the good on the horizontal axis, while the inverse of the slope gives you the opportunity cost of the good on the vertical axis.

a. Constant opportunity cost is described by a straight line (constant slope). If the PPC is linear, it implies that resources are perfectly substitutable in producing pizza and shoes. No matter where you are on the PPC, increasing pizza production will always cost the same number of shoes.

b. A PPC with increasing opportunity costs is drawn with a bowed-outward shape to it, flatter at the top and steeper at the bottom. This shape implies that there are some resources particularly suited to pizza production (like an oven) and some that are better for shoe production (like sewing machines). As we move resources down the PPC to produce more pizza, we would be smart to first allocate the best pizza resources (and weakest shoe resources), thus making our increased pizza big but lost shoe production small. However, when we get closer to maximum shoe production, the only resources we have left are best at shoe-making, so we will gain very few pizzas but lose many shoes. One way to think about this shape is that it gets more difficult (i.e., more costly) to produce something as we produce more of it. Because we see these differences in resources in the real world, this is likely the most realistic depiction of the PPC.

c. If a PPC exhibits decreasing opportunity cost, then it should be drawn as bowed-inward; steeper at the top and flatter at the bottom. This shape also implies that resources are not perfectly substitutable, but it also implies that we would do something counterintuitive when reallocating resources to pizza production: We would select the resources best suited for *shoe* production and use them first for *pizza* production. This decision would cause a sharp decline in shoe production with a very small gain in pizza production. The opportunity cost of making pizza declines as we get closer to the bottom of the PPC, because now we are finally sending strong pizza-making resources to the pizza parlor, thus losing very little shoe production. Because it doesn't make sense to allocate resources in this way, and because we seldom observe opportunity costs falling rather than rising, you would almost never see a PPC drawn this way.

Day 8

a.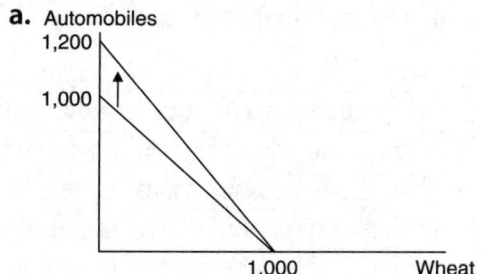

A 20% increase in maximum automobile production moves the vertical intercept up to 1,200 automobiles. Remember that the slope of the PPC gives us the opportunity cost of wheat. Prior to the technology, 1 unit of wheat cost 1 automobile, but now 1 unit of wheat costs 1.2 automobiles. Because automobile-producing technology has improved, devoting resources to wheat costs society more automobiles that could have been produced.

b.

A 25% decrease in maximum wheat production moves the horizontal intercept down to 750 units of wheat. Remember that the inverse of the slope of the PPC gives us the opportunity cost of automobiles. Prior to the drought, 1 automobile costs 1 unit of wheat, but now 1 automobile costs 0.75 units of wheat. Because of the drought that has hampered wheat production, devoting resources to automobiles costs society fewer units of wheat that could have been produced.

c. Automobiles

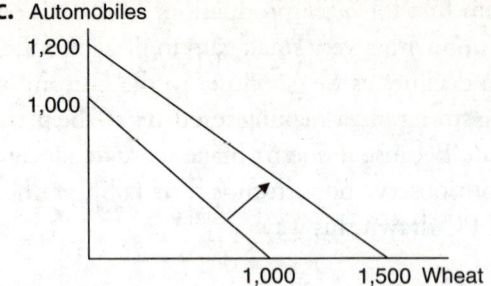

Better technology has improved production of both goods, but not by the same degree. The new opportunity cost of wheat is 0.80 automobiles, a decrease from the original cost of 1 automobile. Since this technology is relatively more useful for growing wheat, devoting more resources to wheat production comes at a lower opportunity cost.

Day 9

A. The following table shows data for the civilian labor force from January 2006 to August 2016. These values are measured in thousands, so the actual value for August 2016 is about 159,463,000 people in the labor force. The percentage change is:
$100 \times (159{,}463 - 150{,}214)/150{,}214 = 6.2\%$

If you found data going back to 1948, you would calculate the percentage change to be about 165%.

YEAR	JAN	FEB	MAR	APR	MAY	JUN	JUL	AUG	SEP	OCT	NOV	DEC
2006	150,214(1)	150,641	150,813	150,881	151,069	151,354	151,377	151,716	151,662	152,041	152,406	152,732
2007	153,144(1)	152,983	153,051	152,435	152,670	153,041	153,054	152,749	153,414	153,183	153,835	153,918
2008	154,063(1)	153,653	153,908	153,769	154,303	154,313	154,469	154,641	154,570	154,876	154,639	154,655
2009	154,210(1)	154,538	154,133	154,509	154,747	154,716	154,502	154,307	153,827	153,784	153,878	153,111
2010	153,484(1)	153,694	153,954	154,622	154,091	153,616	153,691	154,086	153,975	153,635	154,125	153,650
2011	153,263(1)	153,214	153,376	153,543	153,479	153,346	153,288	153,760	154,131	153,961	154,128	153,995
2012	154,351(1)	154,695	154,768	154,557	154,859	155,084	154,943	154,753	155,168	155,539	155,356	155,597
2013	155,666(1)	155,313	155,034	155,365	155,483	155,753	155,662	155,568	155,749	154,694	155,352	155,083
2014	155,285(1)	155,560	156,187	155,376	155,511	155,684	156,090	156,080	156,129	156,363	156,442	156,142
2015	157,025(1)	156,878	156,890	157,032	157,367	156,984	157,115	157,061	156,867	157,096	157,367	157,833
2016	158,335(1)	158,890	159,286	158,924	158,466	158,880	159,287	159,463				

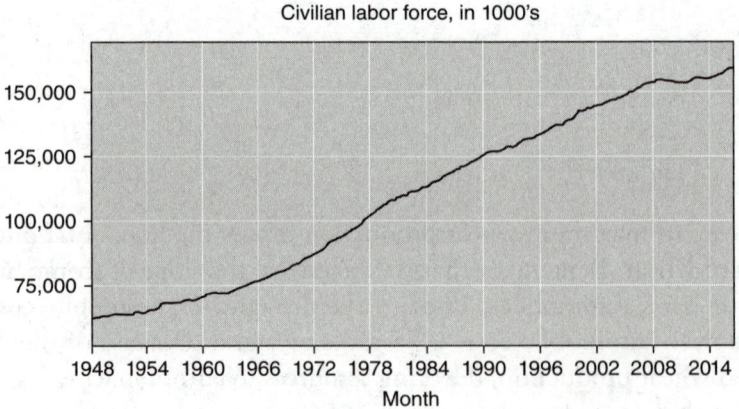

Civilian labor force, in 1000's

452

B. If you found the capital stock data from this data series:

https://fred.stlouisfed.org/series/RKNANPUSA666NRUG#0

then you would see the following graph. These values are measured in millions of 2011 dollars.

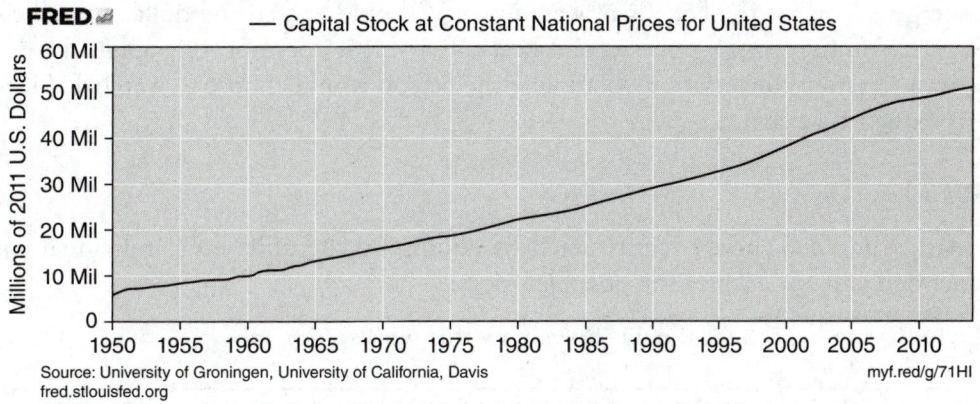

The percentage change in the capital stock from 1950 to 2014 is equal to: 100 × (51,190,644.0 − 5,684,549.5)/5,684,549.5 = 800.5%.

We can see that over a comparable period of time, the stock of capital in the United States has increased by a much larger percentage than has the nation's labor force. Increases in both of these critical economic resources have contributed to the great expansion of the U.S. production possibilities.

Day 10

To measure the benefit of an activity that has no price tag, economists can try to create a hypothetical auction.

Ask this person, "How much money would I need to pay you to stop watching TV and forgo the enjoyment (utility) you are receiving from it? Would you take $1, $5, $10?" Keep increasing the bid until this person accepts a hypothetical compensation to give up doing something he or she enjoys: watching TV. Once you reach this number, you know how much economic value (money) this person places on watching TV. After all, if the person would accept $20 to turn off the TV, watching TV must be worth $20 to him or her.

We can do a similar exercise to try to measure the opportunity cost of not doing a second-best use of our time. You have asked a person to tell you what he or she would be doing if the TV signal suddenly ended and the person could not watch TV during this time. Of course, this person could give you any of dozens of possible activities, but suppose the person tells you that he or she would be playing a game on his or her phone. Now ask this person, "If you were playing a game on your phone, how much money would I need to pay you to stop?" Begin the auction at $1 and gradually raise the hypothetical price until the person accepts a value that would compensate him or her for turning off the game.

If the person would need to be paid $10 to turn off the game, this is the value he or she places on playing the game. Because the person is watching TV at the moment, and not playing the game, then missing the game means the person is sacrificing $10 of potential enjoyment. This is the opportunity cost of watching TV.

If your friend or family member is acting like economists predict, the dollar value he or she gives you for the benefit of watching TV should exceed the dollar value he or she gives you for giving up the second-best activity. If it does not, this opens the door for an interesting conversation about why the person would choose to watch TV if the costs exceed the benefit.

Day 11

A market demand curve is constructed by adding up the units each individual consumer demands, at each of the possible prices.

The following hypothetical data shows how this works.

PRICE PER MOVIE TICKET	QUANTITY DEMANDED BY YOU	QUANTITY DEMANDED FOR FRIEND 1	QUANTITY DEMANDED FOR FRIEND 2	QUANTITY DEMANDED FOR FRIEND 3	QUANTITY DEMANDED FOR FRIEND 4	QUANTITY DEMANDED FOR FRIEND 5	TOTAL Q_d
$6	8	6	10	5	4	2	35
$8	7	5	8	4	3	1	28
$10	6	4	6	3	2	0	21
$12	5	3	4	2	1	0	15
$14	4	2	0	1	0	0	7

You can take the prices in the first column and the total quantity demanded in the last column and draw out the demand curve for the selected good or service. The demand curve for the hypothetical movie ticket example looks like:

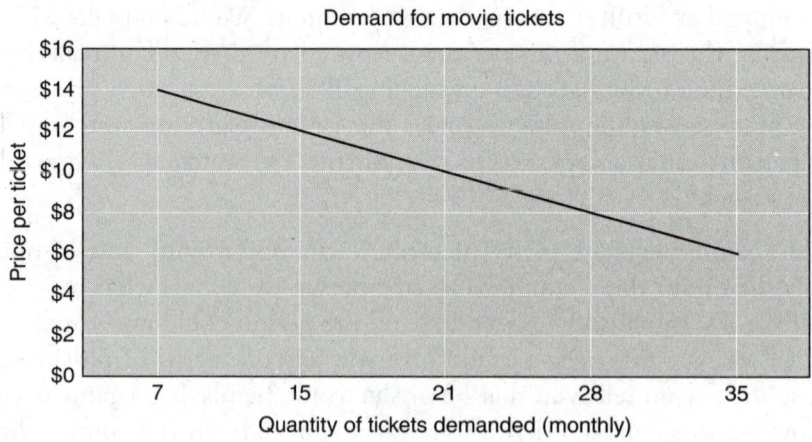

Day 12

a. This is an increase in tastes and preferences, so demand for OJ shifts to the right.

b. This is an increase in the price of a substitute, so demand for OJ shifts to the right.

c. This is a decrease in income, so because OJ is a normal good, demand shifts to the left.

d. An expectation of a higher price of OJ in the future causes demand to shift to the right now.

e. This will not cause a shift in the demand for OJ; it will cause the quantity of OJ to increase downward along the demand curve.

Day 13

a. If we consider Swiss cheese to be a substitute good, a higher price of Swiss will increase demand for cheddar. The demand for cheddar shifts to the right.

b. This is not a shifter. When the price of cheddar falls, the quantity of cheddar demanded increases. This is a movement downward along the curve. Be careful not to call this an "increase in demand," as this would describe a shift.

c. Assuming cheddar is a normal good, higher incomes will shift demand for cheddar to the right. If you argue that cheddar is an inferior good, then you predict a leftward shift.

d. Fear of getting sick weakens the tastes and preferences for cheddar, and this would decrease demand.

e. If you think that crackers are a complementary good to cheddar, then higher cracker prices should decrease the demand for cheddar.

Day 14

A market supply of labor curve is constructed by adding up the hours each individual worker supplies, at each of the possible wages.

The hypothetical data that follows shows how this works.

HOURLY WAGE	QUANTITY OF HOURS SUPPLIED BY YOU	QUANTITY OF HOURS SUPPLIED BY FRIEND 1	QUANTITY OF HOURS SUPPLIED BY FRIEND 2	QUANTITY OF HOURS SUPPLIED BY FRIEND 3	QUANTITY OF HOURS SUPPLIED BY FRIEND 4	QUANTITY OF HOURS SUPPLIED BY FRIEND 5	TOTAL Q_S (HOURS)
$6	6	10	0	12	0	10	38
$8	10	15	10	17	4	20	76
$10	20	20	20	22	15	30	127
$12	25	25	30	27	20	40	167
$14	30	30	40	32	23	50	205

You can take the wages in the first column and the total quantity supplied in the last column and draw out the supply curve for the labor market. The supply curve for the hypothetical data looks like:

Day 15

a. Better technology shifts supply to the right.

b. A higher input price (the paper) shifts supply to the left.

c. The higher price of a related output (self-help books) would decrease the supply of textbooks.

d. Having fewer sellers shifts the supply to the left.

e. This effectively makes it less costly to produce each textbook, so it acts in the same way as a decrease in the price of an input, shifting supply to the right.

Day 16

a. Pumpkins are a key input, so this will increase the supply of pumpkin pies.

b. If apple pies are a substitute output, the supply of pumpkin pies will decrease.

c. Better production technology increases the supply of pumpkin pie.

d. This is not going to shift the supply curve; it will decrease the quantity supplied along the supply curve.

e. With more producers, the supply of pumpkin pie increases.

Day 17

A surplus exists when quantity supplied exceeds quantity demanded, and these are seen at all prices above $4. The size of the surplus is equal to Q_s minus Q_d.

A shortage exists when quantity demanded exceeds quantity supplied, and these are seen at all prices below $4. The size of the shortage is equal to Q_d minus Q_s.

The only price where there is neither a shortage nor a surplus is $4, and this is the market equilibrium price.

PRICE	Q_d	Q_s	SHORTAGE OR SURPLUS
$10	20	110	Surplus = 90 units
$9	25	100	Surplus = 75 units
$8	30	90	Surplus = 60 units
$7	35	80	Surplus = 45 units
$6	40	70	Surplus = 30 units
$5	45	60	Surplus = 15 units
$4	50	50	Equilibrium, $Q_d = Q_s$
$3	55	40	Shortage = 15 units
$2	60	30	Shortage = 30 units
$1	65	20	Shortage = 45 units

Day 18

a. To find the vertical intercept, use $Q_d = 0$ and solve for $P = \$50$. To find the horizontal intercept, use $P = 0$ and solve for $Q_d = 25$.

b. Using $P = \$30$, solve for $Q_d = 10$.

c. Using $Q_d = 15$, solve for $P = \$20$.

d. The new demand curve has a vertical intercept of $100 and a horizontal intercept of 50 units.

e. With the new demand curve, a price of $30 will result in 35 units demanded. This tells us that, holding the price constant, consumers are now willing and able to purchase more of the product.

f. With the new demand curve, a quantity of 15 units results in a price of $70. This tells us that, holding quantity constant, consumers are now willing to pay a higher price for the product.

Day 19

a. The price of a key input is falling, so this would shift the supply of apples to the right, causing a decrease in the price and increase in quantity.

b. A health warning would decrease tastes and preferences for apples, causing a decrease in the demand and eventual decrease in both price and quantity.

c. The price of a substitute good is rising, so demand for apples will increase, causing an increase in both price and quantity.

d. When we combine an increase in the supply with a decrease in the demand for apples, the price will certainly fall, but the change in market quantity will depend on which shift is larger. If the supply shift is larger, quantity will rise. If the demand shift is larger, quantity will fall.

Day 20

a. With more income, assuming pumpkin pie is a normal good, demand for it will shift to the right, increasing price and quantity in the market.

b. If apple pies are a substitute good, demand for pumpkin pies will decrease, causing a decrease in price and quantity.

c. With fewer suppliers, the supply of pumpkin pie will shift to the left, causing an increase in price and decrease in quantity.

d. When we combine an increase in demand with a decrease in supply, the market price will definitely increase. However, the change in quantity depends on which of the shifts is larger. If the demand shift is larger, the quantity will rise. If the supply shift is larger, the quantity will fall.

Day 21

For example, you might ask, "You bought a tube of toothpaste for $2. What is the most you would have paid for the same tube?" A common response might be, "I have no idea." At this point, begin a downward auction by asking, "Would you have paid $6? $5? $4.50?", and so on until you get the willingness to pay value. Complete the table with a few more items this person purchased.

ITEM PURCHASED	HIGHEST PRICE SHOPPER WOULD HAVE PAID (WTP)	ACTUAL PRICE PAID (P)	CONSUMER SURPLUS EARNED (CS = WTP − P)
Toothpaste	$4	$2	$2
			Σ CS =

Day 22

Consumer surplus is the area below the demand curve and above the price. When the demand curve is a straight line, we can calculate consumer surplus as the area of a triangle; we just need to know the dimensions (height and width) of the triangle. To get the height, we need the vertical intercept and the price. The vertical intercept, the price when quantity is zero, is $250, and the current price is given to you as $100. To get the width, we need the quantity of Gizmos demanded. Using a price of $100 in the demand equation, we solve for a quantity of 50 units.

$$\text{Calculate CS} = \tfrac{1}{2} \times (\$150)(50) = \$3{,}750$$

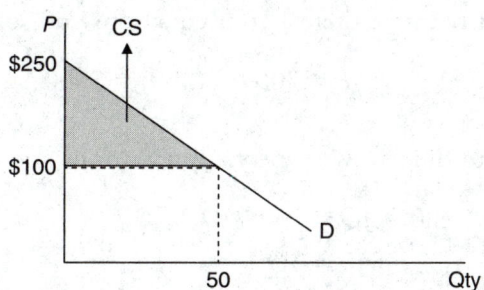

Day 23

Producer surplus is the area above the supply curve and below the price. When the supply curve is a straight line, we can calculate producer surplus as the area of a triangle; we just need to know the dimensions (height and width) of the triangle. To get the height, we need the vertical intercept and the price. The vertical intercept, the price when quantity is zero, is $100, and the current price is given to you as $200. To get the width, we need the quantity of Whodats supplied. Using a price of $200 in the supply equation, we solve for a quantity of 200 units.

$$\text{Calculate PS} = \tfrac{1}{2} \times (\$100)(200) = \$10{,}000$$

Day 24

a. To solve for equilibrium, we simply need to set the equations equal to each other. After all, the price from the demand curve will be the same as the price from the supply curve in equilibrium. You could also rearrange each equation for quantity and set those quantities equal to each other because $Q_d = Q_s$ in equilibrium.

$$700 - 2Q = 100 + Q \quad \text{(Note: There is no need for subscripts on the } Q \text{ variable, as they are the same in equilibrium.)}$$

$$600 = 3Q$$
$$Q = 200$$

Substitute this quantity into either of your equations and solve for price.

$$P = 700 - 2(200) = \$300$$

b. When supply shifts to the left, we expect a higher price and a lower quantity.

$$700 - 2Q = 160 + Q$$
$$540 = 3Q$$
$$Q = 180 \text{ and } P = \$340$$

c. When demand shifts to the right, we expect a higher price and higher quantity.

$$760 - 2Q = 100 + Q$$
$$660 = 3Q$$
$$Q = 220 \text{ and } P = \$320$$

Day 25

a. Set the price from the demand curve equal to the price from the supply curve.

$$12 - \tfrac{1}{4}Q = 3 + \tfrac{1}{2}Q$$
$$9 = \tfrac{3}{4}Q$$
$$Q = 12 \text{ and } P = \$9$$

b. CS = ½($3)(12) = $18

PS = ½ ($6)(12) = $36

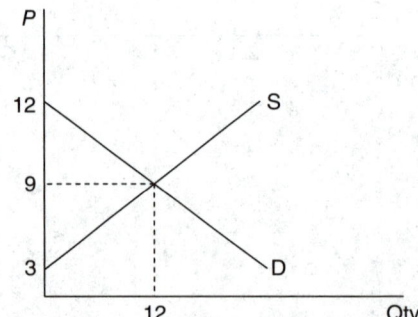

Day 26

Parts (a) and (b) are shown in the following graph:

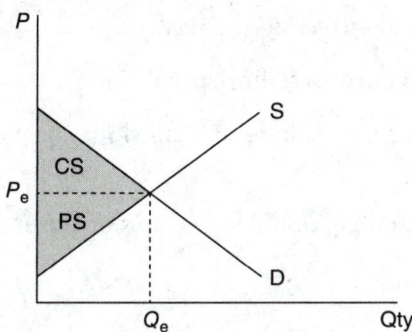

Parts (c) and (d) are shown in the graph below. Because the shaded area represents consumer and producer surplus that is lost, economists call it "deadweight loss". This is a concept you will see in other chapters as you review AP Microeconomics.

Day 27

It is very important to know how the price elasticity of demand is calculated:

$$E_d = (\%\Delta Q_d)/(\%\Delta P)$$

This value will almost always be less than zero because price and quantity demanded go in opposite directions, so we just ignore the negative sign.

a. Gasoline: $E_d = 3\%/5\% = 0.60$, and this is inelastic (less than 1)

b. Broccoli: $E_d = 9\%/6\% = 1.50$, and this is elastic (greater than 1)

c. Wool socks: $E_d = 7.5\%/7.5\% = 1$, and this is unit elastic (equals 1)

Day 28

For this example, I will use restaurant meals as a product that is commonly purchased in a household. Suppose the person you interview estimates that in a typical month about 8 restaurant meals are purchased. Then suppose that if the price of dining out at restaurants increased by 50%, this person responds that only 3 meals would be purchased at restaurants in a month.

$$E_d = (\%\Delta Q_d)/(\%\Delta P)$$

We have already stated that the hypothetical price increase is 50%, so we need to calculate the percentage change in quantity demanded. To calculate the percentage change in quantity demanded, use this formula:

$$\%\Delta Q_d = 100 \times (\text{New } Q_d - \text{Old } Q_d)/(\text{Old } Q_d)$$

Using my hypothetical example,

$$\%\Delta Q_d = 100 \times (3 - 8)/(8) = -62.5\%$$

To complete the calculation of price elasticity of demand, we have:

$$E_d = (\%\Delta Q_d)/(\%\Delta P) = 62.5\%/50\% = 1.25$$

Day 29

Your graph should look something like the one that follows.

a. Perfectly inelastic demand curves are vertical.

b. Perfectly elastic demand curves are horizontal.

c. Relatively elastic demand curves have a small slope, but are still downward sloping (not horizontal).

d. Relatively inelastic demand curves have a steep slope, but are still downward sloping (not vertical).

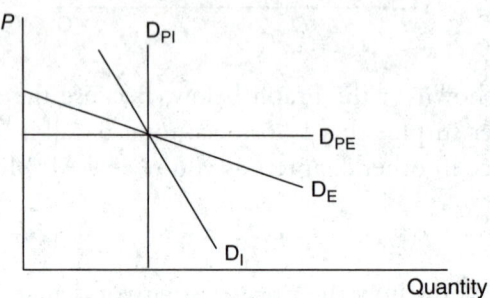

Day 30

a. First we need to determine the quantity of hoozits that would be demanded at each price. To do this, we just use the demand equation provided.

When $P = \$40$,

$$40 = 100 - 2Q_d \text{ and } Q_d = 30.$$

When $P = \$20$,

$$20 = 100 - 2Q_d \text{ and } Q_d = 40.$$

The midpoint approach to calculating price elasticity of demand uses the average price and average quantity between two points on the demand curve. Now that we have our two price and quantity combinations, we can use the price elasticity of demand midpoint formula:

$$E_d = (\Delta Q_d / \Delta P) \times (P_{avg} / Q_{avg})$$

The average price between $40 and $20 is $P_{avg} = \$30$, and the average quantity between 30 and 40 hoozits is $Q_{avg} = 35$.

$$E_d = (10/\$20) \times (\$30/35) = 0.43$$

b. The value of 0.43 tells us that between these two prices the demand is price-inelastic. In fact, it tells us that if the price were to increase by 1%, that quantity of hoozits demanded would decrease by only 0.43%.

Day 31

The completed table is shown as follows. To calculate the total revenue column, you simply multiply price and quantity demanded.

The midpoint approach to calculating price elasticity of demand uses the average price and average quantity between two points on the demand curve.

$$E_d = (\Delta Q_d/\Delta P) \times (P_{avg}/Q_{avg})$$

For example, the average price between $7 and $8 is $7.50, and the average quantity between 0 and 1 is 0.50 units. This leads us to calculate the price elasticity of demand between $7 and $8 as

$$E_d = (\Delta Q_d/\Delta P) \times (P_{avg}/Q_{avg}) = (1/\$1) \times (\$7.50/0.50) = 15$$

PRICE PER UNIT	QUANTITY OF THE GOOD DEMANDED	TOTAL REVENUE = $P \times Q_d$	PRICE ELASTICITY OF DEMAND
$8	0	$0	
$7	1	$7	15.00
$6	2	$12	4.33
$5	3	$15	2.20
$4	4	$16	1.29
$3	5	$15	0.78
$2	6	$12	0.45
$1	7	$7	0.23
$0	8	$0	0.07

Day 32

In the top half of the demand curve (above a price of $4), when the price falls the total revenue rises. The reason this happens is because there is an elastic response to a lower price. For every 1% decrease in the price, quantity demanded rises by *more than* 1%.

In the lower half of the demand curve (below $4), lower prices cause total revenue to fall. This happens because there is an inelastic response to a lower price. For every 1% decrease in the price, quantity demanded rises by *less than* 1%.

Total revenue = $P \times Q_d$, but downward sloping demand curves tell us that price and quantity demanded go in separate directions. When the percentage increase in Q_d outweighs the percentage decrease in P, total revenue will rise. But when the percentage decrease in P is greater than the percentage increase in Q_d, total revenue will fall.

Day 33

Dr. DeBeers, this planned decrease in tuition will not increase total revenue to the college; in fact, total revenue will fall! The price elasticity of demand measures how sensitive consumers, in this case students, are to a change in the price. It is computed with this formula:

$$E_d = (\%\Delta Q_d)/(\%\Delta P)$$

and my research tells me that this is equal to about 0.50. This value tells me that for every 1% decrease in the price (tuition), the quantity demanded (enrollment of students) increases by only 0.5%. In other words your proposed 5% cut in tuition would increase student enrollment by 2.5%.

Total revenue is computed by this formula:

$$TR = P \times Q_d$$

If your price is falling by 5% and quantity demanded is rising by a lesser amount, 2.5%, then total revenue will fall by approximately 2.5%. What you should consider to increase total revenue is a tuition increase, because your customers are not very sensitive to a price change.

Day 34

Remember that the income elasticity of demand tells us how responsive consumers are to a 1% change in income.

$$E_I = (\%\Delta Q_d)/(\%\Delta I)$$

If this value is positive, it means that greater income is associated with greater quantities demanded: a normal good. If it turns out negative, it means that rising income is associated with fewer units demanded: an inferior good.

This allows us to classify eggs and furniture as normal goods, while flour and margarine are inferior goods.

GOOD OR SERVICE	INCOME ELASTICITY OF DEMAND (E_I)	NORMAL OR INFERIOR?
Eggs	0.35	Normal
Flour	−0.37	Inferior
Margarine	−0.21	Inferior
Furniture	1.47	Normal

Interpretations:

- If income rises by 1%, the quantity of eggs demanded will rise by 0.35%.
- If income rises by 1%, the quantity of flour demanded will fall by 0.37%.
- If income rises by 1%, the quantity of margarine demanded will fall by 0.21%.
- If income rises by 1%, the quantity of furniture demanded will rise by 1.47%.

Day 35

The cross-price elasticity of demand tells us how consumers respond in consumption of one product to a change in the price of a second product. The cross-price is calculated with this formula:

$$E_{x,y} = (\%\Delta Q_d \text{ of good } x)/(\%\Delta P \text{ of good } y)$$

If this turns out to be positive, the products are substitutes; if it is negative, the products are complements.

GOOD	CROSS ELASTICITY WITH RESPECT TO A CHANGE IN THE PRICE OF:	CROSS ELASTICITY	SUBSTITUTES OR COMPLEMENTS?
Beef	Pork	0.27	Substitutes
Cereal	Milk	−0.90	Complements
Butter	Margarine	0.67	Substitutes
Potatoes	Meat	−0.50	Complements

Interpretations:

- If the price of pork rises by 1%, the quantity of beef demanded rises by 0.27%.
- If the price of milk rises by 1%, the quantity of cereal demanded falls by 0.90%.
- If the price of margarine rises by 1%, the quantity of butter demanded rises by 0.67%.
- If the price of meat rises by 1%, the quantity of potatoes demanded falls by 0.50%.

Day 36

For this example, I will use tickets to see a movie as a product that is commonly purchased in a household. Suppose the person you interview estimates that in a typical month, the family goes to two movies. If household income were to rise by 50%, suppose this person responds that the family would go to four movies in a month.

$$E_I = (\%\Delta Q_d)/(\%\Delta I)$$

We have already stated that the hypothetical income increase is 50%, so we need to calculate the percentage change in quantity demanded. As a reminder, when we need to calculate the percentage change in quantity demanded, we use this formula:

$$\%\Delta Q_d = 100 \times (\text{New } Q_d - \text{Old } Q_d)/(\text{Old } Q_d)$$

Using my hypothetical example,

$$\%\Delta Q_d = 100 \times (4 - 2)/(2) = 100\%$$

To complete the calculation of price elasticity of demand, we have:

$$E_d = (\%\Delta Q_d)/(\%\Delta P) = 100\%/50\% = 2$$

Day 37

We need to use the price elasticity and cross-price elasticity of demand formulas for each of these problems.

The formulas are:

$$E_d = (\%\Delta Q_d)/(\%\Delta P) \text{ (Recall that we typically ignore the negative sign.)}$$

$$E_{x,y} = (\%\Delta Q_d \text{ of good } x)/(\%\Delta P \text{ of good } y)$$

a. $\%\Delta Q_d/10\% = 0.20$

When we solve for $\%\Delta Q_d = 2\%$, this tells us what happens to the quantity of milk demanded.

b. $E_{x,y} = (\%\Delta Q_d \text{ of good } x)/(\%\Delta P \text{ of good } y) = (\%\Delta Q_d \text{ of cereal})/10\% = -0.80$

Solving for the numerator informs us that cereal consumption will fall by 8% if the price of milk rises by 10%.

c. $E_d = (\%\Delta Q_d)/(\%\Delta P) = 8\%/\%\Delta P = 0.45$

When we solve for the denominator, we see that breakfast cereal manufacturers would need to decrease the price of cereal by about 17.8% to offset the 8% decrease in quantity demanded that was the result of higher milk prices.

Day 38

The price elasticity of supply measures how responsive suppliers are to a change in the price. If the quantity of a product supplied rises greatly with a small increase in the price, we would describe the supply curve as elastic. If the quantity supplied rises by very little or not at all with an increase in the price, we would describe it as inelastic.

The formula is:

$$E_s = (\%\Delta Q_s)/(\%\Delta P)$$

Liz says that she can't do anything about the higher turkey prices right now, presumably because the turkeys are too immature for sale, which tells us that her short-run supply curve is vertical (S_{SR}). However in nine months, the turkeys will be ready, and she can increase her quantity supplied. This long-run supply curve (S_{LR}) will be upward sloping.

Day 39

a. Equilibrium is found at the intersection of supply and demand.

b. Because a price ceiling is a legal maximum price (like rent control), an effective price ceiling must lie below the equilibrium price.

c. At the price ceiling, $Q_d > Q_s$, so a shortage exists.

Day 40

a. Equilibrium is found at the intersection of supply and demand.

b. Because a price floor is a legal minimum price (like a minimum wage), an effective price floor must lie above the equilibrium price.

c. At the price floor $Q_d < Q_s$, so a surplus exists.

Day 41

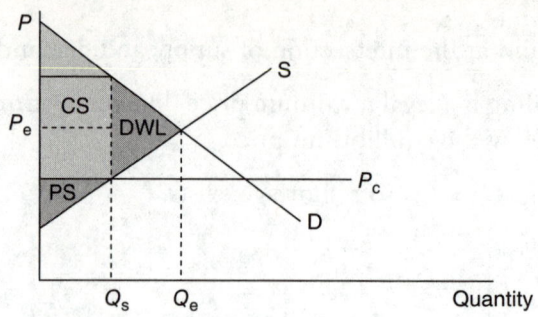

Because the price ceiling is below the equilibrium price (P_e), producers will restrict quantity supplied to Q_s.

Consumer surplus: the area under the demand curve and above P_c.

Producer surplus: the area above the supply curve and below P_c.

Deadweight loss: the area between the demand and supply curves and between Q_s and Q_e.

Day 42

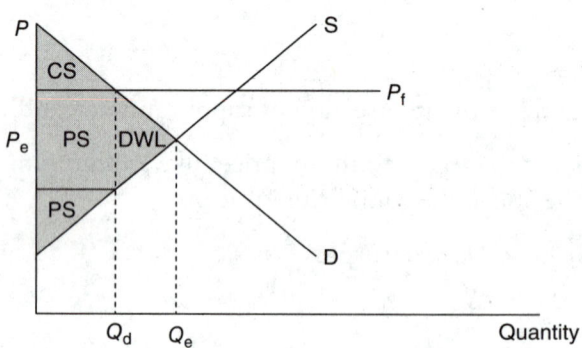

Because the price ceiling is below the equilibrium price (P_e), consumers will wish to buy only quantity demanded of Q_d.

Consumer surplus: the area under the demand curve and above P_f.

Producer surplus: the area above the supply curve and below P_f.

Deadweight loss: the area between the demand and supply curves and between Q_d and Q_e.

Day 43

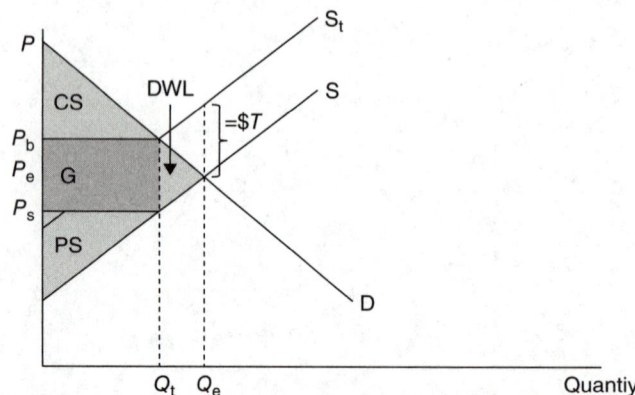

Day 44

This information tells us that demand for cigarettes is price inelastic. When a 10% increase in the price reduces consumption by 4%, the price elasticity of demand is about 0.40. Although there is no information about the price elasticity of supply, when demand for a product like cigarettes is price inelastic, consumers tend to bear a higher incidence of the tax. Of course, the opposite would be true if we discovered that the price elasticity of supply was actually smaller than the price elasticity of demand.

Day 45

If the excise tax on electricity is entirely passed on to the consumers of electricity, the demand curve must be vertical. In the following graph, we see that the original price of electricity is P_e. After a tax of $\$T$ is imposed, the price rises by exactly $\$T$; consumers pay the entire incidence of the tax.

While the demand for electricity, especially in the short run, is very likely inelastic, it is unlikely to be perfectly inelastic. In other words, the demand curve is probably steep, but still downward sloping. If so, the largest share of the tax will fall on the consumers, but not 100% of it.

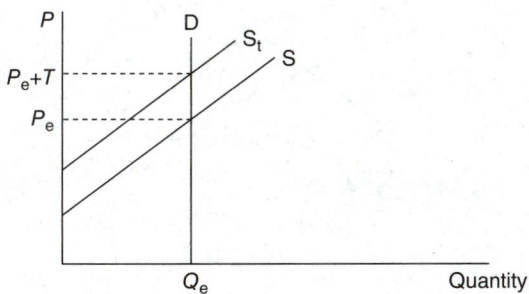

Day 46

	BEFORE THE SUBSIDY	AFTER THE SUBSIDY
Consumer surplus	A + B	A + B + C + F + G
Producer surplus	C + D	B + C + D + E
Government spending	0	−(B + C + E + F + G + H)
Total surplus	A + B + C + D	A + B + C + D − H
Deadweight loss	0	−H

The cost to society, in deadweight loss, is the area labeled "H."

Day 47

At the lower world price, domestic consumers would increase the quantity demanded, but domestic suppliers would reduce quantity supplied. The difference between Q_1 and Q_2 is supplied by foreign producers.

Day 48

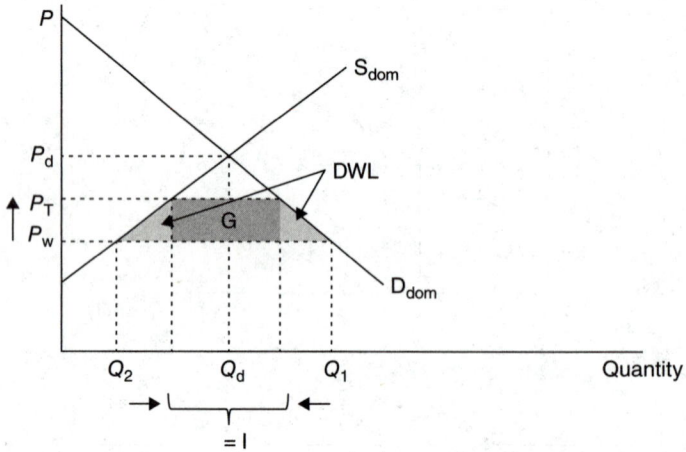

Day 49

Typical losers of import tariffs include domestic buyers of the product and foreign suppliers and their employees.

Typical winners of import tariffs include domestic workers and suppliers of the product.

The domestic government also collects tax revenue.

Day 50

Since Max knows that more than 7 pieces of chocolate will make him sick, his total utility curve begins to fall after a quantity of 7. Marginal utility falls with more chocolate consumed and becomes negative beyond 7 pieces.

Day 51

When we consume something that brings us some amount of happiness, we say that the product provides utility. However, when consumption of a good or service actually makes us unhappy, or even ill, we call it disutility.

Suppose the person that you interview says he or she really dislikes pickles and would never eat a pickle, even if it was free. Since the person claims to never get any utility from pickles, the total utility curve actually falls below zero as more pickles are consumed.

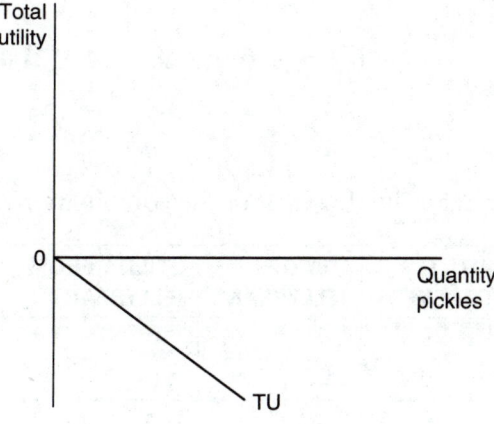

Day 52

a. The table shows marginal utility from successive units consumed. To get total utility, simply add up the marginal utility values.

$$\text{total utility from } 1X = 10$$

$$\text{total utility from } 8Y = 30 + 28 + 24 + 21 + 18 + 16 + 15 + 14 = 166$$

$$\text{total utility} = 176$$

The utility maximization rule is such that all income is spent and

$$MU_x/P_x = MU_y/P_y$$

At this combination:

$$10/\$10 > 14/\$30$$

Since the marginal utility per dollar for good X is greater than it is for good Y, she can increase utility by spending more money on good X and less on good Y.

b. To find the utility maximizing combination, we need to find combinations that spend all of Mary's income and satisfy:

$$MU_x/P_x = MU_y/P_y$$

$$\text{Or } MU_x/\$10 = MU_y/\$30$$

In other words, the marginal utility of good Y must be three times the marginal utility of good X. The combination of 4X and 7Y satisfy both necessary conditions. Total spending on this combination is exactly $250, and the marginal utility of the fourth unit of X is $\frac{1}{3}$ the marginal utility of the seventh unit of good Y.

$$\text{Total utility} = (10 + 7 + 6 + 5) + (30 + 28 + 24 + 21 + 18 + 16 + 15) = 180$$

Day 53

a. Simply add up the total utility for each of the combinations in the table.

QTY OF CRACKERS	TOTAL UTILITY FROM CRACKERS	QTY OF JELLYBEANS	UTILITY FROM JELLYBEANS
0	0	0	0
2	70	1	80
4	130	2	150
6	180	3	210
8	220	4	260
10	250	5	300

# CRACKERS	# JELLYBEANS	TOTAL UTILITY
0	5	300
2	4	330
4	3	340
6	2	330
8	1	300
10	0	250

Theo maximizes his utility with 4 crackers and 3 jellybeans.

b. Marginal utility is the change in total utility divided by the change in consumption.

QTY OF CRACKERS	UTILITY FROM CRACKERS	MU_C	MU_C/P_C	QTY OF JELLYBEANS	UTILITY FROM JELLYBEANS	MU_B	MU_B/P_B
0	0			0	0		
2	70	35	7	1	80	80	8
4	130	30	6	2	150	70	7
6	180	25	5	3	210	60	6
8	220	20	4	4	260	50	5
10	250	15	3	5	300	40	4

Remember the utility max rule is such that all income is spent and:

$$MU_x/P_x = MU_y/P_y$$

The marginal utility per dollar spent is equal in four different combinations, but the only combination where Theo spends his income exactly is 4 crackers and 3 jellybeans. Again, the total utility is 340.

Day 54

Accounting profit begins with total revenue and subtracts only the explicit cost of operating the business. Economic profit also subtracts the opportunity costs of running the shop. Accounting profit shows a profit of $80,000, but when you consider the opportunity costs of running the shop, the economic profit is actually −$10,000. You are better off taking the accountant job and renting the shop.

Day 55

The key to distinguishing a variable cost from a fixed cost is asking whether it increases as more miles are driven (variable) or if it stays the same, even if zero miles are driven (fixed). Here is a sample list.

Variable costs: gasoline, oil, wear and tear on things like tires, belts, and windshield wiper blades

Fixed costs: insurance, licensing, interest payments (if you're repaying a car loan)

Day 56

Once again, the key to distinguishing a variable cost from a fixed cost is asking whether it increases as more nights are spent at the residence (variable) or if it stays the same, even if you were out of town for the entire month (fixed). Here is a sample list.

Variable costs: groceries, electricity, natural gas, water, and other utilities

Fixed costs: cable or satellite TV, Internet service, property taxes, insurance, rent or mortgage payments (if you're repaying a home mortgage)

Day 57

a. It is important to know how marginal product and average product are derived from total product.

$$MP_L = \Delta TP_L/\Delta L$$

$$AP_L = TP_L/L$$

# OF CARPENTERS	TOTAL PRODUCT (# OF CABINETS PER MONTH)	MARGINAL PRODUCT	AVERAGE PRODUCT
0	0	X	X
1	8	8	8
2	18	10	5
3	26	8	8.67
4	32	6	8
5	36	4	7.2
6	38	2	6.33
7	36	−2	5.14

b. If we can ignore the cost of hiring carpenters, then we would want to maximize total number of cabinets made in a month and hire 6.

Day 58

The key to this phenomenon in production is the fact that this is taking place in the short run. In the short run, the quantity of capital (machinery or the size of the production area) is fixed, so adding more labor to this fixed capital creates a problem: ultimately there is not enough capital or space for these additional employees. The total production may continue to rise, but the *marginal* production of the next unit of labor eventually falls.

Day 59

The key to determining what the MP_L curve looks like is to know the relationship between TP_L and MP_L.

Recall that $MP_L = \Delta TP_L/\Delta L$.

Since our graphs plot TP_L on the vertical (y) axis and L on the horizontal (x), the previous equation for MP_L is also the slope of the TP_L curve ($\Delta y/\Delta x$).

Graph A

Graph A, an upward sloping straight line, tells us that the MP_L is a constant value, never rising and never falling. The next worker contributes exactly the same additional output as each of the workers that were employed before.

Graph B

Graph B, with a TP_L that rises and eventually falls, implies that workers hired early have a higher MP_L than those who are hired later. In fact, beyond the point where the TP_L actually falls, the MP_L becomes negative.

Graph C

Graph C, a TP_L curve that keeps rising at a faster and faster rate, tells us that the MP_L of the next worker is even greater than the MP_L of the workers that were hired before.

The graph that makes the most economic sense is B. The MP_L should fall in the short run as additional workers find fewer units of capital to work with, or less work space in which to work.

Day 60

In the short run, there are fixed costs (TFC) that must be paid, even when output is zero. The variable costs (TVC) are zero when output is zero, but increase as output increases.

PRODUCTION (Q)	TFC	TVC	TC	MC
0	$5	$0	$5	n/a
1	5	6	11	6
2	5	9	14	3
3	5	13	18	4
4	5	18	23	5
5	5	25	30	7
6	5	34	39	9
7	5	45	50	11
8	5	58	63	13

The key formulas are:

$$TC = TVC + TFC$$

and

$$MC = (\Delta TC)/(\Delta Q) = (\Delta TVC)/(\Delta Q)$$

Day 61

The following graphs were done using Excel. It is important to see the relationships between these curves.

- The TFC curve is a horizontal line because it doesn't change with output.
- The TC curve lies $5 above the TVC curve because of the $5 of TFC.
- The MC curve is the slope of both TC and TVC curves. At higher levels of output, the TC and TVC get steeper.
- At the lowest levels of output, MC falls, but soon begins to rise and continues rising.

(Continued)

Day 62

The important formulas that you need to use are:

$$AFC = TFC/Q$$
$$AVC = TVC/Q$$
$$ATC = TC/Q$$

PRODUCTION (Q)	TFC	TVC	TC	MC	AFC	AVC	ATC
0	$5	$0	$5		XX	XX	XX
1	5	6	11	$6	$ 5.00	$ 6.00	$ 11.00
2	5	9	14	$3	$ 2.50	$ 4.50	$ 7.00
3	5	13	18	$4	$ 1.67	$ 4.33	$ 6.00
4	5	18	23	$5	$ 1.25	$ 4.50	$ 5.75
5	5	25	30	$7	$ 1.00	$ 5.00	$ 6.00
6	5	34	39	$9	$ 0.83	$ 5.67	$ 6.50
7	5	45	50	$11	$ 0.71	$ 6.43	$ 7.14
8	5	58	63	$13	$ 0.63	$ 7.25	$ 7.88

Day 63

The following graphs were done using Excel. It is important to see the relationships between these curves.

- The AFC curve continues to decline as output rises.
- The AVC and ATC curves are approximately U-shaped.
- The ATC curve lies above the AVC curve by an amount equal to AFC.

- The MC curve rises up and intersects the AVC and ATC curves at approximately their minimum points.

Day 64

Day 65

- Many small independent buyers and sellers
- Firms produce a standardized (identical) product
- No barriers to entry or exit
- Firms are price takers

Day 66

At a price of $230, just multiply by quantity of output to complete the TR column. The profit/loss column is total revenue minus total cost at each quantity.

Compute the level of profit each producer would earn.

OUTPUT (Q)	TOTAL REVENUE = P × Q	PROFIT (+) OR LOSS (−) = TR − TC
0	$ -	$(500.00)
1	$230.00	$(420.00)
2	$460.00	$(240.00)
3	$690.00	$(70.00)
4	$920.00	$80.00
5	$1,150.00	$200.00
6	$1,380.00	$290.00
7	$1,610.00	$340.00
8	$1,840.00	$340.00
9	$2,070.00	$280.00
10	$2,300.00	$150.00

When $P = \$230$, the profit-maximizing output is $Q = 8$.

Redo the total revenue and profit table for a price of $180 and you get the following:

OUTPUT (Q)	TOTAL REVENUE = P × Q	PROFIT (+) OR LOSS (−) = TR − TC
0	$ -	$(500.00)
1	$180.00	$(470.00)
2	$360.00	$(340.00)
3	$540.00	$(220.00)
4	$720.00	$(120.00)
5	$900.00	$(50.00)
6	$1,080.00	$(10.00)
7	$1,260.00	$(10.00)
8	$1,440.00	$(60.00)
9	$1,620.00	$(170.00)
10	$1,800.00	$(350.00)

When $P = \$180$, the firm should produce $Q = 7$ to maximize profits or minimize losses.

Day 67

To use the profit-maximization rule, we must find the level of output where MR = MC. In perfect competition, $P = MR = MC$.

We know that the price is $290, so that is equal to MR. Marginal cost (MC) is calculated by looking at the table. A column for MC has been added to the following table.

When the price is $290, MR = MC at a quantity of 9 bushels. Profit is:

$$\Pi = \$290 \times 9 - \$1{,}790 = \$820$$

What happens when the price falls to $80? At first glance, the profit-maximization rule says that the farmer should produce $Q = 4$ because that is where MC = $80. However, if we calculate profit:

$$\Pi = \$80 \times 4 - \$840 = -\$520$$

Losses of $520 are even worse than what we would lose if we shut down and produced nothing. In that event, we would lose only our fixed costs of $500. In other words, this price is too low to produce any amount of output. Our total revenue of $320 does not pay for our total variable costs of $340 at $Q = 4$. So we are wise to shut down.

OUTPUT (Q)	TFC	TVC	TC	MC
0	$500	$0	$500	XX
1	$500	$150	$650	$150
2	$500	$200	$700	$50
3	$500	$260	$760	$60
4	$500	$340	$840	$80
5	$500	$450	$950	$110
6	$500	$590	$1,090	$140
7	$500	$770	$1,270	$180
8	$500	$1,000	$1,500	$230
9	$500	$1,290	$1,790	$290
10	$500	$1,650	$2,150	$360

Day 68

Make sure that you extend the market price over to the graph of the typical firm, because they are price takers. Also be sure to find Q_f at the point where the $P =$ MR = MC curves intersect. The rectangle of profit should also be labeled.

Day 69

It is important to include the AVC curve and draw the price between ATC and AVC curves. This placement identifies the firm in a loss-minimization situation and not a shutdown situation.

Day 70

a. In the long run, new firms will begin to enter this market. With more suppliers, the market supply curve shifts outward, lowering the market price. With lower and lower prices, the positive economic profits decrease and firms begin to produce fewer units of output. Ultimately, the profits are reduced to zero as the market price is equal to average total cost.

b. In the long run, some existing firms will begin to exit this market. With fewer suppliers, the market supply curve shifts inward, increasing the market price. With rising prices, the negative economic profits increase (become less negative) and firms begin to produce more units of output. Ultimately, the profits are reduced to zero as the market price is equal to average total cost.

c. No matter whether positive or negative profits are happening in the short run, the long-run equilibrium graphs always look like this.

Day 71

- A single producer
- The firm produces a product with no close substitutes
- Barriers to entry exist
- The firm has market power, or the ability to set the price of the product

Day 72

a. The profit-maximization rule is still the same: Find the output where MR = MC. The following table has been extended to allow for calculation of MR and MC. To compute MR, we must first compute total revenue (TR).

OUTPUT (Q UNITS)	PRICE ($P)	TOTAL COST ($)	TOTAL REVENUE (TR = P × Q)	MARGINAL REVENUE (MR = ΔTR/ΔQ)	MARGINAL COST (MC = ΔTC/ΔQ)
0	12	5	$0		
1	11	10	$11	$11	$5
2	10	15	$20	$9	$5
3	9	20	$27	$7	$5
4	8	25	$32	$5	$5
5	7	30	$35	$3	$5
6	6	35	$36	$1	$5
7	5	40	$35	−$1	$5
8	4	45	$32	−$3	$5
9	3	50	$27	−$5	$5
10	2	55	$20	−$7	$5
11	1	60	$11	−$9	$5
12	0	65	$0	−$11	$5

At $Q = 4$, MR = MC = $5. The monopolist would charge $8 to sell those 4 units. Profit is equal to total revenue minus total cost:

$$\Pi = \$32 - \$25 = \$7$$

b. If TFC increases by $1, it will have no effect on MR or MC, so the profit-maximizing output is still 4 units and the price is still $8. However, profit is $1 lower and equal to $6.

c. Deadweight loss is eliminated if price is equal to marginal cost. In the preceding table, $P = MC = \$5$ at an output of 7 units. At this outcome, profits will become losses.

$$\Pi = \$35 - \$40 = -\$5$$

Day 73

When you're drawing a monopoly, remember that the marginal revenue curve is downward sloping and lies below the demand curve. Find Q_m at the intersection of MR = MC, and then go up to the demand curve to find P_m. The area of profit is a rectangle with a height equal to (P_m – ATC) and length of Q_m. It is also helpful to show the MC curve intersecting ATC at the minimum of the ATC curve.

Day 74

- Relatively large number of firms
- Differentiated products
- Easy entry and exit
- Some ability to set the price

Day 75

a. In the long run, new firms will enter this market. The demand for existing firms will shift to the left, decreasing price, output, and profit. Entry of new firms will stop when all firms are breaking even.

b. In the long run, some existing firms will exit this market. The demand for remaining firms will shift to the right, increasing price, output, and profit. Exit of firms will stop when all firms are breaking even.

c. The difficult part of drawing this graph is drawing the demand curve tangent to the ATC curve and having that point of tangency directly above the intersection of MR = MC. I suggest drawing the ATC curve last.

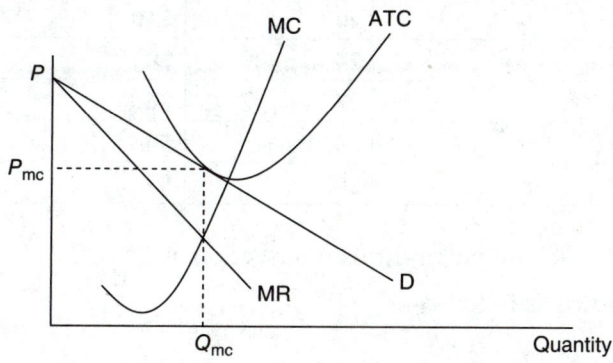

Day 76

a. Hamm has a dominant strategy of "don't build." If Rye is going to build, Hamm earns more profit if they don't build (6 > 5), and if Rye is not going to build, Hamm earns more profit if they don't build (4 > 3). Rye also has a strategy of "don't build." If Hamm is going to build, Rye should not build (7 > 5), and if Hamm is not going to build, Rye earns more profit if they don't build (2 > 1).

b. The Nash equilibrium is that both firms should not build: Hamm earns 4 and Rye earns 2. The choice to not build is each firm's dominant strategy (or best response) to anything the rival would do.

c. Yes, it is an example of a prisoner's dilemma. If the firms could cooperate (or collude) before making their decision, they could both agree to build the factory, and both firms would earn 5.

Day 77

Of course, results are going to vary across different game players, but one successful strategy in a repeated prisoner's dilemma is known as "tit-for-tat." This strategy was developed by Anatol Rapoport and has the advantage of being both simple and effective. The player (you) would begin the game by cooperating, and then in each successive round you adopt the strategy of your rival from the previous round. So if today your rival cheated (played their dominant strategy) and you cooperated, tomorrow you will also cheat as a way of punishing their selfish behavior. If your rival goes back to his or her cooperative ways, so will you, and both players will earn higher profits. Go back to the games and see if this strategy is successful for you.

Day 78

a. This means she sells her product in a perfectly competitive output market and hires labor in a perfectly competitive input market.

b. The completed graph follows. You must first find the marginal product of labor (MP_L) and then multiply by the constant price of a pizza.

QUANTITY OF LABOR (WORKERS)	QUANTITY OF PIZZA	$MRP_L = P \times MP_L$
0	0	
1	9	$2 × 9 = $18
2	15	$12
3	20	$10
4	24	$8
5	27	$6
6	29	$4
7	30	$2

c. Set $W = MRP_L = \$8$ and we find this intersection at $L = 4$

The graph is shown as follows.

d. This doubles the MRP$_L$, shifting the demand for labor outward, and now she will hire L = 6. Adjust the graph accordingly.

Day 79

a. Diesel fuel and semitruck drivers are complementary inputs, so the falling price of fuel should increase the demand for drivers, increasing both wages and employment.

b. More stringent requirements would decrease the supply of teachers, increasing wages but decreasing employment.

c. Rising interest rates usually decrease the demand for capital because firms often borrow to purchase such equipment. Weaker demand for capital equipment should decrease the price of capital and the quantity of capital employed.

d. The rising sea level would inundate existing beachfront property, reducing the supply of it. The reduced supply would increase the price and reduce the quantity of it exchanged in the market.

Day 80

Obviously results are going to vary, but the idea is that you now know there is a good resource out there to provide you with some occupational background and projections.

Day 81

a. The MRP is the price of output ($0.50) multiplied by the MP of each resource.

QTY OF LABOR EMPLOYED	MARGINAL PRODUCT OF LABOR	MRP OF LABOR	QUANTITY OF CAPITAL EMPLOYED	MARGINAL PRODUCT OF CAPITAL	MRP OF CAPITAL
1	20	$10	1	20	$10
2	16	$8	2	18	$9
3	12	$6	3	16	$8
4	10	$5	4	12	$6
5	8	$4	5	8	$4
6	4	$2	6	6	$3
7	2	$1	7	4	$2
8	1	$0.50	8	2	$1

b. The least-cost combination is found when you have produced 144 units of output and:

$$MP_L/w = MP_K/r, \text{ or}$$

$$MP_L/\$1 = MP_K/\$2$$

This means that the MP_K must be twice as large as the MP_L.

At $L = 6$ and $K = 5$, we have:

$4/\$1 = 8/\$2$ and output adds up to 144 units = $(20 + 16 + 12 + 10 + 8 + 4) + (20 + 18 + 16 + 12 + 8)$

c. The profit-maximizing hiring rule is to hire a resource up to the point where the MRP is equal to the resource price.

For labor: $MRP_L = w = \$1$ at $L = 7$

For capital: $MRP_K = r = \$2$ at $K = 7$

d. Total output = $(20 + 16 + 12 + 10 + 8 + 4 + 2) + (20 + 18 + 16 + 12 + 8 + 6 + 4)$
= 156

Profit = TR − TC = ($\$0.50 \times 156$) − ($\$1 \times 7$) − ($\$2 \times 7$) = \$57

Day 82

a. Private good because it is both excludable and rival. It is excludable because sellers of milk will exclude you from having the milk if you refuse to pay. It is rivalrous because once you buy that gallon of milk, another person cannot buy the same gallon.

b. Public good because it is nonexcludable and nonrival. It is nonexcludable because it would be impossible to turn the light on only for the motorists who stop and pay for it, but keep the lamp unlit for those who refuse to pay. It is nonrival because my consumption of the illumination does not reduce your ability to consume the same thing. In other words, when I drive under the light I don't reduce the available units of the light for anyone who drives past it later.

c. Private good. The attorney will not provide me with her advice if I refuse to pay (excludable), and if I'm consuming an hour of the attorney's time, it is one hour that another person cannot consume (rival).

d. Trick question! This is called a "common resource" because it is nonexcludable but also rival. Fish or shellfish are considered nonexcludable because anyone can basically attempt to harvest them. However, they are rival because once I harvest a lobster, you cannot harvest the same lobster. These common resources are often overharvested and create a problem called the "tragedy of the commons."

Day 83

If you've played the game, you surely saw that in the public bunny version of the game, you and the computer rivals harvested all of the bunnies in round one, leaving none to multiply into round two. In the private version, you probably had many more bunnies in round two because you didn't harvest all of them in round one. Economists think that this happens to resources like fish in the ocean because there are no private property rights to the fish. If a person had a fishing pond on their own property, they wouldn't harvest all of the fish in one summer; they would want *their private fish* to multiply so that there were more fish next summer. However, in the open ocean, there are no property rights to the fish; they are common resources. If a person has a boat and their livelihood relies on income from the fish that are caught, they are going to catch as many as possible. Tragically, this spells extinction for the fish and also for the fishing industry.

Day 84

Day 85

Fernando is correct. Payton's apple orchard is surely benefiting from the positive externality that Quinton's bees provide. Fernando would call the pollination services that the bees provide the apple trees as a spillover benefit. Payton receives this benefit but doesn't pay for it. When a positive externality exists in a market, that market will underproduce the product; it fails to produce the quantity where MSB = MSC, and deadweight loss exists. One way to remedy this underproduction is to subsidize either the consumption or the production of the good (bee hives in this case) that is providing these spillover benefits. If Payton were to send Quinton some cash (the subsidy), he could install more beehives. This would benefit his honey production, but it would also benefit Payton's apple production. The subsidy would move the market outcome closer to the socially efficient outcome and eliminate some or all of the deadweight loss.

Day 86

Day 87

According to the IRS tax bracket, this person would pay "$5,183.75 plus 25% of the amount over $37,650." Our single taxpayer has taxable income of $60,000, so she is $22,350 over the lower limit of $37,650. Her tax payment would therefore be calculated as:

$$\begin{aligned}\$22{,}350 \times 25\% &= \$5{,}587.50 \\ &+\ \underline{\$5{,}183.75} \\ &= \$10{,}771.25\end{aligned}$$

Day 88

Of course, the results of this little environmental treasure hunt are going to differ. The point is that you have become a little more familiar and informed about the quality of your local environment.

Day 89

Since both consumers plan to spend $100 on clothing, each consumer would pay $7 in tax (7% of $100). As a fraction of weekly income, those $7 in sales tax are:

Eric: ($7/$1,000) × 100 = 0.70%

Melanie: ($7/$2,000) × 100 = 0.35%

So even though each person spends $7 in sales tax on $100 of clothing, those $7 are a larger share of Eric's income, making a sales tax a regressive tax.

Day 90

The historic distribution of income in the United States shows a clear trend toward a greater share of total income being earned by the top quintile and top 5%, and a decreased share by the lower quintiles. For example:

YEAR	LOWEST FIFTH	SECOND FIFTH	THIRD FIFTH	FOURTH FIFTH	HIGHEST FIFTH	TOP 5%
2015	3.1	8.2	14.3	23.2	51.1	22.1
1995	3.7	9.1	15.2	23.3	48.7	21.0
1985	3.9	9.8	16.2	24.4	45.6	17.6
1975	4.3	10.4	17.0	24.7	43.6	16.5

There are likely several explanations for this trend, and economists will disagree over which is the most important, but the income tax system has become less progressive over this time period. For example, the highest personal income tax bracket was taxed at 70% in 1967, and in 2015 that tax rate was 39.6%. Another possible explanation is that the economy has changed from a manufacturing and farming economy to a high-tech service and information-based economy. More and more jobs in the new economy require advanced degrees, and since education is positively correlated with income, those that receive more education are going to leave those that do not further and further behind.

Among the most highly developed nations, the United States has one of the highest Gini coefficients (41.1), or one of the least equal income distributions. Our largest trading partner and closest neighbor, Canada, has a Gini of 33.7. When nations are ranked by the 2014 Human Development Index, the United States ranks 8th (HDI = 0.915), a very strong showing. However, when the United Nations adjusts for measures of social and economic inequality in the nation, the adjusted HDI falls to 0.760, and this ranks 28th in the world. This drop of 20 spots in the rankings is the largest among the nations classified as having "Very High Human Development."

Appendixes

Further Reading
Websites
Glossary
Important Formulas and Conditions

FURTHER READING

Dodge, Eric, and Melanie Fox. *Economics Demystified.* New York: McGraw-Hill, 2012.

Krugman, Paul, and Robin Wells. *Economics.* 4th ed. New York: Worth Publishers, 2015.

Mankiw, N. Gregory. *Principles of Economics,* 7th ed. Mason, OH: Thomson Southwestern, 2014.

McConnell, Campbell L., Stanley L. Brue, and Sean Flynn. *Economics: Principles, Problems, and Policies,* 20th ed. New York: McGraw-Hill/Irwin, 2014.

WEBSITES

Here is a list of websites that you might find useful in your preparation for the AP Macroeconomics exam.

https://apstudent.collegeboard.org/home

www.economy.com/dismal

www.economist.com/research/Economics

http://www.grokkingecon.com/

www.welkerswikinomics.com/home.html

www.councilforeconed.org

GLOSSARY

absolute advantage The ability to produce more of a good than all other producers.

absolute (or money) prices The price of a good measured in units of currency.

aggregate demand curve The negative relationship between all spending on domestic output and the average price level of that output.

aggregate income The sum of all income earned by suppliers of resources in the economy.

aggregate spending (GDP) The sum of all spending from four sectors of the economy.

aggregate supply curve The positive relationship between the level of domestic output produced and the average price level of that output.

aggregation The process of summing the microeconomic activity of households and firms into a macroeconomic measure of economic activity.

all else equal The assumption that all other variables are held constant so that we can predict how a change in one variable affects a second. Also known as the "ceteris paribus" assumption.

appreciating currency An increase in the price of one currency relative to another currency.

asset demand for money The amount of money demanded as an asset is inversely related to the real interest rate.

assets of a bank Anything owned by the bank or owed to the bank.

automatic stabilizers Fiscal policy mechanisms that automatically regulate, or stabilize, the macroeconomy as it moves through the business cycle.

autonomous consumption The amount of consumption that occurs no matter the level of disposable income.

autonomous investment The level of investment determined by investment demand and independent of GDP.

autonomous saving The amount of saving that occurs no matter the level of disposable income.

balanced-budget multiplier A change in government spending offset by an equal change in taxes results in a multiplier effect equal to one.

balance of payments statement A summary of the payments received by the United States from foreign countries and the payments sent by the United States to foreign countries.

balance sheet or T-account A tabular way to show a bank's assets and liabilities.

base (or reference) year The year that serves as a reference point for constructing a price index and comparing real values over time.

bond A certificate of indebtedness from the issuer to the bond holder.

budget deficit Exists if government spending exceeds the tax revenue collected.

budget surplus Exists if tax revenue collected exceeds government spending.

business cycle The periodic rise and fall in economic activity around its long-term growth trend.

capital (or financial) account This account shows the flow of investment on real or financial assets between a nation and foreigners.

capitalist market system (capitalism) An economic system based upon the fundamentals of private property, freedom, self-interest, and prices.

circular flow of economic activity (or circular flow of goods and services) A model that shows how households and firms circulate resources, goods, and incomes through the economy. This basic model is expanded to include the government and the foreign sector.

Classical school A macroeconomic model that explains how the economy naturally tends to come to full employment in the long run.

closed economy A model assuming no foreign sector (imports and exports).

comparative advantage The ability to produce a good at lower opportunity cost than all other producers.

complementary goods Two goods that provide more utility when consumed together than when consumed separately.

consumer price index (CPI) The price index that measures the average price level of the items in the base year market basket. This is the main measure of consumer inflation.

consumer surplus The difference between a buyer's willingness to pay and the price actually paid.

consumption and saving schedules Tables that show the direct relationships between disposable income and consumption and saving.

consumption function A positive relationship between disposable income and consumption.

consumption possibility frontier The line that illustrates all possible combinations of goods that two nations can consume with specialization and trade.

contraction A period where real GDP is falling.

contractionary fiscal policy Lower government spending or higher net taxes to shift AD to the left to full employment and reduce inflationary pressures.

contractionary monetary policy Decreases in the money supply to increase real interest rates, shift AD to the left to full employment, and reduce inflationary pressures.

cost of living adjustment An annual adjustment to a salary (or pension) so that the purchasing power of that income remains constant. This adjustment is typically based upon the change in the consumer price index.

crowding-out effect Typically the result of government borrowing to fund deficit spending, this is the decline in spending in one sector due to an increase in spending from another sector.

current account This account shows current import and export payments of both goods and services and investment income sent to foreign investors and investment income received by U.S. citizens who invest abroad.

debt financing A firm's way of raising investment funds by issuing bonds to the public.

decision to invest A firm invests in projects if the expected rate of return is at least as great as the real interest rate.

deflation A decline in the overall price level.

demand curve Shows the quantity of a good demanded at all prices.

demand-pull inflation Inflation that results from stronger AD as it increases in the upward-sloping range of AS.

demand schedule A table showing quantity demanded for a good at all prices.

depreciating currency A decrease in the price of one currency relative to another currency.

depression A prolonged, deep trough in the business cycle.

determinants of demand The external factors that shift demand to the left or right.

determinants of supply The external factors that influence supply. When these variables change, the entire supply curve shifts to the left or right.

discount rate The interest rate commercial banks pay on short-term loans from the Fed.

discouraged workers Citizens who have been without work for so long that they become tired of looking for work and drop out of the labor force. Because these citizens are not counted in the ranks of the unemployed, the reported unemployment rate is understated.

disequilibrium Any price where the quantity demanded does not equal the quantity supplied.

disposable income (DI) The income a consumer has to spend or save once he or she has paid out net taxes.

dissaving Another way of saying that saving is less than zero.

domestic price The equilibrium price of a good in a nation without trade.

double counting The mistake of including the value of intermediate stages of production in GDP on top of the value of the final good.

economic growth The increase in an economy's PPF over time.

economics The study of how society allocates scarce resources.

equation of exchange The equation says that nominal GDP ($P \times Q$) is equal to the quantity of money (M) multiplied by the number of times each dollar is spent in a year (V).

equilibrium GDP The level of real GDP where real domestic production is equal to real domestic spending.

equity financing The firm's method of raising funds for investment by issuing shares of stock to the public.

excess demand The difference between quantity demanded and quantity supplied. A shortage.

excess reserves The portion of a deposit that may be loaned to borrowers.

excess supply The difference between quantity supplied and quantity demanded. A surplus.

exchange rate The amount of one currency you must give up to get one unit of the second currency.

expansion A period where real GDP is growing.

expansionary fiscal policy Increases in government spending or lower net taxes meant to shift AD to the right toward full employment and lower the unemployment rate.

expansionary monetary policy Increases in the money supply meant to decrease real interest rates, shift AD to the right toward full employment, and reduce the unemployment rate.

expected rate of return (r) The rate of profit the firm anticipates receiving on investment expenditures.

exports Goods and services produced domestically but sold abroad.

factors of production Inputs or resources that go into the production function to produce goods and services.

fiat money Paper and coin money with no intrinsic value but used to make transactions because the government declares it to be legal tender.

final goods Goods that are ready for their final use by consumers and firms.

financial account See *capital account*.

the firm An organization that employs factors of production to produce a good or service that it hopes to profitably sell.

fiscal policy Deliberate changes in government spending and net tax collection to affect economic output, unemployment, and the price level.

foreign sector substitution effect The process of domestic consumers looking for foreign goods when the domestic price level rises, thus reducing the quantity of domestic output consumed.

fractional reserve banking A system in which only a fraction of the total money deposited in banks is held in reserve.

full employment Exists when the economy is experiencing no cyclical unemployment.

functions of money Money serves as a medium of exchange, a unit of account, and a store of value.

future value If r is the current interest rate, the future value of \$1 invested today for a period of one year is $\$1 \times (1 + r)$.

GDP price deflator The price index that measures the average price level of goods and services that make up GDP.

gross domestic product (GDP) The market value of the final goods and services produced within a nation in a given period of time.

human capital The amount of knowledge and skills that labor can apply to the work that they do.

imports Goods produced abroad but consumed domestically.

income effect Due to a higher price, the change in quantity demanded that results from a change in the consumer's purchasing power (or real income).

inferior goods A good for which demand decreases with an increase in consumer income.

inflation An increase in the overall price level.

inflation rate The percentage change in the price level from one year to the next

inflationary gap The amount by which equilibrium real GDP exceeds full employment GDP.

interest rate effect The process of reduced domestic consumption due to a higher price level causing an increase in the real interest rate.

intermediate goods Goods that require further modification before they are ready for their final use.

investment demand The negative relationship between the real interest rate and the cumulative dollars invested.

investment spending Spending on physical capital, inventories, and new construction.

investment tax credit A reduction in taxes for firms that invest in new capital like a factory or piece of equipment.

Keynesian school A macroeconomic model that believes the economy is unstable and does not naturally move to full employment in the long run.

labor force The sum of all individuals 16 years and older who are either currently employed (E) or unemployed (U). LF = $E + U$.

law of comparative advantage Nations can mutually benefit from trade so long as the relative production costs differ.

law of demand All else equal, when the price of a good rises, the quantity demanded of that good falls.

law of diminishing marginal returns As successive units of a variable input are added to a fixed input, beyond some point the marginal product declines.

law of increasing costs As more of a good is produced, the greater is its opportunity (or marginal) cost.

law of increasing marginal cost As a producer produces more of a good, the marginal cost rises.

This is very similar to the idea of increasing opportunity costs in Chapter 5.

law of supply All else equal, when the price of a good rises, the quantity supplied of that good rises.

liability of a bank Anything owned by depositors or lenders to the bank.

liquidity A measure of how easily an asset can be converted to cash.

loanable funds market A hypothetical market where borrowers (investors) demand more funds at a lower real interest rate and lenders (savers) supply more funds at a higher real interest rate.

long run A period of time long enough for the firm to alter all production inputs, including the plant size.

M1 The most liquid measure of money supply, including cash, checking deposits, and traveler's checks.

M2 $M1$ plus savings deposits, small time deposits, and money market and mutual funds balances.

macroeconomic long run A period of time long enough for input prices to have fully adjusted to market forces, all input and output markets are in equilibrium, and the economy is operating at full employment (GDP_f).

macroeconomic short run A period of time during which the prices of goods and services are changing in their respective markets but the input prices have not yet adjusted to those changes in the product markets.

marginal The next unit, or increment of, an action.

marginal analysis Making decisions based upon weighing the marginal benefits and costs of that action. The rational decision maker chooses an action if the MB ≥ MC.

marginal benefit (MB) The additional benefit received from the consumption of the next unit of a good or service.

marginal cost (MC) The additional cost of producing one more unit of output.

marginal propensity to consume (MPC) The change in consumption caused by a change in disposable income. The slope of the consumption function.

marginal propensity to save (MPS) The change in saving caused by a change in disposable income. The slope of the saving function.

marginal tax rate The rate paid on the last dollar earned, calculated by taking the ratio of the change in taxes divided by the change in income.

market A group with buyers and sellers of a good or service.

market basket A collection of goods and services used to represent what is consumed in the economy.

market economy An economic system in which resources are allocated through the decentralized decisions of firms and consumers.

market equilibrium Exists at the only price where the quantity supplied equals the quantity demanded. Or, it is the only quantity where the price consumers are willing to pay is exactly the price producers are willing to accept.

money demand The negative relationship between the nominal interest rate and the quantity of money demanded as an asset plus the quantity of money demanded for transactions.

money market The interaction of money demand and money supply determines the "price" of money, the nominal interest rate.

money multiplier Equal to one over the reserve ratio, this measures the maximum amount of new checking deposits that can be created by a single dollar of excess reserves.

money supply The fixed quantity of money in circulation at a given point in time as measured by the central bank.

multiplier effect The idea that a change in any component of aggregate demand creates a larger change in GDP.

national debt The accumulation of all annual budget deficits.

natural rate of unemployment The unemployment rate associated with full employment, somewhere between 4 to 6 percent in the United States.

net exports The value of a nation's total exports minus total imports.

net export effect The process of how expansionary fiscal policy decreases net exports due to rising interest rates. Another form of crowding out.

nominal GDP The value of current production at the current prices.

nominal interest rate The interest rate unadjusted for inflation. The opportunity cost of holding money in the money market.

nonmarket transactions Household work or do-it-yourself jobs that are missed by GDP accounting.

nonrenewable resources Natural resources that cannot replenish themselves.

normal goods A good for which demand increases with an increase in consumer income.

official reserves account The Fed's adjustment of a deficit or surplus in the current and capital account by the addition or subtraction of foreign currencies so that the balance of payments is zero.

open market operation (OMO) A tool of monetary policy, it involves the Fed's buying (or selling) of Treasury bonds from (or to) commercial banks and the general public.

opportunity cost The value of the sacrifice made to pursue a course of action.

peak The top of the business cycle where an expansion has ended and is about to turn down.

present value If r is the current interest rate, the present value of \$1 received one year from now is $\$1/(1 + r)$.

price index A measure of the average level of prices in a market basket for a given year, when compared to the prices in a reference (or base) year.

producer surplus The difference between the price received and the marginal cost of producing the good.

production possibilities The different quantities of goods that an economy can produce with a given amount of scarce resources.

production possibility curve or frontier (PPC or PPF) A graphical device that shows the combination of two goods that a nation can efficiently produce with available resources and technology.

productivity The quantity of output that can be produced per worker in a given amount of time.

protective tariff An excise tax levied on an imported good that is produced in the domestic market so that it may be protected from foreign competition.

quantity theory of money The theory that an increase in the money supply will not affect real output and will only result in higher prices.

quota A maximum amount of a good that can be imported into the domestic market.

real GDP The value of current production, but using prices from a fixed point in time.

real rate of interest The cost of borrowing to fund an investment and equal to the nominal interest rate minus the expected rate of inflation.

recession Two or more consecutive quarters of falling real GDP.

recessionary gap The amount by which full employment GDP exceeds equilibrium real GDP.

relative prices The price of one unit of good X measured not in currency, but in the number of units of good Y that must be sacrificed to acquire good X.

renewable resources Natural resources that can replenish themselves if they are not overharvested.

required reserves The minimum amount of deposits that must be held at the bank for withdrawals.

reserve ratio The fraction of total deposits that must be kept on reserve.

resources Also called factors of production, these are commonly grouped into the four categories of labor, physical capital, land or natural resources, and entrepreneurial ability.

revenue tariff An excise tax levied on goods that are not produced in the domestic market.

saving function A positive relationship between disposable income and saving.

scarcity The imbalance between limited productive resources and unlimited human wants.

second-hand sales Final goods and services that are resold.

shortage A situation in which, at the going market price, the quantity demanded exceeds the quantity supplied.

specialization Production of goods, or performance of tasks, based upon comparative advantage.

spending multiplier The amount by which real GDP changes due to a change in spending.

stagflation A situation seen in the macroeconomy when inflation and the unemployment rate are both increasing. Also called cost-push inflation.

sticky prices The case when price levels do not change, especially downward, with changes in AD.

stock A certificate that represents a claim to, or share of, the ownership of a firm.

substitute goods Two goods are consumer substitutes if they provide essentially the same utility to the consumer.

substitution effect The change in quantity demanded resulting from a change in the price of one good relative to the price of other goods.

supply curve Shows the quantity of a good supplied at all prices.

supply schedule A table showing quantity supplied for a good at various prices.

supply shock An economy-wide phenomenon that affects the costs of firms and results in a shifting AS curve.

supply-side fiscal policy Fiscal policy centered on incentives to save and invest to prompt economic growth with very little inflation.

surplus A situation in which, at the going market price, the quantity supplied exceeds the quantity demanded.

tax multiplier The magnitude of the effect that a change in lump sum taxes has on real GDP.

technology A nation's knowledge of how to produce goods in the best possible way.

theory of liquidity preference Keynes' theory that the interest rate adjusts to bring the money market into equilibrium.

total welfare The sum of consumer surplus and producer surplus.

trade-offs The reality of scarce resources implies that individuals, firms, and governments are constantly faced with difficult choices that involve benefits and costs.

transaction demand The amount of money held in order to make transactions.

trough The bottom of the cycle where a contraction has stopped and is about to turn up.

underground economy The unreported or illegal activity, bartering, or informal exchange of cash for goods and services that are not reported in official tabulations of GDP.

velocity of money The average number of times that a dollar is spent in a year.

world price The global equilibrium price of a good when nations engage in trade.

IMPORTANT FORMULAS AND CONDITIONS

Chapter 5

1. Optimal decision making: MB = MC
2. Opportunity cost from a production possibility curve or frontier (PPC or PPF):

   Good X: The slope of the PPC

   Good Y: The inverse of the slope of the PPC

Chapter 6

1. Market equilibrium:

   $Q_d = Q_s$

2. Shortage:

   $Q_d - Q_s$

3. Surplus:

   $Q_s - Q_d$

4. Total welfare:

   = Consumer surplus + Producer surplus

Chapter 7

1. Nominal GDP:

   = Current year production × Current year prices

2. Real GDP:

   $= 100 \times \dfrac{\text{(Nominal GDP)}}{\text{(GDP deflator)}}$

3. Aggregate spending (GDP):

   $= C + I + G + (X - M)$

4. Disposable income (DI):

   = Gross income − Net taxes

5. Net taxes:

   = Taxes paid − Transfers received

6. %Δ real GDP:

   = %Δ nominal GDP − %Δ price index

7. Price index current year:

   = 100 × (Spending current year)/(Spending base year)

8. Consumer inflation rate:

   $= 100 \times (CPI_{New} - CPI_{Old})/CPI_{Old}$

9. Real Income:

   = (Nominal income)/CPI (in hundredths)

10. Nominal interest rate:

    = Real interest rate + Expected inflation

11. Labor force:

    = Employed + Unemployed

12. Unemployment rate:

    = 100 × (Unemployed/Labor force)

Chapter 8

1. Consumption function:

   C = Autonomous consumption + MPC(DI)

2. Saving function:

   S = Autonomous savings + MPS(DI)

3. Marginal propensity to consume (MPC):

   $= \Delta C/\Delta DI$ = Slope of consumption function

4. Marginal propensity to save (MPS):

   $= \Delta S/\Delta DI$ = Slope of saving function

5. MPC + MPS = 1

6. Net exports $(X - M)$:

   = Exports − Imports

7. Equilibrium in the loanable funds market:

    $S = I$

8. Spending multiplier:

    $= 1/(1 - MPC) = 1/MPS$

    $= (\Delta \text{ GDP})/(\Delta \text{ spending})$

9. Tax multiplier (Tm):

    $= MPC \times (\text{Spending multiplier}) = MPC/MPS$

    $= (\Delta \text{ GDP})/(\Delta \text{ taxes})$

10. Balanced-budget multiplier = 1

Chapter 9

1. Macroeconomic short-run equilibrium

    AD = SRAS

2. Macroeconomic long-run equilibrium

    AD = SRAS = LRAS

3. Recessionary gap:

    = Full employment GDP − Current GDP

4. Inflationary gap:

    = Current GDP − Full employment GDP

Chapter 10

1. Budget deficit:

    = Government spending − Net taxes

2. Budget Surplus:

    = Net taxes − Government spending

Chapter 11

1. $M1$ measure of money:

    = Cash + Coins + Checking Deposits + Traveler's checks

2. $M2$ measure of money:

    = $M1$ + Savings deposits + Small (e.g., under $100,000 CDs) time deposits + Money market deposits + Money market mutual funds

3. Present value (PV) of $1 received a year from today:

    $= \$1/(1 + r)$

4. Future Value (FV) of $1 invested today at interest rate r for one year $= \$1 \times (1 + r)$

5. Money demand:

    = Transaction demand + Asset demand

6. Equilibrium in the money market:

    MS = MD

7. Reserve ratio (rr)

    = Required reserves/Total deposits

8. Simple money multiplier:

    $= 1/rr$

Chapter 12

1. Equilibrium in the currency ($) market:

    Q_d for the $ = Q_s of the $

2. Revenue from a tariff:

    = Per unit tariff × Units imported

NOTES

NOTES

NOTES

NOTES

NOTES

Study Smarter and Manage Your Time Better

Create Your Own Personal Study Schedule

Download Your BONUS McGraw-Hill Education AP Planner App

5 Steps to a 5: AP Macroeconomics 2018
Now with extra AP practice questions

Select your exam date

Create your own customized study schedule based on diagnostic test results

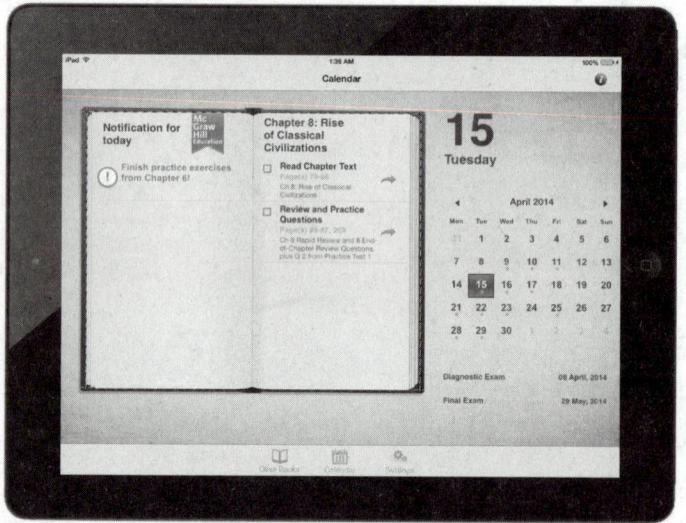

Get a complete, day-by-day study schedule with review and practice assignments

---

AVAILABLE FOR iPHONE, iPAD, AND ANDROID™ DEVICES

SEARCH **MCGRAW-HILL EDUCATION AP PLANNER APP**
IN THE iTUNES APP STORE OR GOOGLE PLAY FOR ANDROID™.